Life after D

APPROACHES TO A CULTURAL AND SOCIAL HISTORY
OF EUROPE DURING THE 1940s AND 1950s

This collection of essays offers a novel approach to the cultural and social history of Europe after the Second World War. In a shift of perspective, it does not conceive of the impressive economic and political stability of the postwar era as a quasi-natural return to previous patterns of societal development but approaches it as an attempt to establish "normality" on the lingering memories of experiencing violence on a hitherto unprecedented scale. It views the relationship of the violence of the 1940s to the apparent "normality" and stability of the 1950s as a key to understanding the history of postwar Europe. Although the history of postwar Germany naturally looms large in this collection, the essays deal with countries across Western and Central Europe, offer comparative perspectives on their subjects, and draw on a wide range of primary and secondary source material.

Richard Bessel is Professor of Twentieth-Century History at the University of York. He is the author of *Political Violence and the Rise of Nazism* (1984) and *Germany after the First World War* (1993), as well as editor of a number of collections, including *Fascist Italy and Nazi Germany: Comparisons and Contrasts* (Cambridge, 1996). Since 1994 he has been co-editor of the journal *German History*.

Dirk Schumann is the Deputy Director of the German Historical Institute, Washington, D.C. He has taught at the Ludwig-Maximilians-Universität in Munich, the Universität Bielefeld, and Emory University. He is the author of *Bayerns Unternehmer in Gesellschaft und Staat, 1834–1914* (1992) and *Politische Gewalt in der Weimarer Republik 1918–1933* (2001).

PUBLICATIONS OF THE GERMAN HISTORICAL INSTITUTE
WASHINGTON, D.C.

Edited by Christof Mauch
with the assistance of David Lazar

The German Historical Institute is a center for advanced study and research whose purpose is to provide a permanent basis for scholarly cooperation among historians from the Federal Republic of Germany and the United States. The Institute conducts, promotes, and supports research into both American and German political, social, economic, and cultural history; into transatlantic migration, especially in the nineteenth and twentieth centuries; and into the history of international relations, with special emphasis on the roles played by the United States and Germany.

Recent books in the series

Norbert Finzsch and Dietmar Schirmer, editors, *Identity and Intolerance: Nationalism, Racism, and Xenophobia in Germany and the United States*

Susan Strasser, Charles McGovern, and Matthias Judt, editors, *Getting and Spending: European and American Consumer Societies in the Twentieth Century*

Carole Fink, Philipp Gassert, and Detlef Junker, editors, *1968: The World Transformed*

Roger Chickering and Stig Förster, editors, *Great War, Total War: Combat and Mobilization on the Western Front*

Manfred F. Boemeke, Gerald D. Feldman, and Elisabeth Glaser, editors, *The Treaty of Versailles: A Reassessment after 75 Years*

Manfred Berg and Martin H. Geyer, editors, *Two Cultures of Rights: The Quest for Inclusion and Participation in Modern America and Germany*

Manfred F. Boemeke, Roger Chickering, and Stig Förster, editors, *Anticipating Total War: The German and American Experiences, 1871–1914*

Hubert Zimmermann, *Money and Security: Troops, Monetary Policy, and West Germany's Relations with the United States and Britain, 1950–1971*

This untitled sketch was drawn by Jack Bessel, then a soldier with the U.S. Army in Europe, toward the end of the Second World War.

Life after Death

APPROACHES TO A CULTURAL AND SOCIAL
HISTORY OF EUROPE DURING THE
1940s AND 1950s

Edited by
RICHARD BESSEL
University of York

DIRK SCHUMANN
German Historical Institute
Washington, D.C.

GERMAN HISTORICAL INSTITUTE
Washington, D.C.
and

CAMBRIDGE
UNIVERSITY PRESS

PUBLISHED BY THE PRESS SYNDICATE OF THE UNIVERSITY OF CAMBRIDGE
The Pitt Building, Trumpington Street, Cambridge, United Kingdom

CAMBRIDGE UNIVERSITY PRESS
The Edinburgh Building, Cambridge CB2 2RU, UK
40 West 20th Street, New York, NY 10011-4211, USA
477 Williamstown Road, Port Melbourne, VIC 3207, Australia
Ruiz de Alarcón 13, 28014 Madrid, Spain
Dock House, The Waterfront, Cape Town 8001, South Africa

http://www.cambridge.org

© The German Historical Institute 2003

First published 2003

Printed in the United States of America

Typeface Bembo 11/13 pt.   *System* LATEX 2$_\varepsilon$ [TB]

A catalog record for this book is available from the British Library.

Library of Congress Cataloging in Publication Data

Life after death : approaches to a cultural and social history of Europe during the 1940s and 1950s /
edited by Richard Bessel, Dirk Schumann.
p.   cm. – (Publications of the German Historical Institute)
Includes bibliographical references and index.
ISBN 0-521-80413-2 – ISBN 0-521-00922-7 (pbk.)
1. Social change – Europe – History – 20th century.   2. Social change – Germany
(West) – History – 20th century.   3. Europe – Social conditions – 20th century.
4. Social conflict – Europe – History – 20th century.   5. Germany – Social conditions –
20th century.   6. Europe – Ethnic relations.   7. Germany (West) – Ethnic relations.
8. Holocaust, Jewish (1939–1945) – Psychological aspects.   9. Reconstruction (1939–1951) –
Europe.   10. Reconstruction (1939–1951) – Germany (West)   I. Bessel, Richard.
II. Schumann, Dirk.   III. Series.

D842.5 .L48   2003
303.4′094′0904–dc21   2002067421

ISBN 0 521 80413 2 hardback
ISBN 0 521 00922 7 paperback

Contents

Contributors

Birgit Beck is Assistant Professor of History at the University of Bern.

Sabine Behrenbeck is Abteilungsleiterin for Sonderforschungsbereiche at the Deutsche Forschungsgemeinschaft in Bonn.

Richard Bessel is Professor of Twentieth-Century History at the University of York.

Paul Betts is Lecturer in History at the University of Sussex.

Joanna Bourke is Professor of History at Birkbeck College, University of London.

Alon Confino is Associate Professor of History at the University of Virginia.

Alice Förster is a psychiatrist and works at the Integrierter forensisch psychiatrischer Dienst at the University of Bern.

Atina Grossmann is Associate Professor of History at The Cooper Union in New York and Associate, Remarque Institute, New York University.

Ido de Haan teaches history at the University of Amsterdam.

Dagmar Herzog is Associate Professor of History at Michigan State University.

Pieter Lagrou is a researcher at the Institut d'Histoire du Temps Présent, Centre National de la Recherche Scientifique, Paris.

Damian van Melis worked until recently at the Institut für Zeitgeschichte, Außenstelle Berlin and is now managing director at the Greven Verlag in Cologne.

Andrea Pető taught until recently at the Central European University in Budapest and is currently visiting Professor in Ethnic and Minority Studies at ELTE in Budapest.

Donald Sassoon is Professor of History at Queen Mary and Westfield College, University of London.

Dirk Schumann is Deputy Director of the German Historical Institute, Washington, D.C.

Pat Thane is Leverhulme Professor of Contemporary British History at the Institute of Historical Research, University of London.

Michael Wildt is a wissenschaftlicher Mitarbeiter at the Institut für Sozialforschung, Hamburg.

Preface

This collection of essays has its origins with a conference that we organized in October 1998 at the IBZ Schloss Gimborn at Marienheide, Germany. We would like to thank the Director of the IBZ, Klaus-Ulrich Nieder, and his deputy, Dr. Peter Lessman-Faust, for their hospitality; they helped tremendously to make the conference a productive and stimulating experience. The German Historical Institutes in London and Washington generously provided the funding for the conference; Prof. Dr. Martin H. Geyer, then Deputy Director at the GHI in Washington, and Dieter H. Schneider, its chief administrator, contributed their organizational experience and skills, without which the conference could not have taken place. We are very grateful for their support. We also wish to thank the GHI, Washington, D.C., for accepting this collection as part of its publication series. The papers presented at the conference have been substantially revised for publication. We would like to thank the two anonymous readers for their critical comments and helpful suggestions, and Dr. Daniel Mattern, Janel Galvanek, and David Lazar at the GHI, Washington, D.C., for their meticulous editorial work.

Introduction

Violence, Normality, and the Construction of Postwar Europe

RICHARD BESSEL AND DIRK SCHUMANN

Works of fiction often express things better than do works of history. At the outset of his remarkably perceptive novel, *Home Fires: An Intimate Portrait of One Middle-Class Family in Postwar America*, Donald Katz writes of his protagonist in 1945:

Sam Goldenberg came back from the war, and now that he had broken the ice with Eve he was able to say that there was only one thing he wanted from the rest of his life: a normal family. That was all a million other guys who'd survived the family degradations of the Depression and the harrowing experiences of the war wanted too.[1]

Hardly a surprising reaction to the horrors of war, and obviously it is a considerable leap from (Jewish) middle-class America to a devastated European continent after the destruction of the "Third Reich." However, this pithy statement points to a major, perhaps *the* major, social and psychological turning point of our century.

The history of the twentieth century revolves around mass death. At its center lies the mass killing and mass murder carried out during the decade roughly from the late 1930s to the late 1940s – during which time more people were killed by their fellow human beings than ever before in the history of humankind. Against the terrible dimensions of the mass death of that decade, the hitherto unimaginable horrors of the First World War and its immediate aftermath appear as merely an antechamber to the house of horrors that arose two decades later. Thus, we find the remarkable contrast between the aftermath of the First World War, when a world profoundly shocked at what it had done found memorable words and cultural expressions with which to describe its shock, and the aftermath of the Second,

---

1 Donald Katz, *Home Fires: An Intimate Portrait of One Middle-Class Family in Postwar America* (New York, 1993), 14–15.

in which it seemed impossible to depict and interpret the suffering and dying on the battlefields, in the bombed cities, and during deportation and flight, the ordeals of occupation and collaboration, and the Shoah in an all-encompassing manner. Although lasting expressions were found for some of these harrowing experiences, they often resulted in silence and a rush to (re)establish "normality."

The First World War and the terrors of the Russian "people's tragedy" of revolution and civil war shocked a world that had convinced itself during the course of a relatively peaceful long nineteenth century that humanity was becoming more civilized; the Second World War, with its campaigns of mass murder that made the lands in the grip of Nazi and Stalinist tyranny the great slaughterhouses of the short twentieth century, went beyond such shock. One may debate whether or not it was possible to write poetry after Auschwitz or whether there remained words, images, and concepts with which that horror could be described adequately, but it is remarkable that the Second World War did not generate poetry, novels, or artistic reflections in quite the same way as did the First: There was no real second-generation Siegfried Sassoon or Erich Maria Remarque. Nor was the violence of the 1940s commemorated in such profoundly moving memorials as those conceived by Edward Lutyens or Heinrich Tessenow for the Great War of 1914–18; the tombs of the unknown soldier contain dead from the First World War, not the Second. The great Soviet war memorials – one thinks of the Mamayev Kurgan at Volgograd/Stalingrad[2] or the Soviet memorial in Berlin-Treptow – impress us with their enormity (and thus the enormity of what they commemorate), not with their profundity. Primo Levi and Elie Wiesel wrote poignant descriptions of the horrors of the Shoah and the suffering of its victims; Heinrich Böll and others described the soldiers' feelings of loneliness and guilt; but the various experiences of violence during the war proved to be too incompatible to be rendered together in a compelling artistic form.

When attempting to understand the postwar transition after 1945, we need therefore to bear in mind that it was the *second* great postwar transition of this century. It proved even more difficult to give "meaning" to what had happened, not only to construct coherent private biographies encompassing the violence but also to develop comprehensive public forms of commemorating the war – in other words, to create private and public

2 See Sabine Rosemarie Arnold, "'Das Beispiel der Heldenstadt wird ewig die Herzen der Völker erfüllen!' Gedanken zum sowjetischen Titenkult am Beispiel des Gedenkkomplexes in Volgograd," in Reinhard Koselleck and Michael Jeismann, eds., *Der politische Totenkult: Kriegerdenkmäler in der Moderne* (Munich, 1994), 351–74.

narratives about the war and violence that were consistent in themselves and compatible with each other. Whereas the search for meaning after mass death may have been necessary and may have made some sense after the first great round of twentieth-century horrors, it was much more difficult, if not impossible, to engage in such a search after the second, even more horrific wave of mass death. After the First World War, it may have been necessary to try to find some meaning in the senselessness of mass death, in the private grief shared by millions. After the Second World War, the horrors of Nazism and Communism, the mass bombing of civilians, the attempts at genocide, and the brutal uprooting of millions of refugees, it was perhaps necessary to do just the opposite: to turn one's back on death and seek to rebuild, in a strangely anesthetised state, "normal" life. Looking specifically at Germany, Reinhart Koselleck has pointed to a profound change in how war and mass death came to be commemorated and understood following the bloodbaths of the 1940s: "The concentration camp memorials make especially clear something that in the Federal Republic [of Germany] also is true for the local memorials to the dead after the Second World War: that death no longer is understood as an answer but only as a question, no longer as providing meaning, only calling out for meaning."[3]

The journey through the slaughterhouses of the 1940s perhaps purged the survivors of the belief that there is an identifiable meaning in mass death, a meaning that can be publicly shared and represented. What remains are deeply disturbing questions and fears, and a desperate flight into normality. This, it must be said, was the dominant motif of the lives of millions who survived the First World War as well as the Second; despite all that was written about disturbed types such as those who found refuge in the paramilitary politics of the Freikorps, the overwhelming desire after the Armistice of 1918 was to return to what were perceived as normal patterns of family, work, and community. However, the shock of the 1940s was so profound and so deep that perhaps there simply was no way to deal with it other than to move on and not look back.

If it was not possible to give mass death a clear meaning, people nevertheless could not escape the memory – in terms of private memories and public commemorations – of what had happened in Europe and beyond. Because hardly a single family in those countries on whose territory war had been fought was left untouched by its violence, their members had to come to

---

3 Reinhart Koselleck, "Der Einfluss der beiden Weltkriege auf das soziale Bewusstsein," in Wolfram Wette, ed., *Der Krieg des kleinen Mannes* (Munich, 1992), 336–7.

terms with the losses that they had experienced. Compared with what had happened in the First World War, however, the composition of the groups of victims of the Second was different. Not only were there millions of ordinary soldiers who had fought and fallen on either side; there also were many more civilian victims than ever before, who had suffered from area bombing, occupation policy, and expulsion from their homes, and there were the Jews and the other victims of the murderous racist policies of the Nazi regime. Yet the experiences, and memory, of the violence often were a complex affair, fitting uneasily into publicly acceptable categories of good and evil. In the countries occupied by German troops, not everybody had been a member of a resistance movement; some had been collaborators, while others had tried to survive without getting involved in either resistance or collaboration. This was true, to some degree, for Germany and its allies as well. Many more people than in the First World War had been traumatized both by what they had endured and by what they had done; the violence of the war – of its battles along the vast and constantly shifting front lines, its incessant air attacks, the brutal acts of occupation policy – neither spared nor could go unnoticed. People had to deal with all these experiences in private, but this also left its public mark on the institutions and rituals of mourning and commemoration. If silence was the public reaction to this challenge, it was a silence occasionally broken and mixed with selective appreciations of the suffering of specific groups of victims. In other words, traumata were not simply repressed but dealt with in different ways; as a result, their long-term impact was different as well, depending on how explicitly they became an issue in private and public strategies of normalization.

This, the shock of the mass violence of the 1940s, more than perhaps anything else is what gave the second half of the short twentieth century – the postwar era that came to an abrupt end with the opening of the Berlin Wall and the collapse of the Soviet Union – its character: Its story is one of life after death. For nearly half a century after the end of the Second World War, Europe lived under the shadow of mass death. The struggle to create a sense of stability and normality after such terrible events and experiences has been, in a deep psychological sense, a story of life after death – a search for an answer to the unarticulated and unanswerable question of how people can live a normal life after mass death, death that overflowed the bounds of private grief and mourning, and became a central feature of public life because it came to be shared by so many people. The end of the 1940s is the great watershed, not simply because it witnessed the beginning of the Cold War and the division of Europe and the world into two hostile blocs as well as the establishment of a new economic order that brought unprecedented prosperity to an unprecedented number of people in the wake of war, but also because it marked a profound transformation of social discourse, practice, and behavior. The first half of the twentieth century was the era of violence and death, in which the nineteenth-century dreams of popular and national sovereignty were realized in twentieth-century nightmares of savagery and genocide; the second half of the twentieth century was an era of *relative* peace and order, but a peace and order that existed under the darkest of shadows: the horrible history of mass murder and the threat of nuclear annihilation.

The subject of this book therefore is pivotal to the history of Europe in the twentieth century: the relationship between the enormous outbursts of violence during the 1940s and the strange conservative normality that characterized so many aspects of life in European societies during the decade that followed. That the 1940s and 1950s form the hinge on which the history of Europe in the twentieth century turns has been most obvious in the political and military spheres. After the defeat of the Axis powers, the political instability that had characterized the European continent after 1914 was replaced by an international system of two competing blocs and remarkably stable political formations for nearly four decades – under the shadow of a nuclear cloud that first appeared in 1945 (announced to President Harry S Truman, who was attending the Potsdam Conference when the first atomic bomb was tested in New Mexico, with a coded message bizarrely appropriate for the dawn of the postwar era: "babies successfully born"). The importance of the 1940s and 1950s as a caesura is scarcely less obvious in the economic sphere. Instead of the expected postwar depression and a return to the economic crises of the interwar period, the post–Second World War period saw the greatest, most sustained economic boom that the world has ever seen, a boom that transformed the lives of millions of people across the European continent, that constituted a social revolution, and that constitutes the background of much of what is discussed in the chapters in this book. That is to say, in many respects the environment surrounding the return to normality in the 1950s was quite extraordinary.

Invoking "normality," however, is not to say that it is easy to define this normality, in terms either of contemporary experience or of historical perspective. For contemporaries, the absence of war and violence was one necessary precondition for establishing normal lives again, but there was no clear-cut model for the normality at which this process was aimed. Most obviously, Germans did not want to rebuild the Germany of the Nazis, although quite a few were ready to admit in the 1950s that until 1939 they had fared fairly well under a regime that had provided them with full employment, *Autobahnen*, and some notion of a consumer society.[4] In France, it did not seem wise simply to re-establish the Third Republic, which had turned out to be so feeble in the face of the German onslaught. Italy could not go back to the Mussolini regime, which was overthrown when defeat as a German ally had become inevitable. This was all the more true for the countries of Eastern Europe, where the victorious Soviet Union soon left no doubt about its determination to prevent the reconstruction of prewar political and social structures. For people in Europe, the shaky world of the interwar years was not something they wanted to get back. Was America the model for rebuilding their societies? The United States had been admired as the beacon of political liberty and economic prosperity by many since the beginning of the century, but it had also been perceived as a country where material values stood above moral ones and where social and racial cleavages deeply divided the society. Many Europeans wished to become consumers as their American counterparts already were, but they wanted to preserve their national traditions, however defined in light of the experiences of war and occupation, and they wanted a smooth transition. A common model of a new society emerged that placed the emphasis on an economic prosperity that was to remove the class conflicts that had marked the late nineteenth century and much of the first half of the twentieth. However, as the wave of youth unrest that occurred in most European countries during the late 1950s made clear, this model did not go uncontested. It was here that the general conservatism of the period proved to be far from universally accepted.

From a historical perspective, the normality of the postwar years also could be gauged in another way. In the 1950s, countries in noncommunist Europe resumed general trends that had marked the three decades before 1914 and had been interrupted by the economic depression and political turmoil of most of the 1920s and early 1930s, and, of course, the Second World War. This was true not only for the return to steady economic growth but also for the democratization of political regimes and the emancipation of women. The extent to which people perceived these trends, according to their generational position, is another matter. However, when contrasting these positive trends of modernization with the enormous violence that occurred in between, it becomes all the more difficult to explain the causes and effects of that violence on the people involved.

4 See Elisabeth Noelle and Erich Peter Neumann, eds., *Jahrbuch der öffentlichen Meinung 1958–1964* (Allensbach, 1965), 230, 233. In October 1951, 42 percent of those interviewed saw the period between 1933 and 1939 as the best Germany had ever had; in May 1959, 41 percent called Hitler until 1939 one of the greatest German statesmen.

The importance of the 1940s and 1950s as a social and psychological turning point is only beginning to be considered seriously. In any attempt to come to grips with the social, psychological, and political history of this century, the terrible violence at its center – and in Europe – cannot be ignored. Of course, not all developments that unfolded after the war were direct results of the conflict. As recent studies of the First World War and its aftermath demonstrate, the continuities of prewar trends and mentalities often were greater than previously assumed. However, there can be little doubt that the social and cultural effects of the mass experience of violence and death during the 1940s were profound and colored all aspects of life during the postwar decades, even when this was not necessarily articulated explicitly. But what precisely these effects may have been, what exactly the connections were between the violence of the 1940s and the normality of the 1950s, remains extremely speculative. Examining these subjects requires the exploration of very difficult historical terrain and involves questions that cannot be addressed solely by reference to the apparently "hard" evidence provided by political and/or economic documentation. It presents a challenging agenda historically, methodologically, and personally.

It is challenging not least because the profound importance and deep consequences of this violence can hardly be grasped if one's vision remains fixed on the cold calculus that has become so familiar a feature of the histories of the "dark continent" during the "age of extremes,"[5] on those terrible abstract numbers of the millions of human beings who were cut down in the killing fields of Eastern Europe and in the extermination camps of the Nazi empire, of the millions who were killed, maimed, or scarred for life on the battlefield or in bombed-out cities, of the millions who were brutally uprooted from their homes and forced to rebuild their lives in new and often strange and even hostile surroundings, of the millions who were subjected to sexual violence, of the millions who would have to lead the rest of their lives without fathers, mothers, sisters, and brothers, and children whose lives had brutally ended in the greatest human slaughter ever.

For a long time research on the late 1940s and 1950s was concentrated on the reconstruction of political and economic structures, especially in Germany. It was centered on the question of how the mistakes made in the treaties of 1919 were avoided after 1945. How were economic and financial structures established that compelled the countries in Central Europe to cooperate, brought the United States into the frame, and provided a

5 This criticism, it should be made clear, cannot be levelled at those fine general texts which have put these phrases into common usage: Eric Hobsbawm, *Age of Extremes: The Short Twentieth Century* (London, 1994); and Mark Mazower, *Dark Continent: Europe's Twentieth Century* (London, 1998).

firm basis for economic growth? How were political systems (re)created that were based on a number of democratic parties while not adopting the severe tensions of the interwar period? Questions such as these did not have as their focus individual experiences, collective memories, or other cultural phenomena such as lifestyles. Research on the victims of the Nazi persecution of the European Jews has demonstrated how difficult it was for them to remember their traumatic experiences and to communicate this to their respective societies. Research on how "ordinary" citizens survived the war and came to terms with it has only begun, reflecting growing interest in the emerging consumer society of the 1950s and its gendered aspects, as well as in the rituals of the public commemoration during the 1950s of war and occupation.

The chapters in this book are therefore situated in a new field of research and attempt to break new ground. Their perspective is interdisciplinary, international, and comparative; together they combine the most recent approaches to the history of the late 1940s and 1950s in Europe. Obviously, not all of them deal with their subjects in the same manner. Some are primarily case studies, asking rather specific questions and drawing on rich source material; others take a broader, more explicitly comparative approach or place particular emphasis on more theoretical questions. It is therefore not surprising that some focus more on the issues related to violence whereas others concentrate more on those related to normality. We would like to have seen all parts of Europe that had been involved in the Second World War fairly equally represented in this book; however, despite our hopes and efforts this proved impossible. Western and Central Europe are overrepresented, whereas Eastern Europe is underrepresented. Nevertheless, we hope that the essays gathered here will stimulate further research in this part of the European continent as well.

As satisfactory methodological concepts have not yet been developed to describe the effects of the large-scale experience of violence on individuals and on whole societies, this book begins with a first, suggestive attempt at filling that gap by linking psychiatric approaches with the social history of the war and early postwar years. In their chapter, Alice Förster and Birgit Beck outline the main features of the psychiatric concept of Post-Traumatic Stress Disorder (PTSD) and then probe how it may be applied to the subject of this book. Originally developed for veterans of the Vietnam War, this concept covers a wide range of symptoms that can be found in many people involved in violence, both as perpetrators and victims. Taking the German society of the 1940s and 1950s as their example, Förster and Beck pose new questions for a number of issues. From this perspective, mental and medical problems become tracers for different degrees of involvement in violence, as silence not only serves as an expression of guilt but also as a strategy of coping in private and public when other paths are not taken.

Public mourning was one way to help individuals come to terms with their experiences of war. Sabine Behrenbeck describes how in both postwar German states, despite their differences, the dead members of the former *Volksgemeinschaft* (national ethnic community) were commemorated in public ceremonies. Whereas in the German Democratic Republic a commemoration calendar emerged that placed the victory of the Soviet troops and the Communist victims of Nazi persecution at center stage, in the Federal Republic public mourning concentrated on the *Volkstrauertag* in November and blurred the distinctions between soldiers and civilians, perpetrators and victims, by eventually including even the German prisoners of war. However, the principal victims of Nazi persecution, the Jews, were not explicitly mentioned, and only after the mid-1960s were they given their own place in the public memory of both German states. To the West German reflections (or lack thereof) on the murder of the Jews, Ido de Haan adds the Dutch and French experiences and concludes that in these countries, too, there was no specific place in public memory for the victims of the Holocaust. In the Netherlands, public discourse focused on the history of occupation and resistance, whereas the persecution of Jews was regarded as a German affair. In France, Jews were defined as part of the republican nation and thus became indistinguishable as part of the resistance movement (although, unlike their counterparts in the Netherlands, they were entitled to receive compensation for the persecution they suffered). De Haan also asserts, however, that public mourning did not progress gradually from silence to memory but rather shifted between the two, depending on the political context.

During the 1940s, women had been affected by wartime violence more than ever before. Atina Grossmann, focusing on Germany, looks at their efforts to reclaim a sense of identity and agency. In doing so, she contrasts the relative unwillingness of German women, who saw themselves as victims of war and occupation, to bear children, with the tremendous upsurge in births among Jewish women survivors in the displaced-persons camps in Germany. For German women, many of whom had been raped, not having children allowed them to re-create the material conditions of normality; for Jewish women survivors, by contrast, bearing children both offered an opportunity to be and feel "normal" and fostered a kind of "productive forgetting" after the horrors of the recent past. Shifting the geographic focus farther east, Andrea Petö discusses the traumatic experience of Hungarian and Austrian women who had been raped by Soviet soldiers at the end of the war. Whereas a public "conspiracy of silence" developed after 1945 owing to the political circumstances, the victims themselves developed an "economy of emotions" that enabled them to distance themselves from the acts of rape. In Hungary, the rapes helped to create a myth of national victimhood, which minimized the Hungarian contribution to Nazi rule in Europe and helped shape an anti–Soviet identity.

In her chapter, Joanna Bourke shifts the attention to men's agency and men's experiences generally, and to the act of killing specifically, and asserts that the evidence testifies not to breakdown but to resilience. Focusing on British (and American) soldiers, she contrasts contemporary fears revolving around the stereotypical figure of the "veteran" – which suggests that returning soldiers, brutalized by their experiences, would pose a serious threat to public order – and the ways soldiers found to distance themselves from the horrors of war and their own behavior by creating out of the chaos and the violence they had inflicted and endured narratives that were both ordered and sensible.

It was in marriage and family that men's and women's experiences and ways to cope with them met. Dagmar Herzog presents the thesis that the 1950s in Germany were less sexually repressed than often portrayed and that the same could be said for the Nazi period. Drawing on a wide range of sources, including marriage counseling texts and opinion polls, Herzog demonstrates that during the late 1940s and early 1950s there was a high level of consent to nonmarital sex, that information on sex practices was easily available, and that the first mail-order service for pornographic material was a great success. This changed only in the mid-1950s, when the influence of conservative forces increased, particularly of the Catholic Church, which had denounced Nazism as too permissive in sexual matters. Pat Thane, setting developments in family life in postwar Europe within a broad social and economic perspective, confirms Herzog's thesis for Britain. There, too, the 1950s brought about a further loosening of the codes of sexual conduct, whereas other features of social life – such as demographic changes and very low unemployment rates after the war – marked a break with prewar experience. Class also mattered: The postwar economic boom and the changes it generated affected the working class most of all, where for the first time parents could expect that their children would have better lives than they did and where working-class families in particular saw a trend toward greater stability in their lives. Michael Wildt, focusing on postwar consumption in West Germany, places his findings in a similar perspective and points to the ruptures as well as the continuities with war and prewar experiences. Anxieties about a possible third world war were ever-present during the 1950s, leading to constant efforts to stockpile extra food at home; and thrift remained a valued quality through the 1950s, although the fact that consumers increasingly bought on credit suggests that things look different when one examines everyday practice. By becoming able to participate in mass consumption, West Germans during the course of the 1950s became westernized and came to accept their new democratic state.

Wartime experiences also were dealt with in the narrative that shaped postwar political culture in a broader sense. Focusing in particular on Spain and Germany, Damian van Melis presents the thesis that the Catholic Church viewed itself as the "victor" among the ruins of the war. Glossing over its silence in the face of Nazi crimes, the Church interpreted the violence of the war as a result of disobedience to God and turning away from the Church, just as the violence of the Spanish Civil War had been perceived as a result of disobedience. The Church was concerned more with reaffirming its traditional worldview and moral rules than with taking serious issue with the violence of the war years, especially the Holocaust. In his contribution, Pieter Lagrou contrasts the First and Second World Wars in France, Belgium, and the Netherlands, and points to the difficulty of constructing homogeneous national memories after 1945. In contrast to the First World War and to the experiences in Eastern Europe during the Second, the actual fighting in the countries he discusses was over very quickly; collaboration and resistance, deportation and persecution of the Jews, not the daily confrontation with violent death, marked most of wartime. He affirms the thesis put forward by Behrenbeck and de Haan that in public remembrance the Jews were excluded from national memory, and suggests a fascinating paradox: In the First World War a relatively homogeneous experience was followed by divergence, whereas the divergent experiences of the Second World War were followed by greater uniformity. Donald Sassoon describes for Italy the problems of constructing a national narrative of the war years that was generally acceptable. There the Communists were virtually in charge of who was in the resistance and its narrative, and they created a national narrative in which most people were unable to recognize themselves and which obliterated the possibility of creating local narratives. Sassoon places particular emphasis on the "myth of the good Italian" who had been involved in the war and in Fascist crimes only by accident, which eventually served as a unifying myth that cut across party lines, although at the price of obliterating the history of Italian anti-Semitism as well as Italy's colonial history.

The last two contributions explore the culture of everyday life, thereby taking up some of the other topics from a different perspective. Drawing on

Walter Benjamin's reflections on art in the industrial age, Paul Betts examines how the legacy of the Bauhaus was used in both Germanies after 1945. In the Federal Republic, an "aesthetization of economics" gave industrial design a new prominence and engendered the shaping of all sorts of consumer products in an explicitly "modern" fashion, whereas the public presentation of politics remained muted. In the GDR, there was no break with the past aesthetization of politics, but there also were efforts to design consumer goods in a manner clearly distinguished from the Nazi years. Alon Confino offers the thesis that the re-emergence of tourism in Germany after 1945 was not, as usually claimed, a hallmark of a new culture of mass consumption. Rather, it was a continuation of a tradition from the 1930s that had been interrupted for six years, but also (as contemporary statements of former German soldiers demonstrated) an attempt to remember the days of war without being politically incorrect. This changed in the course of the 1950s, when a younger generation of tourists who had not been in the Wehrmacht traveled to the sites of Nazi crimes in order to pay respect to the victims.

Altogether, what unites the chapters in this book is their focus not simply on the violence of war but on how to explain and understand the social and cultural history of what followed. It is the relationship between the violence of the 1940s and the normality of the 1950s; it involves an attempt to understand the 1950s as the post-history of the 1940s. Of course, the terms *violence* and *normality* are terribly broad and mask a huge number of exceptions, but they serve as a helpful shorthand that allows us to approach a central aspect of the history of the twentieth century. One of the most striking characteristics of the period that followed the "decade of violence" was its relative peacefulness, stability, and conservatism – not only in terms of politics but also in terms of social and cultural life. If the 1940s may be described as the "decade of violence," the 1950s arguably may be described as the "decade of normality" – a decade in which one saw an apparent "normalization" and stabilization of political, social, and cultural relationships. We can see this in the remarkable – and contrary to longer-term trends – declines in rates of reported crime, divorce, and illegitimacy. Other indications are the triumph of conservative politics of "no experiments," from Adenauer to Macmillan, the conservative tone and content of film and television, the constrained discussion and restrained expression of sexuality, and the circumscribing of gender roles. After the upheavals of the 1940s, people were desperate to put their own worlds back together, to re-establish what they regarded as normality. However, the normality of the 1950s – coming as it did after the greatest outpouring of violence in human history – was anything but normal. It was, both collectively and individually, life after death. Nevertheless, it continues to provide the images of normality to which people refer and compared to which they frequently find their own world wanting – images of a world that now appears to have "fallen apart." That is to say, perceptions of present-day political, social, and cultural developments are conditioned by a remarkable image of a golden age of stability and normality that itself was an amalgam of social, political, and cultural reactions to the violence of the 1940s.

This point highlights why the subject of this book is special: It is as much about ourselves as it is about an objective, detached narrative. We, of the generations born in the 1940s, 1950s, and 1960s, grew up in a postwar world, a world in which mass violence and death was a huge dark shadow of the past and where the present was, by contrast, remarkably benign and sunny. There can be few subjects whereby the observation that the shadowy figures that stare out at us from the tarnished mirror of history are in the final analysis ourselves, more apposite than with the peculiar social and cultural history of Europe after the Second World War. Over the past few decades one of the main preoccupations of modern European historians – and this certainly was true for historians of modern Germany trained during the 1960s and 1970s – was how to explain the path *into* fascism and war: How did the interwar dictators get into power? How did political systems develop that could imprison and murder hundreds of thousands, and finally millions of the people under their control? How did Europe get into a Second World War even more bloody than the First? How was humanity pushed down the road to Treblinka? Relatively little thought was given, until rather recently, to the question that, for us and for the world we inhabit, is probably even more important: How did people emerge from these horrors? We have given enormous thought to how Europeans got into fascism and war; the time has come to understand, in social and cultural as well as political and economic terms, how Europeans got out.

1

Post-Traumatic Stress Disorder and World War II

Can a Psychiatric Concept Help Us Understand Postwar Society?

ALICE FÖRSTER AND BIRGIT BECK

How far can the pervasive violence of World War II, which affected not only combatants but also civilians, help explain the nature of European societies in the 1950s? The research presented in this book spans several countries and approaches this question from a variety of disciplines. The specific point that this chapter proposes to address is whether the understanding of the individual's reaction to life-threatening violence can contribute usefully to the body of research on the German society of the 1950s. This chapter raises questions and generates new hypotheses or tools for future empirical research. The crucial question remains whether it is at all admissible to use medical concepts to generate hypotheses for historical research.

World War II exposed many individuals to extreme and prolonged violence, and works of fiction as well as historical essays and books attempt to describe the way in which ordinary Germans experienced the war. Wolfgang Borchert's play *Draussen vor der Tür* captured the atmosphere of the early postwar years.[1] When it was first broadcast on the radio on February 13, 1947, it elicited a tremendous response from listeners. The play describes the guilt, pain, nightmares, and finally suicide of a returned soldier confronted by various people, such as a former officer and the director of a cabaret, trying to forget the war and return to normality. Returning to "normality" was particularly important in the 1950s.[2] Here, the most important question is what lies beneath the surface of this normality and necessitates maintaining it at all costs.

---

1 Wolfgang Borchert, *Das Gesamtwerk* (Hamburg, 1993), 99–165, 341–3.
2 Ibid., 119–36. Besides Wolfgang Borchert, Heinrich Böll also vividly described the early years in postwar Germany in his tales and novels. See, e.g., "Die Botschaft" (1947), in Bernd Balzer, ed., *Heinrich Böll: Werke. Romane und Erzählungen I 1947–1952*, 3d ed. (Cologne, 1989), 30–5.

Because a great deal has been written about Holocaust survivors and their children, few of whom lived in postwar Germany, we will not deal with this particular aspect of the violence during World War II.[3] In recent years, children not only of perpetrators but also of ordinary Germans have begun talking about their childhood experiences of growing up in postwar Germany.[4] The experience of war and destruction deeply influenced their childhood.[5]

In this chapter, we provide an overview of the literature estimating the proportion of the German population that was exposed to violence in combat as well as in civilian life. According to psychiatric observation, certain traumatic experiences engender specific symptoms. We summarize relevant aspects of the psychiatric literature regarding reaction to combat, atrocities, rape, and life-threatening violence, and then attempt to describe the dimensions of the problem in Germany during World War II from a historical point of view. Moreover, we look at ways to investigate the impact of individual disturbance on the society of the 1950s. First, however, we define the concept of post-traumatic stress disorder (PTSD) before moving on to examine the experiences of people in Germany.

THE PSYCHIATRIC CONCEPT OF PTSD

Since as early as the seventeenth century, reactions to traumatic events have been described in works of fiction. However, medical acknowledgment of such a reaction came much later.[6] Both world wars and the Vietnam War

---

3 See, e.g., Dan Bar-On, "Children of Perpetrators of the Holocaust: Working through One's Own Moral Self," *Psychiatry* 53 (1990): 229–45; Norman Solkoff, "Children of Survivors of the Nazi Holocaust: A Critical Review of the Literature," *American Journal of Orthopsychiatry* 51 (1981): 29–41; Rachel Yehuda et al., "Vulnerability to Posttraumatic Stress Disorder in Adult Offspring of Holocaust Survivors," *American Journal of Psychiatry* 155 (1998): 1163–71.

4 Ingeborg Bruns, *Als Vater aus dem Krieg heimkehrte: Töchter erinnern sich* (Frankfurt am Main, 1991), and Dan Bar-On, *Die Last des Schweigens: Gespräche mit Kindern von Nazi-Tätern*, 2d ed. (Reinbek bei Hamburg, 1996).

5 Bruns, *Vater*, 52: "Mein Vater hat sich nie darüber geäussert, wie die Demütigungen und die Entbehrungen auf ihn gewirkt haben" ("My father never said anything about how the humiliations and privations affected him."); 82: "Als der Krieg kam und mein Vater Soldat werden musste, wurde alles anders. Er hatte kein grosses Interesse mehr an uns Kindern und seine Stimme klang hart" ("When the war began and my father had to become a soldier, everything changed. He no longer had much interest in us children, and his voice sounded harsh."); 89–90: "Ob mein Vater ohne den Krieg, ohne die schrecklichen Erfahrungen, die er doch als Arzt gewiss machen musste und von denen er nie gesprochen hat, ein anderer Vater, ein richtiger Vater hätte sein können? Das einzige was bei ihm sicher war, war, dass man nie sicher sein konnte ob er nicht plötzlich losschlagen oder losschreien würde." ("Could my father have been a different father, a proper father, without the war, without the horrible experiences that he must have had as a doctor and never spoke about? The only thing certain about him was that you could never be certain whether he might suddenly lash out or yell.")

6 Several articles and book chapters give historical reviews of the development of the concept of post-traumatic stress disorder. See L. Stephen O'Brien, *Traumatic Events and Mental Health* (Cambridge, 1998), 1–34; J. David Kinzie and Rupert R. Goetz, "A Century of Controversy Surrounding Post-Traumatic Stress Spectrum Syndromes: The Impact on DSM III and DSM IV," *Journal of Traumatic*

led to systematic research on the psychological reaction to combat. German psychiatric research following World War II focused mainly on the victims of the concentration camps, who were interviewed for compensation claims.[7] Triggered by the Vietnam War, psychiatric research on combat-related reactions to trauma mushroomed in the late 1960s and early 1970s, particularly in the United States. The term *post-traumatic stress disorder* was coined for the symptoms that developed following the experience of "an event that is outside the range of usual human experience and that would be markedly distressing to almost anyone."[8]

The symptoms considered as typical of PTSD are:

- persistent *re-experiencing*, for example, dreams, intrusive recollections of the event, or intense distress at exposure to events that symbolize or resemble an aspect of the traumatic event;
- persistent *avoidance* of stimuli associated with the trauma or *numbing* of general responsiveness, for example, efforts to avoid thoughts, feelings, or activities associated with the trauma, inability to recall important aspects of the trauma, markedly diminished interest in significant activities, feelings of detachment or estrangement from others, restricted range of affect, or sense of foreshortened future; and
- persistent symptoms of *increased arousal*, for example, difficulty falling or staying asleep, irritability or outbursts of anger, difficulty concentrating, hypervigilance, or exaggerated startle response and physiological reactivity on exposure to events that symbolize or resemble an aspect of the traumatic event.[9]

To make a diagnosis of PTSD, at least one symptom of re-experiencing, three of avoidance and numbing, and two of hyperarousal lasting for at least one month are required.

Symptoms of depression and anxiety frequently occur in conjunction with PTSD.[10] Other disorders frequently seen following combat experience

---

Stress 9 (1996): 159–79; Bessel A. van der Kolk, Nan Herron, and Ann Hostetler, "The History of Trauma in Psychiatry," *Psychiatric Clinics of North America* 17 (1994): 583–600.

7 For a review of the German postwar literature on Holocaust survivors, see Klaus D. Hoppe, "Aftermath of Nazi Persecution Reflected in Recent Psychiatric Literature," *International Psychiatry Clinics* 8 (1971): 169–204.

8 This definition of the traumatic event was part of the diagnostic criteria for PTSD in the American Psychiatric Association, ed., *Diagnostic and Statistical Manual of Mental Disorder*, 3d rev. ed. (Washington, D.C., 1987).

9 The symptoms quoted in the text are also from the third revised edition. In the third edition of 1980, when PTSD was first included in the manual, survivors' guilt was also among the symptoms.

10 Susan M. Orsillo et al., "Current and Lifetime Psychiatric Disorder among Veterans with War Zone-Related Posttraumatic Stress Disorder," *Journal of Nervous and Mental Disease* 184 (1996): 307–13. The authors summarize critically the current research on the association of PTSD with other psychiatric disorders and then present their own results on 311 Vietnam veterans. Although lifetime rates for alcohol abuse or dependence were highest among the veterans, they did not differ between those with or without a diagnosis of PTSD.

include drug and alcohol problems, and physical symptoms that are not fully explained by a medical condition.[11] The relation between PTSD and alcohol abuse is complicated: Some view the abuse of alcohol as a consequence of PTSD symptoms, particularly sleep disturbance. However, alcohol and drug abuse can exacerbate symptoms of hyperarousal.

The severity of the trauma determines the percentage of traumatized individuals who will develop typical symptoms of PTSD. In medical research, no distinction is made between civilian and war-related trauma. An American epidemiological study reported a 1-percent history of PTSD in the general population and 3.5 percent in victims of physical attack.[12] Rape and threats to life both seem to increase the likelihood of developing PTSD. A study of 294 female crime victims in Charleston County, South Carolina, found 9.4 percent PTSD among those who experienced no rape, no death-threats, and no injury; among rape victims 28 percent showed evidence of PTSD, even if there had been no life-threat or injury; the percentage rose to 68.8 percent if the victim perceived a threat to life even if she was not injured; that figure rose to 78.6 percent if an injury also was experienced.[13] Rape, particularly when associated with death-threats and injury, elicits very high rates of PTSD. During World War II, rape was not an infrequent occurrence and was often combined with death-threats.

Several studies show that the experiences of prisoners of war (POWs) in Japan, which often involved beatings and/or torture and starvation, carried a particularly high risk of subsequent PTSD. One such study showed that starvation and beatings and/or torture during captivity were predictors of PTSD. Family histories of mental illness, preservice adjustment problems, and severe childhood trauma did not predict the occurrence of PTSD.[14] A retrospective American study that examined World War II Pacific-theater combat veterans found that 78 percent of those who had been POWs had a lifetime diagnosis of PTSD, compared with 29 percent of those with no such experience.[15] The POW experience, particularly in Japanese camps, involved life-threats and, in many cases, the witnessing of atrocities.[16]

---

11 The psychiatric term is somatoform disorder. For a review of the literature, see also O'Brien, *Traumatic Events*, 158–73.

12 John E. Helzer, L. N. Robins, and L. McEnvoy, "Post-Traumatic Stress Disorder in the General Population," *New England Journal of Medicine* 317 (1987): 1630–4.

13 Dean G. Kilpatrick et al., "Victim and Crime Factors Associated with the Development of Crime-Related Post-Traumatic Stress Disorder," *Behaviour Therapy* 20 (1989): 199–214.

14 Nancy Speed et al., "Posttraumatic Stress Disorder as a Consequence of the Prisoner of War Experience," *Journal of Mental and Nervous Disorder* 177 (1989): 147–53.

15 Patricia B. Sutker, Albert N. Allain, and Daniel K. Winstead, "Psychopathology and Psychiatric Diagnoses of World War II Pacific Theatre Prisoner of War Survivors and Combat Veterans," *American Journal of Psychiatry* 150 (1993): 240–5.

16 Brian E. Engdahl et al., "Posttraumatic Stress Disorder in a Community Group of Former Prisoners of War: A Normative Response to Severe Trauma," *American Journal of Psychiatry* 154 (1997): 1576–81.

All studies agree that the more severe the trauma, particularly the more that a person's life has been threatened, the higher the likelihood of developing PTSD. These research findings were incorporated into the most recent edition of the *Diagnostic and Statistical Manual of Mental Disorders* (*DSM IV*), leading to a change in the definition of trauma. The fourth edition of the *DSM* describes the trauma as follows: (1) "the person experienced, witnessed, or was confronted with an event or events that involved actual or threatened death or serious injury, or a threat to the physical integrity of self or others"; and (2) "the person's response involved intense fear, helplessness or horror. Note: In children this may be expressed instead by disorganized or agitated behavior."[17] According to some research, prolonged exposure or repeated exposure to stressors is more likely to cause symptoms.[18]

Some researchers consider participation in atrocities as crucial in the development of PTSD, whereas others regard the subjective appraisal of responsibility as more important in the development of symptoms. The diagnosis of PTSD does not involve a moral judgment, only the presence of certain symptoms following trauma. The concept underlying the definition is biological.[19]

A study of Vietnam veterans shows that, of a list of nine stressful events, participation in atrocities was the strongest predictor of PTSD. The other events included being subjected to enemy fire, being wounded, being attached to a unit in the South Vietnamese army, being surrounded by the enemy, being separated from one's unit, being on combat patrol, having a buddy killed in action, and witnessing atrocities. Statistical methods were used to control for the fact that stressful events often occurred in conjunction. Participation in atrocities increased the risk of PTSD by 42 percent, independent of having experienced any other stressful event. However, there also was a cumulative risk of PTSD with an increasing number of stressful events.[20]

In medical research, no distinction is made between victim and perpetrator as long as a stressor is present and leads to typical symptoms of PTSD. Recent research has focused on the subjective appraisal of traumatic events rather than objective factors.[21] Alan Fontana et al. presented a retrospective

17 American Psychiatric Association, ed., *Diagnostic and Statistical Manual of Mental Disorder*, 4th ed. (Washington, D.C., 1994).
18 Pamela J. Taylor, "Victims and Survivors," in John Gunn and Pamela J. Taylor, *Forensic Psychiatry: Clinical, Legal, and Ethical Issues* (Oxford 1993), 897–8.
19 Rachel Yehuda, "Neuroendocrinology of Trauma and Posttraumatic Stress Disorder," *Review of Psychiatry* 17 (1998): 97–131.
20 Naomi Breslau and Glenn C. Davis, "Posttraumatic Stress Disorder: The Etiologic Specificity of War-Time Stressors," *American Journal of Psychiatry* 144 (1987): 578–83.
21 Alan Fontana, Robert Rosenheck, and Elisabeth Brett, "War Zone Traumas and Posttraumatic Stress Disorder Symptomatology," *Journal of Nervous and Mental Disorder* 180 (1992): 749–55. The authors

study based on 1,709 Vietnam veterans who were treated in the PTSD
Clinical Teams Program of the Department of Veterans' Affairs. The authors attempt to elucidate the relationship between the nature of the stressor
and the ensuing symptoms. The traumatic experiences of the veterans were
divided into four categories: (1) being the target of killing, (2) being the
observer of killing or atrocities, (3) being the agent of killing or atrocities,
and (4) failing to prevent killing. The two latter categories involved feeling
responsible for the killing. The trauma experience itself was divided into
high and low responsibility categories, and the symptoms were the number
of suicide attempts, a general measure of psychiatric distress, and the three
clusters of symptoms relevant for a diagnosis of PTSD (re-experiencing,
hyperarousal, and numbing and avoidance).

The authors found that being the target of an attempt to kill was strongly
related to a diagnosis of PTSD, particularly to symptoms of hyperarousal.
The authors concluded that the subjective experience of being the target of an attempt to kill was associated most uniquely and strongly with
PTSD. This is in keeping with the findings of the previously cited studies
of war veterans and crime victims. The experience of being responsible
for killing others or for failing to prevent harm to others was related to
suicide and psychiatric symptoms not included in the classical definition
of PTSD. Fontana et al. concluded: "Viewed in terms of our classification
of personal responsibility, PTSD appears to be connected most specifically
to traumas low in personal responsibility for their initiation, whereas psychiatric symptoms and suicide appear to be connected more specifically to
traumas high in personal responsibility."[22] This might imply that the subjective appraisal of responsibility determines guilt feelings more strongly
than do objective factors, such as actually participating in atrocities or being a witness. An earlier essay by William B. Gault, a Harvard psychiatrist
who treated Vietnam veterans, lists six factors that in his opinion facilitate the occurrence of slaughter.[23] His definition of slaughter resembles the
one given by Fontana et al. for atrocities. One of the factors is dilution of
responsibility.

Recent data from a group of former World War II veterans who also
had been POWs show that only a small minority ever received treatment
for PTSD although over 50 percent had experienced PTSD during their

---

summarize up-to-date work on cognitive appraisal of danger and the role of moral conflict. They
then present their own data on 1,709 Vietnam veterans.

22 Ibid., 753.

23 William B. Gault, "Some Remarks on Slaughter," *American Journal of Psychiatry* 128 (1971): 450–4.
The six factors are: (1) the enemy is everywhere, (2) the enemy is not human, (3) dilution of
responsibility, (4) the pressure to act, (5) the natural dominance of the psychopath, (6) firepower.

lives and 29 percent still met criteria for it forty to fifty years later. Among those who had been POWs in Japanese camps, 80 percent had a lifetime diagnosis of PTSD.[24] One veteran whose case is described in detail still suffers from intrusive recollections and sleep problems, and he feels distant and mistrustful of people outside his family. Most veterans in the study showed no significant occupational problems. However, a second veteran who was described in detail and still suffered from PTSD describes himself as underachieving at work due to his "personality." As a prisoner, he had survived the Bataan Death March and had witnessed senseless executions and death-threats. His weight had dropped from 150 to 80 pounds. After a long series of life-threatening episodes, he returned home, married, and raised three children with his wife. He was never promoted during thirty-six years at work. He suffered from daily intrusive recollections, frequent nightmares, hypervigilance, and survivor's guilt. His only social contacts outside the family were other POWs. He never had been treated for psychiatric problems prior to participating in the study.

The main conclusion that can be drawn from the work cited thus far is that following severe, life-threatening trauma, psychological problems, particularly PTSD, will develop in more than 50 percent of cases and can persist for long periods of time. Suicide attempts and guilt feelings are most likely to occur in individuals who felt subjectively responsible for killing others or for failing to prevent harm to others. However, only a minority of such traumatized individuals will seek treatment.

Moreover, PTSD affects not only the sufferers themselves but also their families. Zahava Solomon has reviewed the literature on the effect of PTSD on veterans' families.[25] She found that veterans must re-establish their role in the family when they return home, and some symptoms of PTSD can create problems in the process of reintegration. The symptoms she regarded as crucial are the "numbing of responsiveness and reduced involvement with the external world, as seen by diminished interest in significant activities, feelings of detachment or alienation, and constricted affect." Several studies show how Vietnam veterans had difficulties in maintaining close relationships. One study quoted in the review found that veterans who were involved in atrocities suffered from guilt and fear of their violent impulses. There also is some evidence of child-battering and wife-battering. One of the studies found that 50 percent of the couples seeking help reported

---

24 Engdahl et al., "Posttraumatic Stress Disorder," 1576–81.
25 Zahava Solomon, "The Effect of Combat-Related Posttraumatic Stress Disorder on the Family," *Psychiatry* 51 (1988): 323–9.

wife-battery. The incidents were particularly frightening and violent, and had led to professional consultation. Citing the President's Commission on Mental Health of 1978, the review notes that 38 percent of Vietnam veterans' marriages failed within six months of their return from combat. The author asserts that, in the marriages of PTSD sufferers that do not end in divorce, the wife often must bear an enormous psychological burden that can lead to depression and social isolation.[26] In her own study, Solomon found that the wife's mental health is seriously affected by the veteran's trauma-related psychopathology.[27] Moreover, the wife's social functioning also is impaired in several areas. The difficulties encountered by married couples with a spouse, usually the husband, suffering symptoms of PTSD are likely to affect children as well. In her review, Solomon remarks: "A veteran who engaged in actions against women and children may find the transition to the role of husband/father particularly difficult."[28] She also points out: "The natural exuberance and aggressiveness of a growing child, especially a son, may reawaken memories of wartime aggression and provoke excessive rage or guilt over sadistic impulses. The veteran's attempt to control his child's aggressiveness may be out of proportion."[29] Rosenheck and Fontana have investigated the effect of veterans' participation in abusive violence on their children's behavior.[30] Child behavior was assessed by means of a 122–item questionnaire. The main findings of the study were that child behavior was adversely affected by the father's participation in abusive violence and that

---

26 Ibid., 325–6.
27 Z. Solomon et al., "From Front Line to Home Front: A Study of Secondary Traumatisation," *Family Process* 31 (1992): 289–302.
28 Solomon, "Effect," 326.   29 Ibid., 325–6.
30 Robert Rosenheck and Alan Fontana, "Transgenerational Effects of Abusive Violence on the Children of Vietnam Combat Veterans," *Journal of Traumatic Stress* 11 (1998): 734. The authors have developed a questionnaire for combat exposure and abusive violence. The questions regarding abusive violence were as follows:

(1) Were you ever in a combat situation in (or around) Vietnam where you participated in any kind of injury or destruction that seemed necessary then, but that you would consider unnecessary now?

To what extent were you involved in:
(2) Terrorising, wounding, or killing civilians?
(3) Torturing, wounding, or killing hostages or prisoners of war?
(4) Mutilation of bodies of the enemy or civilians?
(5) In combat situations in (or around) Vietnam, women, children, and old people were sometimes seen by our side as the enemy. Were you ever (directly involved) in a situation in Vietnam where women, children, or old people were either injured or killed by American or South Vietnamese (ARVN) soldiers?
(6) In combat situations in (or around) Vietnam, Vietnamese prisoners or civilians were often injured because they were suspected of being enemy sympathisers, or to obtain information, or to avenge the death of American soldiers, or for other reasons. Were you ever (directly involved) in a situation where a Vietnamese prisoner was injured or killed for any reason?

the effect could not be explained fully by PTSD or a range of pre- and postmilitary factors.

In the literature mainly on veterans of the conflicts in Vietnam and Lebanon, there is evidence that the veterans' PTSD symptoms affected their marital relationships, the wives' mental health and social relations, and their children's behavior. Participation in abusive violence in particular seems to affect the behavior of the veterans' children years later, even if PTSD is not present. The questionnaire developed to assess the abusive violence of Vietnam veterans would have been pertinent in exploring the same phenomenon in German World War II veterans involved in partisan warfare or mass murder of Jews in the East.

THE EXPOSURE OF THE GERMAN POPULATION TO VIOLENCE DURING WORLD WAR II

This section discusses the portion of the German population exposed to multiple traumas that were low in personal responsibility, including bombing, rape, and combat situations in which they were the targets. Also addressed is that portion of the German population exposed to trauma high in responsibility, particularly on the eastern front, where a still undetermined number of Wehrmacht soldiers as well as soldiers of the Waffen-SS took part in or witnessed atrocities against Jews and other civilians. At home in Germany, the 1938 pogrom and deportation of Jewish and communist neighbors also exposed many Germans to the experience of witnessing cruelties. What remains unclear is the subjective experience: What proportion of Germans felt that they had failed to prevent a killing and thus experienced a trauma high in responsibility?

Diaries and interviews with children of Nazi perpetrators show evidence of avoidance and difficulties in expressing emotions.[31] Gitta Sereny quotes a railworker who described his wife's reaction to watching the transports to the camps: "There was a period in the beginning when my wife could not function at all, she could not cook, she could not play with the boy, she could not eat and hardly slept. This extreme condition lasted for about three weeks; she then became pathologically indifferent, she did everything like an automaton."[32]

Statistics on the exposure of German soldiers and civilians to violence or atrocities during the war are considered here. Obviously, the proportion of

---

31 Gitta Sereny, *Into that Darkness: From Mercy Killings to Mass Murder* (London, 1991), and Bar-On, *Last*.
32 Sereny, *Into that Darkness*, 150.

Germans who were exposed to violence cannot be calculated exactly. Here, historical methods differ from the often experimental design of research in the natural sciences.[33] As Rüdiger Overmans asserted in his remarks about the civilian and military losses of World War II, different methodological approaches have led to considerable variations in statistical estimates: "The main problem of all available statistics are the different definitions they use, thus not allowing an estimate about all losses."[34] Even a decade later, his statement remains valid and applies to most of the figures that follow. However, the figures can yield an impression of the extent of trauma encountered by German combatants and by civilians.

In 1939, the population of Germany proper was more than 69 million; add the people of Austria and the Sudetenland, and it rose to approximately 79 million.[35] A sizeable proportion of the German population was affected by the war over the following six years. The extent of exposure to traumatic events differed markedly in various subgroups of the population according to their rank in the military structure (for example, Wehrmacht soldiers and Waffen-SS) and the areas where they lived as civilians or fought as soldiers.

Wehrmacht soldiers who took part in the attack on Poland were the first to be involved both in combat and in perpetration of atrocities. At the beginning of September 1939, there were about 4.5 million men in the army, the air force, and the navy, and in 1944 the German armed forces totaled 10 million men.[36] Altogether, more than 17 million men spent time in the Wehrmacht during the Third Reich, and about 13 million of them survived the war.[37] Conscription into the army did not automatically imply front-line

33 Lutz Niethammer, "Fragen – Antworten – Fragen: Methodische Erfahrungen und Erwägungen zur Oral History," in Lutz Niethammer and Alexander von Plato, eds., *Lebensgeschichte und Sozialkultur im Ruhrgebiet 1930 bis 1960*, 3 vols. (Berlin, 1985), vol. 3: *"Wir kriegen jetzt andere Zeiten": Auf der Suche nach der Erfahrung des Volkes in nachfaschistischen Ländern*, 409–10.

34 Rüdiger Overmans, "Die Toten des Zweiten Weltkriegs in Deutschland. Bilanz der Forschung unter besonderer Berücksichtigung der Wehrmacht- und Vertreibungsverluste," in Wolfgang Michalka, ed., *Der Zweite Weltkrieg: Analysen, Grundzüge, Forschungsbilanz* (Munich, 1989), 869. Translation by the authors. Concerning the casualties of the German armed forces, Overmans recently published new statistical data. Rüdiger Overmans, *Deutsche militärische Verluste im Zweiten Weltkrieg* (Munich, 1999).

35 Länderrat des Amerikanischen Besatzungsgebiets, ed., *Statistisches Handbuch von Deutschland 1928–1944* (Munich, 1949), 18, table 4: "Development of the population 1850–1946." See also Peter Marschalck, *Bevölkerungsgeschichte Deutschlands im 19. und 20. Jahrhundert* (Frankfurt am Main, 1984), 149, table 1.7; Dietmar Petzina, Werner Abelshauser, and Anselm Faust, *Sozialgeschichtliches Arbeitsbuch III: Materialien zur Statistik des Deutschen Reiches 1914–1945*, 4 vols. (Munich 1978), 3:22; Bernhard R. Kroener, "Die personellen Ressourcen des Dritten Reiches im Spannungsfeld zwischen Wehrmacht, Bürokratie und Kriegswirtschaft 1939–1942," in Militärgeschichtliches Forschungsamt, ed., *Das Deutsche Reich und der Zweite Weltkrieg*, 6 vols. (Stuttgart, 1979–99), vol. 5/1: "Organisation und Mobilisierung des deutschen Machtbereichs," 750.

36 Rolf-Dieter Müller and Gerd R. Ueberschär, *Kriegsende 1945: Die Zerstörung des Deutschen Reiches* (Frankfurt am Main, 1994), 58, and Kroener, "Ressourcen," 726, 811.

37 Overmans, *Verluste*, 215, 294.

experience and involvement in combat. In fact, in 1939 only 1,131,000 men out of 4.5 million were on active duty, whereas the rest served in the reserves or belonged to the Wehrmacht staff who worked in barracks and factories.[38] It is of great significance for the extent of exposure to combat and atrocities to distinguish among the several fronts at which the soldiers saw action, because the circumstances were not identical with regard to physical and emotional demands. The attack on the Soviet Union on June 22, 1941, was the beginning of a brutal campaign that led to the greatest toll of casualties for the German army. The survivors of this campaign had had to contend with various hardships, including harsh weather conditions, logistical problems, and, more important, the atrocities and dangers of combat and partisan warfare. The average total troop strength of the German armed forces on the eastern front at any one time totaled 3.35 million men,[39] and it can be assumed that a majority of these soldiers were involved in brutal, life-threatening combat on a daily basis.

Surveys on the so-called *Kriegsneurotiker* (war neurotics) are worth mentioning here. Many show that large numbers of troops had previously suffered mental disturbance during the war. According to Karl Heinz Roth, who scrutinized the reports of the *Beratende Psychiater* (advising psychiatrists), before the attack on the Soviet Union in June 1941 suicides had become frequent and the first reports of self-mutilations had surfaced. During the winter of 1941–2, the number of shell-shocked soldiers rose further, and the number of suicides and cases of self-mutilation already exceeded those committed during World War I. After the Battle of Stalingrad, the number of shell-shock sufferers increased dramatically, and by 1944 the entire German army had reported about 20,000 to 30,000 *Kriegsneurotiker*. In the winter of 1944–5, military hospitals alone counted more than 100,000 shell-shock sufferers.[40]

In addition to ordinary forces, the members of the combat units of the SS, the so-called Waffen-SS, and the so-called *Einsatzgruppen* (operation teams) took part not only in the campaigns against Poland and the Soviet Union, but

---

38 Kroener, "Ressourcen," 731.
39 Bernd Wegner, "Der Krieg gegen die Sowjetunion 1942/1943," in Militärgeschichtliches Forschungsamt, ed., *Das Deutsche Reich und der Zweite Weltkrieg*, vol. 6: Horst Boog, *Der globale Krieg. Die Ausweitung zum Weltkrieg und der Wechsel der Initiative 1941–1943* (Stuttgart, 1990), 778.
40 Karl Heinz Roth, "Die Modernisierung der Folter in den beiden Weltkriegen: Der Konflikt der Psychotherapeuten und Schulpsychiater um die deutschen 'Kriegsneurotiker' 1915–1945," *1999: Zeitschrift für Sozialgeschichte des 20. und 21. Jahrhunderts* 3 (1987): 8–75, see esp. 41, 49, 72. His research is based on material from the Bundesarchiv Militärarchiv at Freiburg im Breisgau. See also Gerhard Berger, *Die Beratenden Psychiater des deutschen Heeres 1939 bis 1945* (Frankfurt am Main, 1998), 107–30, 172–7, 238.

also in the mass extermination of Jews in the east. In the summer of 1942, the number of troops in the Waffen-SS totaled 190,000 men,[41] and by the end of the war another 800,000 to 900,000 Germans and men from the Baltic region, Romania, and Hungary had joined these units.[42] Five *Einsatzgruppen*, totaling 2,700 men, operated in the campaign against Poland. After the attack on the Soviet Union, four *Einsatzgruppen* of 600 to 1,000 men each were formed; a total of 4,000 men thus went into action in the Baltic, in Belorussia, Ukraine, Bessarabia, Crimea, and the Caucasus.[43] The members of the Waffen-SS and the *Einsatzgruppen* were the main perpetrators of the mass shootings of men, women, and children. Most participated in or witnessed atrocities. Although many of the perpetrators were deeply influenced by Nazi ideology and were therefore convinced of the necessity of their deeds, there are reports that some could stand participating in such atrocities only under the influence of alcohol.[44] There is no research available showing whether the members of these special units suffered different rates of PTSD or other psychiatric illness or suicide than did the ordinary soldiers of the Wehrmacht. However, according to the American literature on Vietnam veterans, one would expect the highest rates of PTSD in combatants particularly if they took part in atrocities. Perpetrators who qualify for trauma high in responsibility generally have high rates of suicide. However, personal acceptance of responsibility is crucial.[45] There may be a significant difference in this respect between postwar Germany and the post-Vietnam United States.

Not only men served on the western and eastern fronts: A large number of women worked as *Wehrmachtshelferinnen* (female military aides), for example, as secretaries or anti-aircraft auxiliaries. Depending on the circumstances, many of these mainly young women were exposed to combat; however, there is no research on how they coped with their experiences. In the summer of 1944, about 50,000 women and girls were deployed as anti-aircraft auxiliaries, and at the beginning of 1945 the total number of

---

41 Kroener, "Ressourcen," 959, table: Stärkeentwicklung der Wehrmachtteile und der Waffen-SS vom 1. September 1939 bis 1. Juli 1942.

42 Bernd Wegner, "Anmerkungen zur Geschichte der Waffen-SS aus organisations- und funktionsgeschichtlicher Sicht," in Rolf-Dieter Müller and Hans-Erich Volkmann, eds., *Die Wehrmacht: Mythos und Realität* (Munich, 1999), 406n3. See also Overmans, *Verluste*, 215.

43 Helmut Krausnick and Hans-Heinrich Wilhelm, *Die Truppe des Weltanschauungskrieges: Die Einsatzgruppen der Sicherheitspolizei und des SD 1938–1942* (Stuttgart, 1981), 34, 147.

44 A massacre is described by Christopher R. Browning, *Ordinary Men: Reserve Police Battalion 101 and the Final Solution in Poland* (New York, 1993), 55–70; on the significance of alcohol, see 61, 69, 100. Browning also mentions the case of an *SS-Hauptsturmführer* who became ill during the killing activities of his battalion, 114–20.

45 See the section "The Psychiatric Concept of PTSD" at the beginning of this chapter.

auxiliaries for the Wehrmacht amounted to about half a million.[46] Five percent of all internees in the Soviet Union were alleged to be women, and one survey estimates that in 1949, 25,000 women were still held prisoner in Soviet camps.[47]

By the end of 1945, a total of 18.2 million men had been called up to the Wehrmacht and Waffen-SS; out of these, 4.5 million were killed, more than half of them on the eastern front.[48] Eleven million German soldiers and members of the Wehrmacht were captured; of these, more than 3 million were POWs in the Soviet Union and only 2 million returned.[49] One should remember that all these estimates depend on the definition of the status of a POW; indeed, it is unclear who counted as a prisoner of war in these statistics. For instance, women of the Wehrmacht retinue did not have the status of combatants and therefore did not count as POWs when they were captured. Moreover, the place of captivity is not insignificant, as prisoners in the Soviet Union were often bundled off to labor camps where men had to toil in quarries and often were threatened with death or serious injury. One of the long-term consequences of malnutrition was dystrophy, from which many of the POWs in Soviet camps suffered.[50] However, the majority of German soldiers were captured by the Western Allies.[51] The problems encountered by repatriated POWs from the Western Allies have not been examined in detail, as noted in a recent collection edited by Annette Kaminsky.[52] Nevertheless, it is known that long-term separation from their families and the harsh conditions in the labor camps traumatized the POWs and made their reintegration into civilian life difficult. In 1953, there were more than 1.4 million war invalids, half of them seriously disabled. However, the figures do not give us a description of the injuries sustained. Moreover, there is no information on the contribution of psychological factors to the degree of invalidity.[53]

Far more than in World War I, German civilians in World War II were exposed to life-threatening violence. From 1942 onward, the intensified

---

46 Müller and Ueberschär, *Kriegsende*, 31. Also Kroener, "Ressourcen," 726, 811.

47 Stefan Karner, *Im Archipel GUPVI: Kriegsgefangenschaft und Internierung in der Sowjetunion 1941–1956* (Vienna, 1995), 14–15.

48 Overmans, *Verluste*, 293–6.

49 Beate Ihme-Tuchel, "Zwischen Tabu und Propaganda. Hintergründe und Probleme der ostdeutsch-sowjetischen Heimkehrerverhandlungen," in Annette Kaminsky, ed., *Heimkehr 1948* (Munich, 1998), 40, and lower figures in Müller and Ueberschär, *Kriegsende*, 112. See also Overmans, *Verluste*, 286, 292.

50 Karner, *Archipel*, 63–75, 86–94. H. Paul, *Charakterveränderungen durch Kriegsgefangenschaft und Dystrophie* (Bad Godesberg, 1959).

51 Sibylle Meyer and Eva Schulze, *Von Liebe sprach damals keiner: Familienalltag in der Nachkriegszeit* (Munich, 1985), 253, table 5.

52 Kaminsky, *Heimkehr*, 7.   53 Meyer and Schulze, *Liebe*, 257, table 7.

bombing of German cities by Allied forces led to the large-scale destruction of housing and increasingly influenced life on the home front, particularly in the cities. In 1945, a total of 4 million homes had been destroyed in Germany alone. The air raids had killed 600,000 civilians; 900,000 were wounded, and 7.5 million had been made homeless. Some of the people who were bombed out had to live in temporary shelters for years.[54] The areas most severely affected by the bombing were Berlin and the Ruhr area. For instance, in Cologne 70 percent of the housing stock – a total of 176,000 apartments – was destroyed, and in Dortmund and Duisburg more than half of the prewar dwellings were completely annihilated.[55] In Berlin, which had the highest number of casualties, 50,000 died as a result of air raids.[56] In July 1943, in an operation called *Gomorrha*, 3,000 Allied bombers dropped more than 9,000 tons of firebombs and explosive devices on Hamburg within ten days, leaving 40,000 people dead. Sixty-one percent of the city's housing stock was destroyed, and one million people were left homeless.[57] In the last months of the war, Germans in some areas were exposed daily – sometimes several times a day – to air raids, which constituted life-threatening events with low responsibility.[58]

What did daily bombing mean for the residents of a town? It meant blackouts in the evening, a ban on going out, and huddling for hours in air-raid shelters with old and sick people and with screaming children. In some cases, women had to give birth without medical help while the building burned around them and detonations made a terrible noise heralding death.[59] These experiences would fully qualify as traumatic events as defined in *DSM IV*, particularly because many people also witnessed the death or serious injury of their next of kin. There are reports of women who considered suicide because they felt hopeless but did not kill themselves because of the children.[60] An opinion poll in October 1948 documented long-term effects of the bombing. Eight-hundred West Germans over age 18 were

54 Bernd J. Wendt, *Deutschland 1933–1945: Das "Dritte Reich." Handbuch zur Geschichte* (Hannover, 1995), 538, and Müller and Ueberschär, *Kriegsende*, 41.

55 Christian Engeli, "Krieg und Kriegsfolgen in Berlin im Vergleich zu anderen Städten," in Wolfgang Ribbe and Jürgen Schmädeke, eds., *Berlin im Europa der Neuzeit: Ein Tagungsbericht* (Berlin, 1990), 406, table 3.

56 Ibid., 402–3.

57 Ursula Koser-Oppermann, "Evakuiert, umquartiert, einquartiert. Wohnen in der zerstörten Stadt," in Ulrike Jureit and Beate Meyer, eds., *Verletzungen: Lebensgeschichtliche Verarbeitung von Kriegserfahrungen* (Hamburg, 1994), 176.

58 Olaf Groehler, *Bombenkrieg gegen Deutschland* (Berlin, 1990), 259, 319.

59 Sibylle Meyer and Eva Schulze, " 'Als wir wieder zusammen waren, ging der Krieg im Kleinen weiter': Frauen, Männer und Familien im Berlin der vierziger Jahre," in Niethammer and von Plato, *Andere Zeiten*, 309.

60 Ibid., 308.

asked about their dreams: 26 percent of the female interviewees described dreaming about the air raids, 9 percent of the male interviewees reported dreams of the firing line at the front, and 3 percent of those reporting dreams felt tormented by them.[61]

However, the end of the bombing and the end of the war did not bring an end to the horror and pain. In the winter of 1944–5, women and girls, particularly in the eastern regions of Germany, suffered another traumatic experience when they became the victims of mass rapes. Current research on the topic is scant because it was not discussed in public until recently. Helke Sander and Barbara Johr tried to establish figures for Berlin using estimates and projections, and they came to the conclusion that between April and September of 1945, after the invasion of the Red Army, nearly 110,000 of 1.4 million female residents of the city were raped. About 7 percent of all women in Berlin were raped, regardless of their age or appearance. Over one thousand children were born as a result of the rapes, while the number of abortions cannot be estimated due to the high proportion of unreported cases.[62] According to Gerhard Reichling's estimates, about 1.4 million women and girls were raped in East Prussia, Eastern Pomerania, Brandenburg, and Silesia. However, his estimates, as well as those of Sander and Johr, have not been replicated and their methodology is not always clear.[63] There is no doubt that rape associated with threat to life is considered a major trauma in the psychiatric literature and leads to PTSD in more than 70 percent of the cases.[64] There is corroborating evidence from the historical literature that rape was considered traumatic by the German women who experienced it. Asked about their war experiences, women explained that they could not reveal to their husbands the terrible experience of being raped and that they tried to forget it.[65]

Another traumatic experience often associated with threat to life and the death of relatives was flight from the advancing Red Army. Often with little or no notice, the refugees had to leave behind most of their belongings and undertake a dangerous and arduous journey to western Germany with

---

61 Elisabeth Noelle and Erich P. Neumann, eds., *Jahrbuch der öffentlichen Meinung 1947–1955*, 2d ed. (Allensbach, 1956), 9. Between 1947 and 1955, the "Institut für Demoskopie" at Allensbach interviewed different strata of the West German population. They used a questionnaire including 2,176 questions. The results as well as the questions are published in the book (v).

62 Helke Sander and Barbara Johr, eds., *Befreier und Befreite: Krieg, Vergewaltigungen, Kinder* (Frankfurt am Main, 1995), 54.

63 For Gerhard Reichling's figures, see ibid., 58–60.

64 Kilpatrick et al., "Victim."

65 Erika M. Hoerning, "Frauen als Kriegsbeute: Der Zwei-Fronten-Krieg. Beispiele aus Berlin," in Niethammer and von Plato, *Andere Zeiten*, 327–44. See also Sander and Johr, *Befreier und Befreite*, 90, 92, 95.

young children and elderly or sick family members. Between 1945 and 1950, nearly 7 million refugees and expellees from the eastern areas of Germany and nearly 4 million Germans from Czechoslovakia, the Baltic region, Poland, Hungary, Yugoslavia, and Romania moved to the western zones of occupation. In addition, more than two million died during their flight or were reported missing.[66]

It was this experience in particular that was remembered publicly in Germany in the late 1940s and 1950s. Far from being put aside in silence, the horrors of expulsion and flight were used as a political tool in the discussion about the crimes of Nazi Germany. They served to prove that Germans themselves had suffered and to equate their victimization with that of the Jews and other victims of Nazi policy. The West German government, for example, funded a massive research project that centered on about 11,000 eyewitness accounts and was published in eight volumes from the mid-1950s onward.[67] How this selective public memory of the war years influenced the way individuals came to terms with expulsion and flight and other victimizing events is far from clear, however, and needs closer examination.

In 1952, the Allensbach Institute asked 535 young German men about their experiences during World War II. The answers give us a good impression of the proportion of participants who had experienced traumatic events: 58 percent of the interviewees had to worry about family members; 51 percent lost family members; 41 percent had experienced air raids; 36 percent had a father or brother who had been a POW for a long period; 21 percent were bombed out with their family; 21 percent had to flee or were deported after the war; and 19 percent had a family member who was disabled.[68] Also in 1952, another group of two thousand West German women and men over eighteen years of age was asked about their health, and 31 percent of the interviewees stated that they had nervous problems.[69]

CONCLUSIONS AND OUTLOOK

There is strong evidence from the historical literature that millions of German civilians, particularly in the East, were exposed to multiple traumas

---

66 Gerhard Reichling, *Die Heimatvertriebenen im Spiegel der Statistik* (Berlin, 1958), 347. Müller and Ueberschär, *Kriegsende*, 123. The traumatic experiences of children were also discussed at the beginning of the 1950s: Volker Ackermann, "Deutsche Flüchtlingskinder nach 1945," in Dittmar Dahlmann, ed., *Kinder und Jugendliche in Krieg und Revolution: Vom Dreissigjährigen Krieg bis zu den Kindersoldaten Afrikas* (Paderborn, 2000), 145–67.

67 Cf. Robert G. Moeller, "War Stories: The Search for a Usable Past in the Federal Republic of Germany," *American Historical Review* 101 (1996): 1008–48.

68 Noelle and Neumann, *Jahrbuch*, 23. The interviewees could give more than one answer. See also 114 about mentality and the question if one can recognize a person who took part in the war.

69 Ibid., 6.

such as bombing, rape, witnessing the death of relatives, and flight from the advancing Red Army. Although we cannot be sure how many were involved in combat and/or atrocities, it is safe to conclude that almost half the adult German population had some first-hand experience of threat to life, death of a relative, or rape.

Is it permissible to draw conclusions from epidemiological findings from the Vietnam or other wars to generate hypotheses about World War II? Such an approach would not be at all unusual in medical research. Rape and death-threats are regarded as stressors that can cause functional brain changes, which then can lead to symptoms of PTSD in war or peace and across cultures. There is no methodological problem in generating hypotheses from a civilian traumatic situation, such as rape in an inner city, to understand a war-related trauma, for example, PTSD in women who were raped in Bosnia. We are fully aware of how difficult it is to use data from medical epidemiological studies in order to generate hypotheses about social phenomena. In medical research, no distinction is made between life-threatening violence in different cultures or whether the life-threatening event is civilian or war-related. Other variables deemed crucial in medicine, such as genetic vulnerability, are not part of the social science concepts.[70] The assumption is that an event "that is outside the range of usual human experience and that would be markedly distressing to almost anyone" will lead to changes in brain function or even morphology, which in turn will elicit symptoms. Several factors such as duration and severity of the trauma, previous trauma, and previous mental illness can increase or diminish the risk of developing symptoms. Moreover, an event can be equally distressing to the perpetrator as to the victim of violence. It is germane to medical and particularly forensic research to avoid moral judgment. The term *post-traumatic stress disorder*, which describes symptoms following trauma, does not necessarily imply that the sufferer is a victim. Some symptoms occur in perpetrators of violence who were also exposed to life-threatening events.[71]

Having pointed out a range of differences in medical, biological, and social science concepts, we wonder if it makes sense to use medical findings about reaction to trauma in order to understand a society in which the majority has experienced severe trauma. We believe that it can be useful as long as one is constantly aware of the pitfalls. Neither author is a specialist on postwar Germany; however, we believe that it could be interesting to explore how symptoms translate into social phenomena. The research on families

---

70 For a review of epidemiological research of post-traumatic stress disorder, see O'Brien, *Traumatic Events*, 53–82. In the chapter the occurrence of disorder following a range of civilian and war-related trauma is described.

71 See note 22 to this chapter.

of Vietnam veterans could be used to generate testable hypotheses about patterns of behavior in families with one or more traumatized members. Contemporary diaries or other sources could be used to investigate whether similar behavioral patterns can be found in the 1950s and to generate new hypotheses regarding how such behavior could have influenced society. We are fully aware that the task of bridging the gap between what constitutes individual behavior and its influence on the nuclear family and explaining social phenomena remains unresolved. Only further discussion can help us find solutions.

There is some circumstantial evidence from the 1952 Allensbach opinion poll, which does not include combat experience, that psychological problems were not infrequent. In the same year, 31 percent of a sample of two thousand West German men and women complained of nervous problems, although we do not know what percentage was trauma related, and we have no information that would allow us to make a diagnosis.

There is no doubt that, considering the severity of the traumatic events particularly in the East and on the eastern front, one would expect up to 70 percent of those who were refugees from the East or soldiers on the eastern front to develop PTSD either on its own or combined with other psychological problems, particularly alcohol abuse. We would also expect, as described for Vietnam veterans, higher divorce rates.

However, even assuming that, given a certain trauma, symptoms of PTSD occur at similar levels independent of cultural influences, the way one deals with such traumatized individuals is strongly dependent on social factors. Furthermore, how the trauma experience and subsequent pathology influence a society depends on the interaction between illness variables and social phenomena. Shell-shocked soldiers were treated differently in Germany and Great Britain during World War II. In Britain, they received group therapy; in Germany, electroshock treatments.[72] Vietnam veterans were more likely to get help with their own and their families' psychological problems than were veterans of World War II in America and elsewhere. In Germany after the war, doctors, psychologists, welfare workers, and church representatives turned their attention to soldiers returning from the front. Of foremost importance here, however, was treating dystrophy, and professional psychiatric help was given only to very few POWs. A more intense study of the examinations carried out at that time could contribute to an explanation of the

---

72 Edgar Jones and Simon Wessely, "The Effect of Total War on British Psychiatry," in Roger Chickering and Stig Förster, eds., *The Shadows of Total War: Europe, East Asia, and the United States, 1919–1939* (New York, 2002).

problem of trauma.[73] Only interdisciplinary research can investigate these areas further and add to the substantial body of relevant research generated by individual disciplines.

Our review of the literature shows how difficult it would be to try to make precise estimates of the proportion of the population affected by symptoms of post-traumatic stress disorder in Germany. A more viable aim would be to compare a low-trauma with a high-trauma group. Relevant stressors and symptoms could be chosen from the psychiatric literature; for example, suicide and suicide attempts could be regarded as markers for taking part in atrocities.[74] One could compare the rates of suicide and suicide attempts of members of the Wehrmacht who were unlikely to have witnessed atrocities with those in *Einsatzgruppen* who were certainly involved in atrocities. One could also compare divorce rates in members of the *Einsatzgruppen*, in soldiers with high combat exposure, and in soldiers with low combat exposure.

Although the ideal of the happy family was strongly upheld in the 1950s, this image was in stark contrast to the reality of high divorce rates. Between 1946 and 1950, the divorce rate rose. In 1939, the rate was 7.5 per 10,000 inhabitants; in 1946, it rose to 9.9 percent, and to 18.9 in 1948.[75] In 1950, there were 84,740 divorces in the Federal Republic of Germany; five years later, however, the number had nearly halved, to 48,277.[76] Historical research so far has offered several explanations for the postwar rise in divorce rates: One is that people married shortly before or soon after the outbreak of the war. Many couples were separated for years, making an ordinary married life impossible. As one woman pointed out: "Naturally I knew it would be difficult. We had not lived together properly yet. Half a year of marriage and then the war. It was not a proper marriage, and what it means to have children and what their needs are he never realized during his leave."[77] Moreover, numerous war weddings did not last for long because the couples often married in order to be provided for in worse times. Nevertheless, one can assume that some of the divorces resulted from the

---

73 Leonid Ischenin, *Die deutschen Heimkehrer und die Massnahmen zu ihrer Eingliederung unter Berücksichtigung der Umsiedler aus dem Osten* (Cologne, 1966), 126–34; *Extreme Lebensverhältnisse und ihre Folgen. Handbuch der ärztlichen Erfahrungen aus der Gefangenschaft*, Schriftenreihe des ärztlich-wissenschaftlichen Beirates des Verbandes der Heimkehrer Deutschlands e.V. (Bad Godesberg, 1964). See also Robert G. Moeller, "'The Last Soldier of the Great War' and Tales of Family Reunions in the Federal Republic of Germany," *Signs: Journal of Women in Culture and Society* 24 (1998): 129–45.
74 See the section "The Psychiatric Concept of PTSD" at the beginning of this chapter.
75 Meyer and Schulze, *Liebe*, 249, table 2.
76 Ralf Rytlewski and Manfred Opp de Hipt, *Die Bundesrepublik Deutschland in Zahlen 1945/49–1980: Ein sozialgeschichtliches Arbeitsbuch* (Munich, 1987), 46.
77 Bruns, *Vater*, 11. Translation by the authors.

difficulties both partners had after the war coping with their different and often traumatic experiences. Indications to this effect may be found in the numerous interviews with women and men who were asked about their postwar experiences and who often talked about the changed character of their husband, wife, or parent.[78] One woman remembered her father: "He never talked about what he really did or experienced. He was burdened by it, but you could not get him to talk about it."[79] In this case, not even the family could get the former soldier to talk about what had happened – perhaps it had been too terrible for him. In her book about women's memories of their fathers' return from the war, Ingeborg Bruns describes how some of the men behaved like patriarchs and tried to dominate their families. In a few cases, violence against wives and children occurred.[80] Moreover, most of these women remembered that their parents never talked about their experiences in the Third Reich.[81]

By comparing divorce rates among the three groups of soldiers who differed in their exposure to combat and atrocities but probably not with regard to other relevant factors, one could investigate the role of trauma exposure. Such archive-based research could be supplemented by interviews with surviving soldiers and their children. Within the framework of oral history, one could get a better and more systematic account of the personal experience of the war generation and the effect it had on their children. This could contribute to a better understanding of the children's behavior later on. Especially the 1960s could be investigated in this light.[82]

Ethical problems can arise when one interviews traumatized individuals. These are well described by Lutz Niethammer, who points out that interviews with traumatized people should not be done without psychological help.[83] We suggest that collaboration between historians and psychiatrists could help overcome some of the methodological and ethical problems when trying to develop valid and reliable interviews of former soldiers

---

78 Meyer and Schulze, *Krieg.* Also Jureit and Meyer, *Verletzungen.*
79 Bruns, *Vater,* 24. Translation by the authors.   80 Ibid., 38, 52, 180.
81 In one case, a woman remarked: "Warum aber haben Vater und Mutter nie über ihre persönlichen Erfahrungen, nie über ihre Gedanken und Gefühle zu Geschehnissen im Dritten Reich gesprochen? . . . Wer hat eigentlich unseren Eltern geholfen, mit dem Schrecklichen zurechtzukommen, das da in ihr Leben eingebrochen war? Niemand! Man hat es verdrängt und totgeschwiegen. Aber es war doch da!" ("But why did father and mother never speak about their personal experiences, never about their thoughts and feelings about what happened during the Third Reich? . . . Who actually helped our parents come to terms with the horror that disrupted their lives? Nobody! People repressed it and kept silent. But it was there.") (ibid., 40).
82 Barbara Willenbacher, "Zerrüttung und Bewährung der Nachkriegs-Familie," in Martin Broszat, Klaus-Dietmar Henke, and Hans Woller, eds., *Von Stalingrad zur Währungsreform: Zur Sozialgeschichte des Umbruchs in Deutschland* (Munich, 1988), 595–618.
83 Niethammer, "Fragen," 403.

and their children. From several detailed studies of individual experiences of trauma and its influence on marriage and children, one could generate further hypotheses about how the experience of violence and subsequent symptoms of PTSD helped to shape the society of the 1950s as it was experienced by our parents and has been described in detail by historians and sociologists.

2

Between Pain and Silence

Remembering the Victims of Violence in Germany after 1949

SABINE BEHRENBECK

When a war ends, coming to terms with its violence and its victims is one of the most important and urgent tasks postwar society must perform. After 1945 Germany had to cope with the deaths of about seven million soldiers and roughly half a million civilians, many killed in air raids. In addition, there was an unknown number of refugees and prisoners of war. At the same time, the German people were confronted with the moral and political consequences of a military catastrophe, the destruction of many towns, occupation, and the undeniable crimes that the Nazi regime and the Wehrmacht had committed during the war.

In the context of these crimes and the experience of total war, the former interpretation of the fallen soldiers as heroic and patriotic warriors, serving in a just and noble cause, could no longer be maintained as a master narrative. Looking back at the years before 1945, most Germans had very ambivalent emotions: They remembered rather good times for themselves – compared to the postwar years the 1930s appeared normal – but no longer could deny the horrible times for the victims of German aggression and persecution.[1] In this respect, it is of great interest to ask what period Germans perceived as the era of violence, who was seen as victims and who as perpetrators of violence. In short: What was the legacy of war in the German mind?

These are the questions I try to answer in this chapter. I analyze the memory strategies that were supposed to overcome the traumatic experiences and find a path from war to postwar, from violence to normality.[2]

---

1 In 1951, a remarkably large number of West Germans considered the years before the war to be the best time of their lives. Bundesarchiv, Koblenz (BAK) B145/4221: Institut für Demoskopie, "Das politische Klima: Ein Bericht über die politische Stimmung im Bundesgebiet." I am indebted to Michael Geyer for this reference.

2 The term *traumatic experience* is used in this essay in a broader sense than the psychopathological definition. See Elisabeth Domansky and Harald Welzer, "Die alltägliche Tradierung von Geschichte,"

My research is based on the official media of social memory (such as public remembrance days, rituals, and memorials dedicated to the war dead) because we know only little about the memory of families or informal communities.[3]

I closely examine three aspects: the problem of ends and beginnings or, in other words, of rupture and continuity to distinguish the violent era from "normal" times;[4] the problem of the "conversion" or redefinition of social values and behavior; and the problem of making sense of the war experience and of reconstructing the memory of the victims of violence. This chapter has two main sections: The first deals with the commemoration of war linked to special historical dates, the second with the commemoration of victims of violence on special remembrance days and at special sites. However, before going into detail, some general remarks about the relationship between memory and violence may be helpful.

Coming to terms with a traumatic past cannot be handled casually. This is why the construction of a social memory[5] after the Second World War caused severe problems for German society. A crucial role was played by the fact that memories of a violent experience differ fundamentally from other biographical or historical events. They are accompanied by strong negative feelings (fear, disorientation, mourning, pain, shame) and therefore have to overcome defensive strategies (forgetting, denial, suppression).

However, there are also motives for overcoming this resistance. For a community it can be important not to forget because this keeps alive the desire for revenge or the claims for restitution. Ruling elites often use a particular memory of a catastrophic event to emphasize the merits of the status quo or to exemplify the decadence or criminality of the former regime and the necessity for the new. And sometimes a society is simply unable to

in Elisabeth Domansky and Harald Welzer, eds., *Eine offene Geschichte: Zur kommunikativen Tradierung der nationalsozialistischen Vergangenheit* (Tübingen, 1999), 7–25.

3 Elizabeth Heineman, "The Hour of the Woman: Memories of Germany's 'Crisis Years' and West German National Identity," *American Historical Review* 101 (1996): 354–95.

4 On the political level, the end of the Third Reich was simultaneously the beginning of occupation and the collapse of the nation-state, which meant the division of Germany and the founding of two German states only four years later. On the military level, the Cold War started just when the battles of World War II had finished. And in the moral sphere there was an experience of rupture as well: The legal proceedings in Nuremberg against the major war criminals demonstrated that actions which had been judged as exploits or at least had been left unpunished under Nazi rule now were condemned as crimes against humanity. See the astute essay of Tim Mason, "Ends and Beginnings," *History Workshop: A Journal of Socialist and Feminist Historians*, no. 30 (autumn 1990): 134–50.

5 Maurice Halbwachs, *Das Gedächtnis und seine sozialen Bedingungen* (1925; Frankfurt am Main, 1985); Jan Assmann, *Das kulturelle Gedächtnis: Schrift, Erinnerung und politische Identität in frühen Hochkulturen* (Munich, 1999); Peter Burke, "Geschichte als soziales Gedächtnis," in Aleida Assmann and Dietrich Harth, eds., *Mnemosyne: Formen und Funktionen der kulturellen Erinnerung* (Frankfurt am Main, 1991), 289–304.

forget as long as there is no master narrative that makes sense of a confusing experience.

For the individual, remembering a trauma can be therapeutic and can help one leave behind a painful past. However, working through a traumatic experience means recalling violent emotions and therefore may require the assistance of others.[6] Collective commemoration can shape individual memories of a traumatic experience: By remembering with others, violence can lose some of its immediate horror and pain can be relieved. Within a community, the victim of violence may feel more secure and consoled because his or her trauma receives attention and the injury is recognized. Such a commemoration means that the group clearly takes the victim's side. Being reminded by others or being forced to remember something cannot replace empathy and compassion. In Germany after 1945, any commemoration of the victims of Nazi crimes and the war of annihilation would have presumed that the German people as a single, united "community of memory" had accepted the perspective of the victims and opponents of the Third Reich. This would have meant recollecting the crimes themselves and those responsible for them. We know that reality in the 1950s was different.

One reason for this was that the Germans had their own traumatic experiences and their own victims, most of them in the years between 1939 and 1948. Consequently, there was a tension between the wish to remember one's own pain and losses and the wish to forget what the Germans had done to other peoples during the war. The different groups of victims divided the survivors of war into different "communities of memory," and thereby continued the antagonism (and solidarity) of wartime. German memory thus was divided along many different lines: chronological (before versus after 1945), geographical (east versus west), as well as actors (victims versus perpetrators).

This chapter covers mainly the first decade after the foundation of both postwar German states. There are three reasons for this. First, the immediate postwar era was anything but a period of normality in Germany; it was perceived primarily as part of the era of violence.[7] Although the war had ended, the emergency situation remained or even grew more difficult for the civilian population as well as for the prisoners of war. The capitulation was followed by the "difficult years" between 1945 and 1948–9 that still occupy a prominent place in the "communicated memory" of nearly every German

---

6 Brigitte Rauschenbach, ed., *Erinnern, Wiederholen, Durcharbeiten: Zur Psycho-Analyse deutscher Wenden* (Berlin, 1992).
7 Martin Broszat, Klaus-Dietmar Henke, and Hans Woller, eds., *Von Stalingrad zur Währungsreform: Zur Sozialgeschichte des Umbruchs in Deutschland* (Munich, 1988).

family. In the private sphere, stories of hunger, cold, and privation, and of the varied efforts to procure the necessities of life were told and repeated. Indeed, the Germans were traumatized less by war than by the postwar privations.[8] "The war years were so good, in other words, because the postwar years were so bad."[9] Thus, the years between 1945 and 1949 can be seen as a "state of transition" marking the border between past and future. Violence still threatened, and people longed for a normal life. After the foundation of the Federal Republic in the west and the Democratic Republic in the east a period began when normality was actively propounded. Significantly, no remembrance day or site commemorates this period between the end of the war and the founding of the two German states.[10] Despite its deep impact on collective German memory, this time was not accorded recognition as an historical era in its own right.

Second, as a result of the war the Germans lost their national narrative and common political and ethical orientation to make sense of the past. The first years after 1945 were characterized by the search for a new interpretive framework. From a psychological perspective, the postwar years can be seen as a latent period when German society became aware of what had happened and suffered a loss of meaning, whereas the first postwar decade can be interpreted as the era when a new culture of memory was in the making.[11] The end of the war made it both possible and necessary to rearrange time in the private and public spheres. To mark and to act out this special moment of transition, societies often create rites of passage. But transition is hard to endure over the long haul; it arouses the desire to put an end to all the changes, renewal, and insecurity as well as to return to normality, security, and routine. Public practices of commemoration, such as anniversaries and monuments, are meant to demonstrate that the past is over because it has

---

8 Sibylle Meyer and Eva Schulze, eds., *Wie wir das alles geschafft haben: Alleinstehende Frauen berichten über ihr Leben nach 1945* (Munich, 1984).

9 Michael Geyer, "Cold-War Angst: The Case of West-German Opposition to Rearmament and Nuclear Weapons," in Hanna Schissler, ed., *The Miracle Years: A Cultural History of West Germany, 1949–1968* (Princeton, N.J., 2001); Vera Neumann, *Nicht der Rede wert: Die Privatisierung der Kriegsfolgen in der frühen Bundesrepublik: Lebensgeschichtliche Erinnerungen* (Münster, 1999); Elisabeth Domansky, "A Lost War: World War II in Postwar German Memory," in Alvin H. Rosenfeld, ed., *Thinking About the Holocaust: After Half a Century* (Bloomington, Ind., 1997), 240: German national identity was shaped and marked not by the war but by its aftermath.

10 Exceptions are the West Berlin statue in the Volkspark Hasenheide, showing a sitting woman to remind one of the rubble women (Katharina Singer, 1954) and the East Berlin bronze statues of "Trümmerfrau" and "Aufbauhelfer" (Fritz Cremer, 1958) near the Red City Hall, which were supposed to stress the heroic aspect of rebuilding a new Germany after defeat more than the need and privation of the first postwar years.

11 Bernhard Giesen, "National Identity as Trauma: The German Case," in Bo Stråth, ed., *Myth and Memory in the Constructon of Community: Historical Patterns in Europe and Beyond* (Brussels, 2000), 229, 241.

become a part of history and collective memory. Thus, after 1949 new memorial days and sites of memory were created to commemorate the war and at the same time to end this precarious state of transition and return to normality. I shall discuss and compare these new days and sites in East and West Germany in order to see what kind of self-image and master narrative about the war and its victims was constructed in both German societies.

Third, after 1949 public commemoration had different aims and conditions than before, and the actors of social memory and the stories about the past changed. In the first postwar years, the Germans were surrounded by reminders of the past: by the destruction all around, by the Allied occupation, by the victims, and by non-Nazi and anti-Nazi politicians.[12] Furthermore, the German public was confronted with horrible details of the Nazi death camps. However, at that time there was no shared and official practice of memory. Without a German government representing the whole population, the most important agents of memory were the family, the village or municipality, and different competing groups of survivors and Nazi opponents.[13] The victims and opponents of the Nazi regime not only had traumatic experiences differing from those of the majority of Germans, but they also formed a distinct group of commemoration. During the Third Reich they had been separated as culturally, socially, or racially different from the German *Volksgemeinschaft* (national ethnic community). Therefore, the victims among them were remembered as members of a different community, not as a part of the community as a whole.[14] Thus, instead of a single shared social memory, different commemorations communicated different stories about the past that had only one aspect in common: grief and mourning. The beginning of the Cold War and the founding of two separate German states ended the relative openness of the postwar years, with their multiplicity of memories and restored traditions. After 1949, the politics of interpreting the past were in the hands of German politicians, and then split into two different kinds of commemorative practice. The political leaders in both societies tried to legitimize each new political system by undertaking their own interpretation of the German past. Here, the difficulties of and obstacles facing these interpretations are discussed.

The theoretical approach used in this chapter to explain the various memory strategies is based on the concept of "memory" as a creative act, the

---

12 Jeffrey Herf, *Divided Memory: The Nazi Past in the Two Germanys* (Cambridge, Mass., 1997).
13 Publicly discussed were issues as *Wiedergutmachung*, definitions of heroes and victims of war, modes of official memory and the place of the Holocaust in memory. See Herf, *Divided Memory*, 71.
14 Dan Diner, *Kreisläufe: Nationalsozialismus und Gedächtnis* (Berlin, 1995), 56–8.

result of constructing fragments of experience.[15] In this context, to take possession of the past means to forget as well as to remember.[16] The culture of memory can be seen as a process of constructing a past from which a society would like to progress. This "invention of traditions" is a strategy of breaking with a historical continuity that threatened the present.[17] However, in the aftermath of World War II not only continuity but also discontinuity was threatening.

The main problem for survivors of the war was perhaps not the ability to remember but rather the inability to forget.[18] This problem united the victims and the perpetrators of crimes and violence.[19] The inability to construct the past according to the needs of the present, its lack of plasticity, caused a long-lasting obsession with it. The various efforts to deal with the past had different consequences in both parts of Germany. However, East and West Germany had one thing in common: The forced harmonization of inconsistent memories produced a blind spot for what was not remembered. "Silence or marginalization, not denial, became the dominant mode of avoiding an uncomfortable past."[20]

COMMEMORATING THE ERA OF VIOLENCE: REMEMBRANCE DAYS

Following World War II it was impossible to continue older traditions of public commemoration in Germany because the war had lacked moral justification. In the eyes of the anti-Hitler coalition, German aggression and the country's war aims were seen as criminal and barbarous, and the genocide perpetrated against Jews and other groups had meant a fundamental break with civilization.[21] From their perspective, the rupture had taken place with the Nazi seizure of power on January 30, 1933, and yet the military defeat of the Third Reich offered a chance for a new start.

In contrast, the majority of Germans – whether they had sympathized with the Nazi regime, openly supported it, benefited from its actions, or were indifferent toward it – experienced 1945 as a deep rupture in history: the abolition of the German Reich, the humiliating subjugation of enemy occupation, and the loss of political sovereignty. From their perspective the

15 Daniel L. Schacter, *Searching for Memory: The Brain, the Mind, and the Past* (New York, 1996).
16 See Domansky and Welzer, "Die alltägliche Tradierung von Geschichte," 7–25.
17 Heinz Dieter Kittsteiner, "Vom Nutzen und Nachteil des Vergessens für die Geschichte," in Gary Smith and Hinderk M. Emrich, eds., *Vom Nutzen des Vergessens* (Berlin, 1996), 140.
18 Elisabeth Domansky points out that in Germany war memories were not encoded in safe narratives and therefore left open wounds. See Domansky, "Lost War," 235.
19 See Pieter Lagrou's chapter in this book.
20 Herf, *Divided Memory*, 71.   21 Giesen, "National Identity as Trauma," 241.

break of 1945 had only negative connotations; thus there was no consensus about a continuity or discontinuity of the past. To regain an international reputation it was a crucial issue for German politics to insist on the difference before and after the fundamental break, marked by the "zero hour." However, at the same time the Germans had to be converted to democracy, which made it important to draw attention to genuine democratic traditions in German history.

Consequently, politicians in both German states, all of whom had non-Nazi credentials, faced the double task of first insisting on the break with the past and then filling the void with "good" aspects of the German heritage, thereby rescuing German national identity and some traditions.[22] In this context they had to decide how best to remember and commemorate the war that had just ended.

REMEMBERING THE WAR IN EAST GERMANY

In the German Democratic Republic (GDR), the new socialist government stressed the rupture and fundamental change that East German society had experienced after 1945. The Socialist Unity Party (SED) invented new occasions of commemoration to underscore the difference between the new socialist system and the Third Reich. The period of World War II thus served as the watershed between the two eras. Its beginning and its end became occasions for annual commemorations and social "rites of passage" into a new and better Germany.

Following the example of the Soviet Union, the anniversary of the beginning of World War II on September 1, 1939, was celebrated in East Germany as the "International Day of Peace."[23] Well-organized mass meetings in Berlin were supposed to demonstrate the end of militarism and fascism in the GDR. However, not just the capital was involved; the provincial areas celebrated too. For example, in 1956 a nine-day "Festival of Peace and Friendship" took place in the border town of Görlitz while citizens of the neighboring states, Poland and Czechoslovakia, were invited to protest together against Western preparations for nuclear war.[24] On this day the Germans had the opportunity to demonstrate their new, purified attitude of

---

22 Helmut Dubiel, *Niemand ist frei von der Geschichte: Die nationalsozialistische Herrschaft in den Debatten des Deutschen Bundestages* (Munich, 1999).

23 Already in the first years after World War I the left-wing parties celebrated the anniversary of the beginning of war (Aug. 3, 1914) as a "day of peace." See Jeffrey Verhey, *The Spirit of 1914: Militarism, Myth, and Mobilization in Germany* (Cambridge, 2000).

24 *Neues Deutschland*, Sept. 2, 1956.

pacifism with a symbolic walk into the new era of peace and reconciliation with their former enemies and new friends.[25] However, because communism was based on a dialectical theory, the character of this International Day of Peace was also rather combative, because marching for peace at the same time meant fighting against "Western preparations for a new atomic war." Therefore, on September 2, 1956, all German patriots were called on to join this "passionate protest," as the General Secretary of the German Peace Council, Heinz Willmann, called it.[26]

From 1950 onward, the anniversary of the end of war in 1945 formed a memorial day as well. In East Germany, May 8 was celebrated as a day of liberation and a day of thanks to the liberator, the Red Army.[27] This tradition was widespread in Eastern Europe because the Soviet Union forced every country in its bloc to celebrate the occasion.[28] But the GDR was exceptionally eager to contribute: During the 1950s a remembrance ritual was established all over the country involving festive hours in government offices, factories, and schools, mass meetings, and marches of delegations laying wreaths at local war cemeteries or memorials of the Red Army while the population was called on to line up and decorate the streets. The program of the day ended with cultural events and entertainment. The central site of celebration was the Soviet war memorial in Berlin-Treptow, erected in 1948 by order of the Soviet Military Council and handed over to the Berlin city government on September 2, 1949. In the center of a gigantic construction site stood a huge figure, a Red Army soldier, holding a child in his arms and treading on the swastika.[29] This heroic figure became a widespread symbol for the master narrative of the historic caesura of 1945, published in school books, journals, and calendars.[30]

---

25 It is difficult to say whether the participants in these meetings volunteered to show their genuine pacifism. However, we have to remember that the need to ban war was a widespread view in postwar Germany. But perhaps this dominant anti-military consensus was more an attitude of "without-me" (Ohne-mich-Haltung) than a pacifist conviction. See Geyer, "Cold-War Angst."
26 *Neues Deutschland*, Sept. 2, 1956.
27 Matthias Kitsche, "Die Geschichte eines Staatsfeiertages: Der 7. Oktober in der DDR (1950–1989)," Ph.D. diss., University of Cologne, 1990, 17.
28 Volker Ackermann, "Zweierlei Gedenken: Der 8. Mai 1945 in der Erinnerung der Bundesrepublik Deutschland und der DDR," in Holger Afflerbach and Christoph Cornelissen, eds., *Sieger und Besiegte: Materielle und ideelle Neuorientierung nach 1945* (Tübingen, 1997), 315.
29 Aktives Museum Faschismus und Widerstand e.V. and Neue Gesellschaft für Bildende Kunst, eds., *Erhalten, Zerstören, Verändern? Denkmäler der DDR in Ost-Berlin. Eine dokumentarische Ausstellung* (Berlin, 1990), 68–70.
30 *Erhalten, Zerstören, Verändern?* 68–70. See also Monika Gibas, " 'Auferstanden aus Ruinen und der Zukunft zugewandt!' Politische Feier- und Gedenktage der DDR," in Sabine Behrenbeck and Alexander Nuetzenadel, eds., *Inszenierungen des Nationalstaats: Politische Feiern in Italien und Deutschland seit 1860/1871* (Cologne, 2000), 191–220.

East German Communist leaders used May 8 to present themselves, highly decorated by the state they controlled, to honor the dead of the Red Army and the fighters of the antifascist resistance.[31] A ceremony took place in the German State Opera, where prominent speakers commemorated the historic event and its consequences: "By destroying fascism the Soviet soldiers have opened the door to a happy future for Germans. In this way, for the first time in their history the Germans got a chance to join the path of peace, democracy, and friendship with all peaceful people of the world. The regime of [Konrad] Adenauer on the contrary, under the protection from American foreign rule, takes the path of restoring the power of those well-known warmongers and therefore is completely isolated."[32]

From 1958 onward the liturgy was embedded in a "Week of the German-Soviet Friendship," with many cultural festivities and sporting events. The day was characterized by the atmosphere of a folk festival, which tended to overwhelm the commemoration of the dead heroes and victims.[33] However, this element of entertainment corresponded to the official message of a joint victory over fascism and capitalism. It also reminded people of good relations with the Russian people in earlier times, such as the era of the Wars of Liberation, when Prussian and Russian soldiers together fought against Napoleon.[34]

May 8 was meant to remind people not of unconditional surrender or military defeat but of the victory over Hitler and the losses suffered by the Red Army. World War II was remembered as the war that – after the endless pain and martyrdom of the Soviet people – brought about the final triumph of socialism. This was the perspective of the victorious Soviet Union and of the German Communist leaders who returned from Moscow. However, this view of the past was one from outside the German *Volksgemeinschaft*. For the majority of the East German population it could hardly be deduced from

---

31 *Neues Deutschland*, May 9, 1953. The offical memory practiced in the GDR did not reflect the Nazi ritual traditions and the mentality of the *Volksgemeinschaft* because it claimed to be motivated by antifascism. Those antagonistic sources and interpretive frames could not avoid some similarities to the aesthetics and rituals of the Third Reich. On this issue, see Winfried Ranke, "Linke Unschuld? – Unbefangener oder unbedachter Umgang mit fragwürdig gewordener Vergangenheit," in Dieter Vorsteher, ed., *Parteiauftrag: Ein neues Deutschland. Bilder, Rituale und Symbole der frühen DDR* (Munich, 1997), 94–112, in contrast to Gibas, "Auferstanden aus Ruinen und der Zukunft zugewandt!"

32 *Neues Deutschland*, May 9, 1953.

33 Gibas, "Auferstanden aus Ruinen und der Zukunft zugewandt!" 210.

34 Whereas in the first postwar years the Prussian military traditions were rejected, from 1952 a selective appropriation of Prussian traditions took place. This was obvious at the 140th anniversary of the "Battle of the Nations" of 1813 that saw a splendid display. Harald Blum, "Zu Ikonographie und Bedeutung von Darstellungen der Befreiungskriege 1813/14 in der Staatsrepräsentation der DDR," in Vorsteher, ed., *Parteiauftrag: Ein neues Deutschland*, 162–74.

one's own experiences, but it offered the chance to distance oneself from "Hitler's War" and "Nazi crimes." By means of the antifascist foundational myth – claiming that Communist resistance contributed to final victory – the whole population was invited to identify with their former enemies and the opponents of the Nazi regime, who now were the representatives of a "better" Germany. All "bad" German traditions were to be found in West Germany, whereas the roots of all good democratic and peaceful traditions were transferred to the GDR.[35]

May 8 demonstrated that the line between good and evil was a political one during the Cold War. Therefore, it was inopportune to investigate and to publish the details of violence and war crimes insofar as one's own population was concerned. Whereas fascism allegedly had been eradicated in East Germany after 1945, the Federal Republic was deemed responsible for all past and present evils because it remained a capitalist – and that meant a militarist and fascist – state.[36] East Germany therefore denied any responsibility for World War II and the Holocaust. Both supposedly belonged to the prehistory of West Germany and could be forgotten in the GDR.[37] To demonstrate that Nazism was a universal problem of bourgeois-capitalist democracy, the GDR confronted the international public with embarrassing news about the West German political and administrative elites and their Nazi past, but did not demand such truth about its own population. This selective silence excluded individual suffering and guilt as well, and focused on military and political victory.[38]

The message behind May 8 was to leave the past behind, to ignore recent errors and faults, and to move together toward the socialist future. The

---

35 See Eve Rosenhaft, "The Uses of Remembrance: The Legacy of Communist Resistance in the German Democratic Republik," in Francis R. Nicosia and Lawrence D. Stokes, eds., _Germans against Nazism: Nonconformity, Opposition, and Resistance in the Third Reich: Essays in Honour of Peter Hoffmann_ (New York, 1990), 369–88; Antonia Grunenberg, _Antifaschismus – ein deutscher Mythos_ (Reinbek bei Hamburg, 1993).

36 The East German antifascism was first of all anticaptalism. See Sigrid Meuschel, "Legitimationsstrategien in der DDR und in der Bundesrepublik," in Christoph Klessmann, Hans Misselwitz, and Günter Wichert, eds., _Deutsche Vergangenheiten – eine gemeinsame Herausforderung: Der schwierige Umgang mit der doppelten Nachkriegsgeschichte_ (Berlin, 1999), 115–27; Rainer M. Lepsius, "Das Erbe des Nationalsozialismus und die politische Kultur der Nachfolgestaaten des 'Grossdeutschen Reiches,'" in Rainer Lepsius, _Demokratie in Deutschland. Soziologisch-historische Konstellationsanalysen: Ausgewählte Aufsätze_ (Göttingen, 1993), 229–45.

37 See Elisabeth Domansky, "'Kristallnacht,' the Holocaust, and German Unity: The Meaning of November 9 as an Anniversary in Germany," _History and Memory_ 4, no. 1 (spring–summer 1992): 60–94, and by the same author "Die gespaltene Erinnerung," in Manuel Köppen, ed., _Kunst und Literatur nach Auschwitz_ (Berlin, 1993), 178–96.

38 Alf Lüdtke, "Histories of Mourning: Flowers and Stones for the War Dead, Confusion for the Living – Vignettes from East and West Germany," in Gerald Sider and Gavin Smith, eds., _Between History and Histories: The Making of Silences and Commemorations_ (Toronto, 1997), 174.

persecuted Communists functioned as social "decontaminators" of the Nazi past. They were able to rehabilitate everybody of goodwill in East Germany. Thus, the evaluation of the individual's past depended on behavior in the present. By showing the right political attitude, one could find forgiveness for failures during the war. And, unlike the practice of the Catholic Church, the GDR granted general absolution without requiring confession of one's sins.

The annual celebrations of May 8 were intended as a sign of gratitude to the Red Army for having beaten the Nazi dictator and liberating the Germans from a kind of "foreign power." However, considering the violent excesses in which the soldiers of the occupation army had indulged up to 1949 in the Soviet zone of occupation, the long-term internment of many Germans in former Nazi concentration camps, and the thousands of POWs still in Soviet hands, it is unlikely that this gratitude accorded with the real feelings of the majority of the population.[39] In this context the mass rituals can be considered part of the "education dictatorship" of the SED.[40] The funeral wreaths laid at monuments for the fallen heroes of the Red Army and the antifascist resistance were part of this *Volkspädagogik* (countrywide re-education). By worshipping the liberators as heroes on the occasion of May 8, the terror and violence they had brought to Germany were supposed to be forgotten. The ritual revealed implicitly and involuntarily that the alleged break with the past and the purification did not mirror reality; otherwise, popular expression of this kind would have taken place spontaneously and in everyday life.

REMEMBERING THE WAR IN WEST GERMANY

The new West German state defined its new identity and bolstered its legitimacy vis-à-vis both the past and the present: The Federal Republic asserted its break with the Nazi regime and its difference from the socialist regime to the east. Not only did the Federal Republic avoid celebrating

---

39 In both parts of Germany only a minority of people held the opinion that the military defeat of Germany meant a liberation (Giesen, "National Identity as Trauma," 240). Surveys in the Western occupation zones and later the Federal Republic showed a broad agreement with the Nazi ideology. Why should this have been different in East Germany? (See Meuschel, "Legitimationsstrategien in der DDR und in der Bundesrepublik," 115.) However, there might have been more moral scruples about expressing such an opinion publicly.

40 Jürgen Danyel, "Die Opfer- und Verfolgtenperspektive als Gründungskonsens? Zum Umgang mit der Widerstandstradition und der Schuldfrage in der DDR," in Jürgen Danyel, ed., *Die geteilte Vergangenheit: Zum Umgang mit Nationalsozialismus und Widerstand in den beiden deutschen Staaten* (Berlin, 1995), 34.

the same historical events as the Nazis had, but it also consciously chose commemorative moments different from those chosen by the GDR. Like in East Germany, the invention of traditions in West Germany claimed to focus on the "good democratic traditions" in German history, such as the revolution of 1848 and the Weimar Republic. However, because it had accepted the status of legal successor to the German Reich, the Federal Republic found it hard to select only those parts of the national heritage that suited its current political agenda. Space for symbolic action was very limited.

Because of the festival customs in East Germany, the dates marking the end of World War II were of little use to West Germany in demonstrating discontinuity and difference. The war assumed a different meaning in the collective memory in West Germany. This was obvious at the anniversaries of the beginning and the end of the war. In the Federal Republic there was no public commemoration of September 1. Not even the newspapers mentioned this anniversary in their lead articles. The widespread and popular attitude of antimilitarism in the 1950s neither formed a political movement nor served to organize special rituals and ceremonies to publicly demonstrate pacifism.[41]

In the Federal Republic the line between violence and normality was not marked by the events of May 8, 1945, either. In the 1950s, May 8 was considered the day of unconditional surrender and military defeat.[42] The ruling politicians saw no reason for celebrations or even speeches of remembrance in parliament. The political exploitation of the event in the GDR made it especially difficult to acknowledge this date. When the first federal president, Theodor Heuss, suggested that the young republic should celebrate the fact that on this very date in 1949 the Parliamentary Council had ratified the West German Basic Law, the idea of linking the new democratic constitution to this German "day of shame" did not find acceptance either in parliament or among the public.[43] In 1955, the Bundestag discussed the possibility of celebrating this day as a German "Independence Day"; this was after the Federal Republic had gained full sovereignty with the treaties of Paris on May 5.[44] However, there was no majority support for

---

41 The movement of peace marches at Easter was transferred to Germany only in the 1960s. Following the discussion about nuclear weapons for the Bundeswehr in 1957, a "Kampf dem Atomtod"–movement formed and used May 1 as a day for protest campaigns. See Geyer, "Cold-War Angst."

42 Dubiel, *Niemand ist frei von der Geschichte*, 52–5; Peter Reichel, *Politik mit der Erinnerung: Gedächtnisorte im Streit um die nationalsozialistische Vergangenheit* (Munich, 1995), 275–95.

43 Edgar Wolfrum, *Geschichtspolitik in der Bundesrepublik Deutschland. Der Weg zur bundesrepublikanischen Erinnerung 1948–1990* (Darmstadt, 1999), 59; Dubiel, *Niemand ist frei von der Geschichte*, 52.

44 "Wird der Tag der Souveränität gefeiert?" *Frankfurter Allgemeine Zeitung*, Apr. 15, 1955.

this plan.[45] The paradox of resurrection and annihilation still overburdened the collective practices of memory.[46]

The year 1955 was very important for the memory of the war. In the minds of many West Germans the end of war was not a single event but a period of about ten years. It only began when the battles ended; it continued with the founding of the new state in 1949; and it was completed by the end of occupation in 1955.[47] Similar to the national holiday in Austria that commemorates the date when the last foreign soldiers left Austrian territory in 1955,[48] in West Germany, May 8, 1955, was the true "Day of Liberation." In conjunction with the acquisition of sovereignty, the Federal Republic joined NATO. Because a new (cold) war was developing, this year also saw rearmament and the foundation of both the National People's Army (Nationale Volksarmee or NVA) in the East and the Bundeswehr in the West. Nevertheless, in contrast to the GDR's memorial days, with their "Honor Parades of the German-Soviet Fraternity in Arms," the West German military kept a very low profile at state ceremonies. Officers and troops remained on the sidelines – with one exception: the Day of Mourning (*Volkstrauertag*). Public commemoration of the "victims of war and violence" took place on this day.

The West Germans could have underlined the difference between past and present had they decided to commemorate the resistance against Hitler, particularly the conspiracy of July 20, 1944. However, during the 1950s the German resistance movement was very controversial. In fact, from 1951 onward small ceremonies took place at the memorial in Berlin's Stauffenbergstrasse, at the site of the former Reich War Ministry. Official ceremonies were not held in the Bundestag until 1964.[49] Only a small political elite assembled on the anniversary of that day to remind people of those "German

---

45 "'Würdiger Staatsakt' geplant," *Hamburger Abendblatt*, Apr. 21, 1955. See also Florian Altenhöner, "Der 8. Mai: (K)ein Feiertag. Zu einer Ausstellung der Fachschaft Geschichte," in Konvent der Philipps-Universität Marburg, ed., *Die Philipps-Universität im Nationalsozialismus: Veranstaltungen der Philipps-Universität zum 50. Jahrestag des Kriegsendes 8. Mai 1995* (Marburg, 1996), 80–1.

46 It took until the end of the 1960s before the perception of May 8 changed from defeat to liberation. Perhaps it was no accident that in 1967 the liberation day was dropped as a work-free holiday in the GDR; it could no longer serve as a weapon in the Cold War. See Wolfrum, "Die Unfähigkeit zu feiern? Der 8. Mai und der 17. Juni in der bundesrepublikanischen Erinnerungskultur," in Behrenbeck and Nuetzenadel, eds., *Inszenierungen des Nationalstaats*, 221–41.

47 In this same year the Soviet Union declared the end of the state of war with Germany and consequently released all POWs and all internees who wanted to return home. Thus, the end of war was finally reached in 1955.

48 Gustav Spann, "Zur Geschichte des österreichischen Nationalfeiertages," *Beiträge zur historischen Sozialkunde*, no. 1 (1996): 27–34.

49 See Reichel, *Politik mit der Erinnerung*, 296–310; Gerd R. Ueberschär, ed., *Der 20. Juli 1944: Bewertung und Rezeption des deutschen Widerstands gegen das NS-Regime* (Cologne, 1994); Regina Holler, *20. Juli 1944: Vermächtnis oder Alibi?* (Munich, 1994).

members of the Christian aristocracy" who represented the moral integrity of a "different Germany" during the Nazi tyranny.[50] The vast majority of the population viewed the attempt to kill the "Führer" as treason, and the memory of those officers had to be protected against defamation. The disagreement about this event showed that even after 1945 the solidarity of the Nazi *Volksgemeinschaft* was stronger than compassion for and solidarity with the Third Reich's victims.

The West German government instead chose the East Berlin insurrection of June 17, 1953, for its national holiday. The workers killed on that day were immediately presented as martyrs for freedom and reunification.[51] Celebrating this rebellion against the East German regime could, in the government's view, compensate for discussion of the crimes of the Nazi state. Speakers on June 17 often saw it in relation to July 20: The East German rebellion demonstrated that the Germans had learned from the past and were now willing to fight for freedom and self-government. Whereas July 20 had been an insurrection of the elites, June 17 was considered a rebellion of the whole people.

June 17 was highly popular until the 1960s because it made possible the expression of regret about the national division without talking about its cause, the rise of National Socialism. Remembering the victims of totalitarian terror allowed people to view Nazi rule as based on terror, not acknowledging that it was a popular rule all the same. The victims of the 1953 insurrection were equated not only with war victims; they were even linked to higher causes. Mourning for the war dead thus could be transferred to the victims of the current fight against totalitarianism.

REMEMBERING THE VICTIMS OF WAR AND VIOLENCE

In the initial postwar years, public commemoration of the war dead had been prescribed by the occupation powers, who felt responsible for and tried to control the process of denazification of the German people.[52] On May 13,

---

50 Andreas Woell, " 'Wegweisend für das deutsche Volk' – Der 20. Juli 1944: Öffentliche Erinnerung und Vergangenheitsbewältigung in der Bundesrepublik," in Helmut Koenig, Michael Kohlstrunk, and Andreas Woell, eds., *Vergangenheitsbewältigung am Ende des zwanzigsten Jahrhunderts* (Opladen, 1998), 17–37; Ueberschär, ed., *Der 20. Juli 1944*.

51 Wolfrum, *Geschichtspolitik in der Bundesrepublik Deutschland*; Christoph Meyer, *Die deutschlandpolitische Doppelstrategie: Wilhelm Wolfgang Schütz und das Kuratorium Unteilbares Deutschland* (Landsberg am Lech, 1997).

52 In the first month after defeat, an anti-Nazi consensus dominated West German society as well. See Norbert Frei, *Vergangenheitspolitik: Die Anfänge der Bundesrepublik und die NS-Vergangenheit* (Munich, 1997), 14. However, this attitude toward a political and social reconstruction lasted only until 1946–7. Subsequently the fight against the remnants of the Third Reich changed into a struggle against the

1946, the Allied Control Council passed a directive (Allied Directive no. 30) against Nazi propaganda and ideology that was intended to uproot the glorification of war and militarism in Germany. Under the directive, it was prohibited to plan or erect monuments and memorials of any kind that were meant to keep alive the German military tradition, or to awaken militarism, which could serve to glorify war. Existing objects of this kind had to be destroyed by January 1, 1947.[53] Exempted were memorials for dead members of regular units of the Wehrmacht and individual gravestones. In these cases only Nazi symbols (such as the swastika) were to be eliminated.

These instructions were interpreted differently in the two Germanies. In both countries there was great reluctance to commemorate fallen German soldiers with public monuments and ceremonies. A cult of the fallen heroes, which developed in the aftermath of World War I and during the Third Reich, did not repeat itself after 1945.[54] Nevertheless, each German state established its own Day of Mourning for the victims of war and violence.

WAR MEMORIALS AND REMEMBRANCE DAYS IN EAST GERMANY

Neither on May 8 nor on any other annual public holiday were German war victims – with exception of the antifascist fighters and Communist martyrs – the objects of public celebration in East Germany. No monuments or celebrations were dedicated to the fallen soldiers of the Wehrmacht, the civilian victims of air raids, or the dead expellees from east of the Oder-Neisse line. Regular soldiers were not explicitly accused of being perpetrators but were simply ignored and not deemed worthy of public commemoration.[55] The civilians who had been killed would have reminded people of the war crimes

iniquities of denazification. See Detlef Garbe, "Äusserliche Abkehr, Erinnerungsverweigerung und 'Vergangenheitsbewältigung': Der Umgang mit dem Nationalsozialismus in der frühen Bundesrepublik," in Axel Schildt and Arnold Sywottek, eds., *Modernisierung im Wiederaufbau: Die westdeutsche Gesellschaft der 50er Jahre* (Bonn, 1993), 696.

53 "Vom Zeitpunkt des Inkrafttretens dieser Direktive an ist untersagt und als gesetzwidrig erklärt die Planung... die Errichtung ... von Gedenksteinen, Denkmälern, Gedenktafeln... die darauf abzielen, die deutsche militärische Tradition zu bewahren und lebendig zu erhalten, den Militarismus wachzurufen oder die Erinnerung an die nationalsozialistische Partei aufrechtzuerhalten, oder ihrem Wesen nach in der Verherrlichung von kriegerischen Ereignissen bestehen," *Amtsblatt des Kontrollrats in Deutschland*, no. 7, May 31, 1946.

54 Sabine Behrenbeck, *Der Kult um die toten Helden: Nationalsozialistische Mythen, Riten und Symbole 1923 bis 1945* (Vierow bei Greifswald, 1996), 600.

55 In both parts of Germany after the war, a gap of memory opened and swallowed the remembrance of the violence committed by German soldiers. Silence after the war was meant to keep this violence secret. See Klaus Latzel, "Tote Erinnerung ohne letzte Instanz. Feldpostbriefe von der Ostfront: Die nationalsozialistische Propaganda formte Wahrnehmung, aber keinen Sinn," *Frankfurter Allgemeine Zeitung*, Jan. 23, 1999.

committed by the Red Army and were therefore better forgotten or at least not publicly remembered.[56]

In the first few years after issuance of Allied Directive no. 30, the administration of the Soviet occupation zone did not feel it had the authority to allow construction of monuments for the fallen Wehrmacht soldiers. However, even after the founding of the GDR the new state did not erect memorials for members of the Wehrmacht or for the civilian war dead. Local communities were forbidden to erect such monuments.[57] The graves of German soldiers on East German territory were left to the care of private citizens, the churches, or the Red Cross, whereas care for the national *Mahn- und Gedenkstätten* (monuments and memorial sites) lay in the hands of the state.[58] Instead of the fallen soldiers of the Wehrmacht, it was the soldiers of the Red Army and the Communist fighters against Nazism who were honored by public memorials.

The designs for these memorials copied monuments of victory that the Russians had earlier constructed in their occupation zone in the 1940s. These included the huge monuments in or near Berlin (Tiergarten, Treptow, Karlshorst, and Schönholzer Heide).[59] In addition to these central monuments in the capital city, the Red Army covered Eastern Germany with more than 600 monuments and sites of memory dedicated to the Soviet victims of war and violence.[60] As after World War I, when war memorials were built in every local community, East German communities again got such memorials but not dedicated to their own war dead.

---

56 Norman M. Naimark, *The Russians in Germany: A History of the Soviet Zone of Occupation, 1945–1949* (Cambridge, Mass., 1995); Atina Grossmann, "A Question of Silence: The Rape of German Women by Occupation Soldiers," in Robert G. Moeller, ed., *West Germany Under Construction: Politics, Society, and Culture in the Adenauer Era* (Ann Arbor, Mich., 1997), 35–52.

57 Apparently there was a directive of the Interior Ministry on April 17, 1950, to this effect, by which it reserved to itself all decisions about changes to political memorials, but this directive cannot be traced. See Hubertus Tim Adam, "Nationale Totenbeschwörungen: Über den Umgang der DDR mit monumentalen Zeugnissen der deutschen Vergangenheit," in Katrin Keller and Hans-Dieter Schmid, eds., *Vom Kult zur Kulisse: Das Voelkerschlachtdenkmal als Gegenstand der Geschichtskultur* (Leipzig, 1995), 176n109. In any case, local communities and federal state authorities did not feel themselves empowered to act independently in these matters.

58 Meinhold Lurz, *Kriegerdenkmäler in Deutschland*, 4 vols. (Heidelberg, 1985–6), vol. 4: *Bundesrepublik*, 138.

59 For a comprehensive treatment, see *Erhalten, Zerstören, Verändern?* 22–3, 67ff. The monument in the Tiergarten was unveiled already in November 1945 as a victory monument. Karlshorst was not set up as a "Museum of the Unconditional Surrender" until the 1960s. Treptow and Schönholz, on the other hand, were sites of mourning and simultaneously symbolized the self-understanding of an international mission of liberation. On this, see Jacqueline Hénard, "Profane Altäre: Wohin mit den sowjetischen Kriegerdenkmälern?" *Frankfurter Allgemeine Zeitung*, Dec. 4, 1993, and Jeannette Otto, "Das letzte Standbein wackelt: Den sowjetischen Ehrenmalen drohen Verfall, Umgestaltung, Ausgrenzung," in *Die Zeit*, Sept. 10, 1998.

60 Inventar des Bundesinnenministeriums, quoted in Hénard, "Profane Altäre."

This situation was forced on the East German population and did not signify a sudden mental shift from being Nazi followers to being antifascists. Compelled to participate in the official cult for the "heroes of socialism," the actual commitment of the East Germans was low. In 1949, the members of the Association of those Persecuted by the Nazi Regime (Vereinigung der Verfolgten des Nazi-Regimes or VVN) were shocked by the refusal of the population to take part in the inauguration of a memorial for murdered antifascists.[61] Although long-term effects of these educational policies on the population cannot be ruled out, in the 1950s their impact was rather small.

Everyday life witnessed very different private and semipublic practices. Around 1950, Protestant pastors and local churches established a large war cemetery both for the soldiers who fell in the Battle of Berlin during the last days of the war and for the refugees who fled from the Red Army. Corpses from the battlefields were transferred to a central site near the village of Halbe, where the soldiers were reburied in common and mass graves. The cemetery was meant to be a resting place for the dead regardless of confession or nationality.[62] In his letter to the Brandenburg Interior Ministry, Otto Dibelius, bishop of the Protestant Church of Berlin-Brandenburg, stressed that the public, the press, and the population of the region should be excluded from this process,[63] bowing to the government's initial wish to keep the project a secret. In the late 1950s, however, the state assumed responsibility for the Halbe site. Associations from the area, such as sports clubs, school classes, and work brigades, visited the cemetery throughout the year to lay wreaths and flowers. Official West German delegations were granted permission to visit the cemetery on the World Day of Peace, the first Sunday in September.

The battlefields on GDR soil were not completely cleared of fallen Wehrmacht soldiers. Some were buried in individual graves or in small groups. The graves appeared well kept even after forty-five years, decorated with flowers and even tombstones by the inhabitants of the surrounding villages.[64] One woman, asked about her motives for caring for the graves of unknown German soldiers, replied: "I lost two sons on the eastern front

---

61 Ralf Kessler and Hartmut Rüdiger Peter, "Antifaschisten in der SBZ. Zwischen elitärem Selbstverständnis und politischer Instrumentalisierung," *Vierteljahrshefte für Zeitgeschichte* 43, no. 4 (1995): 619; Elke Reuter and Detlef Nasel, *Das kurze Leben der VVN von 1947 bis 1953: Die Geschichte der Vereinigung der Verfolgten des Naziregimes in der sowjetischen Besatzungszone und in der DDR* (Berlin, 1997).

62 Alf Lüdtke, "Histories of Mourning," 152–5.   63 Ibid., 153n7.

64 Ibid., 165–6.

during the war. And I must take care of this grave. I am pretty sure that someone has done the same for my sons in Russia."[65] Unable to reach the location where her loved ones were buried, she used the graves nearby as a substitute and thus created her own mourning site. Initiatives of this kind reveal that state ceremonies and memorials devoted solely to the antifascist war victims did not satisfy the needs of the population. The blind spot in the official memory of the GDR left a gap that was filled by private initiative.

In contrast to these semiprivate initiatives, what were the official ceremonies like during the 1950s? The official day of remembrance for the victims of fascism, the *Opfer des Faschismus-Tag* (*OdF-Tag*), was celebrated every year on the second Sunday in September. The tradition grew from a mass meeting in Berlin-Neukölln on September 9, 1945, one of the first mass rallies after the war. It had been organized by international prisoner associations, which demanded moral and political leadership.[66] However, in 1948 this no longer could be tolerated by the SED because such a policy was not compatible with the new strategy of ending denazification and integrating former Nazis. As a consequence, in 1953 the VVN was forced to dissolve itself. This was the end, too, of a spontaneous and broad culture of memory in East Germany. Nevertheless, the *OdF-Tag*, with its speeches and marches, funeral wreaths, and triangular symbols, was celebrated in East Berlin for more than four decades. Yet as part of official antifascism it degenerated into a cliché.

At first the *OdF-Tag* celebrations obviously did not reflect the convictions of the majority of the population. On the contrary, many returning antifascists complained of popular hostility and contempt. Their claims for compensation were met with ignorance and envy, and soon the former *Volksfremde* (those "alien" to the nation) again felt segregated.[67] At the same time, the victims' associations were not completely homogeneous. The predominance of political prisoners in the *OdF-Tag* committees led to a distinction between fascism's active opponents and its passive victims, a distinction that had an effect on the social welfare system.[68] A person unwilling to participate in the building of the new socialist order would not receive money; rights depended on duties that were performed.[69] In the end, only

---

65 Quoted in ibid., 166.
66 Kessler and Peter, "Antifaschisten in der SBZ," 612.
67 Ibid., 619; Constantin Goschler, "Nachkriegsdeutschland und die Verfolgten des Nationalsozialismus," in Hans-Erich Volkmann, ed., *Ende des Dritten Reiches – Ende des Zweiten Weltkriegs: Eine perspektivische Rückschau* (Munich, 1995), 319.
68 Constantin Goschler, "Paternalismus und Verweigerung: Die DDR und die Wiedergutmachung für jüdische Verfolgte des Nationalsozialismus," *Jahrbuch für Antisemitismusforschung* 2 (1993).
69 Kessler and Peter, "Antifaschisten in der SBZ," 623.

the Communist fighters against the Nazi regime remained because they were the only ones who fit into the antifascist foundational myth.

In terms of organizational expansion, the VVN was supposed to encompass the whole of Germany. Because the SED put pressure on the association to conform, after 1948 Social Democrats in the Western zones sharply disparaged it. Three years later the West German Bundestag banned the association as a Communist front.[70] The *OdF-Tag*, which in the first postwar years had been celebrated all over Germany, thus was replaced by the Day of Mourning in many states of the Federal Republic in 1951–2.[71] This symbolic act was criticized by many who had been persecuted, and indeed this decision pushed them to the margins of public memory for nearly a decade.

WAR MEMORIALS AND REMEMBRANCE DAYS IN WEST GERMANY

A glance at the landscape of memory in the early Federal Republic reveals a homogenous picture, although the government did not directly regulate cultural practices. Immediately after the end of the war some local communities planned memorials to remember their war dead, as had been common in the aftermath of previous wars. However, the governments of individual federal states rejected these applications, indicating that their priority lay with reconstruction and that there was a lack of spare building materials and labor.[72] The present was supposed to take precedence over the past. A few years later, priorities changed, however. The mid-1950s witnessed a boom in the construction of memorials dedicated to fallen soldiers – not by accident, because this was the period of remilitarization and the creation of the West German army.[73]

---

70 Goschler, "Nachkriegsdeutschland," 323–4. To be sure, the federal *Länder* applied this ban in a rather lax manner – presumably out of reverence for the many persecuted people who were innocently caught up in the Communist machinations. Accordingly, Federal Interior Minister Schröder felt compelled to bring a prosecution before the Federal Constitutional Court in 1959. See *Frankfurter Allgemeine Zeitung*, Nov. 25, 1959.

71 Constantin Goschler, *Wiedergutmachung: Westdeutschland und die Verfolgten des Nationalsozialismus 1945–1954* (Munich, 1992), 217ff. An occupation ban (*Berufsverbot*) for members of VVN already was issued in 1950. In that year the victims of fascism were remembered together with the victims of the *Volksgemeinschaft* on September 7. The connection with the OdF-Day remained only a matter of the proximity on the calendar; instead, the occasion of the holiday was the establishment of the Federal Republic (the first sitting of the Bundestag and Bundesrat). See Sabine Behrenbeck, "Rituale des Zwiespalts: Politische Feiertage in Ost und West," in *Zeichen und Mythen in Ost und West*, Rostocker Philosophische Manuskripte, n.s. no. 6 (Rostock, 1999), 50–2.

72 Lurz, *Kriegerdenkmäler in Deutschland*, 4:115–16, 127.

73 Ibid., 4:305, 492. Sabine Behrenbeck, "Heldenkult oder Friedensmahnung? Kriegerdenkmale nach beiden Weltkriegen," in Gottfried Niethardt and Dieter Riesenberger, eds., *Lernen aus dem Krieg? Deutsche Nachkriegszeiten 1918/1945* (Munich, 1992), 344–64.

Thus, in the early postwar years dead Wehrmacht soldiers received no monuments of their own (or at most small plaques affixed to older war memorials). Meanwhile, commemorations of other war victims were taking place in the GDR. The international prisoners association – supported by the Allied military authorities – planned and designed memorials to their dead comrades immediately after the liberation of the camps during the 1940s.[74] Architecture, symbols, and the surrounding landscape were used to create monuments for concentration camp survivors, for their resistance and heroism was an internationally understandable language. The memorials often included symbols of victory – such as pillars, columns, and obelisks – crowned by symbols such as the Soviet red star. In the inscriptions the victims accuse their tormentors without regard to politics and explicitly name the causes of pain and death in the camps.

After 1949, West German society responded to these "victory monuments" in two ways.[75] Once they had taken responsibility for the erection of prisoners' monuments, local communities often changed the designs and established their own symbols.[76] The new designs were meant to represent a different experience of war and violence. This strategy of remembrance was followed by erecting new memorials to the civilian victims of war. Crosses, mourning angels, and pietas for the innocent victims of air raids and expulsion reminded viewers of the violence and pain the German people had suffered. This practice of memory seemed inoffensive and in agreement with the Allied directive. In nearly 90 percent of the monuments religious symbols of consolation and resurrection were employed.[77] The memorials articulated grief for the casualties, all interpreted as victims of the war (not of the enemy). The actions of German soldiers were ignored; they were remembered neither as heroes nor as criminals but as "decent Germans" whose bravery was misused and abused by a diabolical regime. A political meaning could no longer be found in wartime death, but it was still worshipped as a sacrifice for the community. This perspective was the fruit

---

74 Adolf Rieth, *Den Opfern der Gewalt: KZ-Opfermale der europäischen Völker* (Tübingen, 1968); *Gedenkstätten für die Opfer des Nationalsozialismus: Eine Dokumentation*, vol. 1: Ulrike Puvogel and Martin Stankowski, *Baden-Württemberg, Bayern, Bremen, Hamburg, Hessen, Niedersachsen, Nordrhein-Westfalen, Rheinland-Pfalz, Saarland, Schleswig-Holstein* (Berlin, 1995). It would be interesting to compare in detail these memorials on the terrain of former concentration camps with the memorials for the civilian war victims which the Germans constructed in the postwar years.

75 Adolf Rieth, *Denkmal ohne Pathos: Totenmale des Zweiten Weltkriegs in Südwürttemberg-Hohenzollern, mit einer geschichtlichen Einleitung* (Tübingen, 1967), 29.

76 For example, at the war cemetery in Stukenbrock in Westphalia the Red Flag of the Soviet Union that had been fixed at the top of an obelisk was replaced by a Christian cross once the Germans had to care for the cemetery. See Puvogel and Stankowski, *Gedenkstätten für die Opfer des Nationalsozialismus*, 596. Arbeitskreis "Blumen für Stukenbrock e.V." ed., *Protokoll Stukenbrock* (Bielefeld, 1985), 10–14.

77 Lurz, *Kriegerdenkmäler in Deutschland*, 4:217.

of the West German *Vergangenheitspolitik* of the 1950s, wherein bystanders and perpetrators were integrated and the responsibility of the whole society for war and Nazism was obscured.[78]

There also was a third strategy of remembrance for calling attention to German losses. Between 1950 and 1955 a new kind of memorial was spontaneously created: the POW memorial.[79] These were dedicated to prisoners still living and served as a political appeal to the Allies to release them. In contrast to the memorials for the German war dead, mostly placed in churchyards or on the periphery of public spaces in an atmosphere of quiet and seclusion, the monuments to German POWs were placed right at the center.[80] The prominent public commemoration of the POWs sought to end the state of war by means of an exchange of war prisoners.

Parallel to these symbolic actions in the 1950s, the policy of remembrance broadened the definition of war victims. In 1952, the West German government enacted a law regarding the construction of graves for the war dead.[81] It extended the scope of the *Ruherecht* (right of repose) from soldiers to include POWs and victims of postwar tribulations. The maintenance costs for the graves were paid by the state, which delegated the practical work to the Volksbund deutsche Kriegsgräberfürsorge e.V. – a private association. The label "war dead" thus came to include displaced persons, victims of the concentration camps, and civil internees, as well as murdered inmates of asylums, refugees and expellees, and even Wehrmacht soldiers whom the Nazis had executed.[82] The inscription "For the victims of war and violence" was common to many memorials throughout the 1950s.

The official policy of remembrance attempted to link the memory of the Germans' own casualties to the memory of the victims of Nazi terror. Politicians were not consistent and fair in so doing and gave preference to German victims. To explain this discrepancy we must take a closer look at the most important West German remembrance day, the Day of Mourning.

The traditional Day of Mourning had been established in 1919 for the purpose of remembering the fallen soldiers of World War I. The day was

78 Meuschel, "Legitimationsstrategien in der DDR und in der Bundesrepublik," 116.
79 Siegfried Seeger, "Wandlungen in der Einstellung zum Krieg, dargestellt an den westfälischen Ehren-malen für die Kriegstoten," Ph.D. diss., University of Münster, 1962, 64; Lurz, *Kriegerdenkmäler in Deutschland*, 4:188.
80 Seeger, *Wandlungen in der Einstellung zum Krieg*, 64.
81 In 1950 the care of graves of concentration-camp victims was transferred from the Allied military authorities to the German authorities. Only after 1965, however, did they receive the same care as the fallen soldiers. See Rieth, *Denkmal ohne Pathos*, 29.
82 Lurz, *Kriegerdenkmäler in Deutschland*, 4:32, 42.

originally commemorated in late November. The Nazis redefined the holiday in 1934: It became the "Heroes' Remembrance Day" (*Heldengedenktag*)
and was celebrated in springtime to serve as a sign of hope and resurrection.[83] After the end of the Third Reich the *Heldengedenktag* tradition was
continued in the different states and regions of West Germany. It assumed
the function of commemorating the victims of war. On February 18, 1951,
the Bundestag observed a commemorative hour to remember the deaths of
all victims of the war, those who had died in battles, air raids, concentration
camps, and in the expulsions from Eastern Europe.[84]

One year later the Ministry of the Interior proclaimed a new agreement about the *Volkstrauertag*: The Federal Republic would celebrate it
on the second Sunday before the first day of Advent. To distinguish it
from the *Heldengedenktag* of the Third Reich, the *Volkstrauertag* was shifted
from a Sunday in spring to November, the traditional month of mourning and meditation. The government did not, however, declare this a
work-free holiday. As in the Weimar Republic, it was not the government
but a private association dedicated to the case of war graves (Volksbund
deutsche Kriegsgräberfürsorge) that established a commemorative hour in
the Bundestag. Similar observances took place in every local community,
with speeches, music, and funeral rituals.

In his speech of 1951, Herman Ehlers, the president of the Bundestag,
emphasized the lack of a heroic cult of fallen soldiers as proof of the
"conversion" that the German people had undergone. As a consequence
of bitter experiences, the overwhelming majority of the people had turned
away from the worship of violence. Unlike in former times, when Nazi propaganda had misused the Heroes' Remembrance Day to prepare for a new
war, the German people now were unwilling to allow any political action
that could lead to war to take place under the pretense of remembering the
dead. Nor were the Germans willing to accept restrictions on their ways of
remembering the dead. It would be foolish to believe that a people could
be forced to change its nominally militaristic character by being prevented
from honoring its dead.[85] The Allied directive of 1946 banning public symbols of militarism and Nazism thus was misinterpreted as an immoral attack
on the Germans' right to commemorate their war victims. In this context,
remembering the pain and losses of the German population was meant to
demonstrate to the victors that the Germans had paid enough. In death

---

83 Behrenbeck, *Der Kult um die toten Helden*, 291–9.
84 *Die Welt*, Feb. 19, 1951.
85 Bundestag President Hermann Ehlers on February 18, 1951, Redemanuskript auf Mikrofilm, Presse-
und Informationsamt der Bundesregierung.

and mourning all humans were equal – such was the tone of many public speeches. Therefore, no differences were accepted between the war dead of all kinds and all nations. For the political aim, "integration by memory," it was important to neglect the circumstances of death. In 1952, Chancellor Konrad Adenauer therefore warned: "Don't forget the dead and their dependents, remember that we all have to bear pain and that this pain demands unity."[86]

Ehlers's speech was characteristic of the predominant attitude among the West Germans. It neither lacked a clear statement about German responsibility nor advocated a clear break with the past; it demonstrated that the integration of all Germans through a general self-perception as "victims" seemed more important than actual conversion. This hampered the integration of the anti-Nazi resistance, and the language of the memorials was dominated by self-victimization and the obsession with one's own pain and losses.

On the 1952 *Volkstrauertag*, West German President Theodor Heuss used the ceremonial hour in parliament to assert that the grief and sorrow that German women felt was the same as that of American, French, British, Italian, or even Russian women. Thus, pain perhaps could act as a bridge between former enemies.[87] Heuss did not intend to equate the losses of all nations but rather to assume the perspective of the Germans and draw attention to the pain of others who had also suffered. However, he and many other prominent speakers often forgot those victims of violence who had no surviving relatives and no existing community to remember them.

In 1955, ten years after the war, the commemoration of the *Volkstrauertag* was expanded to include the fallen soldiers of both world wars, as well as POWs. The rituals adopted a genuinely military character and returned to older national traditions. They took place at war cemeteries or war monuments and were attended by NATO representatives, members of the West German Border Control Force, regular police, and politicians. One day before the *Volkstrauertag* in 1955, on the birthday of General Gerhard Johann von Scharnhorst (November 12), the first soldiers of the new West German army were presented to the public. The establishment of the Bundeswehr made it necessary to define new national values worth dying for.

The situation seemed to call for religious justification, and the speeches during the official celebration in the Bundestag were given by two Christian dignitaries: Cardinal Josef Frings, Catholic bishop of Cologne, and Otto

---

86 *Der Mittag*, Düsseldorf, Nov. 17, 1952.
87 *Die Neue Zeitung* (Frankfurt/Munich), Nov. 17, 1952.

Dibelius, Protestant bishop of Berlin-Brandenburg. They discussed the contemporary tension between the longing for peace and the need to protect the fatherland. Dibelius called on Germans to respect the soldiers of the new army, who protected their country and prevented war by their very presence.[88] Neither mentioned the contrast with the aggressive nature of previous German armies; rather, they stressed the continuity of past and present armed forces.

Vice Chancellor Franz Blücher asserted that the soldiers of the recent war had died for a good and respectable fatherland, and that the living should not let them down. He asked the public not to find guilt with the individual when a common fate had to be borne by all. The Germans should make their state a safe haven for freedom, and for that reason they should claim their right to reunification – not for themselves but to secure peace in the world.[89] The victims of Nazi terror were either not even mentioned or were subsumed under the casualties of total war.

Thus, by 1955 the prospect of continuity in German commemorative practice seemed to have lost much of its menace. Interpreting war as an anonymous fate meant that nobody could be held responsible for it. Overcoming the division of Germany could be presented as an altruistic service to the cause of world peace. Occasions like this offered (West) Germans a narrative to forget the Third Reich by remembering the consequences of its politics, by feeling sorrow about one's own fate but not regretting one's own faults.

By 1960 we get a first impression of the gradual change that had taken place during the 1950s. On November 13, President Heinrich Lübke spoke at the parliamentary commemoration. He began his speech by remembering "not only the fallen soldiers, but also the countless human beings who perished." He called it a duty to find meaning in their deaths, and there could be no consolation without facing the truth. An honest view of the past would bring forth many things to be ashamed of, but silence was no way to overcome the burden. The people who fought against Hitler knew why they suffered, but the German people, forced to fight as an instrument of evil, still had to answer that question. They should have known that this war was a criminal one, but not everyone was strong enough to resist the dictator and his regime. Only by taking a clear view of the tangled web of guilt, fear, innocence, and uncertain conscience could one pay proper respect to the millions of victims. "Their [the German soldiers'] sacrifice

---

88 *Bonner Generalanzeiger*, Nov. 14, 1955.
89 *Bulletin*, Presse- und Informationsamt der Bundesregierung, Bonn, Nov. 18, 1955.

for the *Heimat* did not lose its worth only because they served Hitler. . . . The meaning of their death lies in the future. We have to see that man never again can be used as an instrument of power. . . . We have to understand the value of freedom."[90]

The values had changed: The war victims called for freedom, not for peace – perhaps because peace now seemed more secure – and the victims of the *Volksgemeinschaft* no longer predominated among the victims of Nazi terror.[91] The search for the meaning of death in war was finally brought into the context of guilt and responsibility for warfare. Like the memorials after 1945, the cultural practices of memory no longer answered the question of meaning but asked the living to make sense of death in war.[92] This memorialization related the past with the future and attempted to remodel it in the present.

CONCLUSION

In the first decade after the end of World War II, the two postwar German states used holidays and public ceremonies to differentiate themselves from the Third Reich, to help them break with the past. But when did that fundamental change occur, and how did it happen? What transformed the Nazi *Volksgemeinschaft* into a people worthy of joining the union of free and peaceful nations? In the 1950s, the shape of the social and moral, political and individual spheres was seen as a successfully completed process, not as an ongoing task. After 1949, politicians in both East and West Germany proclaimed the "end of the postwar period," not least because of a successful transition. The Germans presented themselves as a peace-loving people, as innocent, and as abused by the demonic Führer. In East Germany – embodied in the opponents and victors of Nazism – it was claimed that a society of perpetrators had been transformed into a new humane order guided by the values of peace and socialism. In West Germany, the early postwar years – denazification and re-education, particularly during the years of hunger and privation – were presented as a time of atonement that had somehow changed people and absolved the Germans of their "sins." As a result, the majority of Germans felt they had reestablished moral equality with the victorious powers.

---

90 Redemanuskript für den Rundfunk vom 13. November 1960, Presse- und Informationsamtes der Bundesregierung, Bonn, Mikrofilm.
91 Geyer, "Cold-War Angst."
92 Reinhart Koselleck, "Kriegerdenkmale als Identitätsstiftung der Überlebenden," in Odo Marquart and Karlheinz Stierle, eds., *Identität* (Munich, 1979), 255–76.

In West Germany the consequences, not the causes, of World War II dominated public memory at the beginning of the 1950s. The majority did not want to be reminded that the war was the real cause of contemporary plight but rather interpreted the postwar tribulations as victors' revenge. Conservative politicians felt obliged to heal the wounds of a divided and disoriented people, and therefore maintained a discreet silence about perpetrators and bystanders. In this way they failed to declare their solidarity with the victims of the Nazi regime.[93] Having realized that democracy had to be established among a mostly undemocratic people, many politicians were convinced that such a public stance would damage the process of democratization.[94] The only possibility for reintegrating enemies and opponents seemed to lie in the construction of a community of common fate: victims of war and violence. The specific conditions of individual pain had to be ignored: The story of war and violence was narrated in terms of honor and shame but not of guilt, confession, and atonement. The narrative perspective was one of complicity, not of resistance or persecution. To be released from political responsibility, one's own victims and losses were set against the victims of the Nazi terror as if painful experience could suspend the reason why one had been victimized. In the face of death, all men were supposed to be equal. In their pain, both victims and perpetrators were supposed to become members of the same community of remembrance. Those who insisted on a difference were declared to be "inhumane." German losses were remembered in order to silence those who would accuse Germans of complicity. Memorials and speeches therefore employed the language of religious lamentation for the dead. The negative consequence of denying the diversity of death in war was a loss of concrete memories flowing from individual experience into social memory. Coming to terms with the trauma became a problem that was relegated to the private sphere.[95]

In East Germany the SED emphasized the end of the war, not warfare and war aims. Its foundational myth propagated that from 1918 onward international communism had fought hard to achieve final victory. Stressing the outcome of the war, the shortcomings and failures of the German people (and of the anti-Nazi resistance) could be forgotten; public memory could be focused on the Soviet victors of the war and on the history

---

93 Dubiel, *Niemand ist frei von der Geschichte*, 64–6, 42; Herf, *Divided Memory*, 241. Instead of a public discourse about guilt and responsibility for war crimes and genocide, a coalition of silence formed the first common identity. Giesen, "National Identity as Trauma," 242.

94 That this was the only possible way to establish and stabilize democracy in West Germany is stressed by Hermann Lübbe, "Der Nationalsozialismus im deutschen Nachkriegsbewusstsein," *Historische Zeitschrift*, no. 236 (1983): 579–99.

95 Neumann, *Nicht der Rede wert*.

of socialism triumphant. Struggle, heroism, and sacrifice were stressed instead of genocide, slavery, and victimization. The antifascist foundational myth served to turn the suppressed mourning for the fallen soldiers of the Wehrmacht toward the fighters for socialism. However, the self-legitimation of the GDR was based on the generalization of an antifascist experience that contrasted with a "normal" German biography during the Third Reich.[96] Public reflection about a "normal life" under Nazi rule did not take place. The Nazi war crimes were presented as part of *West* German history. In this way the traumatic experience was converted into victory, but the problem of coming to terms with the past was not sincerely addressed.

Thus, in neither part of Germany was the whole spectrum of experiences of violence and war reflected in the media of social memory. Only a fraction of the biographical experience was communicated or found its way into public symbols and rituals of remembrance.

With regard to public memory, the two German states worked like "communicating channels." That which was suppressed in GDR rituals (the war dead of the Nazi *Volksgemeinschaft*, the POWs, and the internees) was remembered all the more in the Federal Republic. And those victims outside official commemoration of West Germany (such as the Communist resistance to Hitler or Red Army casualties) enjoyed the spotlight in East Germany's ceremonies. Both states commemorated the Jewish victims of the Holocaust in a secondary way, and both shared a blind spot in their collective memory: the non-Jewish victims of persecution (gypsies, homosexuals, beggars, and so forth), who always had been excluded from the community. Public ritual thus did not serve to integrate the former *Volksfremde* but indeed reaffirmed the social ties of the Nazi *Volksgemeinschaft*. However, both societies kept silent about war as a personal experience of violence.[97]

In West Germany the story of postwar integration and normalization was often told in metaphors of deep wounds that needed time and tranquility to heal.[98] Silence and consensus instead of conflict and separation were the therapy used to cure the Germans of their violent past. Nazi rule was presented in terms of rape (the female segment of the population was "seduced" by the Führer); later, it was the victors "penetrating" the Germans from outside (coming over them in air raids or occupation). In any case, the Germans

---

96 Diner, *Kreisläufe*, 79.
97 Exceptions in Robert G. Moeller, "War Stories: The Search for a Usable Past in the Federal Republic of Germany," *American Historical Review* 101 (1996): 1008–48.
98 Dubiel, *Niemand ist frei von der Geschichte*, 64.

were presented as helpless victims of violent actions, suffering injury even after the war.

The narrative of the surviving victims of Nazi terror and their genuine experience of German violence was later forgotten in favor of a collective identity that could offer self-respect to the survivors. Auschwitz was not an integrative symbol in the 1950s, nor was the memory of the Holocaust constitutive for the Federal Republic as it would become in the 1990s.[99] This era was vaguely remembered as a "terrible guilt that was loaded on the shoulders of the German people by a criminal regime."[100] The persecution of the Jews formed a memory gap at that time. Until the late 1970s there was no German public holiday commemorating Jewish victims. Neither the liberation of the concentration camps, for example, Auschwitz on January 27, 1945, nor the "Night of Broken Glass" (*Reichskristallnacht*) on November 9, 1938, were appropriate occasions for commemoration.[101] Only decades after the end of the war did the Germans begin to understand that there was a connection between guilt and honor, between candor about the past and moving toward a better future. Having lost the war, it seemed as if the Germans lost portions of their memory, too. In any case, the process of rediscovering the whole German past still continues.

---

99 Frank Schirrmacher, *Frankfurter Allgemeine Zeitung*, Dec. 14, 1998. Another example is the speech of Bundestag President Wolfgang Thierse on November 9, 1999: "Die Erinnerung an die Schrecken der NS-Zeit bleibe lebensnotwendig für Deutsche," *Der Tagesspiegel*, Nov. 10, 1999. The Holocaust was not used at all in the 1950s to exemplify the singularity of the German nation as a traumatic reference point for German identity (Bernhard Giesen, *Triumph and Trauma* [Berkeley, Calif., 2000]); this only occurred later. The Holocaust hardly played any role in the memory of the 1950s in either German state.

100 Paul Löbe, Sept. 7, 1949, quoted by Dubiel, *Niemand ist frei von der Geschichte*, 39.

101 Yet this lapse of memory was noted in 1955. See the article "Kristallnacht" in the *Frankfurter Allgemeine Zeitung* of Nov. 9, 1955. There it was written: "Whoever stirs up the wounds of the past does not make himself popular. But it seems necessary precisely in the – not simply materially – well-restored atmosphere of our life to remember the difference between forgiving and forgetting. . . . But not if we remember this historical fact [the tremendous extent of the persecution of the Jews in Germany], in order to resurrect a collective accusation. Most Germans learned about what occurred in the extermination camps only after the war. The Night of Broken Glass in 1938, however, was experienced by an entire people – with anger, with indignation, with indifference, with satisfaction. On that night, however, the darkness of evil finally fell over Germany. That should stick in our memory, even the memory of those whose moral comfort always makes do with seeing guilt only in the eyes of the others." See Y. Michal Bodemann, *Gedächtnistheater: Die jüdische Gemeinschaft und ihre deutsche Erfindung* (Hamburg, 1996); Domansky, " 'Kristallnacht,' the Holocaust, and German Unity," 60–94.

3

Paths of Normalization after the Persecution of the Jews

The Netherlands, France, and West Germany in the 1950s

IDO DE HAAN

In the conclusion to his book *Fallen Soldiers*, George Mosse discusses the difference between World Wars I and II. World War I was still a soldiers' war. Even though many families lost their conscripted sons, they died as soldiers in the trenches, relatively far removed from the home front. World War II was much more a civilians' war, "a different kind of war that would blur the distinction between the front line and the home front."[1] The violence of World War II was not only massive but also omnipresent. It pervaded all circles of society and made itself felt even in the remotest corners of the nations involved.

At least in the Western European context, the clearest instance of this all-pervasive violence is the persecution of Jews. It would be a mistake to restrict the episode of anti-Jewish violence to the industrial killing by the *Einsatzgruppen* and in the death camps in Eastern Europe. Not only did the violence begin much earlier than the first operations of *Einsatzgruppen* in the summer of 1941, it also extended far further west. German Jews were already victimized in the second half of the 1930s, while other Western European Jews experienced a potential threat, and sometimes even actual aggression, when the anti-Jewish climate also overtook other countries. At the end of the 1930s, Jews in Belgium, France, and the Netherlands were confronted with social exclusion, verbal aggression, and in some cases even physical violence.[2]

---

1 George L. Mosse, *Fallen Soldiers: Reshaping the Memory of the World Wars* (Oxford, 1990), 222, 201.
2 See Ido de Haan, "The Netherlands and the Novemberpogrom," *Jahrbuch für Antisemitismusforschung* 8 (1999): 155–76; Lieven Saerens, "Antwerp's Attitude Toward the Jews from 1918 to 1940 and Its Implications for the Period of the Occupation," in Dan Michman, ed., *Belgium and the Holocaust: Jews, Belgians, Germans* (Jerusalem, 1998), 159–94; Anne Grynberg, "Les camps français, des non-lieux de mémoire," in Dimitri Nicolaïdis, ed., *Oublier nos crimes: L'amnésie nationale, une spécificité française?* (Paris, 1994), 52–69.

The persecution and killing of Jews took place in the vicinity of their fellow citizens. Even if the Jewish fate in the death camps was unimaginable, the injustice and cruelty of the persecution that led to their deaths was obvious. However, it is now commonly assumed that only a few of the many witnesses of the persecution of the Jews gave testimony about it after the defeat of the Nazis. According to a widely held opinion, a deafening silence settled over the history of the persecution and blocked both the punishment of the perpetrators as well as the recognition of their victims. And, so the argument continues, only after a long delay was the memory of the persecution recovered and the horrible fate of the Jews acknowledged.

This picture of the way in which the persecution of the Jews has been forgotten and remembered describes both a general historical mechanism and a universal normative model for dealing with the horrors of the past. By comparing the memory of the persecution in the Netherlands, West Germany, and France, I question both aspects. There seems to be not one general, but many specific historical dynamics in the development of public recollections of large-scale violence. These different dynamics have resulted in different kinds of "normality." Instead of a general model of normalization, the comparison of three Western European countries suggests there are different paths of normalization.

TRAUMA AND NORMALIZATION

The starting point for the argument that there is a general historical dynamic and a universal model of normalization is the psychological notion of trauma. A few examples suffice to show how often these psychological notions are used to discuss the memory of the persecution of the Jews. For instance, in a recent reflection on "the long shadows of Vichy," Jürg Altwegg discusses "the return of the repressed." Only recently, Altwegg argues, was the historical lie of the postwar period unmasked: "The trauma became visible: 1940 and the dark years afterward."[3] Discussing the collective memory of concentration camps in West Germany, Claudia Koonz argues that it was clouded by the "post-traumatic oblivion of *Stunde Null*."[4] "Massive denial was blatant in the historical work of the late forties and fifties," Saul Friedländer

---

3 Jürgen Altwegg, *Die langen Schatten von Vichy: Frankreich, Deutschland und die Rückkehr des Verdrängten* (Munich, 1998), 9.

4 Claudia Koonz, "Between Memory and Oblivion: Concentration Camps in German Memory," in John R. Gillis, ed., *Commemorations: The Politics of National Identity* (Princeton, N.J., 1994), 265.

argues with respect to Germany.[5] Especially in the Netherlands, the trope of trauma is frequently invoked to discuss the persecution of the Jews. It is sometimes connected to what is called the Dutch "second national trauma," that is, the Indonesian decolonization.[6]

Much of this is pop psychology and is sometimes used to argue that it involved an irrational reaction, "with an emotional intensity out of proportion to the objective values."[7] Sometimes "national traumas" are equated with a given formative experience on a national scale and considered "[s]erious disruptions of the tranquility of everyday life [that] tend to be remembered and to become embedded in a collective perception of society as moral community."[8] Yet, in the context of the memory of the destruction of the European Jewry, the invocation of the concept of trauma implies a more complex line of thought.[9]

The psychology of traumatic memory indeed starts with a disruptive event, such as the paradigmatic railway accidents and bombings. According to late-nineteenth-century psychiatrists, physical harm and intense fear can lead to a serious dislocation of normal mental functions. The pathological state results not from the shock itself but from the perpetuation of the defense mechanism that the shock calls into existence. Traumatic experiences are not so much repressed but rather dissociated from the conscious mental order. They result in a second, alternating or subconscious, or, according to some theorists, even in a second personality, inaccessible without the help of a professional therapist.[10] People suffering from mental trauma are thus unable to master the traumatizing experience or the defense mechanism that hides the experience from view. As Sigmund Freud asserted, they do not remember, only act out; reproduce the event not as memory, but as act.[11]

---

5 Saul Friedländer, *Memory, History, and the Extermination of the Jews of Europe* (Bloomington, Ind., 1993), 124.

6 Cf. Ido de Haan, "The Construction of a National Trauma: The Memory of the Persecution of the Jews in the Netherlands," *Netherland's Journal of Social Sciences* 34, no. 2 (1998): 196–217.

7 Arend Lijphart, *The Trauma of Decolonization: The Dutch and West New Guinea* (New Haven, Conn., 1966), 7–8.

8 Arthur G. Neal, *National Trauma and Collective Memory: Major Events in the American Century* (New York, 1998), 36.

9 I rely here on Allan Young, *The Harmony of Illusions: Inventing Post-Traumatic Stress Disorder* (Princeton, N.J., 1995), 13–85; Hans Binneveld, *From Shellshock to Combat Stress: A Comparative History of Military Psychiatry* (Amsterdam, 1997), passim; Bessel A. van der Kolk and Onno van der Hart, "The Intrusive Past: The Flexibility of Memory and the Engraving of Trauma," in Cathy Caruth, ed., *Trauma: Explorations in Memory* (Baltimore, 1995), 158–82; Cathy Caruth, *Unclaimed Experience: Trauma, Narrative, and History* (Baltimore, 1996).

10 See also Ian Hacking, *Rewriting the Soul: Multiple Personality and the Sciences of Memory* (Princeton, N.J., 1995).

11 Sigmund Freud, "Erinnern, Wiederholen und Durcharbeiten," in Sigmund Freud, *Gesammelte Werke: Chronlogisch geordnet*, 18 vols. (1914; Frankfurt am Main, 1947), 10:129.

It remains society's Other, an *onverwerkt verleden, un passé qui ne passe pas* –
an unmasterable past.[12]

The essence of traumatic memory concerns the lack of a shared frame
of reference in which the memory – in this case, of persecution – can
be grasped. As Friedländer formulates the problem, "the catastrophe of
European Jewry has not been incorporated into any compelling framework
of meaning."[13] The solution then is to find such a framework, to "assem-
ble an organized, detailed, verbal account, oriented in time and historical
context."[14] Only when this historical framework is developed will the witness of the event become capable of speaking out. As Shosanna Felman and
Dori Laub argue, only then is the victim able not only to testify but in a
more fundamental sense to experience the assault.[15] Thus, normalization
of a traumatic experience is not simply assimilation, but rather an incor-
poration of the event into a cognitive framework that first and foremost
encompasses the perspective of the victim, both in his or her role as object
of violence and as involuntary subject in violent engagements.

This line of thought forms the basis of a universal theory of normalization. In this vein, Gesine Schwan argues in *Politik und Schuld* that silenced
feelings of guilt have inhibited the political culture of the Federal Republic from developing democratic virtues and have frustrated the growth of
the social capital of trust that is needed to ensure democratic stability.[16] In
her proposals to overcome silence, she points to a normative conception of
democracy in which political stability can only result from rational legitimation through open political debate. Guilt needs to be recognized, misdeeds to
be acknowledged, before democratic trust can be re-established. Therefore,
the argument that the persecution caused trauma, the result of which was the
repression of the memory of the event, might be considered a "general
theory of normalization." Such a theory not only explains the mechanism
by which societies cope with mass violence; it also offers a criterion to
distinguish between pathological reconstruction and a beneficial, rational
normalization of social and political relations.

12 David Barnouw, Madelon de Keizer, and Gerrold van der Stroom, eds., *1940–1945: Onverwerkt
   verleden? Lezingen van het symposium georganiseerd door het Rijksinstituut voor Oorlogsdocumentatie, 7 en 8
   mei 1985* (Utrecht, 1985); Charles S. Maier, *The Unmasterable Past: History, Holocaust, and German
   National Identity* (Cambridge, Mass., 1988); Éric Conan and Henry Rousso, *Vichy, un passé qui ne
   passe pas* (Paris, 1996).
13 Friedländer, *Memory, History, and the Extermination of the Jews*, 43.
14 Judith L. Herman, *Trauma and Recovery: From Domestic Abuse to Political Terror* (London, 1992), 177.
15 Shosanna Felman and Dori Laub, *Testimony: Crises of Witnessing in Literature, Psychoanalysis, and History*
   (New York, 1992).
16 Gesine Schwan, *Politik und Schuld: Die zerstörische Macht des Schweigens* (Frankfurt am Main, 1997).

I doubt any such theory is viable, but in any case the psychological model of trauma and repression is not. Indeed, there is a prima facie similarity in the development of public memory (or the lack of memory) of persecution in different countries. Everywhere the remembrance of the persecution of Jews had to compete with economic and social reconstruction, the new political polarization of the Cold War, and of course with the attempts of the perpetrators to cover up their crimes. Yet, by subsuming all these processes under the same label of trauma, one tends to disregard the different experiences involved.[17]

The notion of traumatic memory wrongly suggests that all memories are alike. The guilt felt by passive bystanders is different from the fear of disclosure of former perpetrators. Both differ from the maneuvering of political elites between a sincere wish to break with the past and the desire to court as many voters as possible, including those who participated in the crimes of the former regime. And all these experiences differ radically from those of the victims of persecution, who sometimes were struck dumb by the immensity of their suffering but who also cried out their pain and often found that nobody cared to listen.

These memories not only differ, they also can compete. The recollection of the past is at stake in political controversies in the present, and memories are ammunition in the struggle for power and recognition. Typically, memories of the persecutions become a public issue as a result of political scandals, when an unexpected revelation of former involvement or contemporary neglect of the violence against Jews subverts political and social reputations.[18] This implies that the development of public memories must be investigated in the context of societal cleavages and power bases. Obviously, these contexts differ nationally. Consequently, the persecution of the Jews has been remembered in altogether different ways, as I show here by comparing the Netherlands, West Germany, and France. In the first decades after the war, there developed in each of these countries not a psychological dynamic of trauma, pathological silence, and slow recovery of memory, but a shifting political compromise between silence and speaking out.

To explain this shifting compromise, there are numerous factors one should take into account. Recent studies deal with one or more of the following issues: the specific nature of the persecution in the national context;

---

17 Henry Rousso, *Le syndrome de Vichy (1944–198...)* (Paris, 1987), 13; Alfred Grosser, *Le crime et la mémoire* (Paris, 1989), 87.

18 Rousso, *Le syndrome*, 13–14, 234; Marianne Schwab-Trapp, *Zur Begründung von Legitimität in NS-Konflikten: Eine Fallanalyse* (Siegen, 1992); Ido de Haan, *Na de ondergang: De herinnering aan de Jodenvervolging in Nederland 1945–1995* (The Hague, 1997), 101–2.

the interests and strategies of political reconstruction of old and new elites; the postwar position of the former resistance; the treatment of members and collaborators of the Nazi regime; the material restitutions and social recognition of the victims of persecution; the nature and power of the postwar Jewish community; the tradition of national commemoration; the media of cultural reproduction, such as education, mass media, and academic historiography; and the pressure of other national powers and the international community. Some of these factors play an important role in all nations, such as the political purge and reconstruction, the position and recognition of the postwar Jewish community, and the official commemorations of the war period. However, both the structure and weight of these various factors differ and thus contribute to the diverging paths of normalization followed in each of these nations.

THE NETHERLANDS

The commemorative atmosphere in the Netherlands immediately after the war is well characterized by two events. The first took place in February 1946. Queen Wilhelmina gave the city of Amsterdam permission to add the words "heroic, determined, charitable" to its coat of arms in gratitude to the solidarity of the Amsterdam population with the Jews during the strike of February 1941. Some weeks later the Ministry of Interior ordered that there would be no celebration on the actual day of liberation, May 5, because that was a Sunday, the day on which the Christian obligation to rest had to be honored. And because Saturday was a working day, festivities had to be restricted to the afternoon of May 4.[19] Both events characterize the return to normality that Dutch elites wanted to enforce. They envisaged the war as an interlude in the national history, in which the Dutch collectively and bravely resisted the foreign invader. Now that the Germans were defeated, the citizens had to look forward and work hard to rebuild the country.

For most people the promise of abundant employment was an attractive prospect after the years of economic depression and shortages. The war years had brought most people some discomfort, but only after the pressure to enter the *Arbeitseinsatz* became stronger and the lack of food and fuel more severe in the last year of the war had suffering become more widespread. The shortages remained even after the defeat of the German forces, and the rationing of goods ended in the early 1950s. Then a slow but steady rise of

---

19 Martin Harlaar and Jan Pieter Koster, *Stilstaan bij de oorlog: De gemeente Amsterdam en de Tweede Wereldoorlog 1945–1995* (Bussum, 1995), 20.

the standard of living began. The officially promoted middle-class ideal of a job, a home of one's own, a refrigerator, and eventually cars and vacations abroad increasingly became a reality for the majority of the population. The war period indeed seemed to be an interlude in a historical continuity.[20]

This was even true for those who were subjected to the purge. In an international perspective, the Netherlands were purged on a rather large scale. There were files on some 400,000 people (of a population of 10 million), and some 150,000 people were arrested. Over 60,000 were sentenced to imprisonment and the loss of citizenship, and there were 152 death sentences, 40 of which were carried out. The death sentence was applied mainly in cases where collaboration had led to the death of Netherlanders; in most instances these were Jews. However, soon after the purge started the courts became more lenient. In 1947 the first groups were pardoned; in the early 1950s even people whose death sentences had been commuted to life imprisonment were released. All released convicts received some form of social and psychological help to re-integrate into Dutch society.[21]

For the remainder of the Jewish community, the officially proclaimed *Wederopbouw* (reconstruction) was a very frustrating experience. After the German invasion, over 100,000 Jews were deported and killed; around 34,000 in Sobibor and the others mainly in Auschwitz. Nearly 80 percent of the Dutch Jews did not survive: This percentage is the highest in all of Western Europe and is comparable to the percentages in Eastern Europe, the heartland of the Holocaust. Moreover, Dutch Jewish casualties comprised half of the total number of victims in the Netherlands. A few thousand Jews had been able to flee abroad; some 17,000 survived the persecution in hiding; and around 5,500 survived the deportations, camps, and death marches.[22]

After the German capitulation, Dutch Jewish survivors received almost no help and even less recognition for their fate. Their return from the camps was delayed due to the chaotic repatriation of almost half a million other displaced Dutch citizens. While other national relief organizations quickly

20 Ido de Haan, *Zelfbestuur en staatsbeheer: Het politieke debat over burgerschap en rechtsstaat in de twintigste eeuw* (Amsterdam, 1993), 88–97.
21 August D. Belinfante, *In plaats van bijltjesdag: De geschiedenis van de Bijzondere Rechtspleging na de Tweede Wereldoorlog* (Assen, 1978); Peter Romijn, *Snel, streng en rechtvaardig: Politiek beleid inzake de bestraffing en reclassering van "foute" Nederlanders, 1945–1955* (Groningen, 1989); Peter Romijn and Gerhard Hirschfeld, "Die Ahndung der Kollaboration in den Niederlanden," in Klaus-Dietmar Henke and Hans Woller, eds., *Politische Säuberung in Europa: Die Abrechnung mit Faschismus und Kollaboration nach dem Zweiten Weltkrieg* (Munich, 1991), 281–310.
22 Peter Romijn, "De oorlog (1940–1945)," in Hans J.C.H. Blom, Renate Fuks-Mansfeld, and Ivo Schöffer, eds., *Geschiedenis van de Joden in Nederland* (Amsterdam, 1995), 319ff; Jozeph Michman, Hartog Beem, and Dan Michman, *Pinkas: Geschiedenis van de joodse gemeenschap in Nederland* (Amsterdam, 1992), 173.

reached the camps in the east and began to organize the return of their people, the Dutch deportees waited for weeks and even months, often in vain. Many returned on their own initiative or with the help of foreign organizations.[23] Their reception on Dutch soil was cold and frustrating. Many of the Jewish survivors of Auschwitz were first taken to Odessa and traveled further by boat to Marseille. In France they were welcomed together with the other *deportés* and received as heroes. Yet, on the Dutch border they were subjected to degrading physical and political scrutiny and in some cases were housed in camps with former members of the Dutch National Socialist Movement (NSB). In other cases "on arrival at the train station, they played an old record of the *Wilhelmus* [the national anthem], and that was all."[24]

Once home, Jewish survivors began, often in vain, to search for friends and family and for their homes and personal belongings. Numerous are the stories of Jews who, before their deportation, had given their belongings to neighbors or acquaintances for safekeeping, only to find out that the latter had sold them or refused to give them back. Although it is clear that many were bona fide, the number of people who were not was at least considerable, given the fact that there was a word for them, *bewariërs*.[25]

The legal framework for the restitution of property was devised during the war by the government in exile. Nevertheless, it turned out to be a tedious process. One of the main obstacles was the fact that the deported Jews were officially missing. Only in 1949 did the government issue death certificates for those listed by the Red Cross as killed. Moreover, in many cases the present owner argued that he or she had acquired the goods in good faith.[26] Some cases were never resolved, sometimes because Jews no longer were willing to protect their own interests, which involved painful and frustrating

---

23 Conny Kristel, "'De moeizame terugkeer': De repatriëring van de Nederlandse overlevenden uit de Duitse concentratiekampen," *Oorlogsdocumentatie '40–'45: Jaarboek voor het Rijksinstituut voor Oorlogsdocumentatie* (1989): 77–100; Pieter Lagrou, "Le retour des survivants des camps de concentration aux Pays-Bas et en Belgique: de l'ostracisme à l'héroïsation," in Marie-Anne Matard-Bonucci and Edouard Lynch, eds., *La libération des camps et le retour des déportés: L'histoire en souffrance* (Brussels, 1995), 250–69; Pieter Lagrou, *The Legacy of Nazi Occupation: Patriotic Memory and National Recovery in Western Europe, 1945–1965* (Cambridge, 2000).

24 Ab Caransa, quoted in Michal Citroen, *U wordt door niemand verwacht: Nederlandse joden na kampen en onderduik* (Amsterdam, 1999), 53; see also Dienke Hondius, *Terugkeer: Antisemitisme in Nederland rond de bevrijding* (The Hague, 1998), 119–32.

25 This is a contraction of *bewaren*, to keep in custody, and *ariër*, Aryan. It seems its conceptualization dates from the early days of the persecution, when Jews were no longer allowed to exercise most of their civil rights. It was only at the end of the war that the term received a negative connotation.

26 Louis de Jong, *Het Koninkrijk der Nederlanden in de Tweede Wereldoorlog* (The Hague, 1988), 650ff; A. J. van Schie, "Restitution of Economic Rights after 1945," in Jozeph Michman and Tirtsa Levie, eds., *Dutch Jewish History: Proceedings of the Symposium on the History of the Jews in the Netherlands [1982]* (Jerusalem, 1984), 401–20.

encounters with civil servants and insurance companies. In recent years, in the slipstream of the international search for Jewish possessions, it again has become clear that formalism and bureaucratic callousness, as much as outright aggression and antisemitism, held Jews back from reclaiming their possessions.[27]

The Dutch government took the position that no distinction should be made between Jewish and other Dutch citizens, because that was considered a racist perspective. This position led to neglect of the revelations that Jews were exclusively targeted for destruction. After the defeat of the German forces, that same ill-conceived egalitarianism was the reason Jews had no right to special compensation. Former members of the resistance had a right to a special pension because, the government argued, their activities had made them de facto servants of the Dutch state. Jews, however, were considered passive victims for which the state held no special obligation.[28]

Dutch Jews had very limited means to protest this treatment. After 1945, there were only a few survivors, and this small group was very much divided. Before the war the Jewish community was split along cultural, religious, and political lines, and by difference in social class.[29] After 1945, these divisions persisted and may even have been deepened by the rifts resulting from attempts to unite the Jewish community into one religious organization. Finally, few Jews were still willing to engage Dutch society. More than 5,000 Jews migrated abroad, whereas many of those who stayed retreated into the private sphere of home and family.[30]

This is not to say Jews were silent. In cases of gross injustice, Jews voiced their objections. The most important instance was the controversy surrounding Jewish orphans between 1945 and 1949. The committee deciding their fate was dominated by Protestant members of the former resistance. In line with the official doctrine of individual equality, they argued that it was generally not in the interest of the children to grant custody to Jewish foster parents. They said this would mean not only a second separation, this time from the Gentiles who had protected them during the war, but the children would also be exposed to the future predicaments that Jews were expected to

27 See the examples in Citroen, *U wordt door niemand verwacht.*
28 Cf. Pieter Lagrou, "Victims of Genocide and National Memory: Belgium, France, and the Netherlands, 1945–1965," *Past and Present* 154 (1998): 209.
29 Jaap Meijer, *Hoge hoeden, lage standaarden: De Nederlandse joden tussen 1933 en 1940* (Baarn, 1969); Hans J.C.H. Blom and Joel J. Cahen, "Joodse Nederlanders, Nederlandse joden en joden in Nederland (1870–1940)," in Blom, Fuks-Mansfeld, and Schöffer, eds., *Geschiedenis van de Joden*, 247–310.
30 Chaya Brasz, "Bevrijdingsjaren – jaren van bevrijding? De strijd om de opbouw van joods leven," in *Le-Ezrath Ha-am. Het Volk ter Hulpe. Het eerste joodse blad in 1945 Eindhoven-Amsterdam* (Assen, 1985), xvii–xli; Chaya Brasz, "Na de Tweede Wereldoorlog: van kerkgenootschap tot culturele minderheid," in Blom, Fuks-Mansfeld, and Schöffer, eds., *Geschiedenis van de Joden*, 349–403.

encounter. However, most Jewish representatives on the committee argued that their opponents intended to convert the children to Christianity. This suspicion was strengthened by the abduction of two Jewish girls, who were taken to a Catholic cloister in Belgium, and the subsequent trials of the kidnappers in the early 1950s, when the comparable Finaly Affair in France re-awakened interest in the Dutch girls. In the end, in 40 percent of 1,004 cases custody was awarded to Gentile foster parents.[31]

In this and other cases, Jewish protests were voiced by small and often ineffective organizations. In custody cases, the reconstructed Nederlands Israëlietisch Kerkgenootschap (NIK), the orthodox organization, was most active. The struggle for restitution of material goods was fought by individual lawyers. In the immediate postwar years, Jews were represented by the Zionist-oriented Jewish Co-ordination Committee (JCC), which also had a strong influence in the founding of the national organization for Jewish Social Work (JMW). However, the JCC was dissolved after its leaders left for Israel; the JMW focused mainly on individual care; and the NIK soon restricted its activities to spiritual affairs. In most cases, the representation of collective Jewish interests was completely lacking. As a result, a number of collective rights Jews had held before 1940, such as exceptions from the rules for business hours, allowances for ritual slaughter, and the subsidization of synagogue construction, were only partially restored.[32]

As a result of their weak position and ineffective organization, Jews contributed only sparsely and individually to public remembrance of the persecution.[33] Some published eyewitness accounts of their deportation and internment, but interest soon waned. Initially publishers refused to publish the diary of Anne Frank, and it was only after the international acclaim in the mid-1950s that sales began to rise. Even then, the book did not acquire the same sacrosanct centrality there as in the rest of the world.[34]

---

31 Joel S. Fishman, "Jewish War Orphans in the Netherlands – The Guardianship Issue 1945–1950," *Wiener Library Bulletin* 27, n.s. 30–1 (1973–4): 31–6; Joel S. Fishman, "The Anneke Beekman Affair and the Dutch News Media," *Jewish Social Studies* 40 (1978): 3–24; Joel S. Fishman, "The War Orphan Controversy in the Netherlands: Majority – Minority Relations," in Michman and Levie, eds., *Dutch Jewish History*, 421–32.

32 Joop Sanders, "Opbouw en continuïteit na 1945," in Michman, Beem, and Michman, *Pinkas*, 235, 265.

33 Ido de Haan, "Tekens in de stad: De herinnering aan de Jodenvervolging in Amsterdam," in Herman Beliën and Monique van Hoogstraten, eds., *Herinneringen en historische visies: De betekenis van vijfenvijftig jaar Februaristaking in Amsterdam* (Amsterdam, 1996), 63–91.

34 Henriëtte Boas, "Jewish Figures in Post-war Dutch Literature," *Jewish Journal of Sociology* 5, no. 1 (1963): 55–83; Jo Melkman, *Geliefde vijand: Het beeld van de Jood in de naoorlogse Nederlandse literatuur* (Amsterdam, 1964); Dick H. Schram, "Taal behoudt de feiten. De verwerking van de Tweede Wereldoorlog in de literatuur," in Dick Schram and Cor Geljon, eds., *Overal sporen: De verwerking van de Tweede Wereldoorlog in literatuur en kunst* (Amsterdam, 1990), 93–126.

Most remarkable is the early development of the Dutch historiography of the persecution. Two extensive studies had appeared by 1950, one of which was published as part of a semiofficial series on the history of the war period. However, these historical works were characterized by a sharp distinction between the history of the persecution, which was considered a strictly German-Jewish affair, and the history of occupation and resistance, which was viewed a truly Dutch story. The separation between Jews and non-Jews was thus re-enacted in the historiography of the persecution.[35]

So far, the isolated position of Dutch Jews seems to confirm the impression that the fate of the Jews was dissociated from collective memory and that the story of the persecution was silenced in the Dutch society of the 1950s. Yet the fact that Jews had little say did not automatically imply that the memory of their persecution was silenced. On the contrary, it had a central position in the attempts to bestow historical legitimacy on postwar political positions.

The political elites of the first decade aimed at a "nationalization" of the resistance.[36] Individual members of the resistance claimed a prominent role in the postwar society, yet only Communists and right-wing grassroots organizations favored a political role for their resistance organizations. A considerable part of the prewar elite, who had kept aloof during the war, abhorred this veteran activism. Together with the leaders of the largest resistance organizations they presented the resistance as a national movement. Thus, in one gesture, they ideologically disarmed the claims of radical resistance organizations and created a historical legitimation for their new prominence.

The essence of this ideological maneuver was the argument that the Dutch resistance had been first and foremost a spiritual affair. Indeed, the armed or material resistance had been limited, but the main reason for this move was to equate the mentality of the resistance with the spirit of freedom that was supposed to characterize the Dutch nation. The opposite of this spirit was a German "anti-spirit," which was exemplified most strongly by the persecution of the Jews. In commemorative speeches, schoolbooks, and other popular representations of the 1950s, one always referred to the "disgusting adoration of the race" by the "Teutonic hordes." Awareness of

---

35 Cf. Conny Kristel, " 'A Sacred Duty': The Holocaust in Dutch historiography," in *The Low Countries: Arts and Society in Flanders and the Netherlands. A Yearbook* (1994–5): 186–94; Conny Kristel, *Geschiedenis als opdracht: Abel Herzberg, Jacques Presser en Loe de Jong over de jodenvervolging* (Amsterdam, 1998); De Haan, *Na de ondergang*, 51.

36 Pieter Lagrou, "Patriotten en Regenten: Het parochiale patriottisme van de naoorlogse Nederlandse illegaliteit, 1945–1980," in *Oorlogsdocumentatie '40–'45: Zesde Jaarboek van het Rijksinstituut voor Oorlogsdocumentatie* (1995): 10–47.

the persecution therefore was always coupled with a strongly anti-German sentiment, expressed in popular sayings and in aggression toward German visitors, which German tourists have encountered ever since the opening of the border in 1954.[37]

Awareness of the persecution was heightened by the fact that, notably, Communists objected to the nationalization of the resistance. They claimed to be the only group who had actually cared about the Jews, even though they legitimated their resistance in antifascist and anticapitalist terms. The most vehement episodes in this struggle over the legacy of the resistance focused on the commemoration of the strike of February 1941. The Communists claimed the strike as their most remarkable exploit. The queen's gesture to the city of Amsterdam was an essential move in the transference of the spirit of the resistance from particular, politically subversive groups to the community as a whole.[38]

The memory of the persecution was at stake in other controversies as well. As in other countries, the conviction of and amnesty for war criminals and collaborators led to fierce debates. Opponents of a forgiving policy often referred to the crimes against Jews. However, between 1950 and 1964 most of those convicted for the persecution of Jews received pardons and were released from prison, including the Dutch members of the Kolonne Henneicke who had specialized in Jew-hunting. The handling of these cases went almost unnoticed, but the case of four German officials, three of whom had been directly responsible for the deportation of the Dutch Jews, attracted a lot of attention. In the early 1950s their death sentences were commuted to life imprisonment. A series of debates on their parole followed, which finally ended when the last two prisoners were released from prison in 1989, long after war criminals elsewhere in Europe had been freed.[39]

The involvement of Dutch officials and citizens in the violence against Jews was seldom discussed in this period. Just beneath the surface of public debate, in letters to the editor, remarks in literary works and elsewhere in daily life, there were colloquial references to the collaboration of the registration office, of streetcar and railway personnel, and especially of

---

37 De Haan, *Na de ondergang*, 21–3, 77–8; Friso Wielenga, *West-Duitsland: partner uit noodzaak. Nederland en de Bondsrepubliek 1949–1955* (Utrecht, 1989), 345.

38 Selma Leydesdorff, "The Mythology of 'Solidarity,' as Shown by the Memory of the February Strike of 1941," in Jozeph Michman, ed., *Dutch Jewish History III* (Assen, 1993), 353–69; Susan Legêne, "Dans van een dokwerker: Standbeeld en geschiedbeeld van de Februaristaking," in Beliën and Hoogstraten, *Herinnering en historische visies*, 36–62.

39 Belinfante, *In plaats van bijltjesdag*; Romijn, *Snel, streng en rechtvaardig*; Romijn and Hirschfeld, "Die Ahndung der Kollaboration."

the police. These sentiments sometimes surfaced, for instance in 1956 when it was revealed that the mayor of The Hague had been responsible for the deportation of a Jewish family in 1943. Until his resignation six months later, the newspapers discussed daily the case and the broader issues of the persecution of the Jews, the role of Dutch authorities, and the (lack of) Dutch resistance against the deportation of Jewish citizens.

A remarkable aspect of these struggles was that Jews played little or no part in the reproduction of the memory of their persecution. Dutch Jews had little say in the recollection of their fate; the memory of the persecution was not silenced but rather publicly represented for mainly political motives. This was an essential component of the postwar political culture of the Netherlands, which as a result was loaded with ambiguous sentiments. National pride in the solidarity with Jews had to compete with feelings of guilt for having done too little; officially proclaimed egalitarianism stood next to suspicions about the moral standards of the establishment and of the majority of the population.

WEST GERMANY

One of the key moments in the West German encounter with the memory of the persecution was Chancellor Konrad Adenauer's speech before the Bundestag on September 27, 1951, when he asserted that many Germans had risked their lives to save the Jews, but that "in the name of the German people, however, unspeakable crimes were committed that require moral and material restitution."[40] Adenauer's statement contained many of the elements that make it so difficult to interpret the postwar *Vergangenheitspolitik*.[41] Those who argue that West German elites and the population at large were unable to face the past are confronted by authors stating that there was a sincere effort to cope with the crimes and losses of the exterminatory policies of Nazi Germany.[42] However, as in the Dutch case, I believe it is possible in this case as well to have your cake and eat it too. The memory of the persecution was in some ways concealed, yet in other ways placed at the center of public attention.

---

40 Quoted in Jeffrey Herf, *Divided Memory: The Nazi Past in the Two Germanys* (Cambridge, Mass., 1997), 282.
41 Norbert Frei, *Vergangenheitspolitik: Die Anfänge der Bundesrepublik und die NS-Vergangenheit* (Munich, 1996).
42 See, e.g., the debate between Ralph Giordano, *Die zweite Schuld oder Von der Last ein Deutscher zu sein* (Hamburg, 1987), and Manfred Kittel, *Die Legende von der "Zweiten Schuld": Vergangenheitsbewältigung in der Ära Adenauer* (Berlin, 1993).

A crucial factor in the normalization of the West German society was international control and pressure.[43] The Allied victory was military as well as ideological and constituted a complete delegitimization of Germany's political culture. Until 1949, the occupying forces directly controlled the way in which Germans were supposed to confront the crimes that were committed in their midst and to make the transition to a democratic society. The denazification of society and public administration was pursued most vigorously in the American zone of occupation, where it soon led to bureaucratic chaos. The political elites for a democratic Germany had to be recruited from anti-Nazi or at least previously neutral ranks. Yet denazification soon came to a complete standstill and was even reversed when it began to function as a mechanism for the political whitewashing of former Nazis.[44]

A second factor in the international control of West Germany's politics of the past was the re-education program. Besides courses and discussions in the POW camps, the Allies employed a "pedagogy of horror" by taking German citizens into the concentration camps and forcing them to help remove and bury the corpses. Germans also were forced to acknowledge the violence that was committed by viewing exhibits and the movie *Die Todesmühlen*, showing not only the machinery of death but also German citizens witnessing these events after the liberation of the camps, as if to exemplify the required moral and emotional reaction.[45]

The third factor in foreign influence concerned the perpetration of war crimes and crimes against humanity, culminating in the trials of Nuremberg, Lüneburg, and a number of places in the French zone. These trials soon met with hostility and suspicion because they were perceived as victor's justice. Some of this criticism was shared by the Allies, especially in the British zone. Moreover, the Western Allies sincerely expected that the German courts would proceed with the trials and would be able to convict the remaining war criminals. However, immediately after the founding of the Federal Republic, the number of convictions by German courts dropped dramatically, from 1,523 in 1949 to 191 in 1951 and to 21 in 1955.[46]

---

43 See Ulrich Brochhagen, *Nach Nürnberg: Vergangenheitsbewältigung und Westintegration in der Ära Adenauer* (Berlin, 1999).

44 Klaus-Dietmar Henke, "Die Trennung vom Nationalsozialismus. Selbstzerstörung, politische Säuberung, 'Entnazifizierung,' Strafverfolgung," in Henke and Woller, eds., *Politische Säuberung in Europa*, 41ff; Frei, *Vergangenheitspolitik*, 54–69.

45 Kittel, *Die Legende*, 47; Marie-Anne Matard-Bonucci, "La pédagogie de l'horreur," in Bonucci and Lynch, eds., *La libération des camps*, 61–73.

46 Brochhagen, *Nach Nürnberg*, 191–4; Henry Friedlander, "The Deportation of the German Jews: Postwar German Trials of Nazi Criminals," *Leo Baeck Institute Yearbook* 24 (1984): 201–26.

International pressure on the German population specifically lacked attention to the persecution of Jews, and it was sometimes actively suppressed. For instance, the administration in the French zone rejected special treatment of Jewish claims because it was feared that it would feed German antisemitism.[47] After the liberation of Bergen Belsen in the British zone, it was never made explicit that the majority of the surviving camp inmates were Jews, because the British Ministry of Information demanded special attention to the victimization of non-Jewish Germans in the camps.[48] Also, in most of the trials the persecution of Jews was not the central concern in the indictments against war criminals.

Notwithstanding the marginal concern for the fate of Jews, the Allied authorities closely monitored the German attitude toward Jews. Notably in Bavaria, Americans observed a new rise in antisemitism.[49] In the summer of 1949, the American High Commissioner declared the attitude toward Jews to be the touchstone for the democratic mentality of the German people. His speech invited a positive response from the new political elite, but it also caused a vehemently antisemitic reaction and an equally massive counterprotest of Jewish displaced persons (DPs) in the streets of Munich.[50]

This ambivalence is characteristic of the reaction of the German population and leadership in the immediate postwar era. The new Federal Republic under Adenauer's leadership expressed a sincere desire to break with the past. However, there were two ways to do this: Adenauer preferred the strategy of the *Schlussstrich*. He wanted to outlaw all signs of re-emergent Nazism and to suppress new Nazi organizations, but he extended suppression to a debate about the crimes committed in the Nazi era. Denazification efforts had to stop, and in his first declaration as chancellor he announced that Germany would plead for amnesty for convicted war criminals. In this speech he made clear that Jews were not his greatest concern. While he remained silent about Jewish persecution, he waxed eloquent about the German prisoners of war (POWs) and expellees.[51]

However, the "Adenauer era" was not completely dominated by the chancellor's outlook. As Jeffrey Herf stresses, an alternative to a radical

---

47 Rainer Hudemann, "Anfänge der Wiedergutmachung: Französische Besatzungszone 1945–1950," *Geschichte und Gesellschaft* 13 (1987): 202.

48 Tony Kushner, *The Holocaust and the Liberal Imagination: A Social and Cultural History* (Oxford, 1994), 216.

49 Quoted by Frank Stern, *Im Anfang war Auschwitz: Antisemitismus und Philosemitismus im deutschen Nachkrieg* (Gerlingen, 1991), 126.

50 Stern, *Im Anfang*, 264, 303–4; Frank Stern, "Im Anfang war Auschwitz: Besatzer, Deutsche und Juden in der Nachkriegszeit," in *Erinnern oder Verweigern: Das Schwierige Thema Nationalsozialismus*, special issue of *Dachauer Hefte* 6 (1994): 40–1.

51 See Stern, *Im Anfang*, 306–7; Herf, *Divided Memory*, 272; Frei, *Vergangenheitspolitik*, 27–8, 401.

Schlussstrich was proposed by the Free Democrat Theodor Heuss, the Social Democrat Kurt Schumacher, and more left-wing politicians. They argued that only confrontation with the past could lead to a sincere break with the Nazi era. At the first congress of the Social Democratic Party in 1946, Schumacher argued that "our first thoughts concern the dead," among them first of all "the victims of fascism among our own people," the victims of war, bombing, and hunger, but also "the Jews, who fell victim to the bestial racial madness of the Hitler dictatorship." In his inaugural address as federal president in 1949, Heuss voiced his "concern that many people in Germany ... want to forget too quickly. We must reserve a feeling for the traces of what led us to where we find ourselves today."[52] Heuss thereby set the tone for commemorative speeches in Germany. He also seems to have installed a commemorative division of labor, in which the federal president acted as the nation's conscience, stressing the nation's *Betroffenheit* by the persecution of the Jews and counterbalancing the chancellor's political expediency in dealing with the past.[53]

The ambivalent reaction in the political arena to the persecution of Jews extended outside high politics, into the public spheres of civil associations and popular moods. For most people, the persecution of Jews may not have been their first concern. Following Lutz Niethammer's research on life histories, for many people the 1950s were a return to a normality that never was normal. They compared their current situation after the *Währungsreform* only with the latter part of the war years, forgetting both the period of want and joblessness of the early 1930s, and the slow improvement of living conditions in the period up to 1943.[54] However, if only because of the international pressure and the political calculation of the postwar elites in response to this pressure, the memory of the persecution had to be confronted in some way.

It was clear that anti-Jewish attitudes and routines had not simply disappeared after the downfall of the Nazi regime. Norbert Frei discusses, for example, the affair concerning Wolfgang Hedler, a right-wing member of the Bundestag who, in a speech in November 1949, supposedly argued that Germany bore no guilt for starting the war, that the resistance had consisted of traitors, and that one could disagree about the question whether gassing the Jews had been the most appropriate method: "Perhaps there would have

---

52 Quoted in Herf, *Divided Memory*, 239, 249.
53 Ian Buruma, *Het loon van de schuld: Herinneringen aan de oorlog in Duitsland en Japan* (Amsterdam, 1994), 250–1.
54 Lutz Niethammer, "'Normalisierung' im Westen: Erinnerungsspuren in den 50er Jahren," in Dan Diner, ed., *Ist der Nationalsozialismus Geschichte? Zu Historisierung und Historikerstreit* (Frankfurt am Main, 1987), 153–84.

been other ways to get rid of them."[55] After Hedler was put on trial and acquitted, a debate arose on the need for a juridical protection of the democratic debate against extremist opinions. At the same time, extreme right-wing parties were able to win substantial electoral support and became more vociferous in their radical ideology. Efforts to ban national-socialist parties led to the abolition of the Sozialistische Reichspartei in 1952.[56] However, in daily life antisemitic opinions continued to be expressed, and perhaps even gained in strength as older anti-Jewish stereotypes were fed by new anxieties about blame or even revenge by the Jews against their former oppressors. Also more concealed forms of anti-Jewish opinions, often cloaked as anti-Americanism, remained prevalent.[57]

Another part of West German society wanted to discuss the persecution of Jews, confess its *Betroffenheit*, and repair the damage that had been done. In the immediate postwar years, the persecution became the subject of historiographical, philosophical, and literary reflection. Much of this work, such as that by Eugen Kogon, Karl Jaspers, or Heinrich Böll, presented itself as the voice of the other Germany, the one that had resisted Nazism, and stressed the moral conscience of the individual who refused to participate in a criminal system. More directly concerned with the persecution were the works of Paul Celan, whose *Todesfuge* (1952) soon became a standard element in many commemorative practices; and of course the diary of Anne Frank. The diary's first German edition in 1950 did not sell well; only after the story was produced as a play and a film, and after a pocket edition was released in 1955, did its sales explode. Other productions were more successful, such as the frequently staged play by Gotthold E. Lessing, *Nathan der Weise* (1779), exemplifying Jewish wisdom and counterbalancing the antisemitic stereotypes of the period before.[58]

Germans tried to find a new rapport with the Jews in their midst in other respects as well. The churches were very reluctant to think about their accommodating attitude toward Nazi Germany or to distance themselves from their religiously inspired anti-Judaism. The German Catholic Church

55 Frei, *Vergangenheitspolitik*, 309.   56 Kittel, *Die Legende*, 235ff.

57 Stern, *Im Anfang*, 100–10; Anna J. and Richard L. Merrit, *Public Opinion in Semi-Sovereign Germany HIGOC Survey, 1949–1955* (Urbana, Ill., 1980); Werner Bergmann and Rainer Erb, *Antisemitismus in der Bundesrepublik Deutschland: Ergebnisse der empirischen Forschung von 1946–1989* (Opladen, 1991), 231–73; Dan Diner, *Verkehrte Welten: Antiamerikanismus in Deutschland. Ein historischer Essay* (Frankfurt am Main, 1993).

58 Jean-Paul Bier, *Auschwitz et les nouvelles littératures allemandes* (Brussels, 1979); Jean-Paul Bier, "Paradigms and Dilemmas in the Literary Awareness of West Germany, with Regard to the Persecution and Murder of the Jews," in Asher Cohn, Joav Gelber, and Charlotte Wardi, eds., *Comprehending the Holocaust: Historical and Literary Research* (Frankfurt am Main, 1988), 279–301.

followed the opinions of the Vatican and reflected on the Nazi period after the Second Vatican Council. Whereas individual members of the Protestant churches did speak out about their anger and feelings of guilt, the "Remark on the Jewish Question" of the Protestant Evangelical Church of 1948 still held on to the traditional point of view, according to which "the curse on Israel is the incessant confirmation of the truth and reality of God's word and the firm warning of God to his flock." Yet, two years later the Evangelical Synod declared that it shared the guilt for the misery brought on the Jewish people. It called for a rejection of antisemitism and promoted fraternization with the Jews.[59]

American pressure also was decisive in this case. In 1949 the Council for Christians and Jews was founded with the help of an American representative of the International Council. A year later the Council organized a week of fraternization – again after an American example – which was the beginning of the institutionalization of the Christian-Jewish encounter. Many of the activists in these circles, such as the theologian Hans Joachim Schoeps and the philosopher Theodor Adorno, became important spokespersons for the memory of the persecution.

During the same period, a number of scientists and writers were aroused by new anti-Semitic scandals, along with the end of official denazification and the lack of a constructive attitude toward Jewish claims for recognition. Adopting the notion of collective shame, which Heuss had introduced as an alternative to the less favorable collective guilt, Erich Lüth, the editor of the journal for the Christian-Jewish encounter *Zusammenarbeit*, called for a campaign for "Peace with Israel." They received much support from Christian-Jewish councils, universities, and radio stations.[60]

These and other events created the atmosphere in which Adenauer finally acknowledged the involvement of many Germans in the persecution of the Jews of Europe. Even though he considered it necessary at the same time to court the right-wing members of his constituency by frequently referring to the *Vertriebenen* and German POWs, he opened the way for negotiations on *Wiedergutmachung* with the Israeli government and the Diaspora – the Conference on Jewish Material Claims Against Germany.

The *Wiedergutmachung* not only compensated some of the material losses Jews had suffered but also strengthened the representation of Jewish interests in West Germany. Contrary to the expectation that Jews would not want to live in Germany, soon after 1945 the Jewish community became relatively

---

59 Quoted in Stern, *Im Anfang*, 277–9; see also Grosser, *Le crime et la mémoire*, 113–15.
60 Stern, *Im Anfang*, 323.

numerous and well organized, represented by the Central Council of Jews in Germany (Zentralrat der Juden in Deutschland), founded in 1950. In the first months after the German defeat more than 200,000 Jews remained on German soil, mainly in the same camps as before, and often in little improved conditions. Moreover, their numbers were growing due to the influx of Eastern European Jews who had fled new waves of anti-Semitism. Aided by Zionist relief organizations, most left for Palestine, yet in 1950 it turned out that some 12,000 Jews had opted to stay. Moreover, some Jews returned from abroad, both from the Allied countries where they had found a safe haven and from Palestine. The social and cultural composition of the new community was remarkably different than before. In contrast to the pre-1933 Jews who had tried to be outstanding German citizens, the new community mainly consisted of Yiddish-speaking Jews with little urge to assimilate into German society. Another sign of the much greater distance was the significant number of Jews emigrating from Germany. Their number remained stable at around 26,000 people because there was an equal number of immigrants.[61]

In comparison to the Dutch Jews, German Jews were well organized and more combative. They protested against the re-emergence of Nazism and often found the American authorities on their side. The most important difference from the Dutch situation was the fact that Germans needed the Jews to prove that they were developing the required democratic mentality. The demand of the occupying forces that the new political establishment have an impeccable reputation led to a search for proof of good behavior. The most convincing *Persilschein* was the testimony of a Jew, and even better a testimony of help given to Jews. As it was stated by right-wing author Ernst von Salomon in his satirical novel on American denazification, *Fragebogen* (1951): "Jedem sein geretteter Jude" – "each his own rescued Jew."

A good relationship with the Jewish community was a valuable political asset on a collective level as well. Thus, the immediate reason for the campaign for peace with Israel had been the refusal of Israeli Prime Minister David Ben Gurion to follow the Allied authorities in ending the state of war with Germany in the spring of 1951. Tom Segev even argues that the formulation of Adenauer's speech of September 1951 was suggested by the Israeli Ministry of Foreign Affairs because only then would Ben Gurion be

---

61 Monika Richarz, "Juden in der Bundesrepublik Deutschland und in der Deutschen Demokratischen Republik seit 1945," in Micha Brumlik et al., eds., *Jüdisches Leben in Deutschland seit 1945* (Frankfurt am Main, 1986), 13–30; Bernard Wasserstein, *Vanishing Diaspora: The Jews in Europe Since 1945* (London, 1996), 44; Stern, *Im Anfang*, 91.

able to face the opposition in Israel against starting official negotiations with West Germany on monetary compensation.[62]

The way in which the German political elites and the population at large confronted the persecution of the Jews was therefore ambiguous. Adenauer's efforts to negotiate a *Wiedergutmachung* settlement with the Israeli government and the representatives of the Jews in the Diaspora was undoubtedly motivated by political expediency, or, as his biographer called it, "sound state craft in the face of the big influence of the Jews in the United States."[63] The commemoration of the persecution of the Jews was often half-hearted, ritualistic, and less sincere in its balancing act between consideration for the Jewish suffering and the courting of *Vertriebenen* and POWs. The relationship between Germans and Jews was – and still is – tense: a negative symbiosis, as Dan Diner has called it.[64]

Be that as it may, it is obvious that the model of trauma and recovery, silence and speech, does not apply. Not only was there a lot of talking about the persecution, even when it was not all sincere or truthful, but at least a number of people made an effort to keep the memory of the persecution alive.[65] As a result, the idea of *nie wieder Auschwitz* became a constitutive idea of the Federal Republic. The call "never to forget" was shared by the majority of the new political elite and at least a substantial part of the population. The most moderate liberals, like Heuss, and the most radical critical intellectuals, like Adorno, shared the idea that education about the persecution was the best way to arm the new democracy against the horrors of its past.[66] Normality in the West Germany of the 1950s meant a continuous struggle over the implications of the memory of the persecution.

---

62 Tom Segev, *The Seventh Million: The Israelis and the Holocaust* (New York, 1993), 203.
63 Quoted in Stern, *Im Anfang*, 331.
64 Dan Diner, "Negative Symbiose – Deutsche und Juden nach Auschwitz," in Brumlik et al., eds., *Jüdisches Leben in Deutschland*, 243–57; see also Eckhard Jesse, "Philosemitismus, Antisemitismus und Anti-Antisemitismus: Vergangenheitsbewältigung und Tabus," in Uwe Backes, Eckhard Jesse, and Rainer Zitelmann, eds., *Die Schatten der Vergangenheit: Impulse zur Historisierung des Nationalsozialismus* (Frankfurt am Main, 1990), 543–67; Frank Stern, "Antagonistic Memories: The Post-War Survival and Alienation of Jews and Germans," in Luisa Passerini, ed., *Memory and Totalitarianism: International Yearbook of Oral History and Life Stories I* (Oxford, 1992), 21–43; Wolfgang Benz, "Nachkriegsgesellschaft und Nationalsozialismus: Erinnerung, Amnesie, Abwehr," in *Erinnern oder Verweigern: Das Schwierige Thema Nationalsozialismus*, special issue of *Dachauer Hefte* 6 (1994): 12–24; Martin Geyer and Miriam Hansen, "German-Jewish Memory and National Conscience," in Geoffrey H. Hartman, ed., *Holocaust Remembrance: The Shapes of Memory* (Oxford, 1994), 175–90.
65 Herf, *Divided Memory*, 334; Grosser, *Le Crime et la Mémoire*, 121–4.
66 Alf Lüdtke, "Coming to Terms with the Past: Illusions of Remembering, Ways of Forgetting Nazism in Germany," *Journal of Modern History* 65 (1993): 552.

FRANCE

The French memory of the persecution of the Jews was completely dominated and even clouded by the problematic legacy of Vichy. This becomes
immediately clear when one is looking for a key moment of the French
confrontation with the persecution. The first that imposes itself is Charles
de Gaulle's speech of August 1944, when he claimed that the liberation
should be considered a moment of national recovery. The return of the
deportees in the spring of 1945 might have been an even more impressive
event. In contrast to the Netherlands, they received a warm welcome, and
their return was the occasion for enthusiastic celebration.[67] In the summer
of 1945, a third key moment occurred with the trial of Marshal Philippe
Pétain, whose death sentence was soon commuted to life imprisonment.
Characteristic of all three moments is that an explicit reference to the fate
of the Jews was mostly lacking. The persecution of the Jews was a relatively
minor point in comparison to the crisis of the French nation that the Vichy
regime had caused.

From a quantitative perspective, the persecution of the Jews in France was
less severe than in Germany or the Netherlands. The Jewish community in
France before 1940 numbered 300,000 people; after 1933 there was a massive
influx of Jewish refugees. Around 75,000 Jews were deported, of whom only
2,500 survived, together with the remaining 75 percent that had been able
to escape deportation. Yet the deportation of Jews was qualitatively different
from that in the Netherlands, since the French regime of Vichy had itself
created the legal framework for the exclusion of Jews. Actually, this process
had already started before 1940, with the internment of the predominantly
Jewish refugees from Germany.[68]

Nevertheless, the anti-Jewish policy of the Vichy government was only
one aspect of the crisis of the French nation in the war period. The French
had suffered from shortages and material losses on a much larger scale than
during World War I.[69] More important, the German occupation had left
deep rifts in French society, dividing not only Vichyistes from the rest of
France: Vichy also re-awakened the conflicts of the Dreyfus Affair between
Catholics and secularists, between left and right, and it created new divisions between the internal *Résistants* and De Gaulle's national liberation

---

67 Lagrou, "Victims of Genocide," 187; Matard-Bonucci and Lynch, eds., *La libération des camps*.
68 Grynberg, "Les camps français, des non-lieux de mémoire," in Nicolaïdis, ed., *Oublier nos crimes*,
   52–69; Renée Poznanski, *Les Juifs en France pendant la Seconde Guerre mondiale* (Paris, 1997), 43–6.
69 François Bédarida, "World War II and Social Change in France," in Arthur Marwick, ed., *Total War
   and Social Change* (New York, 1988), 82.

army, between Gaullistes and Communists.[70] De Gaulle's invocation in August 1944 of "the whole of France, France defending itself, the only France, the true France, the eternal France" was an attempt not only to claim victory for himself but also to overcome the deep divisions that Vichy had created.

One element of this national reconstruction was the purge of Nazi collaborators. Some 126,000 people were indicted, of whom some 40,000 were sentenced to prison, more than 50,000 lost their citizenship rights, and 12,000 civil servants were fired. There were 7,037 death sentences handed down, 791 of which were carried out. In these trials, racism was a crime separate from collaboration with the enemy. Pétain was accused, among other things, of having issued "those horrible racial laws" and "outlawing complete categories of French citizens." Antisemitism was also grounds to indict ideological leaders of the Vichy regime and a central concern in the trials against Pierre Laval, René Bousquet, and lower-ranking police officers involved in the management of the transit camp at Drancy. However, not only did many of these trials end in a lenient sentence or acquittal; some of the accused also claimed that their antisemitism was of genuine French origin and therefore could not be considered proof of an unpatriotic attitude. Moreover, the majority of these sentences were applied in the first months of the purge. Like in the Netherlands, later trials often ended with more lenient sentences. Finally, amnesty was applied as rigorously as in the Netherlands: Within five years 90 percent of those convicted were released, and after 1958 only nineteen people remained imprisoned until the final releases in 1964.[71]

The Vichy period, and with it the persecution of the Jews, was marginalized in other respects as well. The scarce historiography of that time presented the Vichy period as an aberration of French history, as the emergence of an anti-France. Raymond Aron's highly influential history of Vichy France considered its anti-Jewish legislation as an extension of the German policies for which primarily Laval had been responsible. Some even followed the Pétainist defense that Vichy had kept the German policies in check.[72] The memory of the Vichy was also marginalized as a result of the increased weight given to the commemoration of World War I. The high esteem

---

70 Rousso, *Le syndrome de Vichy,* 313ff.

71 Henry Rousso, "L'Épuration: Die politische Säuberung in Frankreich," in Henke and Woller, eds., *Politische Säuberung in Europa,* 192–240; Henry Rousso, "Une justice impossible: L'épuration et la politique antijuive de Vichy," *Annales* 3 (1993): 745–70.

72 Renée Poznanski, "Vichy et les Juifs: Des marges de l'histoire au coeur de son écriture," in Jean-Pierre Azéma and François Bédarida, eds., *Le Regime de Vichy et les Français* (Paris, 1992), 59–60.

of the veterans of this war had always been considerable, but after 1945 it expanded even further as an unintended consequence of the contested nature of the history of World War II. This process was furthered by de Gaulle's decision of April 1959 to abolish the celebration of the German capitulation on May 8 as a national holiday.[73] The second most important commemoration after Bastille Day thus remained that of the end of World War I, on November 11. In this way, the marginalization of Vichy also created a niche for former Vichyistes to honor the hero of the Great War, Pétain.

This commemorative mould had been essentially a Gaullist invention for the re-integration of the supporters of Vichy in the French nation, and, subsequently, for the reconstruction of the right wing of French politics under de Gaulle's leadership. It stressed the strength of an eternal France and equated *la Résistance* against the Germans not with any group in particular but with the French people in general. Like in the Netherlands, this nationalization of the resistance estranged many individual resistance fighters and was rejected most notably by the Communists,[74] who were among the major contestants in the political arena after 1945. Following their failure to found a centrist "party of the resistance," the Communists remained the only party that directly appealed to the resistance by calling themselves the "party of the 75,000 executed militants."

Communists also dominated the first national federation of former "patriot" deportees and resistance fighters. In Buchenwald, some French deportees objected to the Communist domination and prepared the foundation of a competing federation limited to the members of *la Résistance*.[75] Both federations were able to exact pensions for their own constituency. Paradoxically, the latter federation, appealing to the nationalized resistance, was the more restrictive one because it included only actual resistance fighters. The Communist-led Fédération Nationale des Déportés et Internés Résistants et Patriotes aimed at including all who had been deported, including the Jews. Contrary to the Netherlands, where Jews were not entitled to the same pensions as former resistance fighters, the French Jews were officially recognized as part of the broad category of *la Déportation*.

According to Annette Wieviorka, this was at least partly an attempt by the Communists to confiscate the dramatic reputation of deportation to Auschwitz for political goals.[76] It subsumed the specific fate of the Jews into

---

73 Rousso, *Le syndrome de Vichy*, 85. 74 Lagrou, *Victims of genocide*, 195–6.
75 Annette Wieviorka, *Déportation et genocide: Entre mémoire et l'oubli* (Paris, 1992), 124–5.
76 Wieviorka, *Déportation et génocide*, 136–8; see also Jean-Michael Chaumont, *La concurrence des victims: Génocide, identité, reconnaissance* (Paris, 1997).

a general complaint against the barbarism of German fascism. The clearest example of this perspective was developed in Alain Resnais's documentary movie *Nuit et Brouillard* (1956), which introduced a mass audience to the images of the death camps, which since then have become icons of modern barbarism. The most remarkable aspect of the film, however, was that it mentioned only in passing that Jews were the main victims in these camps.

The persecution of Jews thus was to a considerable extent a nonissue in France of the 1950s. Jews themselves did very little to protest this situation. Many endorsed their subordinate position in the group of deportees because they defined themselves as Communists first. For Annie Kriegel this was a matter of substitution after the period of Vichy: "Being deprived of our Frenchness, that consisted of universality, we regained this universalist position quite naturally by becoming Communist."[77] Even when the Communist Party itself became antisemitic, Communist Jews like Kriegel continued to put their Communist identity first.

Others who objected to the Communist confiscation of the memory of the persecution still refused to identify themselves as Jews. David Rousset, author of the successful *L'Univers Concentrationnaire* (1946), urged other deportees to join his protest against the Stalinist camps and caused many Jewish deportees to leave the Communist *Fédération*. However, Rousset did not object to the neglect of Jewish victimization but, on the contrary, wanted to generalize the memory of the persecution even more.[78]

The refusal to identify with a Jewish cause was deeply ingrained in the worldview of the French "citizen of Israelite origin." Like the prewar Jewish community in Germany, French Jews were proud to be outstanding members of the French Republic.[79] Unlike German Jewry, the French Jews persisted in this attitude after 1945 and were strengthened in this conviction by the relentless attempts to outlaw Vichy as an "anti-France." Raymond Aron's history of Vichy thus expressed not only a hegemonic historical image of postwar France but also the ideals of the mainstream of French Jewry.[80]

---

77 Quoted in Maurice Szafran, *Les Juifs dans la politique française: De 1945 à nos jours* (Paris, 1990), 103.
78 Wieviorka, *Déportation et génocide*, 135; Annette Wieviorka, "Jewish Identity in the First Accounts by Extermination Camps Survivors from France," *Yale French Studies* 85 (1994): 145.
79 Pierre Birnbaum, *Les fous de la République: Histoire politique des Juifs d'État de Gambetta à Vichy* (Paris, 1992); Pierre Birnbaum, "Between Social and Political Emancipation: Remarks on the History of Jews in France," in Pierre Birnbaum and Ira Katznelson, eds., *Paths of Emancipation: Jews, States, and Citizenship* (Princeton, N.J., 1994), 94–127.
80 Robert I. Cohen, "The Fate of the French Jewry in World War II in Historical Writing (1944–1983)," in Yisrael Gutman and Gideon Greif, eds., *The Historiography of the Holocaust Period: Proceeding of the Fifth Yad Vashem International Historical Conference* (Jerusalem, 1988), 83.

The ultimate Frenchness of the French Jews frustrated their attempts to reclaim their rights after 1945. Just like the Dutch Jews, many French Jews had lost their goods and belongings. They also lacked the organizational support to successfully fight for their rights. Only in the case of Jewish orphans did the rabbis participate in protests against attempts to baptize Jewish children because this was considered to be a religious matter.[81] In most other cases, individual Jews were left to their own devices. Moreover, Jews were confronted with antisemitism, for instance by the Fédération des locataires de bonne foi (Federation of Renters of Good Faith), who resisted the claims of Jews on their property.[82] Later on, in the mid-1950s, anti-Jewish sentiments were mobilized by the Poujadist movement, which attacked Jewish Prime Minister Pierre Mendès-France and warned of "the too large influence of the Jews in France."[83]

The rather weak position of the French Jews was all the more problematic because they were confronted with the arrival of some 40,000 Jewish refugees from Eastern Europe. Like in Germany, these Jews were less open to assimilation and more combative. Many wrote down their memories of the persecution, although most of them were in Yiddish and thus remained inaccessible to a wider audience. Some publications were in French, such as the early historiography of the persecution, published by the Centre de recherche et de documentation juive contemporain (CDJC). Although La Brévaire de la Haine (1951), by Léon Poliakov, one of CDJC's founders, received a wider audience, most other publications were little noticed, while the CDJC itself remained marginal to the academic historical profession.[84] The CDJC also took the initiative to create a monument to commemorate the persecution of the Jews, which was unveiled in 1956, but very few people participated in meetings to commemorate the persecution.[85] The Vélodrome d'Hiver, where Parisian Jews were interned before their deportation, was abandoned and later used as a place for political rallies, including the meeting in 1956 when Pierre Poujade made his anti-Semitic attack.[86]

The persecution of the Jews thus remained a nonissue in the public sphere. Political elites were trying to overcome the legacy of Vichy and

---

81 Szafran, Les Juifs, 65–74.
82 David Weinberg, "France," in David S. Wyman, ed., The World Reacts to the Holocaust (Baltimore, 1996), 16.
83 Szafran, Les Juifs, 77.
84 Wieviorka, Déportation et génocide, 415–23; Annette Wieviorka, "Déportation et genocide: Le cas français. Essai d'historiographie," in Matard-Bonucci and Lynch, eds., La libération des camps, 231–7.
85 Weinberg, France, 21.   86 Szafran, Les Juifs, 77.

considered the persecution an issue of secondary importance. The Jews did not protest this. They received some recognition for their suffering as members of the deportation, but more important, they considered claiming a special position as an unwanted break with their republican convictions. The most remarkable example of this situation occurred in 1959, when *Les derniers des justes* by André Schwarz-Bart received France's highest literary award, the *Prix Goncourt*. Although the French could read for the first time how French police assisted in the deportation of French Jews, the political message of the book remained unnoticed. While non-Jews read it only as a work of literature, French Jews rejected the book because it identified Jewishness not with the respectable republican Israelite but with the Eastern European tradition of religious mysticism.[87] This attitude would change at the end of the 1960s, when Jews finally discovered *le droit à la différence* and began to reconsider their Jewish identity and their place in French society.

PATHS OF NORMALIZATION

To conclude, I have three observations: The first is the obvious point that the development and position of the public memory of the persecution of Jews depended very much on the political and cultural context. In the Netherlands and West Germany, making reference to the persecution served as a means of political legitimation and opposition, but in different ways. In the Netherlands, the memory of the persecution served to underline the brutality of the Nazi regime and the righteousness of the Dutch people and its leaders, or in the Communist version, of the small groups that actually resisted the German forces. In West Germany, addressing the persecution of Jews was a means to respond to international pressure and a way to break with the Nazi past. Much more than in the Netherlands the persecution of Jews in Germany was a constitutive myth, not in the sense that it was untrue but that it was sacred. In France, however, referring to the persecution played no role whatsoever in legitimating the postwar regime. The most dangerous ghost from the French past was not German antisemitism, but Vichy; its greatest vice not the persecution of the Jews but undermining the integrity of the nation.

My second observation is that the notion of silence needs to be qualified. To begin with, one must distinguish between the silence of officials and

---

87 Ronnie Scharfman, "Exiled from the Shoah: André and Simone Schwarz-Bart's *Un plat de proc aux bananes vertes*," in Lawrence D. Kritzman, ed., *Auschwitz and After: Race, Culture, and "the Jewish Question" in France* (New York, 1995), 250–63; Szafran, *Les Juifs*, 79.

the lack of voice of Jewish survivors. The fact that Jews were unable to speak, or that they received no attention for what they had to say, does not automatically imply that the memory of the persecution was altogether silenced. This happened only in France, where Jews showed little interest in telling the story of their persecution, and those who did found no niche in the public sphere, no spokespersons to tell their stories on their behalf. The situation was different in West Germany, where the story Jews had to tell was often heard because Jews were well organized as a separate group, because many officials cared to listen, and because international intervention had placed a high symbolic value on the memory of the persecution and the goodwill of the Jewish community. In the Netherlands, we find a third outcome: Jews encountered much difficulty in making themselves heard, yet their fate was often represented by contesting elites and members of the former resistance. Even though Jews were silenced, their spokespersons were not.

This leads to my last observation: The psychological sequence of trauma, repression, and recovery is too crude to address the complexity of the ways in which societies deal with mass violence. What matters is not the simple distinction between silence and voice but the multifarious ways in which some speak and others are silenced, and the resulting uneasy balance between concealment and disclosure of the horrors of the past. Some kind of normalization of the memory of the persecution developed in all three countries. In the Netherlands, the persecution was remembered as a German aberration that unfortunately had infected some members of Dutch society. In West Germany, it formed a permanent source of public distress but also presented an opportunity for displaying moral and political sensitivity. In France, it was indeed repressed, both by Jews who wanted to enforce a return to a republican normality and by non-Jews who wanted to return to the true France.

Considering the diverse paths of normalization, why do many people now suppose there is only one right way for a society to respond to its own history? Why has the psychology of traumatic memory become so popular? To answer these questions, we must look, not at the 1940s and 1950s but at the 1960s. Just as the forms of memory were socially and culturally determined by the normalization in the 1950s, these forms changed as a result of the cultural transformation of the 1960s. In short: Personal growth, a change of mentality, and the flourishing of one's inner life became central concerns; psychic distress no longer was conceived as a sign of individual abnormality but of social and political failure; and silence instead of free debate was considered a pathological means of solving personal and social problems. From this perspective, the development of memory of persecution was reconstructed as a history of repression and recovery. However, good reasons for not adopting the perspective of the 1960s is an altogether different story.[88]

---

88 See Kirby Farrell, *Post-Traumatic Culture: Injury and Interpretation in the Nineties* (Baltimore, 1998), 21–33; Pamela Ballinger, "The Culture of Survivors: Post-traumatic Stress Disorder and Traumatic Memory," *History and Memory* 10, no. 1 (1998): 99–132; De Haan, "Construction of a National Trauma."

4

Trauma, Memory, and Motherhood

Germans and Jewish Displaced Persons in Post-Nazi Germany, 1945–1949

ATINA GROSSMANN

DIFFERENT VOICES ON *ARMES DEUTSCHLAND*

May 8: Germany has capitulated. It held out six years against a world of enemies, it will recover again (*wieder hochkommen*). . . . Dear God – Berlin has had to endure so much, let this be over with.

May 18: And now witchhunts against the Nazis are being orchestrated. In the *Täglichen Rundschau* big reports about the death camp in Auschwitz. Even if only a small part is true, and I fear it is all true, then the rage of the entire world against the Nazis is understandable. Poor Germany (*armes Deutschland*)!

In May 1945, a middle-aged woman physician with excellent antifascist credentials, veteran of the Weimar campaigns for birth control and abortion reform, faced the defeat of Nazi Germany and the first press reports about Auschwitz and the death camps. She was not shocked or disbelieving; she could imagine and would not try to deny the horrors of which the Nazis were capable. Her response: to sigh for "poor Germany" (*armes Deutschland*) – an apparent victim – and look forward to the day when Germany – and especially her beloved metropolis Berlin – would revive (*wieder hochkommen*).[1]

Five years later, in a 1950 report for the American Jewish journal *Commentary* on "The Aftermath of Nazi Rule," Hannah Arendt diagnosed in Germans an "absence of mourning for the dead, or in the apathy with which they [Germans] react, or rather fail to react, to the fate of the refugees in their midst . . . a deep-rooted, stubborn, and at times vicious refusal to face and come to terms with what really happened." Now a visitor from the United States, the land of the victors, Arendt lamented the pervasive

---

An earlier version of this essay appeared in *Archiv für Sozialgeschichte* 38 (Oct. 1998): 230–54.

1 Anne-Marie Durand-Wever, "Als die Russen kamen: Tagebuch einer Berliner Ärztin," unpublished diary, with kind permission of Madeleine Durand-Noll, 36, 51.

self-pity that allowed no reaction to her insistent revelation that she was a German Jew and that continually invoked the image of *armes Deutschland* as the miserable and sacrificial victim – *Opfer* in its double sense – of history.[2]

As Arendt pointed out with her customary acerbity, most Germans after 1945 understood themselves as victims and not as victimizers. The persecution and extermination of Jews, while initially widely and graphically documented in the German (albeit occupier-licensed) press, often in reportages on early trials of Nazis, seems nonetheless absent, or at best obscured and distorted, in immediate postwar public and private discourse.[3] This putative lack of memory or "amnesia" has become a truism for the "silent fifties" in West Germany, the years of nation-building and economic miracle, supposedly broken only by the sea change of the 1960s.[4] In the early occupation period from 1945 to 1946 – often described as the "zero hour" and the "hour of the women" – processions past naked emaciated corpses in liberated camps, denazification procedures, press reports and film images of "death mills," and the Nuremberg trials assured that the immediate past of Nazi crimes remained very much in the present. But despite the lack of "silence," indeed the remarkable amount of discussion about precisely the issues of memory, commemoration, guilt, and complicity that continue to agitate historical and public debate in (and about) Germany, for most Germans the more powerful impressions – the stuff of which memories were made – derived from other more direct experiences of war and defeat.

In the midst of a ruined physical and political landscape, and in the absence of a legitimate national past or clear national boundaries, or for that matter, legitimized rulers or markets, female experiences such as rape,

2 Hannah Arendt, "The Aftermath of Nazi Rule: Report from Germany," *Commentary* 10 (Oct. 1950): 342–3. Here Arendt obviously anticipates Alexander and Margarete Mitscherlich's famous discussion of the German "inability to mourn" in *Die Unfähigkeit zu Trauern* (Munich, 1967).

3 See, e.g., the extensive coverage in the daily press during the fall and winter of 1945–6 of the Belsen trial in Lüneberg in the British zone, the Dachau trial in the American zone, the Hademar Clinic trial in Nuremberg (on charges of "euthanasia"), and the Nuremberg trials beginning in November 1945. For Berlin and a representative sampling of reportage in both the Soviet and the American sectors, see especially *Tägliche Rundschau, Berliner Zeitung*, and *Der Tagesspiegel*. For a highly problematic analysis of divergent occupier and German interpretations of the war and its aftermath, see Dagmar Barnouw, *Germany 1945: Views of War and Violence* (Bloomington, Ind., 1996).

4 See Wolfgang Benz, "Postwar Society and National Socialism: Remembrance, Amnesia, Rejection," *Tel Aviver Jahrbuch für deutsche Geschichte* 19 (1990): 1–12. The impression of "amnesia" in the 1950s has now been forcefully challenged by a host of scholars. See among many others Michael Geyer and Miriam Hansen, "German-Jewish Memory and National Consciousness," in Geoffrey H. Hartman, ed., *Holocaust Remembrance: The Shapes of Memory* (Cambridge, Mass., 1994), 175–90; Alf Lüdtke, "'Coming to Terms with the Past': Illusions of Remembering, Ways of Forgetting Nazism in West Germany," *Journal of Modern History* 65 (Sept. 1993): 542–72; and Jeffrey Herf, *Divided Memory: The Nazi Past in the Two Germanys* (Cambridge, Mass., 1997).

abortion, childbirth, caring for malnourished and sick children, and grief over the dying and dead, as well as relations with occupiers and returning German soldiers and prisoners of war, became especially powerful markers of German victimization and defeat. They also signaled the urgent need for healthy reconstruction.

Clearly, rapidly constructed and tenaciously remembered narratives of victimization worked not only to block confrontation with recent Nazi crimes but most importantly (and efficiently) to manage the chaos of the immediate postwar years and eventually to authorize reconstruction of German nationhood and national identity. (Ernst Renan in his famous 1882 disquisition "What Is a Nation" had already noted that "the essence of a nation is that all individuals have many things in common, and also that they have forgotten many things.")[5] But during the early "pre- or non-national," or at least non-state, years of military occupation from 1945 to 1949, these narratives did not stand alone.[6] They competed with and were contested by those posed by other protagonists who shared territory with defeated Germans, such as the Soviet, American, and British victors or Jewish survivors gathered in displaced persons (DP) camps. Given the lack of a sovereign German state and the lack of clarity about what it might mean to identify as German, it seems especially important to analyze stories of victimization from a vantage point that is not exclusively "German." Moreover, because our understanding of post-Nazi Germany has finally become more gendered,[7] it becomes all the more necessary to consider the notion of "the hour of the women" and the particular association of postwar victimization with female experience from multiple non-German as well as German perspectives. If the history of postwar Germany is, as we have increasingly acknowledged, not only a story of men, it is also not only a German story.

I aim then, in this chapter, to reflect on two separate but inextricably interwoven and highly gendered stories about the meanings of sexuality, motherhood, and childbirth in the wake of National Socialism, war, and genocide. These are stories about the reconstruction of identity and community, maybe even desire, in the wake of violence and trauma in which – to

5 Ernst Renan, "What Is a Nation," in Geoff Eley and Ronald Grigor Suny, eds., *Becoming National: A Reader* (New York, 1996), 45.
6 For a useful discussion of the ambiguities and vagueness of the term *nation*, see Clifford Geertz, *Die Welt in Stücken: Kultur und Politik am Ende des 20. Jahrhunderts* (Vienna, 1996), 37–67.
7 Two recent outstanding examples, from American historians, are Elizabeth Heineman, "The Hour of the Woman: Memories of Germany's 'Crisis Years' and West German National Identity," *American Historical Review* 101, no. 2 (Apr. 1996): 354–95, and Robert G. Moeller, "War Stories: The Search for a Usable Past in the Federal Republic of Germany," *American Historical Review* 101, no. 4 (Oct. 1996): 1008–48. See also "Stunde Null: Kontinuitäten und Brüche," *Ariadne: Almanach des Archivs der deutschen Frauenbewegung* 27 (May 1995).

put it crudely or polemically – Germans appear as victims and Jews as survivors (and Allies as victors). But they are also stories in which the binaries
of those categories emerge as highly complicated and mixed up. In order to
illustrate these points, I focus on two "multinational" sites where post-Nazi
occupied Germany presents itself as a highly diverse and contradictory terrain of "border crossers" (*Grenzgänger*): the DP camps for Jewish survivors
in the American and British zones of occupation, and Berlin, the former
Reich capital, occupied by the four Allied victors.

BORDER CROSSERS (*GRENZGÄNGER*) IN BERLIN, 1945–1948

My initial focus is on Berlin, certainly not typical but exemplary for my
purposes, and located usefully at the intersection of East and West. Conquered by the Soviets in April–May 1945, Berlin became a polyglot city of
Grenzgänger (border crossers) in four sectors after July 1945; a kind of laboratory of international understanding, as U.S. Military Government officials
initially preferred to put it, in which the precarious relations among the victorious powers and the management of the incoming tide of refugees commanded virtually as much attention as the occupied Berliners themselves.[8]
The "greatest collection of rubble in the world" (*grösste[r] Trümmerhaufen
der Welt*), as its inhabitants sarcastically dubbed it,[9] was a city of women,
refugees, and foreigners. Of a population of about three million (2,600,000
in May), over 60 percent was female in 1945–6. Berlin was filled with returning soldiers and prisoners of war, liberated slave laborers from many
different countries, German expellees and refugees from the East, repatriated political exiles (especially Communists returning to work with the
Soviet Military Administration, SMAD), Jews emerging from hiding, forced
labor, or concentration camps, and Allied troops (including a highly visible
handful of former German Jews).[10]

By July 1945, huge numbers of displaced persons of multiple nationalities
(some estimates are as high as half a million) were streaming into some
fifty transit camps in Berlin. Some fifteen thousand mostly ethnic German
refugees from Soviet- and Polish-occupied territories in the East poured into
the city daily, at the same time that Allied officials struggled to repatriate

8 American Military Government officer John Maginnis referred in February 1947 to "a record
   of successful international adjustments and sympathetic understanding." Major General John J.
   Maginnis, *Military Government Journal. Normandy to Berlin*, ed. Robert A. Hart (Amherst, Mass., 1971),
   345.
9 *Berlin: Kampf um Freiheit und Selbstverwaltung 1945–1946* (Berlin, 1961), 10.
10 See, e.g., Hans Speier, *From the Ashes of Disgrace: A Journal from Germany 1945–1955* (Amherst,
   Mass., 1981).

freed foreign laborers, prisoners of war, and concentration camp inmates.[11] It is worth remembering that by 1945 the presence of foreigners in Berlin was nothing new; after all, 7.5 million non-Germans had been mobilized and coerced into the Nazi war economy before May 1945.[12]

There were also some 6,000–7,000 Jews (or "partial" Jews) in Berlin (a high proportion of the 15,000 who survived within the entire Reich, but only a fraction of the 160,000 who had been registered in Berlin in 1932).[13] Their ranks were soon swelled by the "illegal infiltration" of Polish Jewish refugees fleeing renewed persecution. Starting in November 1945, the flight of East European Jewish survivors reached a high point after the pogrom in Kielce, Poland, on July 4, 1946, in which a charge of ritual murder led to the massacre of at least forty Jews who had tried to return to their hometown. About 250 arrived daily in the U.S. sector via the "open secret" of the underground Zionist *Bricha* network, seeking routes out of Europe and especially to Palestine.[14] Indeed, the apparent presence of so many Jews, the formerly hidden and the newly arrived, so soon after the end of

11 See Maginnis, *Military Government Journal*, 278–9. See also Landesarchiv Berlin (LAB) OMGUS 4/24–1/4.

12 By the end of the war, foreigners composed almost a quarter of the labor force in Germany. Mark Roseman, "World War II and Social Change in Germany," in Arthur Marwick, ed., *Total War and Social Change* (London, 1988), 63, 71. For a vivid picture of the immediate postwar period in Berlin, see the many microfilms of the Zeitgeschichtliche Sammlung (LAZ) of the Landesarchiv Berlin.

13 These figures, taken from Frank Stern, "Antagonistic Memories: The Post-War Survival and Alienation of Jews and Germans," in Luisa Passerini, ed., *Memory and Totalitarianism,* vol. 1: *International Yearbook of Oral History and Life Stories* (New York, 1992), 23, are necessarily imprecise. To the total of ca. 15,000 Jews (of a pre-1933 Jewish population of about half a million) who survived within the Reich must be added perhaps 50,000 Jewish forced laborers who were liberated on German territory at the end of the war. Andreas Nachama, "Nach der Befreiung: Jüdisches Leben in Berlin 1945–1953," in Reinhard Rürup, ed., *Jüdische Geschichte in Berlin: Essays und Studien* (Berlin, 1995), 268–9, quotes other reports estimating that there were about 7,000 Jews in Berlin. Fifteen hundred had survived the camps, 1,250 had been "U-boats" in hiding, and ca. 4,250 had been spared deportation because they lived in mixed marriages; of these, 2,250 were so-called star-wearers while the rest were privileged due to their Christian-identified children. Stern's corresponding figures are 1,155 camp survivors, 1,050 "illegals," and 2,000 mixed marriage partners, and another 1,600 exempted from wearing the star. Nachama also counts the pre-Nazi Jewish population of Berlin as about 200,000, which presumably includes those not officially registered as Jews.

14 See Nachama, "Nach der Brefreiung," 272, and Angelika Königseder, "Durchgangsstation Berlin: Jüdische DPs 1945–1948," *Überlebt und unterwegs: Jüdische Displaced Persons in Nachkriegsdeutschland, Fritz Bauer Institut Jahrbuch 1997* (Frankfurt am Main, 1997), 189–206. See also Maginnis, *Military Government Journal*, 323–9, for a detailed (and candid) discussion of the Polish Jewish refugee crisis and the considerable problems it posed for the Allied *Kommandatura* and especially the American occupiers. On Kielce, see Abraham J. Peck, "Jewish Survivors of the Holocaust in Germany: Revolutionary Vanguard or Remnants of a Destroyed People?" *Tel Aviver Jahrbuch für deutsche Geschichte* 19 (1990): 35. On the *Bricha* network which transported Jews into the American zone of Germany and Italy for eventual *Aliyah* to Palestine, see esp. Yehudah Bauer, *Flight and Rescue: Bricha* (New York, 1970); also I. F. Stone, *Underground to Palestine and Reflections Thirty Years Later* (New York, 1978), and Idith Zertal, *From Catastrophe to Power: Holocaust Survivors and the Emergence of Israel* (Berkeley, Calif., 1998).

the regime that had promised to make Germany *judenrein*, so unnerved the journalist Margaret Boveri that on May 9, one day after the unconditional surrender, she commented in a surprised and somewhat irritated tone on her encounter with a young "Rabbi" bicycling through the ruins:

So it is no wonder that important positions are crawling (*wimmelt*) with Jews, they have simply climbed out of obscurity. Reinforcements however are also supposedly coming from East Europe, especially from Poland – those who are smuggling themselves in with the refugee treks.[15]

In the next months and years U.S.- and British-occupied Germany would become a temporary home for some quarter of a million Jewish survivors, leading to many more such unexpected and difficult encounters. Astonishingly, between May and September the victors had managed to repatriate about six of the seven million displaced persons they had found in the occupied areas; a significant number of those who remained uprooted were Jewish survivors.[16] It seemed at times that as difficult as it was to comprehend that European Jewry had been subjected to systematic extermination, that genocide had indeed taken place, it was almost more difficult to grasp that there were in fact survivors – several hundred thousand – who required recognition and care. As numerous contemporary observers had already noted, "it belonged to the ironies of history that Germany, of all places, became under the occupation of the Allied powers a sheltering haven for several hundred thousand Jews."[17]

During this liminal interregnum of occupation and military government from 1945 to 1949, and particularly during the turbulent first two years, defeated Germans, together with hundreds of thousands of their former enemies and victims, became literal border crossers on the surreal stage of a broken country. This was especially evident in carved-up and bombed-out Berlin. Ruth Andreas-Friedrich titled her diary of war's end "Schauplatz Berlin," and Curt Riess, a Berlin Jew who had returned as an American journalist, depicted his former hometown as "hardly like a city anymore, more like a stage on which the backdrops are just standing around."[18] The U.S.

---

15 Margaret Boveri, *Tage des Überlebens: Berlin 1945* (1968; Munich, 1985), 128. Remarkably, Boveri opted to leave this section in her revised diary when she published it in 1968.

16 Zorach Wahrhaftig, *Uprooted: Jewish Refugees and Displaced Persons After Liberation, From War to Peace no. 5* (New York, 1946). Altogether, Allied armies had to cope with over seven million DPs in occupied territories, plus some twelve million ethnic German expellees. See also Leonard Dinnerstein, *America and the Survivors of the Holocaust* (New York, 1982).

17 Michael Brenner, "East European and German Jews in Postwar Germany 1945–50," in Y. Michal Bodemann, ed., *Jews, Germans, Memory: Reconstructions of Jewish Life in Germany* (Ann Arbor, Mich., 1996), 50.

18 Ruth Andreas-Friedrich, *Schauplatz Berlin. Tagebuchaufzeichnungen 1945 bis 1948* (Frankfurt am Main, 1984); Curt Riess, *Berlin-Berlin 1945–1953* (Berlin, 1953), 174. The notion of Berlin in ruins

diplomat Robert Murphy recorded his impressions when the Americans moved into the city in July 1945: "Two months after their surrender, Berliners still were moving about in a dazed condition. They had endured not only thousand-plane raids for years, but also weeks of Russian close-range artillery fire. In addition to three million Germans in Berlin, thousands of displaced persons were roaming around the shattered city."[19] After accusing his Soviet allies of having created in Berlin "another Nanking, with Russians instead of Japanese doing the raping, murdering, and looting," Colonel Frank Howley, the American commander, remembered in 1950:

Berlin in late July was still a shambles from the effects of Allied bombing, especially incendiary raids, and of Russian street fighting, but the Russians already had put large squads of German women to work clearing the rubble in various parts of the city. As the women wearily passed the fallen bricks from hand to hand, in a long human chain, they presumably were spurred on to heroic efforts by the great posters the Russians had erected to assure the Germans that they had not been conquered but "liberated" by the Communists from their Fascist oppressors.[20]

Inhabitants moved between Allied occupation sectors and their varied models of denazification, democratization, and reconstruction. Germans in Berlin also moved between identities as victims or perpetrators, liberated or conquered. They appeared as rightfully subjugated former citizens of a criminal regime, or as hapless victims of Nazi betrayal, Anglo-American bombings, and Soviet plunder and rape. Rather quickly, they also surfaced as plucky survivors fascinated with the number of cubic centimeters of ruins to be methodically cleaned up, cheering the premiere of the Philharmonic or the re-opening of the much worried-about Berlin Zoo. Especially in the early occupation period through 1947, much that would seem settled by the 1950s, after the formation of the Federal Republic and the German Democratic Republic, was still open and fluid; nothing about the postwar order was fixed.

At a moment when survival and the reinvention of national and ethnic communities had such high political and cultural priority, women were especially visible, and issues of reproduction – literally birth and death – were brought to the fore both in public policy and in personal accounts. Moreover,

---

as a kind of surreal theatrical or operatic stage set was invoked by many observers – and filmmakers – at war's end. See the large number of films made in the ruins (*Trümmerfilme*); exemplary perhaps are Roberto Rossellini's *Germania Anno Zero*, Billy Wilder's *A Foreign Affair*, and early DEFA films such as Wolfgang Staudte's *Die Mörder sind Unter Uns*.

19 Robert Murphy, *Diplomat Among Warriors* (New York, 1964), 264. Former ambassador Murphy became political advisor to the U.S. Military Government in Germany.

20 Frank Howley, *Berlin Command* (New York, 1950), 65. An extraordinary number of Berlin's occupiers published memoirs.

given the indeterminacy of viable categories of citizenship or identity (as continually reworked in rationing or denazification classifications, for example), reproduction, motherhood, and sexuality loomed intriguingly large as crucial discourses for organizing the past, understanding the present, and imagining the future.[21]

VICTIMS AND VICTORS: RAPE, ABORTION, AND MOTHERHOOD IN BERLIN

I begin with the example of rape, probably the most dramatic form of gendered victimization and one which has – after years of remarkable inattention – begun to receive a good deal of notice.[22] Let me just reiterate briefly that, whatever the estimates, and they vary wildly – perhaps one out of every three of about 1.5 million women in Berlin – it is unquestionably the case that mass rapes of civilian German women by the Red Army signaled the end of the war and the defeat of Nazi Germany.[23] The notorious days of "mass rapes" from April 24 to May 8, 1945, were an integral part of the final bitter battle for Berlin. The continuing (if not as massive) experience and fear of rape for at least months and probably several years thereafter,[24] as well as the often repeated recollections, inscribed indelibly in the memory of many German women (and of the men who were unable/unwilling to

21 For a fine general discussion of the West German case, see Heineman, "The Hour of the Woman."
22 See, e.g., *Heimatmuseum Charlottenburg Ausstellung: Worüber kaum gesprochen wurde: Frauen und alliierte Soldaten; 3. September bis 15. Oktober 1995* (Berlin, 1995); and Helke Sander and Barbara Johr, eds., *Befreier und Befreite: Krieg, Vergewaltigungen, Kinder* (Munich, 1992). For earlier feminist analyses, see Ingrid Schmidt-Harzbach, "Eine Woche im April. Berlin 1945. Vergewaltigung als Massenschicksal," *Feministische Studien* 5 (1984): 51–62; Erika M. Hoerning, "Frauen als Kriegsbeute: Der Zwei-Fronten Krieg. Beispiele aus Berlin," in Lutz Niethammer and Alexander von Plato, eds., *"Wir kriegen jetzt andere Zeiten": Auf der Suche nach der Erfahrung des Volkes in antifaschistischen Ländern. Lebensgeschichte und Sozialkultur im Ruhrgebiet 1930 bis 1960 Bd. 3* (Berlin, 1985), 327–46; and Annemarie Tröger, "Between Rape and Prostitution: Survival Strategies and Chances of Emancipation for Berlin Women after World II," in Judith Friedlander et al., eds., *Women in Culture and Politics: A Century of Change* (Bloomington, Ind., 1986), 97–117. On the thorny problems of historicizing rape at war's end, see Atina Grossmann, "A Question of Silence: The Rape of German Women by Occupation Soldiers," *October* 72 (Spring 1995): 43–63, reprinted in Robert G. Moeller, ed., *West Germany Under Construction: Politics, Society, and Culture in the Adenauer Era* (Ann Arbor, Mich., 1997), 33–52.
23 Barbara Johr, "Die Ereignisee in Zahlen," in Sander and Johr, *Befreier und Befreite*, 48, 54–5, 59. Andreas-Friedrich, *Schauplatz*, noted, "The municipal physicians (*Amtsärzte*) are meeting in the Charité, with Sauerbruch as chair. Behind closed doors and in the absence of the responsible occupying power. Half of all Berlin women have been raped, their reports confirm" (94). See also Erich Kuby, *Die Russen in Berlin 1945* (Munich), 312–13, and especially Norman M. Naimark, *The Russians in Germany: A History of the Soviet Zone of Occupation, 1945–1949* (Cambridge, Mass., 1995), 69–90.
24 Naimark, *Russians in Germany*, 88, suggests that the Red Army rapes continued, "at least through 1947."

protect them) a firm conviction of their own victimization. At the same time, they retained a sense of their superiority over the vanquisher from the East who came to "liberate" them.

Rapes of German women by Red Army soldiers also secured a particularly potent place in postwar memories of victimization because they represented the one, and certainly in Berlin the only, instance in which Goebbels's relentless anti-Bolshevik propaganda turned out to be substantially correct. As Berliners emerged from their cellars during the piercingly beautiful spring of 1945, the Soviets did not kill everyone on sight, deport them to Siberia, or burn down the city. As the musician Karla Hoecker reported with genuine surprise in one of the many diaries composed by women at war's end: "The Russians, who must hate and fear us, leave the majority of the German civilian population entirely alone – that they don't transport us off in droves!"[25] In fact, the SMAD moved quickly and efficiently to organize municipal government, restore basic services, and nurture a lively political and cultural life.[26] In regard to violence against women, however, the Nazi *Greuelgeschichten* (horror stories) were largely confirmed.

Women's continuing (and undeniable) sense of unjust victimization was exacerbated by a nagging perception that the experience of massive sexual assault was quickly and lastingly silenced or tabooized – as anticommunist propaganda, as the normal byproduct of a vicious war, or, in the "antifascist" narrative, downplayed as understandable retribution.[27] However, after May 1945 there was no lack of discussion or documentation about rape. If anything, we find a plethora of speech in many different voices: detailed police and medical reports, statements by Communist Party, SMAD, and then U.S. authorities. Most concretely, the Communist and Soviet-dominated *Magistrat* (municipal government) recognized the problem and its public health consequences early (on May 20) by authorizing a moratorium on the long-standing and controversial antiabortion paragraph 218 of the penal code (as well as by instituting harsh venereal disease screening and treatment). This liberalized abortion policy was instituted despite

---

25 Karla Hoecker (mit einem Vorwort von Ingeborg Drewitz), *Beschreibung eines Jahres: Berliner Notizen 1945* (Berlin, 1984), 42. See also Susanne zur Nieden, *Alltag im Ausnahmezustand: Frauentagebücher im zerstörten Deutschland 1943–1945* (Berlin, 1993).

26 See Wolfgang Schivelbusch's engaging study of postwar and pre–Cold War cultural politics, *In a Cold Crater: Cultural and Intellectual Life in Berlin, 1945–1948* (Berkeley, Calif., 1998).

27 This was certainly expressed in the lively discussions surrounding Helke Sander's film *Befreier und Befreite* which explicitly claimed to "break the silence" around Soviet rapes of German women. See the special issue of *October* 72 (spring 1995) on "Berlin 1945: War and Rape, 'Liberators Take Liberties.'"

some grumbling on the part of doctors and clear but irrelevant protest from Walter Ulbricht, the new German Communist Party (Kommunistische Partei Deutschlands or KPD) leader who had flown into the embattled and smoldering city from Moscow on May 1: "The gentlemen doctors should be reminded to exercise a bit of restraint in this matter," he laconically remarked. But the very statement shows how widespread the practice already was.[28]

Drawing on a mixed legacy of Weimar and National Socialist maternalist, population policy, and racial discourses, as well as on occupation policy, women seeking to terminate pregnancies told their stories in highly specific terms. By the thousands, they reported to authorities in medical commissions attached to district health offices, which then sanctioned abortions right up to the very last months of pregnancy. Women also retold rape stories in astonishing quantity in diaries and memoirs; never before had German women put pen to paper as copiously as they did in April and May 1945, when – and in many cases only when – they faced defeat. Both in private statements and official affidavits, women deployed a wide range of direct and indirect vocabulary – *Schändung* (violation), *Vergewaltigung* (rape), *Übergriff* (encroachment), *Überfall* (attack) – to denote the "it" (*es*) that had been endured.[29] Sometimes they recounted stories of surprising escape or reprieve; often they resorted to generalities and passive voice (the awful scenes went on all night, we all had to submit) – or referred specifically to the horrific experiences of neighbors, mothers, and sisters that they themselves had supposedly been spared.[30] "But many fewer escaped than was later claimed," Curt Riess asserted a few years later.[31] Public conversation about rape, common in the early postwar period, was indeed curtailed in both West and East once conditions had normalized. But rape stories continued to circulate and indeed were repeatedly invoked or alluded to by contemporary chroniclers, both German and occupier.[32] Moreover, the importance of Berlin as the conquered capital and the millions of refugees from the East

---

28 Bundes archiv, Berlin, Stiftung Archiv der Parteien und Massenorganisationen der DDR, hereafter BArch (Sapmo), Nachlass Walter Ulbricht (hereafter NL) 182/246, Besprechung Gen. Ulbricht mit je 1 Genossen aus jedem Verwaltungsbezirk, Berlin, May 20, 1945, 47. See also LAB Rep 12. Acc 902/Nr.5, Dienstbesprechungen der Amtsärzte 1945–6.
29 See zur Nieden, *Alltag im Ausnahmezustand*, esp. 74, 95–6.
30 A wide range of literature about wartime rape, including from the recent conflict in former Yugoslavia, makes similar observations about the ways in which women describe and circumscribe their experiences. See, e.g., Shana Swiss M.D. and Joan E. Giller, "Rape as a Crime of War: A Medical Perspective," *Journal of the American Medical Association* (hereafter JAMA) 270 (Aug. 4, 1993): 612–15.
31 Riess, *Berlin-Berlin*, 10.
32 Howley, *Berlin Command*, 11, referred to the "atrocious crimes" of the Soviets. For a rather melodramatic summary of many such accounts of destroyed Berlin, see Douglas Botting, *In the Ruins of the Reich* (London, 1985).

who poured into western Germany assured the centrality of rape stories in memories of defeat even in areas where there had never been a Red Army soldier.

In the Berlin stories that I work with, maternal and rape experiences were often closely connected; in these stories of victimization, the terminology of *Opfer* clearly carries the double meaning absent in the English term: the negative connotation of "victim" but also a more positive, redeeming, and even heroic sense of sacrifice. Women reported offering themselves in order to protect their young daughters: "They wanted to take my then 10-year-old girl. What mother would have done such a thing? So I could only sacrifice myself instead."[33] Or: "My heart was pounding but I believe my soul was dead. He ripped open the door, placed the revolver on the night table, and lay down beside me in bed. The anxiety about my sleeping child let me endure everything."[34] In another oft-repeated but somewhat different scenario, women recounted trying to take advantage of the Soviet troops' repeatedly observed kindness to children by clutching a young child to their bodies or taking children along wherever they went. In one version, a mother remembered that she pinched her baby in the behind to make him cry piteously, said the child was very ill, and the soldiers let her go.[35] And sometimes women explicitly interpreted the rapes as a kind of revenge; the soldiers, they recollected, called, "*Dawai, Dawai* [Russian for "Move along!"]. Your man wanted war, then German women want what we want."[36]

However, rape stories came – and this is central to the "not only a German story" aspect of my project – not only from these victims, but from those marked (in other contexts) as survivors and victors, that is, from Jews and antifascists who welcomed the Red Army. As Gabriele Vallentin, the sister of the executed Jewish Communist Judith Auer, wrote bitterly: "What became of Goebbels's 'horror-stories'? Reality! . . . Many committed Communists turned their back on the party. They were not prepared for this random vindictiveness."[37] Disappointment and disillusionment with the Red Army *Befreier* (liberators) and its clear connection to rape are surprisingly

---

33 LAB 240/2651/655/1, report by Erna Köhnke. The following three texts are from an essay contest sponsored by the Berlin Senat in 1976: "Preisausschreiben. Berlin 1945. Wie ich es erlebte." 812 contributors, most of them women, wrote about the period from May 1945 to the end of the blockade in June 1949. For further analysis of rape, abortion, and motherhood in postwar Berlin, see Grossmann, "A Question of Silence."
34 LAB 240/2651/131/1, report by Gertrud Strubel.
35 LAB 240/2641/83/1, report by Erna Beck.
36 LAB 240/2651/644/4, report by Elli Fallner.
37 LAB Acc 2421. Gabrielle Vallentin, "Die Einnahme von Berlin Durch die Rote Armee vor Zehn Jahren. Wie ich Sie Selbst Erlebt Habe," 1955, p. 30.

explicit in the complaints of Communist activists about the damaging effect that Soviet soldiers' behavior was having on an otherwise not unreceptive (and indeed somewhat relieved) local populace. One unhappy comrade wrote:

Men and women from the working population say to us over and over again: We had so hoped that it would finally become better, we were so happy that the Red Army was coming, and now, they are behaving just like the SS and the NSDAP always told us they would. We cannot understand this. The hope that things will get better, which we have promised people over and over again; most of them no longer have that hope.

Or even, as frustrated Communist organizers reported:

The mood in the population has become very bad due to these incidents. . . . One woman on the street said to me today, while telling me how the Red Army had again been at their home at night, raping women, "In that regard we had it better with the SS, at least in that respect they left us women alone."[38]

Antifascist activists, many of them recently released from Nazi concentration camps, despaired of their potentially promising political work as the Soviets' liberator image was rapidly dismantled:

For us, who fought against fascism for twelve long years, the concentration camps were no sanitoria and when we now have to watch, as the workers are more and more disappointed, we too could despair . . . if we did not have our strong faith in the party leadership of the KPD.[39]

Rank-and-file Communists pleaded with their leaders that "even the Red Army soldiers, now that the war is already over for eight weeks, absolutely must discipline themselves."[40] But they presented themselves as motivated less by outrage at the crimes than by bitterness over the problems it posed for their efforts at political organization. In their desperation, one group of comrades helpfully suggested that the army set up brothels staffed with "bourgeois" and Nazi women to relieve the pressure.[41] Party documents also make perfectly clear that rape by Red Army forces presented very concrete material problems. The much needed harvest was endangered not only by the plunder of farm animals and equipment but also because women were afraid to work in the fields. Female activists were even so bold as to counter SMAD criticism of women's inadequate political involvement by protesting

---

38 BArch(Sapmo) NL 182/853, p. 30.
39 BArch(Sapmo) NL 182/853, p. 97. See also report from Köpenick, 842, p. 132.
40 BArch(Sapmo) NL 182/852, p. 134. Report from the comrades in Köpenick.
41 BArch(Sapmo) NL 182/852, p. 132. To ZK from KPD Tegel-Süd, June 29, 1945. Naimark, *Russians in Germany*, 119, also cites this example.

that women did not attend meetings because they were simply afraid to walk the streets after dark.[42]

Far from imposing total silence, Communists and Soviet military author-ities – certainly in the immediate postwar years from 1945 until 1947 – found many ways of talking about and acknowledging the massive incidence of rape. They tried simultaneously to deny, minimize, justify, shift responsibil-ity for, and contain them. Beyond the public-health response of organizing abortion and venereal disease treatment, KPD and SMAD officials also de-ployed a wide range of rhetorical and political strategies. They freely ad-mitted violations, "excesses," abuses, and unfortunate incidents (*Übergriffe, Auswüchse, unglückliche Vorfälle*), and vowed to get them under control (or to demand that the Soviet army do so). But they also trivialized rape as an inevitable part of normal brutal warfare, as comparable to Allied excesses, and as understandable if not entirely excusable in view of the atrocities per-petrated on the Russians by the Germans: "We cannot and will not try to provide justifications [for rape], even if we do have explanations and could answer the question by referring to all the havoc that Hitler wreaked in the Soviet Union."[43]

Despite all efforts at containment, rapes figured prominently as public-relations and political-control problems because they provoked anti-Soviet sentiment, especially among women, youth, and dedicated anti-Nazis, pre-cisely those groups considered most likely to support a new socialist and democratic peace-loving Germany. Such protestations notwithstanding, it was generally if not explicitly acknowledged that the KPD's embarrassing loss to the SPD (Social Democratic Party) in Berlin's first free elections in 1946 was due in no small part to a majority female electorate remembering and responding to the actions of the Soviet "friends" (*Freunde*).[44]

For their part, German Communist leaders and the SMAD continually complained about German unwillingness to focus on their own guilt or complicity, noting that calls for *Wiedergutmachung* (referring to reparations to the Soviet Union) or discussions of responsibility and guilt were met with "icy silence" (*geradezu eisiges Schweigen*).[45] The clear implication always was that the Germans should be happy to have gotten off as easily as they did. Even in regard to rape, both the SMAD and the KPD/SED contended that women would have had more of a right to complain if, rather than

---

42 See BArch(Sapmo) DFD (Demokratischer Frauenbund Deutschlands) BV 1, Gründung des zentralen Frauenauschuss beim Magistrat der Stadt Berlin, 102. See also NL 182/853, p. 105. See also Naimark, *Russians in Germany*, 116–21.
43 BArch(Sapmo) NL 182/856, p. 27; *Der Funktionär*, KPD Bezirk Thüringen, Oct. 1945.
44 See, among many sources, Naimark, *Russians in Germany*, 119–21.
45 BArch(Sapmo) NL 182/853, p. 39.

senselessly battling the Red Army to the bitter end right into the center of Berlin, the German working class had fought fascism for even a day or two, thereby preserving some German honor and credibility vis-à-vis the Soviets. One Communist leader petulantly remarked that those who supported the war and the attack on the Soviet Union could not stand there later and cry "*Pfui.*" He added: "War is not a socializing tool."[46] But there was little popular sympathy for Ulbricht's perhaps irrefutable logic in an early leaflet promising swift punishment for "excesses": "Had they [the Soviets] exacted revenge eye for an eye (*gleiches mit gleichem*), German *Volk*, what would have happened to you?"[47]

Even three years later, in 1948, when two overflowing meetings were held in the Haus der Kulturen der Sowjetunion to discuss the ever sensitive subject "about the Russians and about us," the issue most on the minds of the predominantly female audience was Soviet soldiers' violations. The SED argued that the memory of rape as the most dramatic example of abuse by the victors was whipped up and kept alive by Western propaganda. In a standard construction, used both negatively and positively, of the Soviets as more impulsively "natural" and primitively "hot-blooded" than the defeated Germans, the SED ideologue Wolfgang Harich insisted that the Soviet rapes were mere expressions of victor's excess (*Überschwung des Sieges*), as compared to German crimes, which were "cold-blooded actions of master-race consciousness."[48] The topic was abandoned after two crowded, four-hour-long meetings threatened to get out of control. Discussion of the topic could be publicly restrained but not eliminated.

The continuing prominence of rape in German narratives of victimization was certainly not due to Cold War propaganda by the Western Allies, as suggested by the SED. The Americans had their own problems with rape by GIs and, more importantly, with fraternization and casual prostitution. Indeed, there is a remarkably similar rhetoric of anxiety in the American debate about the negative and corrupting effects of servicemen's looting, brawling, raping, and general "sexual antics" on both occupier and occupied.[49] In the early occupation years, U.S. officials were far from seizing

---

46 Wolfgang Harich, *Tägliche Rundschau*, no. 291, Dec. 12, 1948, p. 3.
47 BArch(Sapmo) NL 182/853, p. 10. Aufruf der KPD.
48 Harich, *Tägliche Rundschau*, p. 3. I am indebted to Norman Naimark's work for steering me to this source.
49 Harold Zink, *The United States in Germany, 1944–1955* (Princeton, N.J., 1957), 138. Among many contemporary sources on relations between American occupiers and German women (rape, fraternization, and venereal disease), see also Julian Bach Jr., *America's Germany: An Account of the Occupation* (New York, 1946), especially "GIs Between the Sheets," 71–83; Bud Hutton and Andy Rooney, *Conquerors' Peace: A Report to the American Stockholders* (Garden City, N.Y., 1947); Earl F. Ziemke,

on rape stories to discredit their Soviet allies and competitors, whom they described in 1946 as "hard bargaining, hard playing, hard drinking, hard bodied, and hard headed."[50] The Soviets were viewed not only as barbarian rapists but also as tough fighters and exotic celebrators who could drink, eat, and copulate prodigiously – often to the frustration of U.S. colleagues unable to match their levels of consumption.[51] Noting that "our army has done a little on occasion," William Shirer remarked in his *End of a Berlin Diary* on November 2, 1945 that:

taking into account that the Soviet troops had been in the field constantly fighting for two to three years and that capturing Berlin was a costly operation and that some of the Russian divisions were made up of very inferior material, not to mention a weird assortment of Asiatic troops, then the amount of raping by Russian troops here apparently was not above the average to be expected.[52]

The U.S. occupiers in Berlin downplayed German anxieties about hunger, homelessness, suicide, and disease, and especially crime and disorder (including a high level of violence by returning German soldiers against their families, as well as assaults by Soviets, Poles, and Ukrainians). The Americans noted with a touch of sarcasm that the crime rate per capita in 1945–6 Berlin was lower than that of most cities in the United States, especially New York![53] Indeed, the threat of violence and disease was generally identified with "outsiders" and refugees clamoring for entry into Berlin.[54] This process of official marginalization and privatized retelling left much room for rape stories to proliferate and shape memories. As one woman wrote for

The U.S. Army in the Occupation of Germany 1944–1946 (Washington, D.C., 1975); and Hans Habe, *Our Love Affair with Germany* (New York, 1953).

50 *6 Month Report* (Jan. 4–July 3, 1946), U.S. Army Military Government, Report to the Commanding General U.S. Headquarters Berlin District, p. 8. By 1950, with the Cold War in full swing, Frank Howley, who had been the American commander in Berlin, had changed his view of the Soviets: "We went to Berlin in 1945, thinking only of the Russians as big, jolly, balalaika-playing fellows, who drank prodigious quantities of vodka and liked to wrestle in the drawing room. We know now – or should know – that we were hopelessly naive." Howley, *Berlin Command*, 11.

51 Howley, *Berlin Command*, Maginnis, *Military Government Journal*, and Murphy, *Diplomat*, among others, all make this point.

52 William L. Shirer, *End of a Berlin Diary* (New York, 1947), 148. It was clearly acknowledged, however, that the incidence of outright rape (as opposed to various levels of sexual "fraternization") was much lower among U.S. occupiers. See, for example, Hutton and Rooney, *Conquerors' Peace*, and Zink, *The United States in Germany*.

53 *6 Month Report*, p. 8. See the detailed Berlin police reports on rape, prostitution, drug addiction, and especially family suicides and murders in LAB (Breite Strasse) Rep 9/241, Polizeipräsident 1945–1948.

54 LAB Rep 12. Acc 902/Nr.5, Dienstbesprechungen der Amtsärzte 1945/6, files demonstrate clearly the anxiety about refugees and displaced persons, the attempts to deny them entry or at least limit the resources available to them, as well as to blame them (rather than "legitimate" Berliners) for the spread of social disorder and infectious diseases.

an essay contest sponsored by the Berlin Senate in 1976 on "Berlin 1945: How I experienced it": "To write more about this would mean to reawaken terrible experiences which one would like to forget, but which in fact are constantly reawakened in one's deepest inner self."[55] In immediate reports and in later memoirs, women reported over and over that the cry "Frau komm" still rang in their ears.[56]

Rape was, of course, by no means the only traumatic event that contributed to German women's perceptions of victimization. In some ways, rape came as just one more event (sometimes the worst, but sometimes not) in a series of horrible deprivations and humiliations of war and especially conquest; for mothers, not comparable to the loss of children. Rape – itself signified by a variety of generalized expressions – was integrated into a whole range of other violations and abuses (the ubiquitous term *Missbrauch*), including plunder and demontage, hunger, homelessness, disease (especially infant and child mortality), the harsh treatment of German prisoners of war in the Soviet Union, the perceived arbitrary injustices of denazification, and the expulsions from the eastern territories. "Flight is women's business, just as the war was men's work," Ilse Langner noted in her postwar novel, *Flucht Ohne Ziel* (Flight Without Destination).[57]

After the initial burst of reporting on rape and despair, many accounts of German (especially Berlin) women's experiences at war's end have portrayed sturdy, fresh-faced women wielding shovels and clad in trousers and kerchiefs (think of Hildegard Knef in postwar films). Or reporters presented young "furlines," driven by material need and moral degeneration, eager to fraternize; and provided apocalyptic accounts of Berlin's wild trade in rumors, sex, and black-market goods.[58] Only in the last several years have these rather heroic or salacious versions been displaced by the early stories of German women as victims of mass rape. Indeed, in most immediate postwar sources the *Trümmerfrauen* (rubble women) are hardly heroines; they appear as resentful and reluctant conscript labor tainted by having been Nazis or Nazi wives, or as hungry mothers desperate to escape the so-called *Himmelfahrt* (journey to heaven) category 5 ration cards assigned to "unproductive" housewives.

Just as the city's landscape was marked by theatrical contrasts between the utterly destroyed and the eerily intact, official reports by occupiers

---

55 LAB Rep. 240/2651/655/1, report by Erna Köhnke.
56 See, e.g., LAB Rep 2651/2/184/1, report by Erna Kadzloch on the cry "Frau komm und Uri Uri."
57 Ilse Langner, *Flucht ohne Ziel: Tagebuch – Roman Frühjahr 1945* (Würzburg, 1984), 123. See also Heineman, "Hour of the Woman," and Moeller, "War Stories."
58 For a summary (and good bibliography) of such dramatic versions, see Botting, *In the Ruins*.

and German authorities stressing how remarkably quickly Berlin began to function again (in large part due to women's valiant cleanup efforts) contrasted sharply with women's own accounts. Memoirs and diaries relate bitter experiences of rape, lack of fuel and food, suicide, and disease such as dysentery, typhus, typhoid, and diphtheria, which claimed particularly children as their victims.[59] Berliners cherished images of themselves as plucky, good-humored survivors: "Berlin lebt auf!" (Berlin revives!) the *Berliner Zeitung* proclaimed on Monday, May 21, 1945, and other headlines announced, "Berlin ist wieder da" (Berlin is back!). The still irrepressible Berliner *Schnauze* (cynical wit) reported in a tone of ironic suffering, "Germany, Germany, without everything (*ohne alles*), without butter, without fat, and the little bit of marmalade is eaten up by the occupiers."[60] But despite all efforts to revive the "Berliner Luft" of the Golden Twenties,[61] the pervasive picture was one of relentless misery (*trostlose Not*). Municipal officials themselves frequently emphasized how needy the city was in order to argue for improved occupation conditions, at times so much so that U.S. military authorities countered what they deemed to be persistent German "whining" by labeling fears about starvation as "bushwah."[62]

Contemporary reports (whether by foreign observers, occupiers, or Berliners themselves) present a virtually unanimous portrait of a thoroughly "whipped and beaten" population, self-pitying, broken, in the grip of what one today might identify as mass clinical depression. A major symptom was the inability or unwillingness to bear children – as reflected in high abortion and low birth rates.[63] Berliners were described as listless and apathetic; they were dully, sullenly willing to clean up and rebuild, to "look forward," but were neither insightful into the root causes of their misery nor remorseful about their own agency or responsibility.[64] Amazingly, the *Berliner Zeitung*,

---

59 There were at least 15,000 deaths due to epidemic diseases from May to December 1945 (plus a very high venereal disease rate). Municipal and occupation officials were more likely to stress the rapidity and efficacy of public health measures such as mass immunizations, examinations, and disinfection. For a brief overview, see Dieter Hanauske, ed., *Die Sitzungsprotokolle des Magistrats der Stadt Berlin 1945/46* (Berlin, 1995), 74.

60 Quote is from LAB/Rep. 240. Acc. 2651/748. Irmgard Heidleberg had submitted her mother's diary.

61 See, among others, Schivelbusch, *In a Cold Crater*, on efforts to bring back into the public the stars and successes of Weimar culture.

62 Howley, *Berlin Command*, 85.

63 Botting, *In the Ruins*, 109, summarizes many reports: "The wish to have a child is waning. Instead of wanting a child many women are now succumbing to a deep despondency."

64 This portrayal of whining self-pity is especially evident in reports by occupiers, and only really changes to the spunky "Berlin ist wieder da" image with the blockade and the airlift. For an insightful analysis of this "depression" (and the distinctions in the psychoanalytically oriented literature between melancholia and *Trauerarbeit*), see Eric L. Santner, *Stranded Objects: Mourning, Memory, and Film in Postwar Germany* (Ithaca, N.Y., 1990), esp. 1–56.

published by the *Magistrat*, felt it necessary in June 1945 to establish a readers' forum on the topic, "Too much or too little, should the newspapers cover this?" asking whether the Berlin daily press was overreporting news about concentration camps and Nazi crimes.[65] Just weeks after the collapse of the Third Reich, a major daily in the Soviet zone published responses that (among others) invoked *armes Deutschland*: "We have taken on a difficult legacy and must make good again what these criminals [the Nazis] have done. For that, however, we must look forward; only then we can rebuild, and not if we look back on ugly past times." In a rhetoric more commonly associated with the 1980s and 1990s, readers called for a *Schlussstrich* (termination point) to discussions of the Nazi era.[66] As one American Military Government official observed in his diary in 1945:

The Germans in Berlin ... were on very short rations, had only what shelter they could find ... and looked beaten physically and in spirit. But what they were going through as they toiled, clearing up bricks and rubble, did not compare with the hell of Belsen and Buchenwald. Still, I doubted that they knew that.[67]

VICTIMS AND SURVIVORS: JEWS, TRAUMA, AND BABIES

Like the U.S. occupation officer interjecting the experience of the concentration camps into his narrative of German victimization, I too want at this juncture to insert another parallel story that mixes up categories of victims and survivors. The high suicide and abortion rates among German "victims," the sense that having to bear and care for children somehow was an intolerable burden in the months after the defeat, contrasts sharply with the remarkable fertility among the approximately 250,000 Jewish "survivors" or "victims" living in DP camps. In some kind of supreme historical irony, at the same time that Germans bemoaned the high incidence of suicides, infant and child mortality, and abortion, and as German women were desperately seeking to keep alive the children they already had,[68] Jewish DPs in occupied Germany were producing a record number of babies. In 1946, occupied Germany, far from being *judenrein*, counted the highest Jewish

---

65 *Berliner Zeitung*, June 24, 1945, p. 3.   66 *Berliner Zeitung*, June 29, 1945, p. 3.
67 Maginnis, *Military Government Journal*, 258–9.
68 This rhetoric of despair complements the pro-natalist rhetoric immediately deployed in both East and West Germany (only partially but carefully reworked from the Nazi version) in which self-sacrificing motherhood was key to restoring "humanity and culture" to the German Volk. For excellent samples, see BArch(Sapmo) DFD (Demokratischer Frauenbund Deutschlands) BV 7, Zeitungsausschnittssammlung, Probleme der Frauen im Nachkriegsdeutschland, 1945–6.

birthrate in the world. (Some, pointing to the unusually young and fertile population of survivors, say it was the highest overall birthrate.)[69]

The "steady rush of weddings"[70] in the DP camps, sometimes within days to neighbors in the next barrack without necessarily knowing them very well, and the resulting "population explosion" had little to do with the reconstruction of "normal" family life and self-sacrificing maternalism demanded by West Germany (or pronatalist calls for renewing the health of the *Volk* in the East). Neither among Germans nor in the DP camps could one really speak of orderly family life. Indeed, the Jewish DPs were often characterized by a vocabulary similar to that defining the Berliners, whom their occupiers had quickly judged "shocked and apathetic . . . concerned almost exclusively with problems of food and shelter."[71] Jewish relief workers and American military authorities, as well as German observers, saw the DPs as depressive, afflicted with "inertia" and "an air of resignation," and unsuited to any kind of normal life. They regularly and graphically bemoaned the "uncivilized" state of the survivors, oblivious to the most elementary rules of hygiene, uninhibited in regard to the opposite sex, and unwilling to work or take any sort of active initiative. Other reports cited symptoms that today are clearly associated with post-traumatic stress disorders: DPs were labeled "jittery, excitable, anxiety prone."[72] In 1946, the psychiatrist William Niederland, himself a refugee from Nazi Germany, defined such a "survivor syndrome" – which, painfully, would become both a stigmatizing label for people who in many ways eventually became ultrafunctional citizens of their new homelands and a necessary diagnosis for claiming restitution from the future West German government.[73]

Given our own late-twentieth-century inflationary romance with the language and theory of trauma and memory, and its corollary valorization of Holocaust survivors, it is salutary to recall how very unromantic, unappealing, and alien the DP survivors appeared even to those who meant to aid them. Echoing his Military Government colleagues' gloss on the Berliners, Irving Heymont, the American (and as he later revealed, Jewish) commander

69 See among numerous sources, Peck, "Jewish Survivors," 38; Michael Brenner, *Nach dem Holocaust: Juden in Deutschland 1945–1950* (Munich, 1995), 36; and Margarete L. Myers, "Jewish Displaced Persons Reconstructing Individual and Community in the US Zone of Occupied Germany," *Leo Baeck Institute Yearbook* 42 (1997): 306–8.

70 Jacob Biber, *Risen from the Ashes* (San Bernardino, Calif., 1990), 49.

71 *Berlin Sector: A Report by Military Government From July 1, 1945 to September 1, 1949,* 113.

72 Quoted in Alex Grobman, *Rekindling the Flame: American Jewish Chaplains and the Survivors of European Jewry, 1944–1948* (Detroit, 1993), 57. See also Dinnerstein, *America and the Survivors.*

73 On the trauma and trauma diagnoses of Jewish survivors, see, among many other sources, Aaron Haas, *The Aftermath: Living with the Holocaust* (Cambridge, 1995), and Israel W. Charny, *Holding on to Humanity: The Message of Holocaust Survivors. The Shamai Davidson Papers* (New York, 1992).

of the Landsberg DP camp in Bavaria, portrayed his charges: "With a few exceptions, the people of the camp themselves appear demoralized beyond hope of rehabilitation. They appear to be beaten both spiritually and physically with no hopes or incentives for the future."[74] In his autobiographical novel, Hanoch Bartov recalled the reaction of tough Jewish Brigade soldiers from Palestine who entered Germany determined to "hate the butchers of your people – unto all generations!" and fulfill their mission of "the rescue of the Jews, immigration to a free homeland," with "dedication, loyalty, and love for the remnants of the sword and the camps." But despite these "commandments for a Hebrew soldier on German soil" the Brigade men were not prepared for what they found once they actually encountered the remnants they had pledged to avenge and rescue: "I kept telling myself that these were the people we had spoken of for so many years – but I was so far removed from them that electric wire might have separated us."[75] The Israeli historian Idith Zertal has characterized the painful, shocking encounter of the *Yishuv* with the survivors, "between the Jews of Europe and the 'reborn Israel,'" as a kind of "return of the repressed," which provoked the fear and anxiety Freud diagnosed when something that had once been *heimlich*, familiar and homelike, becomes *unheimlich*, frightening and inexplicable.[76] I. F. Stone, the American Jewish leftist journalist who covered the underground route to Palestine as a "participant observer," noted briskly about his first impression of the DPs in the camps: "They were an unattractive lot."[77] As one survivor ruefully stated, "the concentration camp experience is nothing that endears you to people."[78]

Particularly young mothers in the DP camps were in many ways unsuited for motherhood and domesticity. They had come into Nazi ghettos and death camps, partisan encampments, or hiding, as teenagers and had no time to grow up. Their own mothers were generally dead (often killed or selected for death before the survivors' eyes), or they had once had children, who were now lost or murdered. As a shocked American Army rabbi reported back to Jewish agencies in New York: "Almost without exception each is the

74 Jacob Rader Marcus and Abraham J. Peck, eds., *Among the Survivors of the Holocaust – 1945: The Landsberg DP Camp Letters of Major Irving Heymont, United States Army*, Monographs of the American Jewish Archives no. 10 (Cincinnati, 1982), letter to Heymont's wife, Sept. 19, 1945. Heymont graphically describes the camp residents' unwillingness or inability to use the latrines properly and the lack of sexual privacy.

75 Hanoch Bartov, *The Brigade*, trans. David S. Segal (1965; New York, 1968), 56, 148.

76 Idith Zertal, *From Catastrophe to Power: Holocaust Survivors and the Emergence of Israel* (Berkeley, Calif., 1998), 8–9.

77 I. F. Stone, *Underground to Palestine and Reflections Thirty Years Later* (New York, 1978), 24. In general, see Yehudah Bauer, *Out of the Ashes* (Oxford, 1989), and *Flight and Rescue: Bricha* (New York, 1970).

78 Haas, *Aftermath*, 18.

last remaining member of his entire family. . . . Their stories are like terrible nightmares which make one's brain reel and one's heart bleed."[79] In some widely publicized cases children had been appropriated by Christian rescuers who would not give them up or, most painfully, the children themselves did not want to give up their new identities. Some women had simply picked up other families' lost children and made them their own, at least for the duration of the displacement: "Women who have lost entire families . . . one woman who came in with three children not hers nor related to each other — she merely picked them en route — one in one place, one in another — all three had lost their parents."[80]

Relief workers consistently noted this desperate need to recreate some sort of familial or group bonds in a situation where "the overwhelming majority of the Nazi camp survivors are *single* survivors of exterminated families."[81] Meyer Levin, in his searing memoir *In Search*, bitterly reflected on the sentimentalization of the desperate search for lost children:

There were heartbreaking stories of children seeking their mothers; in a few cases they found them, and these cases were so endlessly overplayed in the radio dramas of American Jewish organizations for the next few years that Europe and its DP camps must have seem [sic] to the mind of the American Jew to be one large happy reunion center where every half-hour another distracted mama called out a long-forgotten childish pet name, whereupon a curly haired five-year-old who had disguised her dark eyes for blue eyes in order to survive as a Polish child under the name of Wanda, rushed to the call of *Bubaleh* into mama's arms.[82]

---

79 Letter to Stephen S. Wise, June 22, 1945, Abraham J. Peck, ed., *The Papers of the World Jewish Congress 1945–1950: Liberation and the Saving Remnant*, 23 vols. (New York, 1990), 9:30. On the important role of U.S. military rabbis in dealing with Jewish DPs, see Grobman, *Rekindling the Flame*, and Louis Barish, *Rabbis in Uniform: The Story of the American Jewish Military Chaplain* (New York, 1962). It is important to note that Jewish DPs who had spent difficult war years in the Soviet Union and began arriving in the U.S. zone in large numbers in 1946 were more likely to have survived in intact families.

80 Memorandum from Kalman Stein, Dec. 7, 1945, *Archives of the Holocaust*, 9:146. The problem of reclaiming perhaps 10,000 Jewish orphans who had been saved by Christians was prominently discussed in the immediate postwar period. Altogether, about 150,000 children outside Russia were estimated to have survived. See Wahrhaftig, *Uprooted*, 121.

81 Wahrhaftig, *Uprooted*, 44. Polish Jews who had fled to the Soviet Union and who later entered DP camps in the American zone after experiencing postwar persecution in Poland were more likely to arrive in intact family groups than were survivors of the death camps, ghettos, or partisan groups.

82 Meyer Levin, *In Search: An Autobiography* (New York, 1950), 245. This is precisely what happens in the American film *The Search* (1948, directed by Fred Zinnemann) in which Montgomery Clift plays a U.S. GI who picks up a lost and speechless child, clearly a victim of unspeakable brutality, wandering in the German ruins. At the movie's conclusion, the child is reunited with his concentration camp survivor mother who has been walking through the assembly centers of Europe looking for him. She finally spies him walking past her in a row of children being prepared for *Aliyah* for Palestine. "Karel," she calls out; "Mamischka," he calls out and runs toward her, and the movie fades out. Only there is a twist familiar to Levin, who railed against the universalization and dejudaization of the Holocaust in *The Diary of Anne Frank*: while the other orphans being prepared for emigration out of Europe are Jewish, little blond Karel is the child of anti-Nazi Czech intelligentsia.

His own vision was different. Remarking on a young woman survivor he encountered as he drove through devastated Europe in his U.S. Army jeep, he wrote: "She hadn't been able to save her child, nobody had been able to save the child in this place. And somehow her tragedy seemed more terrible than that of the mothers who went into the gas chambers with their babies clutched to their breasts."[83]

The veritable baby boom of 1946–7 was a phenomenon much more complicated and remarkable than the "manic defense" against catastrophic experience and overwhelming loss diagnosed by contemporary psychiatrists and social workers.[84] "In the midst of the depressed desert life" of the DP camps it was obvious that "a noticeable change occurred: People who had survived singly in all age groups were struck with a strong desire to be married."[85] Levin too sensed that the survivors' primary need was "to seek some link on earth. . . . This came before food and shelter."[86]

The rapid appearance of babies and baby carriages in the dusty streets of DP camps throughout the American and British zones served as a conscious and highly ideologized reminder that "mir szeinen doh," (Yiddish for "we are here"). A *She'erit Hapleitah* (surviving remnant, or more literally, left-over remnant of a remnant) of the Jewish people had survived Nazi genocide and was determined to replace the dead at an astonishingly rapid rate.[87] Despite everything, women who only weeks or months earlier had been emaciated, amenorrheic "living corpses" became pregnant and bore children.[88] Attempting to dramatize many survivors' desperate determination to emigrate to Palestine, Bartley Crum, a U.S. member of an Anglo-American committee on Palestine investigating conditions in the DP camps, claimed that, "In many camps I was told that Jewish women had

---

83 Levin, *In Search*, 270.
84 For a fine analysis of this literature, see Isidor J. Kaminer, " 'On razors edge' – Vom Weiterleben nach dem Überleben," *Fritz Bauer Institut Jahrbuch* (1996): 146–7, 157.
85 Biber, *Risen from the Ashes*, 37.   86 Levin, *In Search*, 183–4.
87 See Juliane Wetzel, "Mir szeinen doh. München und Umgebung als Zuflucht von Überlebenden des Holocaust 1945–1948," in Martin Broszat, ed., *Von Stalingrad zur Währungsreform: Zur Sozialgeschichte des Umbruchs in Deutschland* (Munich, 1988). See also Angelica Königseder and Juliane Wetzel, *Lebensmut im Wartesaal. Die jüdischen DPs (Displaced Persons) in Nachkriegsdeutschland* (Frankfurt am Main, 1994), 104–5, 187, and Peck, "Jewish Survivors," 35–8. The term *She'erit Hapleitah* derives from reworkings of Biblical references to the survivors of the Assyrian conquest.
88 See Zalman Grinberg, "We Are Living Corpses," in *Aufbau*, Aug. 24, 1945. For a strong argument against the view of survivors as "living corpses" and for the agency, and what Peck has called "the revolutionary ideology," of the *She'erit Hapleita* (which focuses on political organization rather than reproduction), see Ze'ev Mankowitz, "The Formation of *She'erit Hapleita*: November 1944–July 1945," *Yad Vashem Studies* 20 (1990): 337–70, and "The Affirmation of Life in She'erith Hapleita," *Holocaust and Genocide Studies* 5, no. 1 (1990): 13–21.

deliberately suffered abortions rather than bear a child on German soil."[89] Remarkably, the opposite was more common; survivors were not deterred even by the knowledge that for purposes of *Aliyah* to Palestine and emigration elsewhere, pregnancy and young children were an obstacle.[90] Major Heymont noticed "that the use of contraceptives is highly frowned upon by the camp people. They believe it is everyone's duty to have as many children as possible in order to increase the numbers of the Jewish community."[91] The American Jewish Distribution Committee (Joint) found itself having to scramble to build Jewish ritual baths for brides (*Mikveh*) and to produce gold wedding rings and wigs for Orthodox wives.[92]

It is plausible then to suggest that this rash of marriages, pregnancies, and babies represented a conscious affirmation of Jewish life. This was true for both men and women; in his memoir *Risen from the Ashes*, Jacob Biber poignantly described the birth of his son, the first baby in Föhrenwald Camp near Munich. Chaim Shalom Dov was named in honor of the first son who had been murdered in his father's arms as the family fled to the forest in the Ukraine, and in celebration of peace and life. While on the run and in hiding after the death of their son, Biber and his wife had "lived like brother and sister," not daring to risk pregnancy, and now "this pleasant surprise was a sign of the continuity of life."[93]

Women especially were determined to claim the domestic reproductive roles that they had once been promised in some long ago and now fantastic past. Women survivors of the death camps, sometimes of medical experiments, were anxious to reassure themselves of their fertility as well as to prove male potency (which, it was widely rumored, had been subjected to emasculating potions in the camps). Pregnancy and childbirth served as definitive material evidence that they had indeed survived.[94] Observers were shocked

---

89 Bartley C. Crum, *Behind the Silken Curtain: A Personal Account of Anglo-American Diplomacy in Palestine and the Middle East* (New York, 1947; reprint, Jerusalem, 1996), 90.

90 Levin, *In Search*, noted, "And the urge to arrive in time for the birth of the child in Eretz was real on every vessel that left for Palestine with its host of pregnant women, some of whom were smuggled onto the ships in their ninth month despite the Haganah regulation making the seventh month the limit" (360). See also Wahrhaftig, *Uprooted*, 52–4.

91 Heymont, *Among the Survivors*, 44.

92 Judith Tydor Baumel, "DPs, Mothers and Pioneers: Women in the She'erit Hapletah," *Jewish History* 11, no. 2 (fall 1997): 103. See also her *Kibbutz Buchenwald: Survivors and Pioneers* (New Brunswick, N.J., 1997).

93 Biber, *Risen from the Ashes*, 1.

94 It is worth noting how many "Holocaust memoirs" actually include (or conclude with) descriptions of the DP camps and experiences of marriage, pregnancy, and childbearing. See, among many memoirs, Sonja Milner, *Survival in War and Peace* (New York, 1984) and Sala Pawlowicz, with Kevin Klose, *I Will Survive* (London, 1947; reprint, 1964). In general, see Dalia Ofer and Lenore J. Weitzman, eds., *Women in the Holocaust* (New Haven, Conn., 1998); also Sybil Milton, "Gender and

by a kind of "hypersexuality" among the mostly youthful inhabitants of the DP camps, who had missed out on the usual processes of adolescent sexual and romantic experimentation. They noted with a certain astonishment, both impressed and appalled, that the "appearance of numbers of new-born babies has become a novel feature of the Jewish DP camps."[95] As many survivors have articulated, they were young and finally freed from constant fear; they wanted to live, to taste the pleasures of youth long denied: "Our young bodies and souls yearned to live."[96]

In one major displaced persons camp, there were only nine babies among 1,281 inhabitants in October 1945. The majority of the survivors were young, and men outnumbered women (approximately sixty to forty); young children and their mothers, along with the elderly, had been automatically marked for death in the Nazi camps. But within several months almost a third of the camp's 2,000 strong population were children, most of them newborn infants. On the grounds of Bergen-Belsen, the former concentration camp that became the center of Jewish life in the British zone, fifteen Jewish babies were born every week; in early February 1948, the birth of the thousandth Belsen baby was celebrated.[97] Marriages were a daily ritual: "By the winter of 1946, a thousand [Jewish] babies were born each month" in the American zone.[98]

Fertility and maternity worked, if you will, as a mode of reidentifying and reconstructing, both of claiming personal agency and an intact individual body, and of constructing a viable new community – after extraordinary trauma, and even in transit. Supported by the traditional religious imperatives of the East European Jewish community in the camps, the reproductive behavior of the *She'erit Hapleitah* could not offer any redemptive meaning

Holocaust – ein offenes Forschungsfeld," Sara R. Horowitz, "Geschlechtsspezifische Erinnerungen an den Holocaust," and Atina Grossmann, "Zwei Erfahrungen im Kontext des Themas 'Gender und Holocaust,'" all in Sigrid Jacobeit and Grit Philipp, eds., *Forschungsschwerpunkt Ravensbrück: Beiträge zur Geschichte des Frauen-Konzentrationslagers* (Berlin, 1997), 124–46.

95 Wahrhaftig, *Uprooted*, 54. Occupation and relief officials, as well as Germans, were often caught between disbelief at the horror and magnitude of the extermination and incomprehension of the fact that there remained, after all, hundreds of thousands of survivors who resisted repatriation and for whom there had to be found not just "relief" but a new life (what was still called "a final solution") outside of Europe. Report by Zorach Wahrhaftig, Nov. 27, 1945, "Life in camps 6 months after liberation," *Archives of the Holocaust*, 9:130.

96 Biber, *Risen from the Ashes*, 46. It is important to note that sexual longing was mixed with a painful sense of inexperience and of having missed out on some crucial adolescent socialization and pleasures. Women especially also had to contend with memories of rape and sexual assault and coercion perpetrated in many settings: by Soviet liberators and other rescuers, partisans and Red Army fighters (Jewish and not) in forest encampments, as well as by Germans and local fascists.

97 See also Myers, "Jewish Displaced Persons," 306–8.

98 Grobman, *Rekindling the Flame*, 17. This baby boom is well portrayed in the American documentary film "The Long Journey Home," Simon Wiesenthal Center, Los Angeles, 1997.

to the catastrophe (*Churban*) that had been experienced. But it did perhaps offer a possible means to "redeem the future"[99] or at least to begin the regenerative work of making and imagining one. Having babies – the most normal of human activities under normal circumstances – now became both miraculous and an entry into "normal" humanity, even if it often seemed to offer only a kind of make-believe normality, a "parallel life" to the memories of the preceding trauma. In that sense, the quick construction of new families could also be interpreted as a kind of genealogical and biological revenge.[100] Jewish infants, born on territory that had been declared *judenrein* to women who had been slated for extermination, were literally dubbed *Maschiachskinder* ("children of the Messiah").[101]

Marriage, pregnancy, and childbirth clearly represented a possible reconstruction of collective, national, and individual identity for the Jewish DPs – the battered survivors of the death camps, ghettos, and partisan groups in Eastern Europe, as well as those tens of thousands of mostly Polish Jews who had spent difficult war years in the Soviet Union. The baby boom was the counterpart, indeed was closely linked to, the passionate political Zionism that gripped virtually all survivors.[102] It offered a means of establishing a new order and a symbolic sense of "home," even and especially in the approximately sixty refugee camps in the U.S. and British zones and in the American sector of Berlin.[103] Indeed, the flip side to the stigmatization of Jewish DPs as both incorrigible and pathetic was a kind of romantic vision of the tough survivor who had emerged like a phoenix from unimaginable devastation. Kathryn Hulme, an adventurous young American war welder turned UNRRA (United Nations Relief and Rehabilitation Administration) worker, described her reaction to the Jewish DPs assigned to her camp,

99 Mankowitz, "The Formation of *She'erit Hapleita*," 351.
100 We might consider such a gendered and broadened notion of "revenge" in light of discussions about the relative lack of vengeful actions by survivors. See, e.g., John Sack, *An Eye for an Eye* (New York, 1993).
101 I am grateful to Samuel Kassow, History Department, Trinity College, Hartford, Connecticut, for this reference.
102 Some, especially recent Israeli, historiography has pointed to an instrumentalization of the Jewish survivors for the Zionist agenda of finally establishing a state of Israel. See especially Tom Segev, *The Seventh Million: The Israelis and the Holocaust*, trans. Haim Watzman (New York, 1993), and Idith Zertal, *From Catastrophe to Power: Holocaust Survivors and the Emergence of Israel* (Berkeley, Calif., 1998), but there can be no doubt that the Zionist fervor in the DP camps was also powerful and genuine, especially among young survivors who had lost their entire families and found a sense of family, community, identity, and pride as well as hope for the future in Zionist peer groups.
103 Comparative anthropological literature is useful in this context. See especially Lisa Malkii's analysis of the ways in which refugee camp settings encourage "construction and reconstruction of [their] history 'as a people' " and the importance of children in that process, in *Purity and Exile: Violence, Memory and National Cosmology Among Hutu Refugees in Tanzania* (Chicago, 1995), 3.

whom she had awaited with "mingled emotions of alarm and compassion." They were hardly the "ashes of a people" announced by so many observers; on the contrary, they were indeed survivors, "charged with the intensest life force I had ever experienced." They – or at least their toughened leaders – were entirely unlike either the docile, well-behaved defeated Germans or the "professional" non-Jewish Polish and Baltic DPs she had worked with previously – "contrary, critical, and demanding." Resorting to nonetheless admiring stereotypes, she described "their wiry bodies . . . smoldering eyes . . . voices unmusical and hoarse . . . their hands moved continuously." In fact, she concluded, "They didn't seem like DPs at all."[104]

Despite the overcrowding, the unappetizing rations, the sometimes humiliating and uncomprehending treatment by military and relief workers who "looked down on us . . . as if we were some kind of vermin or pests,"[105] the DP camps and the new families they housed provided a makeshift therapeutic community for survivors who had "been liberated from death" but not yet "been freed for life."[106] Magda Denes, who had survived in hiding with her mother in Czechoslovakia, remembered her reaction to the chaotic, depressing DP camp where "being processed was a protocol to which we were subjected again and again." She asked a friend: 'Do you think we live in a madhouse?' She looked at me sadly. 'No, my dear,' she said. 'You have never been in a concentration camp. This is normalcy. This is practically heaven.' "[107]

JEWISH DPS IN TRANSIT STATION BERLIN

In Berlin, despite the best efforts of American occupation officials to stem the flow of Jewish refugees and especially to evacuate pregnant women and mothers with young children to the ostensibly better equipped DP camps in West Germany, the numbers of Jewish DPs continued to grow. The U.S. Military Government had initially resisted forming DP camps in Berlin, especially because "the Jewish population resident in Berlin in the main did not desire to have a camp created for them, stating that they had seen enough of camps."[108] Starting in November 1945, however, about 250 to 300 Jewish

---

104 Kathryn Hulme, *The Wild Place* (Boston, 1953), 71, 212–13.
105 Biber, *Risen from the Ashes*, 14.   106 Wahrhaftig, *Uprooted*, 86.
107 Magda Denes, *Castles Burning: A Child's Life in War* (New York, 1997), 304, 316. A recent letter to the editor of the American Jewish magazine *Moment* recalled DP Camp Föhrenwald as "a vibrant Jewish community . . . we needed this transition time after Nazi hell," June 1997, 21.
108 Lt. Col. Harold Mercer, chief of Displaced Persons and Welfare Section (OMG), Feb. 5, 1946, LAB OMGUS 4/20–1/10.

survivors arrived in the officially closed city every day, creating what one U.S. officer termed a "red-hot" crisis.[109] By 1947, over a thousand Jewish infants and children were housed in camps in the American sector, and 6,000–7,000 Polish Jews were settled into DP camps in the American sector. The Soviets forced the *Bricha* underground network to curtail its "flight and rescue" missions in the fall of 1946, but altogether some 32,000 Polish Jews would pass through Berlin from November 1945 through January 1947.[110]

American policy was influenced by an eagle-eyed press and by public opinion campaigns at home. The Harrison Report, commissioned in the summer of 1945 by General Dwight D. Eisenhower, who had been deeply shaken by what he had seen at the liberated death camps, alerted especially American Jewish organizations that "we appear to be treating the Jews as the Nazis treated them except that we do not exterminate them."[111] Much to their annoyance, U.S. Military Government authorities could not as easily, guiltlessly, and unilaterally ban all Jewish DPs from their zone in Berlin as the British and French, and certainly the Soviets, did. The British, preoccupied with the crisis in Palestine, flatly said no; the French, typically, pleaded poverty and lack of resources, and the Soviet general, with "a puckish smile on his face," rather gleefully noted that the refugees all snuck out of their sector into the West anyway.[112] In fact, squabbles about the "Polish Jewish problem held center stage" at a surprising number of Allied *Kommandatura* sessions. The U.S. Military Government officer responsible recalled: "Everyone was irked by the way we were being browbeaten into assuming responsibility for all of the Polish Jews, regardless of what sector of Berlin they were in."[113]

The Americans, in cooperation with UNRRA, eventually made the commitment, as they did throughout their zone, that "reasonable care be taken of these unfortunate people."[114] But they did so with great reluctance and resentment; as Heymont confessed in his memoir about running

---

109 Maginnis, *Military Government Journal*, 326.
110 Nachama, "Nach der Brefreiung," 272. See also Angelika Königseder, "Durchgangsstation Berlin: Jüdische DPs 1945–1948," in Fritz-Bauer-Institut, ed., *Überlebt und unterwegs: Jüdische Displaced Persons in Nachkriegsdeutschland* (Frankfurt am Main, 1997), 189–206. All these numbers are inexact. The Berlin Sector/Public Welfare Branch of the Office of Military Government estimated on June 20, 1947 that there were 8,000 German Jews in Berlin receiving aid from the American Joint Distribution Committee, plus 6,300 Polish Jews in two DP camps. Another memorandum on June 20, 1947 for the Jewish Agency for Palestine counted 8,000 persons in Düppel and 4,000 in Wittenau camps. See LAB OMGUS 4/20–1/10. On confusing statistics, see also Frank Stern, *The Whitewashing of the Yellow Badge: Antisemitism and Philosemitism in Postwar Germany* (Oxford, 1992), 63.
111 Among many sources, Brenner, *Nach dem Holocaust*, 18.
112 Maginnis, *Military Government Journal*, 327.   113 Maginnis, *Military Government Journal*, 326.
114 Mercer, February 5, 1946, OMGUS 4/20–1/10.

the Landsberg camp: "When I raised my right hand and took the oath as an officer, I never dreamed that there were jobs of this sort."[115] In the characteristically rapid turnaround of sentiment in the postwar years, it was the victims of Nazism, still displaced and unruly, who came to be seen even by the victors as the disreputable villains. The Germans, miserable and depressed but trying to rebuild – with their "clean German homes and pretty, accommodating German girls" – came to be viewed as victims, pathetic but appealing, and later, with the Airlift in Berlin, even heroic.[116] Frustrated by Allied indifference to the particular trauma of their experience and what they perceived as favorable treatment for the more orderly Germans, DPs tartly observed that "it is better to be a conquered German than a liberated Jew,"[117] and joked among themselves, "The Germans will never forgive us for what they did to us."[118]

Displaced Persons existed within the "historic triangle" of occupiers, Germans, and Jews,[119] and as the impact of the Harrison Report faded into Cold War politics, it seemed to many that the "guilt of the Germans was forgotten." A worried Zorach Wahrhaftig informed the American and World Jewish Congress that, six months after liberation, the "Jewish DPs are looked upon as intruders, the Germans as the autochthonic population suffering from the plague of DPs."[120] It was directly in response to the mass influx of East European Jewish DPs that, in December 1945, the liberal, U.S.-licensed *Tagesspiegel* editorialized:

So one may hope that the millions of sacrifices (*Opfer*) by the Jews have not been brought in vain, but that rather after hundreds of years of effort it will finally be possible today to solve the Jewish problem in its totality (*das jüdische Problem in seiner Gesamtheit zu lösen* [*sic!*]); namely, on the one hand, through emigration of the homeless Jews and, on the other hand, through the complete assimilation of those Jews who wish to remain in Europe.[121]

---

115 Heymont, *Among the Survivors*, 38.
116 Samuel Gringauz, "Our New German Policy and the DPs. Why Immediate Resettlement Is Imperative," *Commentary* 5 (1948): 510. On shifting U.S. policy, see also Dinnerstein, *America and the Survivors*, and Stern, *The Whitewashing of the Yellow Badge*, 53–157.
117 Quoted in documentary, "The Long Way Home."
118 Norbert Mühlen, *The Return of Germany: A Tale of Two Countries* (Chicago, 1953), 154–5.
119 Frank Stern, "The Historic Triangle: Occupiers, Germans, and Jews in Postwar Germany," *Tel Aviver Jahrbuch für deutsche Geschichte* 19 (1990): 47–76.
120 Report by Zorach Wahrhaftig, Nov. 27, 1945, on "Life in camps 6 months after liberation, "*Archives of the Holocaust*, 9:134. For case studies of relations between Jewish DPs and a local German population in Landsberg, see Angelika Eder, "Jüdische Displaced Persons im deutschen Alltag: Eine Regionalstudie 1945–1950," *Fritz Bauer Institut Jahrbuch* (1997): 163–87, and D. Kohlmannslehner, "Das Verhältnis von Deutschen und jüdischen Displaced Persons in Lager Lampertheim 1945–1949," unpublished paper, Fritz Bauer Institut archives, Frankfurt am Main.
121 K.E., "Juden in Deutschland," *Der Tagesspiegel*, no. 39 (Dec. 5, 1945), 3.

Indeed, Allied and German anxieties about a "flood by Jews from the East" into "countries [Germany and Austria] made *judenrein* by the Nazis"[122] were exacerbated by their high birthrate and obvious lack of assimilation; they reveal a great deal about when and how Jews were specifically defined as victims of Nazi genocide, assigned roles (either uncomfortable or valorized depending on whether one looks West or East) as victims of fascism, or, most prominently, subsumed in the larger category of unwelcome war refugees.[123]

By 1948–9 currency reform, blockade, and airlift sealed the division of Berlin and fundamentally changed its status from vanquished Nazi capital to plucky Cold War ally (this too is a highly gendered process that requires further analysis). Ironically, it was the final division of the city into East and West that also basically eliminated the Jewish DP problem for Berlin. Almost all the stubbornly remaining DPs in Berlin (an estimated 6,500) were flown out to the western U.S. zone in empty airlift planes returning to their base at Rhein-Main; this was another step toward the normalization of divided Berlin. At the same time, however, Berlin maintained a particular status in postwar Jewish life, in part because of the relatively high number of Jews who had survived in the city (most of them spouses in mixed marriages or of mixed ancestry) or had returned from exile or the death camps (especially Shanghai and Theresienstadt). In March 1946, the community counted 7,768 members living in 5,640 households, not including the large numbers who passed through Berlin DP camps.[124]

The city had quickly become a center of revived German-Jewish community, and inevitably also a center of anguished debate about what that might or should mean. The local German-Jewish weekly *Der Weg* chronicled all of this ferment: the divisions among those who had survived underground (often the most hopeful about the possibilities of reconciliation and cooperation for building a new democratic Germany), those who had returned from the camps, and the remigrés; the endless cogitations about whether it was better to stay or to leave, whether to simply administer a small *Liquidationsgemeinde* or attempt to build a new German-Jewish life; the increasing (rather than diminishing) anger and anxiety about continued antisemitism and lack of remorse among Germans. The advertisements and announcements pages of *Der Weg* tell these stories most eloquently. The paper printed notices pleading for any word of lost loved ones, the beginning

---

122 Wahrhaftig, "Life in Camps," 133.
123 The reconstituted Jewish community in Berlin engaged in tense discussions with the SMAD about whether Jews could be classified as resistance fighters, and not just as "victims of fascism" (Opfer des Faschismus). See Nachama, "Nach der Befreiung," 279.
124 *Der Weg*, Jg. 1, Nr. 2 (Mar. 8, 1946), 1. *Der Weg: Zeitschrift für Fragen des Judentums* commenced publication on Mar. 1, 1946 as the voice of the Berlin German Jewish community (*Gemeinde*).

trickle of wedding, birth, and Bar Mitzvah announcements, ads announcing departures for new homelands, and ads offering the services of re- or newly established Jewish doctors, dentists, lawyers, hoteliers, butchers, and antique dealers. Although Berlin had been a crucial entry point, the "first frontier for this Jewish migration from East-Central Europe,"[125] the center of Jewish DP life in occupied Germany had been shifting to large camps near Munich and Frankfurt.

GERMANS AND JEWS: VICTIMIZATION, SURVIVAL, AND MEMORY

Writing about the transitional period of occupation and adjustment, a German woman in Berlin asserted not at all untypically: "1947 our younger son was born and with him for me yet another great worry. It was irresponsible that in this terrible time of need I would put another child into the world."[126] Certainly, young Berlin women reported excitedly on their encounters with well-fed fraternizing GIs, but even the *Fräuleins*, Curt Riess caustically noted, "were only ruins of their former selves, just like the houses in which they now lived out their days."[127] Women's stories were more likely to highlight rape or the terrible hardships of motherhood at war's end: nursing a child through typhoid or diphtheria, the virulent dysentery epidemic of the first winter that killed sixty-five of every one hundred newborns,[128] pushing a wheelbarrow with a dead child in a cardboard box (for lack of coffins) through a bombed-out street, and harrowing accounts of mothers and children separated on the trek west, on the road, or in the packed refugee trains. Gabrielle Vallentin's 1955 account poignantly recalled the Berlin streetcars, where "One saw many such sad pictures; mothers who sat silent and rigid (*stumm und starr*), on their lap a cardboard box in which they had picked up their dead child from the hospital."[129]

In compelling counterpoint to the response of Jewish survivors, it seems that for German women the really quite brief but vivid experiences of victimization narrated over and over so dominated all memory as to seemingly block out all knowledge of what happened before. Another classic

---

125 Wolfgang Jacobmeyer, "Jüdische Überlebende als 'Displaced Persons': Untersuchungen zur Besatzungspolitik in den deutschen Westzonen und zur Zuwanderung osteuropäischer Juden 1945–1947," *Geschichte und Gesellschaft* 9 (1983): 432.

126 LAB Rep 240/2651/98.3. H. Gnädig.

127 Riess, *Berlin-Berlin*, 34. This view contrasted with more cheerful portrayals of women in western Germany, and surely had to do with the experience of mass rape. For fraternization stories, see the interviews in Heimatmuseum Charlottenburg catalog.

128 Maginnis, in *Military Government Journal*, makes this point, 344. On the toll exacted by epidemics, see *Berlin Kampf um Freiheit*, 10.

129 LAB Acc 2421. Vallentin, "Die Einnahme von Berlin," 28.

testimony: "The bombs in winter 1944–5 were bad, but the days that came after were almost impossible to bear."[130] Such sentiments of course were also interpreted more cynically: "What they claim not to have known yesterday they wish to forget again today!" a Jewish observer commented in 1950.[131] The *Frauenleben* page of the *Tagesspiegel* conveyed the ubiquitous despair about the conditions of infants and children: "It is after all the case that we have already broken the habit of the proverbial glance into the baby carriage, which supposedly no woman would deny herself, because what we see there so often makes us so sad."[132]

A few statistics can serve to provoke discussion about the different meanings attached to childbirth and babies by Germans and Jews in the interval immediately after the war's end. Berlin births, which had reached a quite unprecedented high of 74,903 (17.2 per 1,000 population) in 1940, plummeted in 1946 to 22,894 (7.3 per 1,000 population), a development that provoked much anxiety in the press and among medical and social welfare officials agonizing about the need to rebuild a healthy *Volk*.[133] In Bavaria, where there had "never been as many Jews as there were one year after the destruction of European Jewry,"[134] the 1946 Jewish birth rate was 29 per 1,000, versus 7.35 per 1,000 for Germans. The death rate for Jews was much lower, 1.6 versus 8.55, and, at a rate of 27.7 versus 2.8, there also were many more Jewish weddings. The recorded Jewish birth rate in Germany for 1948 – right before the proclamation of the state of Israel on May 16, 1948, and the easing of U.S. immigration regulations that eventually reduced the "problem" to small but highly visible proportions – was a whopping 35.8 per 1,000, which far exceeded anything the Germans had managed in the twentieth century.[135]

The point here is not to make facile comparisons on the basis of statistics that describe two very different populations that had undergone such different and incommensurate experiences and now lived under quite different

---

130 LAB, Rep. 240/2651, Gertrud Strobel, Nr. 131, p.1.

131 Dr. B. Sagalowitz, Report on trip to Germany, April 1950, *Archives of the Holocaust*, 9:377.

132 *Tagesspiegel* Nr. 29 (Nov. 23, 1945), 3.

133 LAB OMGUS 4/24–1/4; also *Berlin in Zahlen*, 128. In 1946, 166 marriages in which the man was Jewish, and 109 in which the woman was Jewish were celebrated (out of a total of 20,903). *Berlin in Zahlen*, 122.

134 Brenner, "East European and German Jews," 49–50. He adds, "Ironically, some places that the Nazis never had to make *judenrein* because Jews had never lived there were eventually populated by several hundreds, if not thousands, of Jews."

135 Jacobmeyer, "Jüdische Überlebende," 437. See also Brenner, *Nach dem Shoah*, 36. For comparative purposes: the German birthrate in 1933 stood at 14.7 (9.9 in Berlin); in the aftermath of the First World War it had reached 25.9 in 1920. Two-thirds of Jewish DPs eventually ended up in Israel; altogether about 100,000 went to the United States and 250,000 to Israel. On the reaction in Israel, see Segev, *The Seventh Million*.

circumstances. I am indeed talking about two groups – "Aryan" Germans (themselves hardly homogeneous) and mostly East European Jewish survivors – whose social histories were dramatically different but who quite unexpectedly (and ironically) found themselves in the same war-torn territory after May 1945. All these striking demographic markers can be related to empirical data, such as the "alarming disparity"[136] of sex ratios among Jewish survivors and the general German population (with a preponderance of males among Jews and women among Germans), the different age structure (most Jewish survivors were young), the higher rations (up to 2,500 calories a day), and guaranteed (if primitive) housing for Jews. Having sex and making babies was a good way to deal with the boredom and loneliness of leading a waiting life – *auf dem Weg* (on the way) – in the transit camps, and with the disappointment at the reality of the long-yearned-for liberation when, as was often and loudly pointed out by the DPs and their advocates, Jewish survivors were once again consigned to living in barracks behind barbed wire.[137]

The radically different reproductive and sexual patterns of Germans and Jews – unsurprising as they may be in light of their divergent social histories and circumstances – were at the time saturated with, and represented as carrying, highly charged political meaning and memory: a process that bears examination for all of us interested in gender, nation, and memory.[138] I would insist that these glaring statistics, and the intense scrutiny to which they were subjected by Germans, the Allies, and Jews, do speak to the blurred and complicated categorizing of victim, victor, and survivor in consciousness and memory after the war and the Holocaust.

Certainly, many Germans conceived of their experience as that of *Opfer*, and they did so in gendered and sexualized terms that focused on birth and abortion rates, infant and child mortality, and rape (as well as male impotence – one would have to look here at the competing images of the "poor infantryman" (*armer Landser*) and broken POW that populated the

---

136 Wahrhaftig, *Uprooted*, 54. As noted earlier, the approximate sex ratio in the DP camps was 60 percent male and 40 percent female; in Berlin at war's end, approximately the opposite (over 60 percent female) ratio applied.

137 See the poignant depictions in the German/Polish co-production "Lang ist Der Weg" (1947). For a critical analysis, see Cilly Kugelmann, "Lang ist der Weg: Eine jüdische-deutsche Film-Kooperation," *Fritz Bauer Institut Jahrbuch 1996*, 353–70.

138 Anthropologists have reminded us that "children are a crucial element in the representation of refugees" (Malkii, *Purity and Exile*, 11). Literary scholars are increasingly admonishing us to interrogate discourses of reproduction as responses to experiences of mass death and crises of futurity. Pressured by the AIDs crisis, queer theory has provided some of the most insightful analyses of cultures of reproduction in relation to loss and death. See Michael Warner, "Repro-culture," unpublished paper, Rutgers University, 1995.

postwar era).[139] I would argue that Jews – certainly in the published record and in political representations – looked to pregnancy and maternity as emblems of survival, as signs that they were more than just "victims" and precisely did not dwell obsessively on the traumatic recent past. DP culture placed a premium on collecting personal histories, on bearing witness for the future. Almost immediately after liberation the first memorials were raised and a day of remembrance proposed; theater, music, cabaret, and press in the refugee camps directly addressed the horrors of the war years. But in its preoccupation with the mundane everydayness of camp life and political association, with all its customary factionalism and bickering, daily life in the DP camps also fostered a kind of productive forgetting. Bearing children worked to mediate this continuous tension between remembering and forgetting. Babies, in their names and in their features, bore the traces of the past, of those who were dead and lost. Indeed, in some significant ways the bearing of new life was not only a signal of survival and hope but also an acknowledgment of the losses that had gone before. Jewish DPs were continually accused of manically "acting out" rather than "working through" their mourning, but because the Jewish religion prohibits naming children after the living, survivors did in their naming practices recognize the deaths of loved ones, whom they had for the most part not been able to bury or even confirm as dead. Certainly, children also represented the future, both imaginatively and in their ever-present demandingness. As the first issue of the DP newsletter *Unsre Hoffnung* stated: "We must turn to today and prepare a better tomorrow, a beautiful and a healthy tomorrow."[140]

In a sense, the German women who underwent abortions carried within their bodies a huge question mark about the future of the nation: Would Germany – as nation, as *Volk* – go on (*wieder hochkommen*), would it be reconstituted and how? None of that was clear at war's end. The question of national identity was indeed on the agenda. Mass rape at the point of defeat of course exacerbated such worries, with all their nationalist and racial implications; the attempt to restore German women's bodily (and genetic)

---

139 For discussions of postwar German male trauma, see Robert G. Moeller, " 'The Last Soldiers of the Great War' and Tales of Family Reunions in the Federal Republic of Germany," *Signs* 24 (1998): 129–45, and Frank Biess, "Survivors of Totalitarianism: Returning POWs and the Reconstruction of Masculine Citizenship in West Germany, 1945–1955," in Hanna Schissler, ed., *The Miracle Years: A Cultural History of West Germany* (Princeton, N.J., 2000), 57–82; also Biess, "The Protracted War: Returning POWs and the Making of East and West German Citizens, 1945–1955," Ph.D. diss., Brown University, 2000.

140 Dieter E. Kesper, "Unsere Hoffnung: Die Zeitung Überlebender des Holocaust im Eschweger Lager 1946" (Eschwege, 1996), in Fritz Bauer Archives, Frankfurt am Main. Newspaper of UNRRA camp in Eschwege, discovered in Heimatarchiv, Nr. 1. June 4, 1946. The published text is a translation of the original Yiddish.

integrity via abortion seemed a necessary precondition for national integrity. If German women were expressing uncertainty about the possibility of a viable nation, Jewish women survivors, living in a kind of extraterritoriality on both German and Allied soil, were prefiguring on their pregnant bodies a kind of imaginary nation that they hoped – at least this is the message of the sources – to realize in Palestine/Eretz Yisroel. Their babies had "red hot" political valence not only for the Allies but also for the Zionists who dominated political and cultural life in the DP camps. The DP press and political actions demanding open emigration from Germany to Palestine invariably foregrounded images of babies and baby carriages.[141] The DP camp newsletters, which reported on cultural life in the camps and on progress toward a Jewish state – written in Yiddish but printed in Roman characters because there was no Hebrew typeset available in occupied Germany – drove their message home with pages of marriage and birth announcements (along with notices searching for lost relatives or details on their death). Meyer Levin was particularly struck by the hectic din of the streets in Berlin, Vienna, and Munich, where DPs congregated and "DP women paraded their babies."[142] It is also crucial to keep in mind that this Jewish baby boom did not simply go on behind the gates of the DP camps, unnoticed by Germans. As the survivors settled in, both inside and outside the camps, Jews gave birth in German hospitals where they were treated by German physicians and nurses; some Jews hired German women as housekeepers and nannies; they sometimes (especially given the surplus of men) dated, had sex with, and even (in a much stigmatized minority of cases) married German women. DP mothers crisscrossed the streets of German towns with their baby carriages; the many Jewish marriages and births in the DP camps were registered in the German *Standesämter* (registry offices).[143]

What are we to make, then, of these contrasting statistics and reports about Jews procreating and Germans aborting – especially if direct comparisons are not appropriate? This leads me to some concluding speculations on the continually vexing question of remembering and forgetting, and its relationship to (gendered) nationmaking, particularly the distinct issues raised by the (increasingly acknowledged) prominence of women's voices in defining the "difficult legacy" of the early postwar period. In a context in which female bodies – raped, aborting, pregnant, mothering – are so clearly both public and private and where neither public nor private is clearly defined or bordered, these German and Jewish stories, taking place, after all,

---

141 See the extraordinary photo collection in *Ein Leben Aufs Neu: The Robinson Album. DP Lager, Juden auf deutschen Boden 1945–1948* (Vienna, 1995).
142 Levin, *In Search*, 398.   143 See Eder, "Regionalstudie."

on the same territory, if not really in the same (nonexistent) nation must, I think, be told together. They must be examined as contrasting survival strategies and differing responses to different wartime traumas, which were in turn given different public meanings by Germans, Allies, and Jews. But they also raise similar and provocative questions about the place of sexuality, pregnancy, childbirth, and motherhood in furnishing possible reconstructions of ethnic or national identity in the wake of Nazism and World War II (or other violent trauma, either individual or collective).

Both Germans and Jews turned to narratives and metaphors of fertility and maternity (in terms of both loss and possibility) to comprehend victimization and survival and to conceptualize and imagine future identities as nation or *Volk*. By looking comparatively at these disparate experiences and the discourses they generated, we can begin to usefully complicate our understanding of gender as a historical category, de-Germanize a German history in which multiculturalism or heterogeneity is too often seen as an invention of the very recent past, and cut through the persistent division between German history and the history of Jews in Germany that still characterizes our work on gender, nation, and memory.

5

Memory and the Narrative of Rape in Budapest and Vienna in 1945

ANDREA PETÖ

In an exhibition in Vienna on Austrian women's lives in 1945 there hung a remarkable picture taken in the Prater in January 1946. It was a photo of a sixteen-year-old girl who was raped and killed by five Russian soldiers, as stated in the police record. The picture is lyrical; even in death her face remains peaceful. Her dress is loose but explicitly suggests sexual violence. The blood on her face is not disturbing. Her hands are gracefully placed. The twisted body resembles both that of Christ being removed from the Cross and the famous picture of the half-naked Zoia Kosmonievskaja, the Soviet Saint.[1] Her body also melts smoothly into the background.

This picture disturbed me. Why exactly was this picture chosen for exhibition from the hundreds of other police photos with less aesthetic but more criminal attributes? It gave a face to the millions of women who died during the so-called peacetime. The photo also radiates a certain peaceful aspect of the victimization of that girl. This led me to do a comparative study of the rape cases of 1945 in Budapest and in Vienna.[2]

Both cities were liberated by the Red Army after heavy fighting. Soviet troops were stationed in Vienna until 1955, but historical and political discourse on the Second World War in these two countries was separated by the Iron Curtain and focused on differences while ignoring obvious similarities. That is the reason why analyzing a single historical event (rapes committed by the soldiers of the Red Army) and the ways in which this

This chapter was prepared with the help of the Central European University Junior Faculty Research Grant. An earlier version was published in "Stimmen des Schweigens. Erinnerungen an Vergewaltigungen in den Haupstädten des 'ersten Opfers' (Wien) und des 'letzten Verbündenten' Hitlers (Budapest)," *Zeitschrift für Geschichtwissenshaften* 10 (1999): 892–914.

1 Rosalinde Sartorti, "On the Making of Heroes, Heroines, and Saints," in Richard Stites, ed., *Culture and Entertainment in Wartime Russia* (Bloomington, Ind., 1995), 176–93.
2 Peter Eppel, ed., *Kriegsende in Wien: Frauenleben 1945*, Sonderaustellung des Historisches Museums der Stadt Wien (Vienna, 1995), 222.

event was discussed or suppressed in the national historiographies of the two countries might enrich our understanding of violence in the Second World War. I have relied very much on the work of Austrian historians when asking similar questions in my interviews in Budapest in order to produce comparative data.[3]

In February 1945, Budapest was liberated from the German occupation troops and their ally, the Hungarian army, saving the lives of the trapped population of Budapest, including the remaining Hungarian Jews. The communist discourse on the justice of war immediately became the dominant one, and it silenced the discourse on justice in war that addressed the atrocities committed by the soldiers of the Red Army while they were liberating Hungary.[4] Social silence on different levels is a common element of the narration of rape cases committed by Soviet soldiers in Budapest and Vienna. The silence itself became a historical fact, and this chapter analyzes who generated this silence on the different levels of narrative in different historical periods, and why. I use the term *narrative* in the sense of storytelling, which is useful in analyzing the phenomenon of rape in a military context. The narratives on rape were never personalized; if they became a part of the public memory, it was by constructing a single, unified group of victims from the women. This is the other reason why stories that emerged due to different historical circumstances should be analyzed in a comparative perspective.

In Hungary, the rapes committed by the soldiers of the Red Army represent a special case of social memory: of different levels of forgetting on the individual and social plane.[5] On the one hand, everybody "privately" knew that rapes had been committed by the Soviet soldiers. Private stories circulated that pointed a finger at the behavior of the Soviet soldiers and justified strong anti-Soviet sentiment. However, on the other hand, this historical fact became part of canonized Hungarian historical knowledge only after 1989, once communism had collapsed. In Austria, the dismantling of

---

3 Inspired by the systematic study by Austrian historians, I asked my friends and their parents about their grandmothers' and mothers' war experience. When I located three women and a man who were raped by the soldiers of the Red Army, I conducted long interviews with them following the introductory question: What happened in those days? The interviewees were interviewed in autumn 1997; they were No. 1, born 1926, journalist; No. 2, born about 1925, administrator; No. 3, born 1924 and died 1999, teacher; and No. 4, a man born 1925, mathematician. I did not use a tape recorder, which is counterproductive in Eastern Europe anyway, but made extensive notes.

4 Michael Walzer, *Just and Unjust Wars: A Moral Argument with Historical Illustrations*, 2d ed. (New York, 1977), 21.

5 For the detailed Hungarian case, see Andrea Petö, "Átvonuló hadsereg, maradandó trauma. Az 1945-ös budapesti nemi erőszak esetek emlékezete" (Passing Army, Lasting Trauma. The Memory of Soviet Rape Cases in Budapest), *Történelmi Szemle* 1–2 (1999): 85–107.

the myth of the first victim and the Waldheim affair led to alternative approaches to the history of the Second World War. I argue that the silence surrounding the massive number of rapes by Soviet soldiers is not a case of amnesia but rather a "conspiracy of silence." As Foucault said, "each regime has a system of truth." In the sometimes conflicting systems of narration on rape, we find different systems of truth depending on the time and the agent of narration. In both countries, collaboration with Nazi Germany served as a means of remembering, and the political discourse dominated by the Cold War colors the picture and determines the unfolding of silence. Specialists in contemporary history also have to wrestle with their "perceptual disadvantage," as Furet pointed out, that is, they are analyzing the very recent past, for which nearly all of us have our own "original" memory. In the "Rankean tradition" of history, the definition of science is that documents are used as sources. Even the "New History" did not give up entirely the "source-bound nature" and rationalist idealism of history writing.

In Central and Eastern Europe, the function of history has been even more problematic. History was defined in a framework through which one sought to find out or to reconstruct how an event actually happened. The event shaped the collective memory and in some cases even legitimized political structures. During the period of communism in Central and Eastern Europe, the past was distorted to legitimize communist rule, and history was reduced to an enforced forgetting. It is crucial to search for the origins and forms of the *mis-memoires*, to use Tony Judt's term.[6] The greatest danger for historical research today can be found in the unchangeable character of historical research. If the historians of the region are still caught in the trap of believing that they must find the "truer" history, there will always be a group of historians who are ready to produce history with the claim that theirs is "the 'truest' history." After the fall of communism in Eastern Europe, private knowledge and private histories were used to challenge official representations in the writing of contemporary history. The unauthorized forms of representations and everyday forms of resistance need to be placed under the focus of a comparative perspective, which provides another reason why linking Vienna and Budapest is useful.

The first systematic studies on the history of rape in countries under Soviet occupation saw as their main task to come up with a specific number of cases – to make the fact visible. We might have hoped to find military,

6 Tony Judt, "The Past Is Another Country: Myth and Memory in Postwar Europe," *Daedalus* 4 (1992): 83–118.

health, criminal, public-administration, or foreign-office documents in both Vienna and Budapest, but few written documents are available. For the Hungarian situation, we find reports by the county heads (*foispan*) about the atrocities, but they are not sufficient to allow us to reconstruct a countrywide picture. The collections of the Vienna archives for 1945 have been lost entirely; the Viennese police did not open their records to researchers. The documents relating to military affairs are in Moscow, where in the collection of the Ministry of Foreign Affairs we find sporadic letters of complaint about the behavior of Soviet soldiers written by both Austrian and Hungarian citizens. The documents of the Ministry of Health in Vienna were lost in the 1960s due to a reorganization of the archive, but in the Hungarian collections we find valuable reports by local health officials. The Budapest archive contains some pieces of information about the health officers and the hospitals' records.

In 1945, the victims of rape remained silent in Austria and in Hungary. After the Second World War, women were concerned with returning to normality, with re-establishing patriarchal society. The period of "matriarchy born in need" was over.[7] Regarding the sexual violence against women in 1945, we can be sure of one fact: Each and every actor – the victim, the perpetrator, the official, the policeman, the soldier – had a common interest in keeping silent about what had happened. The desire to keep the events hidden, combined with the uncertainty of the war years, makes the social phenomenon of rape difficult to study.

The most reliable sources are the reports of the public-health officials, which survived the war or had functioned even during wartime. The consequences of rape were pregnancy and sexually transmitted disease, but if neither of these biological consequences had occurred, then the rape itself remained unrecorded by the officials.

The rough estimates in the literature of the rapes committed by Soviet soldiers in Budapest are based on circumstantial evidence and vary from 5,000 to 200,000. It is widely accepted that 10 percent of the female population in Budapest was raped.[8] However, for the case of Budapest, I argue here that neither is it methodologically possible nor is it the task of this study to emphasize how the debate on the numbers has occupied the space that otherwise would be available for a relevant narrative.

7 See Andrea Pető, *Hungarian Women in Politics, 1945–1951* (Budapest, 2000), and Andrea Pető, "Women's Associations in Hungary: Mobilisation and Demobilisation, 1945–1951," in Claire Duchens and Irene Bandhauer Schöffmann, eds., *When the War Was Over: Women, War, and Peace in Europe 1940–1956* (Leicester, 2000), 132–46.
8 Krisztián Ungváry, *Budapest ostroma* (Siege of Budapest) (Budapest, 1998), 280.

After 1989, when the monopoly of antifascist historiography was questioned, more emphasis was placed on the discourse on the justice *of* war than that on justice *in* war. I argue that the uncertain, wild numbers circulating publicly allowed Hungary to redefine its national identity after the war, creating the myth that Hungary suffered at the hands of not only Nazi Germany but also the Red Army. In Hungary, mentioning the crimes (rape and looting) committed by the Red Army was viewed as a diversion of public attention away from the crimes committed by Hungary as a part of the Nazi war machine. Because the Red Army was stationed in Hungary permanently after 1945, the rapes became a nonissue at the level of public discourse. A predictable development of post-1989 Hungarian historiography has been to stress the martyrdom of Hungary, following the lead of scholarship written and published in the West by Hungarian émigrés who were far away not only from archival sources but also from the monolithic historical explanation of communist historiography. The uncertain, wild estimates allowed both Austria and Hungary to redefine their national identities after the war, creating for Austria the myth of the first victim to suffer not only from Nazi Germany but from the Red Army as well.

The history of war is a history of men in uniform. Women usually appear as victims or as civilians serving on the home front. We know very little about women soldiers, yet in Hungary women served in the military after 1939. There were more than 450,000 women in the German Wehrmacht, excluding those in the medical service. We also have uneven knowledge about women serving as combatants in the Red Army. Consequently, rapes committed against Soviet women soldiers by Hungarian males remained at the level of everyday narrative. However, determining when the war actually ended, and when the pre-existing norms and normality returned, is difficult. Is what happened to that girl in Vienna in January 1946 a war crime? Does it belong to the history of the Second World War? I argue that the answer is "yes."

In 1997, I interviewed women who had been living in Budapest and had been raped during and shortly after the heavy siege of the Hungarian capital in 1945. The interviewees were chosen at random, without an attempt to put together a representative sample. Due to the silence surrounding this phenomenon, I asked only questions of clarification: How did it happen? How many soldiers were there? Were there any consequences? To whom did they afterward tell what had happened to them? How did they explain to themselves the massive number of rapes committed by Soviet soldiers? During the interviews the women very briefly mentioned their own rape-related experiences; they then switched to narrating the experiences of others or to other stories. To my great surprise, their brief descriptions were very similar to the Austrian case.[9] Had there been attempts to collect the stories of raped women in eastern Poland or somewhere else in Eastern Europe, I believe the interviewers would have received very similar brief stories. It is not the event but the narration and silence surrounding the event that are worth analyzing. I use the interviews I conducted in Budapest to demonstrate how the silence around the rapes committed by the Red Army is a built-in element of the narration, an untold story of the Second World War.

THE IMPACT OF RAPE: THE MEDICAL NARRATIVE AFTER 1945

We assume that if a woman became pregnant as a consequence of rape, she opted for abortion. In Hungary, if a "Russian child" was born, the minister of health issued detailed instructions on how the child was to be taken into state custody at the state's cost. In cases where the children were born in the absence of the mother's husband, the husband had the right, upon his return, to send the child to an orphanage if the child was under twelve months of age and if he reported his intention to do so within three days of his return home.[10] In Vienna, the authorities followed Nazi eugenics practices, which stipulated mandatory abortion if the father belonged to another "race." The streets were covered with posters saying that if anybody wanted to be sure about the consequences of the war, they should contact the hospital. It was unclear whether the judicial system of the Austrian First Republic or that of the Third Reich was applicable. Consequently, the mayor's office received letters from gynecologists asking what they should do to help "women in trouble." The notorious paragraph 144, which allowed compulsory sterilization for the purity of the race, was still in force.[11]

The rapes committed by Soviet soldiers led to a change in the Hungarian practice of reproductive rights and in the narrative on reproductive rights,

---

9 Irene Bandhauer Schöffmann and Ela Hornung, "Vom 'Dritten Reich' zur Zweiten Republik: Frauen im Wien der Nachkriegszeit," in David F. Good, Margarete Grandner, and Mary Jo Maynes, eds., *Frauen in Österreich: Beiträge zu ihrer Situation im 19. und 20. Jahrhundert* (Vienna, 1994), 232; and Marianna Baumgartner, "Zwischen Mythos und Realität. Die Nachkriegsvergewaltigungen im sowjetisch besetzten Mostviertel," *Zeitschrift für Landeskunde von Niederösterreich* 2 (1993): 80.

10 Budapest Főváros Levéltára (Archive of City of Budapest), XXVI. 1117. Budapest Székesfovárosi Anya és Kisdedvédelmi Intézet iratai, 97/1946. 8540/1945. I. 3.sz. népjóléti minisztériumi rendelet 1946. január 14.

11 Maria Mesner, *Frauensache? Zur Auseinandersetzung um den Schwangerschaftsabbruch in Österreich nach 1945*, Veröffentlichungen des Ludwig-Boltzmann-Instituts für Geschichte der Gesellschaftswissenschaften, vol. 23 (Vienna, 1994), 36.

which also helped to erase the event from both social and individual memory. The right to choose was accepted in a wider, even religious context. In Budapest, there was the possibility of free, officially approved abortion, which changed how women related to their own bodies. After 1945, there was no dramatic change in the birthrate in Budapest,[12] just a slight increase, which is a normal demographic trend after war. Changes in the birthrate thus will not tell us about the number of rapes.[13] On February 14, 1945, the Budapest National Council suspended the ban on abortion for four months.[14] This upset the equilibrium that had existed previously between the total ban on abortion dating from 1878 and the existing practice whereby abortion was available in order to save the woman's life or where the pregnancy was a consequence of rape. In 1945, Hungarian gynecologists protested that they were obliged to perform abortions against their convictions. We see that this pronatalist argumentation also was supported by gynecologists who previously had run lucrative private abortion clinics. The powerful Hungarian Catholic Church also equated the Soviets with evil and so applied the pro-life principle selectively. However, this opened the door to speaking about women's decisions concerning pregnancies that had resulted from an unpunished crime.[15]

The way in which the decisions of the National Council were publicized in Hungary also increased the secrecy surrounding abortion. The directors of the hospitals were informed in a euphemistic letter that "because of the present serious situation" abortion may be carried out in order to "give proper help to women in trouble."[16] The municipal health officer was expected to produce a certificate that officially authorized the rape victim to go to the hospital for an abortion. After the gynecologist confirmed the pregnancy, women were expected to visit local health officers for the abortion permit. From the minutes of such visits, we can reconstruct a typical case, that of a twenty-six-year-old woman from the small village of

---

12 Budapest Fõváros Levéltára. XXI. 515. b. Reports of the public health officer of Budapest.

13 In Berlin, research has suggested that 20 percent of raped women became pregnant. See Helke Sander and Barbara Johr, *Befreier und Befreite: Krieg, Verwaltigung, Kinder* (Munich, 1992), 52.

14 Thanks for the help of György Németh who shared his ideas and insights about the history of abortion in Hungary. Budapesti Nemzeti Bizottság jegyzõkönyvei 1945–1946 (Minutes of the Budapest National Council) (Budapest, 1976), 33.

15 Concerning the impact of liberalizing abortion in Hungary upon legislation and sexual practices, see Andrea Petõ, "Abortõr perek és 'bajba jutott nok' 1952-ben" (Trials against illegally performed abortions and "women in trouble" in 1952), in Nagy Beata, ed., *Nõk a modern a társadalomban szerk* (Debrecen, 2001).

16 Gyõr Megyei Levéltár Nemzeti Biztottság iratai 1945. április 30. (Documents of the National Council in Gyõr). A copy of the decision of the National Council.

Lébény. This represents a different sort of narrative, a translation of women's experience to the level of medical narrative:[17]

This year on 18 June at 10:00 P.M. I was on my way home from my dressmaker. Two Russian soldiers stopped and raped me. Exactly four weeks after that at 8:00 P.M. I was cycling home parallel to the railway, when I met a Russian who wanted to take my bicycle. I started to cry, then he left with me my bicycle but he raped me. My last menstruation was on 7 June, which usually lasts for 3–4 days and comes regularly every four to six weeks. My expected menstruation did not arrive, and I felt myself pregnant. As I do not want to have a baby against my will, I hereby am applying for a certificate to go to the hospital to get rid of my pregnancy.[18]

This type of medical narration, chosen from more than a dozen such "minutes," illustrates the acceptable, official narrative. Yet in the extensive literature on abortion legislation the analysis of the cause of this major change is still missing; consequence is treated as cause.

The result of the rapes in Vienna and Budapest was a dramatic increase in sexually transmitted diseases. The number of infected women in Vienna doubled; in Budapest, it tripled. Yet not every sexual contact resulted in disease. A comprehensive investigation in Melk, Austria, showed that 30 percent of the total number of women raped were reported to the health authorities as infected.[19] The detailed records of sexually transmitted disease are missing; however, sexually transmitted diseases generally meant two illnesses, gonorrhea and syphilis. In the Soviet Zone in Austria, we see a dramatic increase in the milder form of venereal disease, gonorrhea. This fact can be explained only by the presence of the Red Army, because the local men were mostly absent. Hungary entered the war late, and drafted Hungarian soldiers were not allowed to return home. In the interviews, all the women expressed concern about possible infection, which suggests that this topic had been discussed widely before the final military battles had begun and that the women had been afraid.[20] In the Western zones in Austria, penicillin was readily available and the soldiers often used condoms, which were part of the standard military issue; therefore, sexual contact, which may or may not have reached the same levels as in the Soviet zone, did not cause a dramatic change in the public health of the occupied country. The

---

17 For a social-linguistic analysis of abortion petition, see Atina Grossmann, "A Question of Silence: The Rape of German Women by Occupation Soldiers," in Robert G. Moeller, ed., *West Germany Under Construction: Politics, Society, and Culture in the Adenauer Era* (Ann Arbor, Mich., 1997), 37–9, 46–9.

18 Győr megyei Tisztifőorvos iratai 245/1845. tfo .sz. (Documents of the Health Officer in Győr).

19 Baumgartner, "Zwischen Mythos und Realität," 80.

20 Interviews nos. 2, 3.

soldiers of the Red Army, who had been on the move since 1943 without proper medical facilities, used neither penicillin nor condoms.

Reports of venereal disease are available for Vienna beginning in 1938, after the German occupation and after the Soviet occupation. The reports of the Inter-Allied Commission revealed how the Soviet health authorities simply denied the existence of venereal disease among Soviet soldiers.[21]

The minister of health during Hungary's first postwar government opted for very strict regulation of sexually transmitted diseases.[22] The reporting, distribution of medication, and medical surveillance of sexually transmitted diseases were placed under strict medical control. The necessary health care was free because some "respectable women" also were infected. Thus, when it really became a mass phenomenon, the moral values attached to sexually transmitted diseases changed. This also transformed the view of prostitution, which had previously been the main avenue for the transmission. The alarming increase in sexually transmitted disease by 1946 provided an official argument for strict administrative control. Nevertheless, in 1947, 200,000 cases of venereal disease were reported in Hungary, after the majority of prisoners of war had returned home.[23]

Sexually transmitted disease thus became a public-health issue. The creation of a national network of institutions for treating venereal disease was one of the consequences of the Soviet occupation. The circumstances whereby women had been infected and who had infected them were not mentioned; only the "result" – the disease – was important. Responsibility thus was conveniently placed on women's shoulders. Rape was dealt with not as a moral but as a medical matter, which was controlled and institutionalized. The act, the rape, was shrouded in social silence. The consequence of rape was medicalization and the establishment of treatment institutions.

NARRATION DIVIDED ALONG POLITICAL LINES

The politics of memory is simultaneously an economy of emotions because remembering and coping are closely connected. In the stories of the women I interviewed in Budapest, we find an ideological dividing line. The families

---

21 Part V/A Medical Report. Siegfried Beer and Eduard G. Staudinger, "Die 'Vienna Mission' der Westalliierten im Juni 1945," in Ferdinand Oppl and Karl Fischer, eds., *Studien zur Wiener Geschichte: Jahrbuch des Vereins für Geschichte der Stadt Wien* 50 (Vienna, 1994): 390–1.

22 Magyar Országos Levéltár Népjóléti Miniszterium iratai 6. tétel (Hungarian National Archive, Budapest, Documents of the Ministry of Welfare).

23 György Gortvay, "Egészségvédelem" (Health protection), in Rostás Ilona, ed., *A szociális titkárok első továbbképzési tanfolyamának tananyaga* (Budapest, 1947), 179. The pre-1945 figures on STD are not high in comparison with the 1945 data.

of the Left felt a nearly religious enthusiasm for the approaching Soviets.[24]
For one woman interviewed, a member of the underground communist
movement and a victim of the Nazi regime, being raped by a Soviet soldier
was even more traumatic because she had nurtured illusions about the "New
Soviet Man." She and those like her had been waiting for the "liberators"
to arrive.[25] Even Mátyás Rákosi, the leader of the Hungarian Communist
Party, complained to Dimitrov, the leader of the Comintern, that the orgy of
rape by the Soviet soldiers had destroyed the reputation of the young Communist Party; this was the most important issue for the ambitious communist
politician who had just returned from Moscow.[26]

For women not of the Left, who had expected the horror, it came just as
they had imagined it. In both cases, however, the reaction was silence. Any
negative comments about the Soviet army became highly politicized during
the Cold War. The women whom I interviewed told their own stories in
the impersonal third person; they described what the Soviets did to others,
not to them. As one of them told me: "The weary soldiers entered the
flat and they found a woman there. What do you think happened next?"[27]
Their other, positive experiences with the Soviets – for example, soldiers
distributing bread to the hungry population of Budapest – were described
in the first person.[28] In Vienna, the findings of oral-history research also
suggest that women were sublimating the experience of rape; they referred
to Hollywood movies such as *Dr. Zhivago* or *Gone with the Wind*, distancing themselves from their own experience.[29] As in Budapest, in Vienna,
too, it was those women with a leftist background or those who had been
humiliated because of their poverty who volunteered to accompany the despised Soviet soldiers. Thus, in both cities we find the same divide as far as
narration is concerned.[30]

THE NARRATION OF PROTECTION

Rape affects the position of a woman in the community if the fact becomes
known. In both Budapest and Vienna, in the interviews and according to
public wisdom, the topos of the Soviet soldier is the drunken, armed, and

---

24 For example, the Soviet pavilion of the Budapest International Fair had fallen victim to the relic
    collectors of the underground communist movement in 1941. See Politikatörténeti Intézet Levéltára
    (Archive of the Institute of Political History), Budapest, 867. f. 1/k-91.
25 Interview no. 1.
26 Dokumentumok Rákositól Rákosiról. Selected by Henrik Vass (Documents on Rákosi) *Múltunk*
    1991/2–3, p. 247, 1945. február 19-i levél (Letter of Feb. 19, 1945).
27 Interview no. 3.   28 Interviews nos. 1, 2.
29 Schöffmann and Hornung, "Vom 'Dritten Reich' zur Zweiten Republik," 233.
30 Ibid., 241.

dangerous foreigner, the Other, the enemy. During the siege individual protection strategies proved the most successful. The interviewees blamed neither men nor politics for the rapes. From their stories we know that girls' faces were darkened with dirt, but this did not necessarily help them escape violence.[31] This part of the narration was the most upbeat, describing the individual tricks they employed in hopes of fooling the soldiers. In his recently published memoirs, Mátyás Rákosi, the leader of the Hungarian Communist Party, wrote about the magical protective power of trousers: "Lots of women were wearing clumsy trousers; I was told that women wearing trousers were hated by the Russians."[32] In the ice-cold winter during the weeks of siege, nearly everybody wore trousers. Cross-dressing was not some innocent trick because women wearing men's clothing risked being immediately shot as deserters. If they had the choice, women did not go into the street, or if they did, they disguised themselves as old women. Women hid, pretended to be ill, feigned venereal disease with the help of iodine, feigned menstruation with red ink, or pretended to have tuberculosis.[33] As one of the women interviewed told me: "My mother dressed me as an old woman, put dirt on my face in the hope that the Russians would not hurt a woman very similar to their mothers."[34] Others lay hidden under the bed or asked sick family members to stay in bed to discourage soldiers from searching further. Feigning menstruation or applying dirt was not always sufficient, however. Living in communities offered a higher level of security than did living alone. In Budapest, families, relatives, and acquaintances lived together in cellars – "we survived the siege in a big cellar, when the Russians came in, we hid the girls and women" – but this was not enough to protect them.[35] If rape occurred, the community played an important role in healing the wounds.[36]

Armed resistance offered maximum results with maximum risk. Self-defense was not an acceptable defense according to Soviet army regulations and, to make the distinction even more obvious, Soviet soldiers were not even treated in Hungarian medical institutions.[37] The principle of justified self-defense was not recognized by the Soviet military courts, so those who

---

31 Interviews nos. 2, 4.
32 Mátyás Rákosi, *Visszaemlékezések: 1940–1956* (Memoirs, 1940–1956), ed. István Feitl, Márta Gellériné Lázár, and Levente Sipos, 2 vols. (Budapest, 1997), 1:160.
33 Schöffmann and Hornung, "Vom 'Dritten Reich' zur Zweiten Republik," 230.
34 Interview no. 2.   35 Interview no. 3.
36 Irene Bandhauer-Schöffmann and Ela Hornung, "Der Topos des Sowjetischen Soldaten," in Siegwald Ganglmair, ed., *Lebensgeschichtliche Interviews mit Frauen in Dokumentationsarchiv des österreichen Wiederstandes* (yearbook) (1995): 31.
37 Budapest Fõváros Levéltára (Archive of Budapest) XXVI.1102. Rókus Kórház irata (Files of Rokus Hospital) 800/1945. 1945. február 16-i tisztiorvosi leirat (Memorandum by the health officer on Feb. 16, 1945).

attacked Soviet soldiers faced an immediate death sentence or thirty years' imprisonment.[38]

In 1945, there was no possibility for a victim to lodge a complaint in court against a member of the victorious Red Army. The invading Soviets brought their own court system. In cases of rape, the psychological experience of women and the possibilities of judicial narration do not necessarily match, even in peacetime. If the case reached the court, the woman had to recount the story, had to remember what happened. She had to construct a coherent narrative of her story for the outside world using vocabulary acceptable to the outside world.[39]

The rapes should have been described at the level of the family, but this is the level that was silenced. As the interviewees told me, they did not want to "bother" their male partners with this experience. However, as Primo Levi pointed out, "we speak also because we are invited to do so,"[40] and women were not invited to speak. The loyalty of women to men prevented them from working through the experience. Women whom I interviewed were cautious about translating their experiences onto a personal level. They kept it hidden if the experience of rape questioned their belief in men or in heterosexuality. These stories are simple; the same terms and idioms are repeated no matter where the interview took place. About the actual physical act of rape, women remained silent. "I was lucky," said one of the interviewees, "I did not become either pregnant or sick."[41] The experience remained enclosed within the female body. The experiences of these women remained unrecorded in official historical sources and thus invisible to historians. The women did not consider what happened to them remarkable or unique: "This was not so unique that it would be worth telling," was the excuse one woman gave while she buried this experience deep within herself.

EXPLANATORY FRAMEWORKS

The myths of heterosexual relationships in Europe are loyalty, faithfulness, security, and human progress. The silence of women is a crucial element in any explanatory framework given to the rapes during the Second World War.

---

38 Imre Kovács, *Magyarország megszállása* (Occupation of Hungary) (Budapest, 1990), 246.
39 John Forrester, "Rape, Seduction, Psychoanalysis," in Sylvana Tomaselli and Roy Porter, eds., *Rape: An Historical and Cultural Enquiry* (Oxford, 1986), 72.
40 Primo Levi, *The Drowned and the Saved* (New York, 1989), 150.
41 Interview no. 1.

Men accept sexual violence if it is narrated within either of two frameworks: the archaic-patriarchal or the ideological-patriarchal. In war, women and daughters are expected to be loyal to men, but men are loyal only to their nation and to the army protecting their nation. In this archaic-patriarchal explanatory framework, the woman, as the property of the enemy soldier, is taken by the victor. By raping the women of the enemy, the victorious soldier "destroys" the property of the enemy. The victims thus must keep silent about what happened to them because it was not they but their male kin who were the real victims. Retelling the story simply means giving an extra victory to the perpetrators. Loyalty to their men was stronger than their wish to come to terms with the experience of horror. In 1945, respectability and peace were more important than anything else. Had women tried to understand the experience on their own terms, they would have faced the sanctions of the male world because many men consider rape a part of war, a horrible reality. In their accounts, women replicated the male thought patterns – that is, the justification that "war is war," the most common explanatory factor mentioned in my interviews.[42] However, the previous occupation of Hungary by the Romanian Entente forces in 1919 did not result in mass rape, so vague, rationalizing arguments about the general characteristics of war were not voiced either, despite the fact that there had been equal prejudice against the Romanian army.

The explanation of rape also could be framed in ideological propaganda.[43] The army and the nation represent masculine strength. In the vocabulary describing military activity, expressions relating to sexuality are very often used. During the First World War, France accused Germany of the "Rape of Belgium," using sexual violence as a metaphor for a military campaign against an unprepared country.[44] This does not mean that every soldier commits rape, but it does mean that a soldier may rape as the ultimate proof of his masculinity and loyalty to his army. In war, there is enough opportunity to prove personal bravery. The body of a woman represents the whole community from which the woman comes, so rape signifies victory over the whole community.

EXPLANATIONS IN WAR

Rape was always part of the weaponry of warfare in Europe, and the history of war was always a male narrative. On the level of propaganda, women's

42 Ibid.
43 Erika M. Hoerning, "The Myth of Female Loyalty," *Journal of Psychohistory* 16, no. 1 (1988): 38.
44 See Roy Porter, "Does Rape Have a Historical Meaning?" in Tomaselli and Porter, eds., *Rape*, 232.

achievements on the home front were never comparable to the actions of the heroic soldiers. Women behind the front were expected to protect the family, the home. Violence against the woman's body was not discussed openly because women themselves were blamed for rape: They had not been skillful enough to hide as had their more successful comrades. Silence was to be secured even at the price of murder. A repeated motif in the interviews was a story the women were told at the time about an old man who killed his daughters after they had been raped in order to preserve moral purity and to eliminate the objects of the rape.[45] The stories consisted of topoi from mythological scenes, so they are not where we should search for the truth about the motives of the perpetrators; what is important is why the women thought it was imperative to tell us this story. It was not a narrative of the event that actually took place but rather a story borrowed from somebody else.

The interviews in Budapest revealed the topos of the Soviet soldier as the drunken, armed, and dangerous foreigner, the "Other."[46] This reinforced the sense of Hungary as a borderland, created by the propaganda that it was here that the barbarian East met the civilized West. The role of the protector of Western civilization is one of the well-known historical stereotypes in the case of mostly Catholic countries (Poland, Croatia, Hungary) with a centuries-long tradition of fighting Moslem, "oriental" enemies, such as the Ottomans or Mongols. Gyula Szekfû pointed out that the occupation of Hungary by the Red Army was very similar to the occupation of Hungary by the Ottoman Turks in the sixteenth century: A different, alien culture and political structure was imposed on Hungary by military force after a military defeat.[47] The women of Budapest did not blame the men for what happened to them. In the interviews they also did not mention the short-sighted decisions of the politicians that led to the situation whereby the Soviet soldiers ruled the bodies of women.

There could have been very few doubts about the behavior of the Red Army during occupation for those who had read Ilja Ehrenburg's 1942 manifesto: "Kill! Kill! In the German race there is nothing but evil. Use force and break the racial pride of these Germanic women. Take them as your lawful booty . . . you gallant soldiers of the Red Army!"[48] Nazi war propaganda also had prepared the population for what would happen if the Soviet army won. The Hungarian army fought under the military

---

45 Interview no. 2.   46 Ibid.
47 Gyula Szekfu, *Forradalom utan* (After Revolution) (Budapest, 1947). My thanks to Gábor Gyáni for this reference.
48 Susan Brownmiller, *Against Our Will: Men, Women, and Rape* (New York, 1975), 70.

command of the German army, so the difference between the nations fighting in the occupational Nazi army was blurred in Soviet propaganda. In the case of the Red Army, there also was the politically driven differentiation between real Soviet and other units, such as the Bulgarian or Romanian.[49] Both Nazi Germany and the Hungary of the Horthy regime had prepared the population so that they would not forget their first encounter with the Red Army. Consequently, over fifty years after the event women told their stories as if they were scenes from movies, as if they were somebody else's experiences. The behavior of the Soviet soldiers confirmed the propaganda of the Horthy regime, which frightened the middle classes with the idea that in the Soviet Union women were common property.[50] As one victim said: "Goebbels had been telling us for years that the Russians would rape us.... We couldn't bear the thought that [he] might be right after all."[51] The most influential image in the newsreel was that of the rude Asian-looking soldiers, and when this was actually played out in reality it had an enormous impact.[52]

The fear of the Hungarian population was based on ethnic difference, on fear of the coming "Mongols," as one woman of middle-class origin expressed it. The memory of the fateful invasion of Hungary by the Mongol hordes in 1241–2, which is still a vivid part of the national memory, merged with the memory of the occupation of Hungary by the Tsarist army in 1849. The only written source on the rapes committed during the Mongol occupation is the chronicle by Rogerius, a monk who survived and reported the military campaign dressed as a Mongol soldier. He pointed out not only the genocidal element of the occupation, that the Mongols killed everybody regardless of gender or age for disciplinary purposes, but also that the Mongols especially "found pleasure" in humiliating women.[53] After the occupation in 1945, Soviet propaganda tried to counterbalance this racial element by emphasizing the Slavic character of the Red Army and erecting liberation monuments. In both Hungary and Austria, the population's fear was based on ethnic difference. Although ethnic difference was the common

---

49 Gyula Horn, the Prime Minister of Hungary from 1994 to 1998, and the president of the Hungarian Socialist Party, differentiated in his autobiography between the good Russian soldiers and the bad Romanian soldiers serving together in the Red Army. According to him, the latter were those who committed rape. Gyula Horn, *Cölöpök* (Columns) (Budapest, Zenit Könyvek, 1991), 71. I am greatful to Krisztián Ungváry for this reference.

50 Interview no. 2.   51 Hoerning, "Myth of Female Loyalty," 22.

52 Grossmann, "Question of Silence," 41.

53 See a detailed interpretation of the Mongol invasion in the standard history of Hungary published several times in the 1930s: Hóman Bálint and Szekfû Gyula, *Magyar történet* (Hungarian History), 8 vols. (Budapest, n.d.), 2:135–44.

element, in Hungary the effective anticommunist propaganda was more important, whereas in Vienna racial difference set the tone. The topos of the irresistible Asian horde threatening the civilized West was combined with the threat of communism.

In his book *The Russians in Germany*, Norman Naimark analyzed the rapes committed by Soviet soldiers in the Soviet occupation zone of Germany.[54] He believes that in Hungary the Soviet soldiers were given more freedom to rape than in other countries, but this was still not comparable to Germany, according to the data by Liebman and Michelson. In his explanation, Naimark points out that in Hungary there was no space for Slavic solidarity and that the Hungarians actively took part in the war against the Soviet Union. This argument was often used by those rape victims whom I met and who were close to the Left. "It happened as a revenge for the crimes committed by the Hungarian soldiers in the Soviet Union" – that was the explanation given by one of the Hungarian Communist women interviewed.[55] She rationalized her private history on the politicized public level within the left-wing political explanatory framework. Naimark also points to the importance of personal revenge. The Soviet soldiers saw the higher Hungarian living standards and wanted retribution.

The character of the Soviet army also may have been an explanatory factor. The women interviewed who did not share a left-wing political orientation pointed to the similarity of the Red Army with the Mongol hordes. The front itself was considered to be the most dangerous for women because soldiers facing the threat of death often engaged in improper behavior. Others, like Susan Brownmiller in her classic study, quote the Cold War historian Cornelius Ryan, who pointed out that it was those soldiers who left their own regular fighting units who were the most lenient toward such activity.[56] Zoltan Vas, the Communist mayor of Budapest in 1945, also discouraged those prominent male politicians who had complained about the rapes, saying that this was only a temporary phenomenon, that these were the fighting troops, that elite occupation units were on their way.[57] This distinction was not important to the women I interviewed; they viewed the Red Army as a single, dangerous entity: "The first Russians came in. They were Tatars."[58]

---

54 Norman M. Naimark, *The Russians in Germany: A History of the Soviet Zone of Occupation, 1945–1949* (Cambridge, Mass., 1995), 70.
55 Interview no. 1.
56 Cornelius Ryan, *The Last Battle* (London, 1966), quoted in Susan Brownmiller, *Against Our Will*, 66–7.
57 Kovács, *Magyarország megszállása*, 270.   58 Interview no. 2.

THE END OF SILENCE: FEMINISM AND DEMOCRACY

The public silence about rape has been broken. Brownmiller's book first analyzed rape as war waged by men against women.[59] The first feminist historical investigations in Europe were attempts in Germany to recover the silenced chapters of the war within the general framework of rethinking the history of the Second World War.[60] A new language was born with the second wave of feminism, which describes rape in a different framework.[61] Terminology developed in the late 1970s was used retrospectively to describe women's experiences. Language was created later, decades after the event had taken place, and applied by feminist researchers. Because of this time gap we have to be very careful when using this language to analyze women's narratives. In postwar societies, it was a paradigm of moral decency and respectability that prevailed, not the present-day rape paradigm born of the second wave of feminism, where the woman's consent plays a crucial role.

This twin discourse on rape caused methodological problems. First, because of the lack of written records we have to rely on oral testimony when doing research. The violence against women's bodies can be analyzed only if the woman, the victim, tells us what she was thinking at the moment the event occurred. Our task in the future will be to analyze who narrates or keeps the story silent and why. In the case of the rapes committed by Soviet soldiers, the task is to analyze the interaction among the different levels of silence. The wider acceptance of oral history as a method and as a creator of knowledge also was important. Second, we need an extra level of sensitivity as feminist researchers. The problem for feminists is not necessarily the form of survey or the generation of statistical data "but the ways in which research participants are treated and the care with which researchers attempt to represent the lived experience of the research participants."[62] Compared with the feminists of the second wave, whose terms and concepts we use when discussing sexual violence, the relationship to women's sexuality was different. They distanced themselves from their own bodies.

In Austria, historians of the second wave began to collect what written documents were available and to show the meaning of the Soviet occupation for women, who comprised the majority of the postwar population.

---

59 Brownmiller, *Against Our Will*.

60 Sander and Johr, *Befreier und Befreite*; Stuart Liebman and Annette Michelson, "After the Fall: Women in the House of the Hangmen," *October* 72 (spring 1995): 5–14.

61 Verena Fiegl, *Der Krieg gegen die Frauen: Zum Zusammenhang von Sexismus und Militarismus* (Bielefeld, 1990).

62 Liz Kell, Sheila Burton, and Linda Reagan, "Researching Women's Lives or Studying Women's Oppression: Reflections on What Constitutes Feminist Research," in Mary Jo Maynard, Jane Purvis, and Francis Taylor, eds., *Researching Women's Lives from a Feminist Perspective* (Bristol, 1994), 35.

Investigating everyday life under occupation led them to redefine the myth of Austria as the first victim. Austrian left-wing historians struggled with the contradiction that, if Austria was the first victim and had nothing to do with Nazism as such, how was it that the liberating Soviet soldiers behaved as they did. In comprehensive regional studies, each and every citizen of a particular district was interviewed about his or her experience of the Soviet occupation. Very few women admitted they were rape victims. Instead, they explained in detail that they knew someone to whom this had happened.[63] Surprisingly, men were more eager to tell the story of dishonor in their own family than were women. Again rape, or the narration of rape, became a part of the history of men's war.

The linguistic opposition in the stories – "liberation of Hungary" versus "occupation of Hungary" – reflects the differing political standpoints. The moment of liberation by the Red Army served as lieux de memoires, to use Pierre Nora's term. The official celebration of the liberation of the country, stressing the official image of the heroic Red Army, was counterbalanced by the private counter-memory of 1945 lived as an embodied experience of the survivors. Investigating the history of everyday life, a new trend in Hungarian historiography, led some historians to publish a collection of documents on the liberation of the country. However, this thorough and comprehensive two-volume collection was banned in 1970. Because, as one of the editors told me, a document from a small Hungarian city, Kisujsszallas, where the city council had considered setting up a brothel, argued that "according to its knowledge there were armies of women who will be willing to put themselves at the disposal of the Russians."[64] In Hungary, historical re-evaluation started after 1989, when the Red Army had left the country.[65] Émigré Hungarian historians had been trying to write the missing chapters of the history of the Second World War, focusing mainly on the atrocities committed by Soviet soldiers and the heroic self-sacrificing character of the Second Hungarian Army, which also was the subject of a long and influential documentary film that portrayed the heroism of the Hungarian soldiers fighting as a part of the German war machine.

After 1989 and the collapse of communism, the forgotten past was used as the basis of a new legitimacy, which nowadays has become history it-self. Films, reburials, and recorded memories of the survivors presented to a wider public were all important aspects of analyzing the different lenses

63 Interviews nos. 2, 3.
64 Elek Karsai and Magda Somlyai, eds., Sorsforduló (Change in Life), 2 vols. (Budapest, 1970), 1:223.
65 Krisztián Ungváry, "Szovjet jogsértések Magyarországon" (Violation of Hungarian Laws by the Soviets), Magyar Nemzet, Nov. 29, 1997, 16.

through which history can be viewed. Private knowledge and private histories were used to challenge official representations.[66] Before 1989, novels by Alain Polcz and Gyorgy Konrad, opponents of the forced amnesia of the communist regime, kept alive the memory of the rapes,[67] but the individual memories of women about their rape experience had not been collected. Revising history is a permanent process in which only the groups involved change, and it is these groups which revise memories and rewrite history. The violence of the Red Army is one of the issues that was instrumentalized by historians in political–ideological debates.

After the collapse of the Soviet Union as a military world power, space opened up for rewriting of the military history of Budapest, something that also was necessary to dismantle the official mythology surrounding the heroic Russian army. Re-evaluation of the role of the Hungarian army presents stories in the same framework: victimology. Who is the most honored victim? In this "new" narrative framework, the impersonal, instrumentalized narration of rape is crucial to maintaining the coherence of the historical explanation in this verbal civil war now being waged in what no longer is a bipolar world.[68]

CONCLUSION

The real impact of the rapes committed by the Soviet soldiers was psychological. The judicial systems of the occupied countries collapsed, and the resulting power vacuum did not encourage the submission of legal complaints against the victorious occupying army. Crimes remained unpunished. Uncertainty and powerlessness increased the feeling of subordination because the Soviet army represented an independent legal entity in the occupied territory. A psychological pattern was formed: If we keep silent we can pretend that "that" event did not happen at all.

The Pope recently canonized a Hungarian bishop, Bishop Apor, who was shot and killed in Pannonhalma while trying to protect women who were hiding from drunken Soviet soldiers in the cellar of his monastery. A well-known Hungarian historian pointed out the martyrdom the bishop suffered on behalf of "hundreds of thousands of dishonored Hungarian women."[69] Neither the suffering of women nor the contribution of the

66 See also Andrea Petö, "Európa minding máshol van" (Europe is always somewhere else), *Rubicon* 5–6 (1997): 67–9.

67 Alain Polcz, *Asszony a fronton* (Budapest, 1991); and Gyorgy Konrad, *Cinkos* (Budapest, 1983).

68 Ungváry, *Budapest ostroma*, 275–82.

69 Grgely Jenö, "Boldog Apor Vilmos" (Canonized Apor Vilmos), *Magyar Hírlap*, Nov. 10, 1997, 13.

Catholic Church in keeping the feeling of being "dishonored" alive was mentioned. The figure of the canonized bishop was inflated into that of a heroic male figure, whereas the women were reduced to powerless victims dependent on desexualized male protection. This, it would seem, confirms my argument that the definitions of rape and the honor of women were determined by men, and that hundreds of thousands of men will not hesitate to instrumentalize rape for their own or for national purposes.

6

"Going Home"

The Personal Adjustment of British and American Servicemen after the War

JOANNA BOURKE

War requires some men to commit acts of exceptional violence. They are sent to the front lines not primarily to die for their country, but to kill for it. They are executioners as well as victims, and, as such, inspire fear. For all men – whether they belong to the minority who are required to engage in front-line combat or whether they are the majority working behind the scenes in "support roles" – war disrupts lives in unprecedented ways. Without a doubt, the experience of combat during World War II had a permanent effect on its British and American participants. But what was the nature of this "impact" on combatants? Although historians have analyzed the political and social impact of the war, the psychological impact has been explored less frequently. Despite the difficulties involved in analyzing the copious number of accounts about the war of 1939–45 and its aftermath, it is crucial that an attempt be made to examine the ways in which servicemen themselves attempted to create and recreate themselves upon returning home.

Indisputably, combat experiences were powerful ones – and not wholly negative. Most combatants were able to find positive sides to their war. They frequently describe deep friendships and the excitement of travel. There was virile beauty in much of the technology of war. Even the act of fighting was often said to be thrilling, even sexually so. The removal of souvenirs from the bodies of their victims was indulged in as a way of prolonging the memories of the joys of combat long after the conflict had ended.[1]

However, combat also involved a degree of horror rarely experienced in everyday civilian contexts. War is bloody. The suffering of British and American servicemen during World War II is all too audible. Familiar themes

---

1 For a detailed study, see Joanna Bourke, *An Intimate History of Killing: Face-to-Face Killing in Twentieth Century Warfare* (London, 1999).

include physical, moral, and emotional castration. Certain groups of people bore more than their share of the long-term effects of war; the dead were not present to appreciate their loss in the way that mutilated men were. Although the availability of sulphanamides and penicillin, coupled with faster transportation and improved surgical care, meant that fewer injuries resulted in amputation between 1939 and 1945 than during the conflict of 1914–18, three years after the termination of the conflict there were 45,000 war amputees in Britain.[2] Furthermore, as had happened after World War I, medical and pensioning authorities proved inefficient in caring for limbless veterans. For instance, once again, there were serious delays in supplying them with artificial limbs. In 1945, it would take three months for a man to receive his artificial leg; it took much longer for an artificial arm to be fitted.[3] The emotional effects of losing a limb were exacerbated by these delays. Soldiers who lost an arm were particularly liable to suffer depression, resentment, and anxiety, in comparison with those who had lost a leg, who were more likely to express feelings of morbid euphoria or defiance. Only 8 percent developed what the authorities called the "normal" response, that is, resignation and acceptance.[4] The war had scarcely ended when war amputees began being sidelined. The public response to them rapidly became one of apathy and neglect. Visible signs of mutilation were regarded with disgust, to the chagrin of those who had imagined that their "sacrifice" warranted respect. The title of one autobiography written by a war-disabled veteran tells it all: *No Memorial* (1954).[5]

Not all war wounds were visible. As one ex-soldier put it:

If you have a disability such as a leg or arm off, it's all right. But anything they can't see they don't consider you disabled. They say, "What's wrong with you?" and I say, "so and so." They say "You look alright." About that time I have my own ideas what I would like to do with them.[6]

He did not name his "wound," but a significant minority of servicemen were driven insane by war. According to Major H. A. Palmer, reporting on 12,000 psychiatric war casualties, the nation had as much right to demand that men give their "nerves" for their country as give their limbs, eyes, or

2 Rosalind Ham and Leonard T. Cotton, *Limb Amputation: From Aetiology to Rehabilitation* (London, 1991), 9.

3 Ministry of Pensions, *Artificial Limbs: Report of the Departmental Committee* (London, 1944), 16–17.

4 Ernest Jones, "Psychology and War Conditions," *Psychoanalytic Quarterly* 14 (1945): 15.

5 Anthony Babington, *No Memorial: The Story of a Triumph of Courage over Misfortune and Mind over Body* (London, 1954; reprint, 1988).

6 Unnamed veteran cited by Samuel A. Stouffer et al., *The American Soldier: Combat and Its Aftermath*, 3 vols. (Princeton, N.J., 1949), 2:633.

lives.[7] The statistics are inaccurate, but the best estimates agree that between 20 and 50 percent of casualties during the 1939–45 war were psychiatric. Between September 1939 and June 1944, 118,000 British soldiers were discharged on psychiatric grounds.[8] Of course, not all these men had been rendered psychiatric casualties because of their war experiences. Indeed, only 35 percent of psychiatric casualties were a result of war service, compared with 40 percent arising from "constitutional" factors and 15 percent caused by disease.[9]

Although war madness was an aberrant experience, for those it affected the outcome was devastating. For these men, the war lasted long beyond their term of active service. After the war, their status as "men" and "warriors" had clearly been dealt a severe blow. They often felt guilty for having deserted their comrades in the midst of war.[10] Many people – from employers to family members and friends – suspected that they were cowards or "gold-brickers." The psychiatric examiner for the U.S. Armed Forces in New Haven observed that "an astonishing percentage of otherwise intelligent persons in the community possess an abysmal ignorance of psychiatric conditions, and . . . are prone to ascribe [psychiatric difficulties] to lack of 'guts,' weakness of will, or some other equally erroneous factor."[11] They were housed in mental institutions for the poor or in other hospitals that were overcrowded and understaffed.[12] There even were arguments that such men should be denied pensions. As one doctor summarized it: "All psychiatric opinion is opposed to the granting of pensions to those whose illness is basically emotional in origin."[13] After all, such commentators insisted, pensions rewarded men for their psychological inadequacies.

After returning home, feelings of guilt continued to haunt many combatants. Long after the war, men had nightmares and other guilt reactions over killing. John Garcia was one such man. Forty years after he returned home, he was still able to recall how he had shot a Japanese woman and her child one night: "That still bothers me, that haunts me," he confessed, "I still feel I committed murder. . . . Oh, I still lose nights of sleep because of that

---

7 Major H. A. Palmer, "The Problem of the P & N Casualty – A Study of 12,000 Cases," 1944, 11, in the Contemporary Medical Archives Collection (London), RAMC/466/49.
8 War Cabinet, "Ministerial Committee on the Work of Psychologists and Psychiatrists in the Services. Report by the Expert Committee," Jan. 31, 1945, 8, Public Record Office, London (hereafter PRO), CAB21/915.
9 Ibid. Ten percent were categorized under the label "miscellaneous."
10 George K. Pratt, *Soldier to Civilian: Problems of Readjustment* (New York, 1944), 136.
11 Ibid., 135–6.
12 Robert England, *Twenty Million World War Veterans* (London, 1950), 177.
13 C. M. McCarthy, "The Rehabilitation of War Neurotics," *Medical Journal of Australia* 1, no. 26 (June 29, 1946): 911.

woman I shot. I still lose lots of sleep."[14] Such emotional conflicts made the question "How many men have you killed?" abhorrent to ex-servicemen. Indeed, there is much evidence to suggest that guilt over killing was generally activated only after the war. One explanation for this was provided by Therese Benedek, author of one of the best psychoanalytical studies of the effects of war. In her words,

As long as the danger existed, those feelings were checked. The fear which mobilizes all means for survival shuts off those feelings which, should they enter the mind, would have paralyzing effects upon function. Even after the action is over, repression operates relatively well as long as the soldier lives in the same environment, together with the men who did as he did, who felt as he felt, who "know all about it." However, when the soldier is released from his group and stands alone among civilians the memories of the inhuman hatred and humiliating fear which he felt and the recollection of what he did, or felt capable of doing, separates him, like a wall, from civilians.

For ex-combatants, civilians appeared to reside in a long-gone "world of the Sunday-school."[15]

Their families and friends "at home" were not deaf to these scruples. It was precisely their awareness of the tremendous rite through which "their boys" had passed that worried them. The permanency of men's combat experiences troubled many consciences. They asked how men who had spilt human blood could fail to be permanently transformed by such an abrogation of civilian mores. Numerous criminological studies predicted disaster. Raymond English, author of the immensely popular *The Pursuit of Purpose* (1947), believed that adjustment to civilian life would be extremely difficult because the army "teaches comradeship but kills friendship and love." It "inculcates a certain hardness towards one's personal sufferings, and inevitably towards those of one's fellows.... Perhaps the strongest mental characteristic of men who have served through the war is superficiality." He argued that civilian conventions and beliefs were "smashed out of existence" by military experiences.[16] These fears were heightened by the awareness that men had been bringing "souvenirs" of guns, hand grenades, and bombs into Britain. The fears were sufficiently strong that in February 1946 the government issued a disarmament campaign that included a safe period during which illegal weapons could be handed in without fear of prosecution.[17]

14 John Garcia interviewed in Studs Terkel, *"The Good War": An Oral History of World War Two* (London, 1985), 23–4.
15 Therese Benedek, *Insights and Personality Adjustment: A Study of the Psychological Effects of War* (New York, 1946), 56.
16 Raymond English, *The Pursuit of Purpose: An Essay on Social Morale* (London, 1947), 16–17.
17 PRO WO32/11675.

In some instances, civilians seriously proposed that ex-servicemen be sent to reorientation camps and be required to wear a yellow star as a form of warning.[18] Occasionally servicemen could be heard sharing these fears of brutalization. As one soldier wrote to his wife: "My dear wife: I am writing to tell you that I am a killer. I do not want you to worry, because I am not going to kill you and the kids, but I am a killer." He went on to describe how he had callously slaughtered two German prisoners of war.[19] Without question, "effective combat behavior" required men to act in brutal, bloody ways.

There was little evidence to substantiate such anxieties, however. Sociologists did their best to provide statistical evidence of the impact of combat on men's propensity to commit violent crimes once they returned home.[20] The statistical basis of evidence for brutalization was inherently contradictory. As the eminent criminologist Edwin H. Sutherland noted in 1943,

One theory states that war produces an increase in crimes because of the emotional instability in wartime, and another states that wars produce a decline in crimes because of an upsurge of national feeling. One states that crimes of violence increase in wartime because of the contagion of violence, and another that they decline because of the vicarious satiation of the need for violence.[21]

Even if we put aside such serious criticisms, the conclusions of these studies are ambivalent. For instance, one of the best studies showed that homicide rates did increase after World War II in England, Australia, Scotland, and New Zealand, while remaining unchanged in Canada and declining in Northern Ireland and the United States. This survey also observed that crime rates increased within groups that did not include combatants. Thus, the crime rates of women and older men also increased in those countries experiencing a postwar crime wave.[22] In all likelihood, something other than combat experience affected the rates.

Despite the lack of evidence, the accusation that ex-servicemen were more violent than others is constantly asserted. The popularity of the

---

18 William Manchester, *Goodbye Darkness: A Memoir of the Pacific War* (Boston, 1980), 273.
19 Unnamed man writing to his wife, cited in Robert L. Garrard, "Combat Guilt Reactions," *North Carolina Medical Journal* 10, no. 9 (Sept. 1949): 490.
20 For instance, see Dane Archer and Rosemary Gartner, *Violence and Crime in Cross-National Perspective* (New Haven, Conn., 1984); David Lester, "The Association Between Involvement in War and Rates of Suicide and Homicide," *Journal of Social Psychology* 131, no. 6 (1991): 893–5; David Lester, "War and Personal Violence," in Giorgio Ausenda, ed., *Effects of War on Society* (San Marino, 1992), 211–22; Colonel John J. Marren, "Psychiatric Problems in Troops in Korea During and Following Combat," *U.S. Armed Forces Medical Journal* 7 (May 1956); Jeffrey Streimer and Christopher Tennant, "Psychiatric Aspects of the Vietnam War. The Effect on Combatants," in Kenneth Maddock and Barry Wright, eds., *War: Australia and Vietnam* (Sydney, 1987).
21 Edwin H. Sutherland, "Wartime Crime," in Sutherland, *On Analyzing Crime* (1943; reprint, Chicago, 1973), 120–1.
22 Archer and Gartner, *Violence and Crime.*

"brutalization thesis" has many origins. It is seen by many people to be a potent argument against military aggression. After all, if war is not only concerned with temporary destruction of property and people but has a permanently negative impact on "human nature" itself, this might place yet another restraint on armed conflict. The narrative satisfaction of innocence shattered by a great trauma is also something that can be keenly embraced by combatants and civilians alike. Popular criminal reportage also plays a part by exaggerating the extent of violence carried out by former servicemen. The press applies the description "ex-serviceman" to any man who might have served and subsequently committed a violent crime, irrespective of the nature of that man's service or of any link between his particular action and his war service. In addition, combat films are full of brutalized combatants. The ability of gory bloodletting to appall civilians while leaving combatants unmoved is an effective literary device employed by countless autobiographers.

Unconfirmed reports about the negative long-term effects of war did concern the military, who set out deliberately to emphasize the benefits of life in the army. They stressed new skills, training in leadership, education in patience and resilience, and broadened horizons. Such optimism was not shared by servicemen themselves, who recognized that the skills conferred on them were often of little use in civilian society. In the longer term, war was not an effective recruiting ground for the armed forces. Indeed, after each conflict, the military faced extreme difficulties in maintaining recruitment levels. In America, only about 3 percent of servicemen after World War II said that they would want to make a career out of the army (although as many again said that they would consider returning to the army if they were unemployed).[23] Most servicemen believed that their military experiences had had a negative rather than a positive effect on them. In a survey in November 1945, for example, a representative cross-section of 542 enlisted men in the United States who had served in the army for between one and three years were asked whether the army had "hurt or helped" them. Between 55 and 71 percent agreed with the statement that "On the whole, the army has hurt me more than it has helped me." The proportion agreeing with this statement was highest among high school graduates over twenty-five years of age.[24] Another American survey in December 1944, this time of discharged veterans, showed similarly high levels of discontent. When they were asked, "Do you feel that Army life changed you?" 37 percent reported undesirable changes only, 20 percent reported both

---

23 Stouffer et al., *American Soldier*, 2:598.   24 Ibid., 611.

undesirable and desirable changes, and 22 percent reported desirable changes only. Twenty-one percent either reported no changes or their opinions were not ascertained. The majority of the "changes" these men observed concerned higher levels of nervousness, rather than aggressiveness. The most widely reported negative changes mentioned (reported by 41 percent of the veterans) were that the military life had made them more nervous, high-strung, restless, jumpy, tense, unable to concentrate, and wanting to be "on the go." Only 17 percent claimed the army had made them more irritable, short-tempered, quarrelsome, or belligerent.[25]

In other ways and for other groups, war was regarded as imposing long-term negative traits on combatants. Although, as two prominent officers in the army air force put it, "removal of external prohibitions against killing and even encouragement of human destruction do not develop a killer," ex-servicemen were more liable to rebel against civilian society. They could talk angrily about unrelated civilians and soldiers who had not served overseas.[26] Hostility was directed particularly strongly against politicians, leaders in business and industry, and the trade unions. When over three thousand servicemen in the European theater in August 1945 were asked whether they thought that government leaders would "try to see to it that discharged soldiers get a square deal?" only 39 percent answered "most of them." A similar question about leaders in business, industry, and the trade unions showed only one-quarter were confident of support.[27] The split between veterans and civilians was greater in America (compared with Britain) because of its geographical remoteness from the conflict.[28] This bitterness toward those who had not fought could be acute. Certainly the scope for misunderstanding was wide. As one unnamed soldier recalled:

When we came off the ship here's the Red Cross or the Sally Ann, some girls, they give us a little bag and it has a couple of chocolate bars in it and a comic book. Here, we had gone overseas not much more than children but we were coming back, sure, let's face it, as killers. And they were still treating us as children. Candy and comic books.[29]

As the sociologist August B. Hollingshaw predicted in 1946: "It will be impossible for them to communicate their inner sense of accomplishment

25 Ibid., 631–2.
26 Roy R. Grinker and John P. Spiegel, *Men Under Stress* (London, 1945), 308.
27 Stouffer et al., *American Soldier*, 2:584.
28 Alanson H. Edgerton, *Readjustment or Revolution? A Guide to the Economic, Educational, and Social Readjustment of War Veterans, Ex-War Workers, and Oncoming Youth* (New York, 1946), 83.
29 Unnamed soldier interviewed in Barry Broadfoot, *Six War Years 1939–1945* (Toronto, 1974), 392. See also George K. Pratt, *Soldier to Civilian: Problems of Readjustment* (New York, 1944), 5–6.

in the fine art of killing to civilians."[30] Although elites within society were liable to regard their increased assertiveness in a negative light, we should hesitate before judging the soldiers in similar ways. Ex-servicemen were increasingly willing to regard themselves as part of the polity – indeed, a part that had more rights than the middle- and upper-class men who had managed to find a secure niche at home during the war.

There were negative repercussions from the politicization of servicemen. Racism, for instance, was often reinforced in the context of war. Lasting hatred of the Germans (often conflated as "Nazis") continued long after the war was over and remains a powerful undercurrent in British and American society. Anti-Japanese sentiment, although muted by guilt arising from the bombing of Hiroshima and Nagasaki, also continued. For instance, George MacDonald Fraser eventually became famous for his hilarious stories about the exploits of Private McAuslan, his best-selling Flashman novels, and his scripts for *The Three Musketeers*, *The Four Musketeers*, and the James Bond film *Octopussy*. During the war, he had served in the jungles of Burma, in the largely Cumbrian unit of the 14th Army. His racism not only found expression during the war but was confirmed and strengthened by his experiences. Fraser prided himself on his "killer instinct . . . the murderous impulse of the hunter," and his memoirs contained numerous descriptions of killing (the "jolt of delight" he felt each time he hit a "bastard"). He defended atrocities carried out against the Japanese during World War II. Neither he nor his comrades felt any remorse for mass slaughter – after all (they rationalized), the Japanese were a "no-surrender" enemy who would not hesitate to kill them, and "Japs" were further down the evolutionary scale than Europeans. At one stage in his memoirs he described a unit serving alongside him in Burma. One night, these men callously slaughtered all the Japanese patients. It was not a war crime, in his view, but a legitimate way to rid the world of as many Japanese as possible. He "shrugged, and forgot about it." To anyone who criticized the practice of shooting prisoners, Fraser advised: "Get yourself to the sharp end, against an enemy like the Japanese, encounter a similar incident . . . and let me know how you get on."[31] Even as late as 1992 he unashamedly admitted that he preferred not to sit next to Japanese tourists.

The war did not reduce racism in America either. Many soldiers admitted to sharing many of the antisemitic prejudices of their enemy. For instance, 22 percent of American servicemen stationed in Germany in 1946 reported

---

30 August B. Hollingshaw, "Adjustment to Military Life," *American Journal of Sociology* 2, no. 5 (Mar. 1946): 446.
31 George MacDonald Fraser, *Quartered Safe Out Here: A Recollection of the War in Burma* (London, 1992), xvi, 26, 73, 83, 87, 118, 125–6, 191–2.

that they agreed that the Germans had some good reasons "for being down on the Jews." An additional 10 percent were undecided.[32] One in six white American veterans "expected trouble" between Jews and non-Jews after the war, and they agreed with statements claiming that Jews owned too large a proportion of business, were profiteers, and had dodged the draft. Even those veterans who claimed that their war experiences had made them more favorably disposed toward Jews remained fundamentally antisemitic. As one veteran put it: "There were some Jews [in the Army] that were real white men and they were swell, but back here they are a separate race all by themselves."[33]

A similar story can be told about relationships between black and white Americans. During the war it had been predicted that interracial contact in the army would promote greater tolerance after the war. Although it may have done so for a minority, more typically contact actually reinforced prejudices. White American ex-servicemen generally continued to insist that their black comrades had been poor soldiers and were cowards. On the other side, black servicemen had good reason to be made bitter by their war experiences. First, they had served in segregated units, usually of a noncombatant nature, wherein promotion was exceptionally difficult. Even the single case of a black serviceman being promoted to brigadier-general during the war (General Benjamin O. Davis) was widely believed to have been made possible only by political considerations.[34] Second, certain incidents of discrimination gained an immense amount of publicity, most notoriously the decision by the Red Cross to segregate blood given to black and white soldiers. Finally, there was the recognition that they were being "used": They were welcomed in combat but once they had sacrificed their own limbs and seen their comrades sacrifice their lives, they were repudiated. The diary of one black soldier described it thus:

Take D-days. Everybody is buddies and everybody talk to you. If you don't have a fox hole in a raid maybe a white fellow call you to come get in his hole. That lasts like that during combat until the island start getting secure. Then it all changes. A colored fellow can't get a lift in a jeep and six steps further on they pick up a couple of white fellows. Also colored men can't use the white man's latrine at the base. They gotta dig their own. How that make a fellow feel?[35]

32 A press survey, cited in Stouffer et al., *American Soldier*, 2:571.
33 Unnamed veteran cited in ibid., 638.
34 For instance, see Ruth D. Wilson, *Jim Crow Joins Up: A Study of Negroes in the Armed Forces of the United States* (New York, 1945), 99.
35 Unnamed diary of a black soldier, cited in Lieutenant Colonel Herbert S. Ripley and Major Stewart Wolf, "Mental Illness Among Negro Troops Overseas," *American Journal of Psychiatry* 103 (1946–47): 510.

As a result, the war left a new legacy of bitterness against the army, particular among northern blacks.[36] This bitterness led to powerful protest groups (such as the Committee Against Jim Crow in Military Service and Training) insisting that the "Jim Crow Army" be abolished and that black Americans be integrated. In effect, this was what happened in 1948 when President Harry S Truman issued Executive Order 9981, which officially ended segregation in the military.

Irrespective of ethnic identity, servicemen came home with their minds firmly centered on personal concerns. Time and time again, it was observed that the average soldier was "thinking about himself and his family, not about his country or the world."[37] This is not to deny that adjusting to civilian life, and familial life in particular, was difficult. A detailed examination of families in postwar Stanford showed that veterans often felt bewildered by the weight of the responsibility of readjusting to civilian life: They found it "overwhelming." Those who had been married prior to the war were particularly anxious about returning. Indisputably, it was difficult for married veterans to cope with the fact that their wives had jobs or that their children treated them like strangers. This survey concluded, however, that although these married veterans had been profoundly worried about how they would adjust to marital relations again, three-quarters admitted that the reunion had gone well and that they were experiencing good relations with their wives.[38] Indeed, for many men, despite the drama of their military experiences, the experience of combat had very little impact on their psychological make-up. As one major survey of veterans in Midwestern America concluded:

There is little evidence that these men had been "knocked out of their rut," at least in a practical, developmental sense. They had been exposed to new and unusual situations, and had, in one way or another, adapted themselves to them. They had all undergone some degree of change and growth in the process of adapting. But for the most part the insights that accompanied that growth were either specifically related to the military environment or were broadly philosophical.... there appeared to be little carry-over of this maturation into the immediate problem of readjusting to civilian life, earning a living, or getting ahead socially.[39]

36 Robert W. Smuts, "The Negro Community and the Development of Negro Potential," *Journal of Negro Education* 26 (fall 1957): 461–2.

37 Stouffer et al., *American Soldier*, 2:597.

38 Lois Meek Stolz et al., *Father Relations of War-Born Children: The Effect of Post-War Adjustment of Fathers on the Behaviour and Personality of First Children Born While the Fathers Were at War* (Stanford, Calif., 1954), 30–1. See also Pratt, *Soldier to Civilian*, 172–5.

39 Robert J. Havighurst, Walter H. Eaton, John W. Baughman, and Ernest W. Burgess, *The American Veteran Back Home: A Study of Veteran Readjustment* (New York, 1951), 175–6.

If ex-combatants did admit to any long-term change, it was spoken of as being "hardened," not "brutalized." As John B. Doyle (a Marine who had been decorated for bravery on Guadalcanal) told his family in 1944: "What has [combat] done to me? What does it mean to me? I know that I have not become cruel or callous. I am sure that I am hardened."[40] Time and time again veterans insisted that this process of "hardening" was not translated into brutalization after the war. As one soldier observed:

I saw men overseas do things I don't think I'm even going to tell you about, dreadful things, acts of cruelty, and if you were where the heavy stuff was flying around, for a week, two weeks at a time, you developed a disregard for human life. It was just natural. And yet these men came home and took off their uniforms, hung them in the closet, bought a new outfit or tried to get into the clothes they had when they volunteered, and went right out into life, getting up in the morning, going to work, coming home at night, some going to university, getting married, having fun, just as if there never had been a war on.[41]

Indeed, the letters and diaries of combatants continually testified to a range of positive emotions stimulated by their wartime experiences. War gave many men a unique occasion to express love and respectfulness toward spouses, family members, and friends. Separated from these loved ones and acutely aware of the suffering they must also be enduring, servicemen were liable to become uniquely articulate about their emotions. Wartime experiences increased men's propensity to declare those "finer" feelings of heterosexual love – at least this was the view of George Bassett, a chaplain during World War II. He had expected to discover hidden reservoirs of lust in the men to whom he ministered, assuming that the effect of war would be to encourage the idea that "one woman was as good as another and that a wedding service had little permanent value." Instead, while carrying out the task of censoring their letters, he became aware of hidden reservoirs of tenderness. In his words:

Man after man wrote of a love that was exclusive, speaking of experiences of the past, both physical and spiritual, that bound them together for ever. I am sure now that most men worship at the shrine of one woman and have no desire to change their religion. Their concern for the welfare of those women whom they had left behind was paramount; even their own discomfort on broiling hot decks, or the dangers of sea warfare, or the unpleasantness of sea-sickness ... – these were as nothing compared to their anxious thoughts concerning wife, child, parent, or sweetheart.[42]

40 John B. Doyle cited in Dixon Wecker, *When Johnny Comes Marching Home* (Cambridge, Mass., 1944), 493.
41 Unnamed soldier interviewed in Broadfoot, *Six War Years*, 413.
42 George Bassett, *This Also Happened* (London, 1947), 16.

Distance forced men to express their roles as lover, protector, father, son, or husband in different ways. As one major survey of veterans in Midwestern America concluded:

The military environment causes nostalgia . . . it is implicit in the status of the citizen soldier that he should regard his military surroundings as a very temporary and provisional state of affairs. . . . This nostalgia was expressed in many ways: by the serviceman's endless exchange of hometown reminiscences with his buddies; by an insatiable appetite for newspapers and magazines from the States; and perhaps most of all by the indefatigable letter-writing in which the average serviceman engaged.[43]

Numerous men repeated the words of one veteran who admitted that he and his wife "never could have talked about the things they wrote about, especially in the sexual area" and therefore the war had "salvaged his marriage."[44]

Combatants were not passive moral subjects who (having committed the ultimate transgression) were permanently scarred. Rather, in striving for their concept of a "better world," processes of brutalization were strenuously resisted. This is not to deny that the logic of such resistance was often highly fanciful. For instance, the commonplace distinction made between "hardening" and "brutalization" depended on metaphors of "shedding outer skins" to enable the rebirthing of the "real" man. Life-cycle arguments (in which martial killing was characterized as part of an inevitable cycle of events by which "boys" followed their father's footsteps and were "tested" before being reintegrated into more mature society as peaceable fathers and preparing their own sons for the bloody ritual) represented a moral commitment to a warrior society. The military created a strong feeling of nostalgia for civilian mores. There was disillusionment upon return and readjusting to familial life was often difficult, but the vast majority of servicemen proved content to return to civilian life, confident that despite their experiences in combat they were fundamentally the same men who had left. The most frequent sentiment was summed up by Max Miller, who had served in the Pacific theater of war. When hearing descriptions of the difficult and often dangerous work servicemen had to do in combat zones, civilian listeners used to say: "Think of all the material you'll have to write about afterwards!" For combatants, however, the typical response to such sentiments was "no, no, no, no." Their chief desire was "to think about something else, and quickly, if we could."[45]

---

43 Havighurst et al., *American Veteran Back Home*, 25–6.
44 Unnamed veterans cited in Meek Stolz et al., *Father Relations of War-Born Children*, 31.
45 Max Miller, *It's Tomorrow Out Here* (New York, 1945), 30.

7

Desperately Seeking Normality

Sex and Marriage in the Wake of the War

DAGMAR HERZOG

In the first seven or eight years after the end of World War II, the western German press and publishing landscape was filled with essays and books addressing what was variously called the "marital crisis," the "sexual crisis," or the "sexual misery of our time."[1] One author titled his 1947 book *The Tragedy of the Bedroom*; another writer in 1949 opined that "marriage is sick through and through."[2] Not until the mid-1950s did the hyperventilated fascination with these themes subside. An analysis of the postwar writings on sexual topics suggests not only that the reconstruction of a domesticated heterosexuality was an important component of the transition from fascism to Western democracy, but also that for quite some time it was not at all self-evident what sort of sexual politics would emerge from the wreckage of 1945.

Each contributor to the postwar debates defined the problem of "marital crisis" or "sexual crisis" differently. Some authors referred to the high rates of marital discord in the wake of so many multiyear spousal separations caused by war and postwar imprisonments. News articles, popular advice columns, and professional literature alike repeatedly thematized both the need to help individuals leave unhappy partnerships through divorce *and* the possibility that with mutual effort and sensitivity damaged relationships could be repaired. For other observers the main problem was the painful arithmetic of a several-million-strong "surplus of women" in the wake of an overwhelming

Heartfelt thanks to Y. Michal Bodemann, Geoff Eley, Jeffrey Herf, Julie M. Johnson, and the anonymous readers for their astute criticisms and helpful suggestions.

1 References to the "marital crisis" or "sexual crisis" (*Ehekrise, Ehenot, Sexualkrise*) were ubiquitous in the late 1940s and early 1950s; references to "sexual misery," "sexual need," or "sexual unhappiness" (*sexuelle Not, Sexualnot*) were frequent. The specific phrase "the sexual misery of our time" comes from Franz Hubalek, "Die Sexualnot unserer Tage," *Der Seelsorger* 20 (1949–50): 276.
2 Theodor Hartwig, *Die Tragödie des Schlafzimmers: Beiträge zur Psychologie der Ehe* (Vienna, 1947); Gerhard Fechner, *Die kranke Ehe* (Hamburg, 1949), 10.

number of male war deaths. Here, too, commentators vied with each other to suggest specific solutions.[3] As the best-selling women's magazine *Constanze* acerbically joked, with 1,250 women to every 1,000 men, "which woman, in view of such an oppressive statistical surplus of female marriage partners can still ask, What is the man like? rather than simply, Where, where is the man?"[4] Some, especially Christian authors, sought to validate single women's sense of pain but urged them to find fulfilling lives through sublimation and service to society. A few daring writers recommended experimenting with consenting threesome relationships so that two women might share the same man (although the main tendency was to make titillating references to the possibility of such threesomes while claiming to go on record against them). And a number of energetic female authors declared that sharing a life with a man was not as exciting as it was made out to be and that no one need condescend to the single woman.

The overarching tendency among contemporary commentators, however – and this had tremendous consequences – was both to pity the involuntarily single woman and to aggravate every already married woman's sense of anxiety that she was about to lose her man. In 1950, for example, a contributor to the newly founded scholarly *Zeitschrift für Sexualforschung* (Journal for Sex Research) only exacerbated the atmosphere of competition when he referred to the "threat to healthy, normal marriage created by the current large surplus of women . . . for the excess of female sexuality cannot simply in every case be forced into professional-spiritual sublimation!"[5] An author writing in the semipornographic but also would-be highbrow sex advice journal *Liebe und Ehe* (Love and Marriage) added insult to injury when he defined (what he believed were) increases in female masturbation and lesbian love as indicators of the "statistically unmeasurable extent" of "the sexual misery."[6] And advice authors such as Elisabeth and Carl Lindner marketed suggestions not only for nabbing a husband but also for *keeping* him. Their 1952 book *So Hat Jede Frau Erfolg* (How Every Woman Can Succeed) assured wives that they were facing a new kind of rival – a mistress not out for simple material gain but for "talk, cozy hours . . . tenderness and sexual satisfaction." And they insisted that the best plan for a woman once she had landed a man was to spoil and flatter him, and even if she was unable

3 On the social history of single women in postwar Germany, see the outstanding study by Elizabeth D. Heineman, *What Difference Does a Husband Make?: Women and Marital Status in Nazi and Postwar Germany* (Berkeley, Calif., 1999).
4 See Petra Lund, "Zwei Frauen? Mir Reicht's!" *Constanze* 20 (1948): 7.
5 K. Bier, review of Theodor Bovet's *Die Ehe, ihre Krise und Neuwerdung* (1946), *Zeitschrift für Sexualforschung* 1, nos. 3–4 (1950): 305.
6 Dr. K., "Was halten Sie vom Frauenüberschuss?" *Liebe und Ehe* 2, no. 2 (1950): 12.

to monopolize his body, at least continue to monopolize his heart by acting even more agreeable and making herself even more attractive.[7] The rhetoric of the era, in short, conveyed a sort of impossible double message in which heterosexual coupledom was constantly declared to be *the* ideal and yet also was presented as under perpetual threat.

In the postwar debates about sex and marriage, however, more was at stake than either the issue of high divorce rates or the disproportionate ratio of marriageable women to men. Something far more fundamental appeared to be awry between men and women. Heterosexuality itself was held to be in crisis. Complaints were widespread that there no longer was any erotic pull between the sexes. Notably, moreover, despite the much-lamented dearth of marriageable men in the immediate postwar period – and the concomitant recurrent speculation that this dearth made women of necessity less choosy in the search for a mate – those early postwar years also saw extensive discussion of the liabilities of heterosexual manliness.[8] One reason for this lay in the concrete damage done to men by their experiences during the war and during postwar imprisonments. In contrast to the post–World War I preoccupation with overcoming female frigidity by encouraging men to become better lovers (which was a significant campaign despite its scientifically and morally insupportable eugenicist underpinnings and its anxiety-inducing insistence on building to simultaneous orgasm during penetration), the post–World War II period saw a much more elaborate reflection on male sexual dysfunction.[9] There is some evidence that the new concern with male sexual vulnerability was in fact a specific backlash against the pressure for men to be concerned with women's pleasure.[10] But the factors raised most frequently by post–World War II commentators involved

7 Elisabeth and Carl Lindner, *So Hat Jede Frau Erfolg* (Teufen, 1952), 9, 14, 116, 143–5, 161–2.
8 Postwar German masculinity is beginning to receive its due. See esp. Robert G. Moeller, "War Stories: The Search for a Usable Past in the Federal Republic of Germany," *American Historical Review* 101, no. 4 (Oct. 1996): 1009–48; Robert G. Moeller, "The 'Remasculinization' of Germany in the 1950s: Introduction," Heide Fehrenbach, "Rehabilitating Fatherland: Race and German Remasculinization," Moeller, " 'The Last Soldiers of the Great War' and Tales of Family Reunions in the Federal Republic of Germany," and Uta G. Poiger, "A New, 'Western' Hero? Reconstructing German Masculinity in the 1950s," all in *Signs* 24, no. 1 (autumn 1998); Svenja Goltermann, "Verletzte Körper," paper delivered in Bielefeld, Oct. 6, 1998; and Frank Biess, "Survivors of Totalitarianism: Returning POWs and the Reconstruction of Masculine Citizenship in West Germany, 1945–1955," in Hanna Schissler, ed., *The "Miracle Years": A Cultural History of West Germany 1949 to 1968* (Princeton, N.J., 2001).
9 For a terrific dissection of the post–World War I debate, see Atina Grossmann, *Reforming Sex: The German Movement for Birth Control and Abortion Reform, 1920–1950* (New York, 1995).
10 See, e.g., Emil A. Gutheil, "Störungen der männlichen Potenz und ihre Behandlung," *Der Seelenarzt: Handbuch für seelische Beratung* (Leipzig, 1933), 145–62; and P. Orlowski, "Zur Frage der Pathogenese und der modernen Therapie der sexuellen Störungen beim Manne," *Zeitschrift für Urologie* 31, no. 6 (1937): 374, 380.

malnutrition and the lack (or only intermittent availability) of a heterosexual outlet during the war, and although after a few years doctors were pleased to report that the malnutrition problem had largely been solved, they still openly worried about the difficulty for men in "finding the way back to the woman."[11] Popular and scholarly articles and advice books, as well as advertisements for hormonal and herbal products to alleviate male difficulties, raised the triple specters of premature ejaculation, impotence, and male homosexuality as though they were all aspects of the same phenomenon – an imaginative linkage that is as disturbing as it is indicative of the mentality of the era.

There was one further reason, however, for the heightened concern with the state of heterosexual relations after 1945, and that has to do with the way discussions of sex were intertwined with efforts to come to terms with the recent Nazi past. Across the entire ideological spectrum of opinions on sex, from church-affiliated Christians on the one side to self-styled "healthy" pro-sex sensualists on the other, including mainstream observers and advice-givers in the middle, postwar commentators, far from being silent about Nazism, invoked it with frequency. One important insight that emerges from examining the literature on sex written in the years immediately following the defeat of the Third Reich is that current scholarly assumptions about the Third Reich's own sexual politics are in serious need of revision. And another insight arising from an analysis of this material is that postwar discussions of sex were an important locus not just for the normalization of perceived-to-be-destabilized gender relations but also for the normalization of "Germanness" more generally. What requires attention are the meaning-making processes engaged in by postwar Germans and especially the diverse ways that Nazism was represented in postwar accounts. For it also was within postwar discussions about such seemingly mundane issues as romantic relationships and private happiness that central aspects of the traumatic and shameful past were mastered. Conflicts about sexual matters proved to be key sites for processing the legacies of Nazism.

The prevailing view among scholars at present, so pervasive that no one seems to feel the need to document it more fully but which instead serves as a sort of foundational backdrop to other inquiries, is that the Third Reich was at its core "sex-hostile."[12] Although it is acknowledged that there was

---

11 H. Kilian, "Das Wiedereinleben des Heimkehrers in Familie, Ehe und Beruf," in *Die Sexualität des Heimkehrers*, Beiträge zur Sexualforschung, vol. 11 (Stuttgart, 1957), 34.

12 Joachim Hohmann, *Sexualforschung und -aufklärung in der Weimarer Republik* (Berlin, 1985), 9. There is no reason to single out Hohmann; as Jeffrey Herf pointed out in 1999, most "historians of German society and culture under the Nazis" have proceeded as though "the connection between Nazism and sexual repression" were "intuitively obvious." See Jeffrey Herf, "One-Dimensional Man" (review of

wartime adultery and that the two or three years immediately following the war saw a dramatic upheaval in mores signified by German women's sexual relations with occupation troops and by German couples' inability to formalize romantic relationships due to the constricted economic and housing situations, these phenomena are treated as temporary aberrations in an otherwise tendentially sexually conservative era – an era that is often imagined to run from 1933, when the Nazis took power, to the mid-to-late 1960s, when the student movement and the sexual revolution finally brought relief. Indeed, members of the student movement and their liberal supporters frequently saw sexual conservatism in the postwar era as another indicator, much like the capitalist economy or the repressiveness of the police, for the persistence of "fascist" tendencies in the Federal Republic.

In the Third Reich, there were countless profoundly sexually repressive tendencies: the torture and murder of homosexuals, the incarceration of prostitutes, the forced sterilization of proletarian women whose purported promiscuity was taken as a sign of mental deficiency, the prosecution of Jewish-gentile sex in race defilement trials, the grotesque reproductive experiments, and the sexual sadism in the concentration and death camps. But none of these horrific facts justify the conclusion that the Third Reich was sexually repressive for everyone. What has routinely been downplayed since the 1960s is the evidence that Nazi policy and practice, for regime-loyal or regime-indifferent nonproletarian heterosexual "Aryans," was often anything but repressive. Indeed, the regime's brutality and the pleasures it promised to those it did not persecute were inextricably connected. The stepped-up persecution of homosexuals provided a crucial context for the injunction to heterosexual activity; the abuse and murder of those deemed unworthy of reproduction and life because of their supposed behavioral

Herbert Marcuse, *War, Technology and Fascism), New Republic,* Feb. 1, 1999, 39. For classic analyses of sex under fascism which insist on fascism's antisexuality despite their own marshaling of considerable evidence to the contrary, see George L. Mosse, *Nationalism and Sexuality: Respectability and Abnormal Sexuality in Modern Europe* (New York, 1985); George L. Mosse, *The Image of Man: The Creation of Modern Masculinity* (New York, 1996); and Udo Pini, *Leibeskult und Liebeskitsch: Erotik im Dritten Reich* (Munich, 1992). For attempts to articulate also Nazism's pro-sex agendas, but which are marred by sensationalism, see Hans Peter Bleuel, *Das saubere Reich: Theorie und Praxis des sittlichen Lebens im Dritten Reich* (Bern, 1972); and Hans Dieter Schäfer, *Das gespaltene Bewusstsein: Über deutsche Kultur und Lebenswirklichkeit 1933–1945* (Munich, 1981). For marvelous primary research on sexual ideas in popular culture in the Third Reich – for example, sexual motifs in the lyrics of popular songs – with nuanced attention to both the inciting and the conservative impulses and their ever-shifting interplay in the course of the Third Reich, see Torsten Reters, *Liebe, Ehe und Partnerwahl zur Zeit des Nationalsozialismus: Eine soziologische Semantikanalyse* (Dortmund, 1997). Unfortunately, however, Reters' analysis is also marred by thoughtlessness with regard to the status of homosexuality in the Third Reich. For a superb analysis of the overall state of the scholarship on sexuality under Nazism, see Elizabeth D. Heineman, "Nazism and Sexuality: The Doubly Unspeakable?" *Journal of the History of Sexuality* 11 (2002).

or "racial" characteristics constituted the background against which those classed as superior were enjoined to enjoy their entitlements. Sexually conservative values were preserved through the duration of the Third Reich, especially in the bourgeois middle strata and in church-affiliated circles of all strata, and Nazi spokespeople at many occasions appropriated and actively disseminated sexually conservative values. But these more conservative values were also intensively combated by the regime. What seems puzzlingly inconsistent on the surface actually contains a deeper – and more pernicious – sense.

Under Nazism, discussions of sex consisted of a complex amalgam of diverse, overlapping and mutually reinforcing but also often quite contradictory tendencies. Almost all discussions of sex were inflected by notions of "race" – whether what this term denoted was intended as anti-Jewish or anti-handicapped, or whether its use signaled a vaguer and broader conception of physical health and behavioral norms. Yet beyond that, assumptions and arguments varied widely, from a nudist's insistence that "healthy, beautiful" naked bodies were morally superior to the "overintensification" of titillation induced by partial clothing, to a jurist's agonized circumlocutions in defense of a realm of privacy in which homosexual acts could be acceptable (in the midst of an argument that nonetheless took offense at the implication that someone who did not advocate "merciless harshness" toward homosexuals might be displaying "inadequate racial consciousness").[13] The anti-Semitic newspaper *Der Stürmer* ranted repetitively about male Jews' supposed compulsion toward sexual criminality (including rape, pedophilia, and systematic seduction of "German" girls into prostitution); reading it one could easily get the impression that non-Jews never had sex with each other – even as the paper itself served as a kind of pornography.[14] But some female authors writing in Nazi venues complained more about Nazi men's overeagerness for premarital sex and tried to insist that Germanic tradition demanded premarital chastity.[15] One physician decried what he saw as the unfortunate pressure on men to please women sexually (and, in racially coded terms, blamed this pressure on Jewish doctors); he recommended

---

13 See Hermann Wilke, *Dein "JA" zum Leibe! Sinn und Gestaltung deutscher Leibeszucht* (Berlin, 1939), 96–7; and Graf zu Dohna, review of Rudolf Klare, *Homosexualität und Strafrecht* (Hamburg, 1937), in *Monatsschrift für Kriminalbiologie und Strafrechtsreform* 29, no. 1 (1938): 55–7.

14 See, e.g., "Die blonde Hilde: Der Jude Ernst Landau in Düsseldorf vernichtet blonde deutsche Mädchen," *Der Stürmer* 11, no. 1 (Jan. 1933): 1–2; "Jüdische Mädchenjäger: Rasseschänder Samuel Maier zu 1 1/2 Jahren Zuchthaus verurteilt," *Der Stürmer* 13, no. 17 (Apr. 1935): 8; "Max Strauss: Der Kinderschänder von Karlstadt und Urspringen," *Der Stürmer* 13, no. 29 (July 1935): 1–2; and "Leo Weil: Der Kinderverführer von Karlsruhe," *Der Stürmer* 14, no. 7 (Feb. 1936): 7.

15 Marie Joachimi-Dege's remarks in *Neue Literatur* (May 1935), quoted and discussed in Hans Lüdemann, "Neues Stadium der Frauenbewegung?" *Das Schwarze Korps*, June 19, 1935, 10; "Wie eine Frau es sieht," *Das Schwarze Korps*, July 13, 1944, 4.

to men a return to "'automatic-egotistical' sexual intercourse."[16] Yet another physician theorized elaborately that female orgasms enhanced female fertility – and reported proudly on his (extraordinarily invasive) laboratory experiments proving this point by identifying how far the sperm had traveled three minutes after the conclusion of coitus.[17]

One significant strand of sexual discussion under Nazism was indeed overtly and unapologetically conservative also with respect to so-called Aryans and used references to Jews as a negative counterpoint to underscore the value of a sexually conservative agenda. Thus, for instance, the Nazi physician Ferdinand Hoffmann argued in 1938 that "the demand for the full living-out of sexuality is a typical Jewish-liberal one, and the news should gradually have gotten around, that everything that on the Jewish side has become a battle cry, solely serves disintegrative and not constructive aims. The Jew has never talked us into something that could help us." Hoffmann called for the return to chastity before marriage and insisted on a single standard of premarital abstinence and marital fidelity for both women and men. But this position was a minority one and one profoundly embattled in the Third Reich. (Indeed, Hoffmann himself made his anti-Semitic arguments in the context of complaining that although the populace had largely converted to Nazism in political terms, in sexual terms it was still deeply attached to pleasure-seeking and premarital promiscuity.) Hoffmann was disgusted that many Nazis did not agree with him, challenging them to explain how they could reconcile "their enthusiastically presented National Socialist worldview" with their ongoing "sexual Bolshevism" and fulminating that "it is not acceptable to disguise dirty desires with National Socialist ideas. . . . There are no two sides to the Jewish Question and it is not admissible to damn the Jew in his political, economic, and human manifestation while secretly, for personal convenience, maintaining the customs he has suggested in the realm of love- and sex-life."[18] Hoffmann was certainly not alone in his views. Paul Danzer, writing in the *Völkischer Wille*, a journal concerned with population policy, argued that "whether the Jews . . . exploited our economy, whether they confused our legal life or encouraged social divisions, all that pales before the most serious damage they have done to our *Volk*, the *poisoning of marital- and sex-morality*. . . . Just remember the semitically saturated entertainment and theater literature, the filmmaking of the last decades, and the persistent effort made from that side in the

---

16 Orlowski, "Zur Frage der Pathogenese," 383.
17 B. Belonoschkin, "Weibliche Psyche und Konzeption," *Münchener medizinische Wochenschrift* 88 (1941): 1007–9.
18 Ferdinand Hoffmann, *Sittliche Entartung und Geburtenschwund*, 2d ed. (Munich, 1938), 29, 49–50.

ripping asunder of all moral barriers, the glorification of adultery and sexual uninhibitedness!" And yet Danzer, like Hoffmann, worried openly that the German masses could not have cared less about cleaning up their sexual act.[19] Along related lines, the NSDAP-affiliated physician Dr. Knorr complained vociferously in 1937 that "we have experienced a revolution in ways of understanding the world and a *völkisch* awakening like never before. And yet we thoughtlessly repeat the Jewish or Jewish-influenced vulgarities concerning the relations of the two sexes. . . . It is astonishing how little our great National Socialist revolution has moved forward in this area!"[20] Some Nazi-affiliated writers continued to hold to a conservative agenda during the war years, as for example one military officer, a Major Ellenbeck, not only recommended to the noncommissioned officers under his command that they choose "squeaky clean" (*blitzsaubere*) young women as their wives but also insisted that men too needed to adhere to a standard of premarital chastity; officers must provide a model by avoiding "raunchy jokes," and any man who displayed a double standard of sexual morality "still has the poisonous substances of the Jewish moral perspective . . . sitting in his bones. Out with them!"[21]

Ultimately, however, the sorts of views articulated by Hoffmann were more popular and influential among Christian authors than among his fellow Nazis.[22] It is indicative that Catholic writers complained with regularity that the Third Reich had disappointed them in the realm of sexual mores. In this vein, for instance, one Catholic editor in Württemberg charged that "fleshly lust" and a "spirit of uncleanness" were at work in the Third Reich, and bemoaned the fact that although "at first we believed that morality would improve in the Third Reich – today *this hope* reveals itself *more and more as false*."[23] The far more prevalent tactic in Nazi discussions of sex was to use references to Jews' purportedly shameless and morally reprehensible defense of sexual pleasure-seeking as a technique of disavowal, a strategy for distracting attention from Nazis' own defenses of the very same

---

19 Paul Danzer, "Die Haltung zum anderen Geschlecht als unentbehrliche Grundlage völkischen Aufbaus," in *Streiflichter ins Völkische: Ausgewählte Lesestücke für deutsche Menschen aus dem "Völkischen Willen"* (Berlin, 1936), 5–6.

20 Dr. Knorr, "Eine noch nicht genügend beachtete weltanschauliche und bevölkerungspolitische Gefahr," *Ziel und Weg: Organ des Nationalsozialistischen Deutschen Ärztebundes* 7, no. 22 (Nov. 1937): 570.

21 Major Dr. Ellenbeck, "Der deutsche Unteroffizier und das Thema 'Frauen und Mädchen,'" *Die Zivilversorgung* 47, nos. 19–20 (Oct. 15, 1942): 281–2.

22 See B. van Acken, S.J., "Prüderie – Distanzhalten," *Theologisch-praktische Quartalschrift* 92 (1939): 73–87.

23 Krupka's remarks in *Weg zum Ziel* 18 (1935), quoted and discussed in "Pikanterien im Beichtstuhl," *Das Schwarze Korps*, June 26, 1935, 5.

thing.[24] Without question, romantic and sexual relations between so-called Aryan men and women were extensively monitored, often with profoundly repressive consequences, including prohibitions on marriage, compulsory sterilization, and enforcement of unwanted abortions or denial of desired abortions.[25] But we cannot understand the popular appeal of Nazism if we focus only on its repressiveness.

As Herbert Marcuse observed in the 1940s, when he worked for the American Office of Strategic Services, the effectiveness of Nazi culture also rested on its "abolition" of taboos, its "emancipation of sexual life," and its "inducement" to the pursuit of sexual pleasure. This actually involved a reconfiguration of taboos: What was off limits was not sexual fulfillment; rather, who could have sex and with whom were circumscribed in new ways. As Marcuse noted, Nazism encouraged sexual release and license and worked to link that release and license to racism; Nazism appealed powerfully to yearnings for a no-nonsense earthiness *and* to a hubristic sense of belonging to a "master race." As Marcuse put it, "the destruction of the family, the attack on patriarchalic and monogamic standards and all the similar widely heralded undertakings play upon the latent 'discontent' in civilization, the protest against its restraint and frustration. They appeal to the right of 'nature,' to the healthy and defamed drives of man. . . . They claim to reestablish the 'natural.'" At the same time, however, "the new individual liberties are by their very nature exclusive liberties, the privilege of the healthy and approved." Marcuse certainly pointed out that under Nazism "personal satisfaction has become a controlled political function" and that while "the abolition of these taboos" was "one of the most daring enterprises of National Socialism . . . the liberty or license implied in this abolition serves to intensify the 'Gleichschaltung' [coordination] of individuals into the National Socialist system." Yet he also was quite clear about the inciting effects of Nazism and its encouragement especially of "extra-marital relations between the sexes."[26]

Although Marcuse suggested that the trends he was identifying could not be found in official regime pronouncements or documents but rather needed

24 See Dagmar Herzog, " 'Love Is the Only True Religious Experience in the World': Theorizing Sexuality Under National Socialism," paper delivered at Cornell University, Apr. 12, 2001.
25 An excellent overview and analysis is provided by Gabriele Czarnowski, "Hereditary and Racial Welfare (*Erb- und Rassenpflege*): The Politics of Sexuality and Reproduction in Nazi Germany," *Social Politics* 4, no. 1 (spring 1977): 114–35. Czarnowski notes that between 3 percent and 5 percent of applications for marriage loans were rejected, and that such rejections could also be accompanied by prohibition of the marriage or compulsory sterilization (116–18).
26 Herbert Marcuse, *Technology, War and Fascism: Collected Papers of Herbert Marcuse*, ed. Douglas Kellner, 2 vols. (London, 1998), 1:84–6, 162–3.

to be gleaned from an assessment of social and cultural dynamics, the widely read SS journal *Das schwarze Korps* (The Black Corps) – directed explicitly at the nation's self-understood racial and political elite and one of the regime's prime venues for disseminating its policy views to its most devoted followers – actually provides a very good sense of Nazi strategies with regard to sex. In particular, the journal reveals the brazen self-confidence with which Nazi theorizers took on the Catholic Church's antisexual attitude while elaborating in great detail on their own pro-sex position. In the mid-1930s, for example, Christian campaigns to turn the populace away from Nazism by documenting the Nazis' encouragement of premarital intercourse were a running joke for the journal, which reprinted – and repudiated – the Christian complaints only to confirm, with slight twists emphasizing the grandeur of the Nazis' racial aims, precisely the point that the party was in synch with the populace, especially its youth, on the matter of the benefits and pleasures of premarital encounters. As befits the mindset of a fundamentally opportunistic regime, the journal was carefully contradictory, placing defenses of marriage and critiques of "Marxist" free love and "Jewish" attacks on the family side-by-side with amused diatribes against bourgeois prudery. But the overwhelming message was that although romantic activity needed to take racial concerns into account, heterosexuality was fun, and parents or religious authorities who doubted that were simply out of step with the new age.[27]

In the 1950s, individuals with insider knowledge of the Nazi regime's leadership confirmed the view that Nazism was not just sexually repressive. For example, the much-discussed and -reviewed memoirs of Felix Kersten, Heinrich Himmler's personal physician, published in 1952 in German and 1957 in English, argued that (far from being the uptight "sex critics" they would be portrayed as in later years) both Hitler and Himmler were enthusiastic advocates of bigamous and extramarital sexuality.[28] In 1958, the successful Nazi-era film director Arthur Maria Rabenalt asserted that Nazism's sexual politics were not even as narrowly reproduction-oriented as many may have thought. In Rabenalt's words, "The National Socialist will to

27 See "Offene Antwort auf eine katholische Kritik," *Das schwarze Korps*, Apr. 17, 1935, 1–2; "Ist das Nacktkultur? Herr Stapel entrüstet sich!," *Das schwarze Korps*, Apr. 24, 1935, 12; " '. . . Unzucht in der Soldatenzeit,' " *Das schwarze Korps*, Mar. 5, 1936, 6; "Ehestifter Staat," *Das schwarze Korps*, Mar. 26, 1936, 11; "Das uneheliche Kind," *Das schwarze Korps*, Apr. 9, 1936, 6; and "Anstössig?" *Das schwarze Korps*, Apr. 16, 1936, 13.

28 See Felix Kersten, *Totenkopf und Treue: Heinrich Himmler ohne Uniform* (Hamburg, 1952); translated as *The Kersten Memoirs, 1940–1945* (New York, 1957). Contrast the later representations of Hitler in "Die gefallene Natur," *Der Spiegel*, May 2, 1966, 58; and of Himmler in Dieter Duhm, *Angst im Kapitalismus* (Lampertheim, 1972), 102; and Detlev Peukert, *Inside Nazi Germany: Conformity, Opposition, and Racism in Everyday Life* (New Haven, Conn., 1987), 203–7.

eroticism, the matter-of-fact embrace of sex manifested itself far beyond these functionalist necessities, in a very free-spirited, generous, un-bourgeois way." Rabenalt added that under Nazism "marriage was encouraged and propagated as the cell of state formation, but it was anything but sacrosanct." As long as sexual representations and practices stayed within the official racial guidelines and the leadership's personal taste, he claimed, "the erotic" faced "no limit," and adultery and premarital sexual activity were openly tolerated. In sum, and repeatedly contrasting Nazi attitudes to the (in his view) far more prudish Stalinist ones, Rabenalt characterized the Nazis as vigorous defenders of the "all-powerful sexual drive."[29]

In contrast, then, to current conventional wisdom that treats the Third Reich's sexual politics as a reactionary backlash against the experimentation and openness of the Weimar years, what is most notable about the immediate post–World War II discussion is that *no one* in the later 1940s or 1950s argued that the Third Reich was anti-sex. On the contrary, the most diverse observers expressly remarked on what they saw as a *steady* liberalization of heterosexual sexual mores in the first half of the twentieth century, or even articulated directly their view that it was the *Nazis* who had spurred this liberalization. It is important to note that this singular emphasis on Nazi incitement itself constituted a disavowal and erasure especially of the ways that sexual incitement under Nazism had been inextricable from Nazi racism in all its many anti-Semitic, homophobic, anti-handicapped and class-slanted aspects. Nonetheless, the point holds that no one in the 1940s or 1950s perceived the Nazis – from the national leaders to the SS in the camps, to the pro-Nazi populace – to be especially hung-up. The concept of the repressed fascist was a creation of the 1960s.

Meanwhile, although certainly there were voices in the postwar years that called for even *more* sexual liberality, as well as voices that strove to impose greater value-conservatism, the initial seven or eight postwar years were seen as rather sexually liberal as well. Conservative Christians hostile to the trends of the time, for example, referred to the postwar era as one of "erotic overstimulation and damned sexualism," and complained about what they identified as the "overheated atmosphere" and "the progressive

---

29 Arthur M. Rabenalt, *Film im Zwielicht: Über den unpolitischen Film des Dritten Reiches und die Begrenzung des totalitären Anspruches* (Munich, 1958), 26–9. In addition, in contrast to those who might dismiss all accounts of a pro-sex Third Reich as based on an extrapolation from the "chaos" of the war and immediate postwar years, Rabenalt emphasized the opposite, saying that if it had had any effect at all, the war had brought with it the first hesitations about the overarching trend toward liberalization, because of the concern that incidents of adultery on the home front – or even the perception that they might be occurring – could be damaging to the *Wehrmacht's* morale.

sexualization of the entirety of life."[30] Conservatives saw in the evidence that some eighty sex-aid companies in the Federal Republic attracted tens of thousands of customers each month nothing but "a powerless attempt to extricate oneself from the general apathy and despair."[31] Others argued, as did one contributor to a Catholic reference work on sex, that "in the life of peoples one must speak of a sexual crisis, when lifelong marriage and monogamous marriage are called into question, sexual crimes and perversions grow out of control, and sexual matters take up too broad a space in public. It is incontestable that such a sexual crisis exists now. Marriages are breaking up . . . youth masturbation and extramarital intercourse among youth are becoming increasingly frequent."[32] But as the conservative complaints already suggest, in the years immediately following the war there was decidedly greater openness and generosity in discussion of heterosexuality than in the later 1950s and early 1960s.[33]

It was not only conservatives who thought of postwar Germans as invested in sexual satisfaction. In response to the publication of the first Kinsey report in the United States, for example, reviewers in the German press in 1948 and 1949 could only marvel and scoff at the pathetic prudishness and backwardness of American attitudes. Reviewers declared themselves aghast at what they saw as the puritanical American notion that sexual desire was the preserve of men and pitied the American woman who disliked sex and the American man who employed inadequate sexual skill. All this stood in sharp contrast to the "sexual freedom" and "true eroticism" of the Europeans.[34]

Indeed, one thing that emerges with startling clarity from a reading of postwar sexual discussions is that sex was important to postwar Germans in a way that has gone fundamentally underacknowledged in the extant and otherwise excellent scholarship on postwar gender and family relations.[35]

---

30 Johannes Leppich, " 'Thema 1,' " in Günther Mees and Günter Graf, eds., *Pater Leppich Spricht: Journalisten hören den "roten" Pater* (Düsseldorf, 1952), 44; and "Gefahren und Ursachen des Sexualismus," *Bonifatiusbote* 63, no. 9 (1952): 5.

31 "Gefahren und Ursachen des Sexualismus," 5.

32 Richard Gutzwiller, "Die Überwindung der sexuellen Krise," in Franz Xavier von Hornstein and Adolf Faller, eds., *Gesundes Geschlechtsleben: Handbuch für Ehefragen* (Olten, 1950), 436.

33 I emphasize the heterosexual aspect advisedly, although I would say that despite pervasive homophobia there was a brief window of greater openness around homosexuality as well. This window closed in 1950 with the recommencement of prosecutions of homosexuals in the Federal Republic. See Dieter Schiefelbein, "Wiederbeginn der juristischen Verfolgung homosexueller Männer in der Bundesrepublik Deutschland: Die Homosexuellen-Prozesse in Frankfurt am Main 1950/51," *Zeitschrift für Sexualforschung* 5 (1992): 59–73.

34 See Ha., "Puritanismus und Wirklichkeit: Kinseys 'Sex Report' und sein Widerhall," *Die Weltwoche* 16, no. 765 (1948): 9; and L. M. Lawrence, "Der Kinsey Report," *Merkur* 3, no. 5 (1949): 495–9.

35 In addition to the secondary scholarship cited above, see also Dieter Wirth, "Die Familie in der Nachkriegszeit: Desorganisation oder Stabilität?" in Josef Becker, Theo Stammen, and Peter Waldmann, eds., *Vorgeschichte der Bundesrepublik Deutschland: Zwischen Kapitulation und Grundgesetz*

And far from seeing extramarital arrangements or promiscuity as an effect of the "crisis years" of economic hardship and military occupation, or as a dramatic departure from past behaviors, contemporaries tended to emphasize a sense of continuity in sexual values. In a way that would come to seem unimaginable for those who remember the claustrophobic later 1950s, in the late 1940s and early 1950s sex was "Topic No. 1" (*Thema 1*).[36] The idea that "unsatisfied urges" made people "neurotic" was widely held.[37] Nonmarital heterosexual activity was taken to be not only prevalent but reasonable. And – strikingly, in view of later attitudes – the reality of female desire and capacity for satisfaction were considered well-established facts. In one study, carried out in 1949 by *Constanze* and the Institute for Statistical Market and Opinion Research (ISMA), six out of ten people questioned declared that sex between unmarried adults was not immoral, and fewer than three out of ten insisted that it was.[38] In another, more elaborate 1949 study, done by the weekly paper *Wochenend* and the Institute for Demoscopy in Allensbach, fully 71 percent of those questioned approved of premarital sex and only 16 percent disapproved. Moreover, 52 percent described premarital experience for women as desirable; 28 percent went so far as to assert that it would be detrimental for a woman, sexually speaking, to be a virgin on her wedding day. Meanwhile, 89 percent of the men and 69 percent of the women among the over one thousand people interviewed admitted to having had premarital sex. The sole significant differential variable found by the study had to do with church attendance: That quarter of the population that attended church regularly tended to disapprove more strongly of premarital relations. Yet it is relevant to note that even in this constituency fully 44 percent declared that premarital sex was just fine.[39]

(Munich, 1979); Angela Vogel, "Familie," in Wolfgang Benz, ed., *Die Bundesrepublik Deutschland: Geschichte in drei Bänden*, 3 vols. (Frankfurt am Main, 1983), vol. 2; Barbara Willenbacher, "Zerrüttung und Bewährung der Nachkriegs-Familie," in Martin Broszat et al., *Von Stalingrad zur Währungsreform: Zur Sozialgeschichte des Umbruchs in Deutschland* (Munich, 1988); Karin Stiehr, "Aspekte der gesellschaftlichen und politischen Situation von Frauen in den 50er Jahren," in Barbara Determann et al., eds., *Verdeckte Überlieferungen: Weiblichkeitsbilder zwischen Weimarer Republik, Nationalsozialismus und Fünfziger Jahre* (Frankfurt am Main, 1991); Merith Niehuss, "Kontinuität und Wandel der Familie in den 50er Jahren," in Axel Schildt and Arnold Sywottek, eds., *Modernisierung im Wiederaufbau* (Bonn, 1993); Robert G. Moeller, *Protecting Motherhood: Women and the Family in the Politics of Postwar West Germany* (Berkeley, Calif., 1993); and Maria Hoehn, "GIs, Veronikas, and Lucky Strikes: German Reactions to the American Military Presence in the Rhineland-Palatinate during the 1950s," Ph.D. diss., University of Pennsylvania, 1995.

36 Leppich, "'Thema 1,'" 43; Walter Dittmann, "Die Krisis der Ehe: Die Ansicht des Geistlichen," *Nordwestdeutsche Hefte* 2, no. 10 (1947): 34.
37 Laszlo Hamori, "Die rationalisierte Sexualität," *Aktion* 8 (1951): 48.
38 See Petra Lund, "Muss Liebe amtlich beglaubigt sein?" *Constanze* 1 (1949): 3.
39 On the whole, men and women tended to present similar views, and those between the ages of twenty and fifty were largely in agreement with one another; only those over fifty, especially those

There is no reason to think that these findings simply resulted from unsophisticated sampling techniques.[40] On the contrary, expounding on the sense that heterosexual mores had loosened considerably was a favorite activity across the disciplinary and ideological spectrum. The University of Freiburg jurist Karl Siegfried Bader, for instance, in addressing the founding meeting of the German Association for Sex Research in 1950 asserted as uncontroversial that in the course of the first half of the twentieth century, the rural population had become just as sexually liberal as the urban, and that indeed "the moral code of the bourgeois era is now strongly defended by an ever smaller residual group . . . the old strict order has acquired the taint of the obsolete, the ridiculous." He also stressed that "the transformations of the sexual order were primarily caused by the raising and – at least partial – recognition of a woman's entitlement to the acknowledgement of *her* needs. What distinguishes today's sexual order from that of the beginning of the century is the greater assertion of female sexual rights."[41] As numerous other commentators observed, it was not just that women were claiming their share of sexual pleasure; men, too, no longer valued female virginity as much as they once had. In 1950, for instance, the leading sexologist Hans Giese remarked on "the ever increasing disappearance in the last two or three decades of the significance of female virginity in the erotic imagination of male consciousness."[42] Similar observations were put forward in 1949 in a book on sexual hygiene by Dr. Heinz Graupner. The old double standard,

socialized before 1900, inclined toward greater strictness. See Ludwig von Friedeburg, *Die Umfrage in der Intimsphäre*, Beiträge zur Sexualforschung, vol. 4 (Stuttgart, 1953), 24, 27, 46, 50.

40 It is unlikely that with more advanced techniques the results would have tended toward greater conservatism. The wealth of other interpretive evidence from the era – from both supporters and detractors of the liberalizing trends – suggests the results' representativeness. It is further notable that those who reported on and analyzed the findings clearly did not feel any need to contradict the results. (In addition to Lund and Friedeburg, see also I. Phönix, "Moderne Intimmoral," in Hans Giese and A. Willy, eds., *Mensch, Geschlecht, Gesellschaft: Das Geschlechtsleben unserer Zeit gemeinverständlich dargestellt* (Paris, 1954), 201–9.) Indeed, one of the most noteworthy aspects of Friedeburg's analysis was the way he went on, up front and at length, about the fact that the Germans interviewed in the study had expressed deep commitment to the institution of marriage. In the early 1950s, when he was writing his analysis, this commitment was apparently not self-evident. It is finally also of interest that the numbers endorsing – and admitting having engaged in – premarital sex in West Germany at this time, especially among the women, are considerably higher than the comparable figures from England or the United States. See L. R. England, "Little Kinsey: An Outline of Sex Attitudes in Britain," *Public Opinion Quarterly* 13, no. 4 (1949): 587–600; and for a concise summary of Kinsey's findings for the United States, see John D'Emilio and Estelle B. Freedman, *Intimate Matters: A History of Sexuality in America* (New York, 1988), 286.

41 Karl Siegfried Bader, "Die Veränderung der Sexualordnung und die Konstanz der Sittlichkeits-delikte," *Zeitschrift für Sexualforschung* 1, nos. 3–4 (1950): 217. On the positive reception of Bader's talk see esp. Udo Undeutsch, "Jugendsexualität: Tatsachen und Folgerungen," *Zeitschrift für Sexual-forschung* 1, no. 2 (June–July 1950): 123.

42 Hans Giese, review of Max Marcuse's essay, "Zur Psychologie der Eifersucht und der Psychopatholo-gie ihres Fehlens," *Psyche* 3 (1950), published in *Zeitschrift für Sexualforschung* 1, nos. 3–4 (1950): 307.

he said, was simply falling away: "In the eyes of men, female virginity has lost meaning also with respect to the future wife.... Nowadays it no longer is made into a problem for a girl if her first experience did not lead to marriage. We have to accept this state of affairs, even if we don't like it: It is the general condition of our present."[43]

The change in West Germany that thus requires explanation is the one that took place in the *mid*-1950s. For, as it turns out, all the sexually conservative attitudes now stereotypically associated with the 1950s, particularly with the especially stuffy West German version of them – the obsession with the niceties of proper manners, the prescriptive consignment of sexuality only to marriage, the devaluation of sexuality and hostility to its open discussion and display in general, and the belief in particular that women were less sexual than men and that overt sexual desire and agency on women's part was unrespectable – consisted of convictions that only gradually became consolidated in the course of the 1950s. One of the most remarkable things is that popular magazines in the first years of the 1960s expressed more conservative views on gender and sex than did those in the late 1940s.[44]

In order to better understand how conservative mores became gradually ascendant, it is worthwhile to look more closely at the writings of different constituencies: self-identified Christians arguing against premarital sex, defenders of "free love" singing its praises, and mainstream commentators and advice-givers trying to stake out a middle ground. The evidence that emerges is quite weird and complicated, and it raises important theoretical questions about ideological conflict more generally. Scholars in gender history have done a fair amount of thinking about the ways in which invocations of a notion of "crisis" facilitate efforts to reconstruct social hierarchies. A great deal more thinking needs to go into understanding the role played by the assertion that people are in a state of "misery." In the opening pages of volume 1 of *The History of Sexuality*, Michel Foucault began to sketch the outlines of a conceptual framework for thinking about the powerful effects produced by promises of happiness.[45] And in *The Sexual Fix*, his marvelous introduction to the history of sexuality in Anglo-American culture in the nineteenth and twentieth centuries, the British film and cultural critic

---

43 Heinz Graupner, "Das normale Geschlechtsleben und seine Gefahren," *Liebe und Ehe* 1, no. 2 (1949): 4. This is an excerpt from Graupner, *Geschlechtshygiene und Geschlechtskrankheiten* (Konstanz, 1949).
44 For a classic summary statement of the conservative notions, especially the sexual double standard, see the first several installments of Dr. Christoph Vollmer's "Knigge für Verliebte" in the popular teen magazine *Bravo* in December 1962 and January 1963. Contrast the spirited defense of unmarried love by journalist Petra Lund in 1949 in Lund, "Muss Liebe amtlich beglaubigt sein?" 3.
45 Michel Foucault, *The History of Sexuality*, vol. 1: *An Introduction* (New York, 1980), 3–13.

Stephen Heath elaborated on some of Foucault's insights.[46] But there is far more work ahead of us in making sense of the effects of discourses of sexual happiness in concrete historical contexts.

Precisely the prominence of the Christian churches in West Germany (in contrast to the obvious demotion of the churches' role in the Soviet zone of occupation) was a crucial factor in making sex a constant topic of public debate. In the western zones in the postwar period the churches reacquired tremendous prestige and influence. This was due in part to the American occupiers' (largely mistaken) assumption that the churches had provided something of a bulwark against Nazism – and the occupiers' concomitant decision to allow the churches to run their own denazification procedures.[47] And it was due in part to the choice of the Christian Democrat Konrad Adenauer as the first postwar chancellor of the Federal Republic. Through Adenauer's appointment of Franz-Josef Wuermeling as family minister in 1953, Wuermeling's own particular brand of conservative Catholic values in matters of sex, gender, and family policy soon were ensconced in the law of the land.[48] As one German who had experienced both the Third Reich and its aftermath remembered recently, "people resented that so much, when the Catholic church got power again."[49]

One of the more notable phenomena in the postwar discussion in West Germany is the fact that it was Catholic writers in particular who most frequently highlighted what they saw as a pervasive Nazi incitement to sex. (One important explanation for this is precisely that competition between Catholics and Nazis over sexual matters went back to the Third Reich itself.) Some writers simply railed against Nazi inducements to premarital activity. In the antifascist intellectual (and tendentially Catholic) periodical *Frankfurter Hefte*, for example, Maria Jochum in 1946 criticized the ways unmarried women under Nazism had been "encouraged into extramarital motherhood at all costs or at least into libertinage."[50] The well-known priest Johannes Leppich, in his widely attended open-air sermons, raged against popular denigration of female virginity as just so much "hackneyed Goebbels-claptrap."[51] And the Catholic physician Anton Hofmann, in his

---

46 Stephen Heath, *The Sexual Fix* (New York, 1984).
47 For a comprehensive assessment of just how pliable and nonresistant to Nazism both the Catholic and Protestant churches were despite postwar narratives to the contrary, see Robert P. Ericksen and Susannah Heschel, eds., *Betrayal: German Churches and the Holocaust* (Minneapolis, 1999). See also Dagmar Herzog, "Theology of Betrayal," *Tikkun* 16, no. 3 (May–June 2001): 69–72.
48 For an excellent discussion of Wuermeling's impact, see Stiehr, "Aspekte der gesellschaftlichen und politischen Situation," 122–5.
49 R.S., Washington, D.C., May 1999, communication with the author.
50 Maria Jochum, "Frauenfrage 1946," *Frankfurter Hefte*, June 1946, 25.
51 Leppich, " 'Thema 1,' " 46.

sex-advice book of 1951, criticized the way "NS-schools and the like" had forced "premature sexual contact" on young people under the guise of " 'natural-free experiencing' of the erotic event." But Hofmann also linked Nazi encouragement of sexual activity with Nazism's other crimes. Analyzing what he called "the sexual crisis of the present," Hofmann contended that the disrespect for the spiritual dimension of life evident among people overly obsessed with erotic pleasure was intimately connected with disrespect for the bodies of others and therefore facilitated brutality and mass murder. Or, as he put it, after he lumped together "overvaluation of the body" with "godlessness and cruelty," what needed to be understood was "the paradoxical matter that the same person who raises the body to dizzying heights can in an instant sacrifice the bodies of a hundred thousand others."[52]

Another strategy, however, was to adapt the public's evident preoccupation with sexual happiness to a Christian message. Catholics and Protestants alike tried to make the case that – contrary to Nazi-fostered clichés – Christianity was actually *pro*-pleasure. Indeed, one of the main strategies among postwar Christian writers was to argue that Christian, marital sex was especially ecstatic, that it in fact offered more pleasure than secular vice. Protestant physician Theodor Bovet, for example, liked to announce that "for the Christian there is no contradiction between eros and divine love."[53] Catholic theologian Franz Arnold, in complaining about what he saw as the Nazi stereotype that Christianity encouraged a "negation of nature . . . a defamation of eros and sex" (and lamenting that this "widely held notion" had "survived the downfall of the Third Reich and its blood-mythos"), also argued that marital sex was a great thing.[54] In the "fundamental biblical texts," Arnold contended, "sexual pleasure within marriage is considered to be the God-willed *creation-ecstasy* of those who carry on the work of the Creator in accordance with His thoughts."[55]

Related themes were evident in Hans Wirtz's best-selling sex-advice book for Catholics, *Vom Eros zur Ehe* (From Eros to Marriage, 1946), which managed to get the apostolic imprimatur but was also a paean to the joys of wedded sex. Daring the church fathers to presume to know what God wanted now that Drs. Smulders, Knaus, and Ogino had discovered how women's cycles actually worked and hence had been able to develop the

---

52 Anton Christian Hofmann, *Die Natürlichkeit der christlichen Ehe* (Munich, 1951), 5, 9–10, 38–9.
53 Theodor Bovet, "Die Ehe, ihre Krise und Neuwerdung," *Universitas* 2, no. 2 (1947): 161.
54 Franz Arnold, "Sinnlichkeit und Sexualität im Lichte von Theologie und Seelsorge," in *Über das Wesen der Sexualität*, Beiträge zur Sexualforschung, vol. 1 (Stuttgart, 1952), 1.
55 Franz Arnold, "Das eheliche Geheimnis in Theologie und Seelsorge," *Universitas* 2, no. 10 (1947): 1155, 1158. Arnold in fact departed from Catholic Church teaching in contending that birth control was acceptable within marriage.

rhythm method, Wirtz slyly asked "who could know" whether maybe God Himself "in our present conditions" might not be in favor of a bit more emphasis on what used to be called "the secondary purpose" of marriage – that is, sexual communion (and not just reproduction). In Wirtz's view, sexual satisfaction for both partners was essential to a healthy marriage; Wirtz encouraged husbands to become ever more expert at bringing their wives to orgasm. Although always invoking various church authorities, insisting that church law be honored, and claiming to advocate the reconciliation of spirit and flesh, Wirtz repeatedly also referred to the "weakness of the flesh," "the incredible force of the drives," the strength of "the sexual motor," the "revolt of the blood against the spirit," and "the giving of a thousand joys," as well as to the idea that "*eros* and *sexus* are essential to marriage. They are its *center*, not a side realm. They are the main point."[56]

The key to these arguments was the sanctity of marriage, and this of course provided a major contrast to Nazism. But what remains interesting are the innovative ways that church-affiliated authors made their arguments for keeping all this delightful, God-willed sexual activity within marriage. Hofmann, for example, who was a defender of women's "equal right" to the "rapturous haze" of orgasm (his argument against coitus interruptus was not just that preventing pregnancy was against church law but also that it deprived the woman of climax), also stated in his book that if a man engaged in sexual activity before marriage, he ran the risk of having difficulty achieving erections all through his many years of marriage. In general, Hofmann warned, "the full, blissful richness of sexual love can only remain preserved undiminished for that person who has not violated it with untamed greed."[57] Bovet was even more blunt: "Happy love is only possible within marriage." In his sex-advice book specifically for girls, Bovet declared that whoever "wants to experience the whole pleasure of love [*die ganze Lust der Liebe*] cannot even consider experiencing it outside of marriage. It is as impossible as harvesting grapes during the snows of March. Only those who do not have an inkling of or do not respect mature love-lust can allow themselves to preempt it prematurely." Indeed, Bovet went so far as to assert that "the majority of girls who wish for or tolerate premarital intercourse are not somehow especially passionate but on the contrary are those who repress their feelings or are indeed frigid."[58]

56 Hans Wirtz, *Vom Eros zur Ehe: Die naturgetreue Lebensgemeinschaft* (Heidelberg, 1946), 7, 227, 231, 246, 248, 256–7.
57 Hofmann, *Die Natürlichkeit*, 50, 79, 81, 83.
58 Theodor Bovet, *Die werdende Frau* (Bern, 1962), 20–1; the book previously appeared in Switzerland in 1944, and was first published in Germany in 1950.

Christian writers, meanwhile, also exhibited disturbing continuities with Nazism. Catholic Werner Schöllgen, for example, not only offered the factually false but pro-orgasmic argument that "often the actual source of a woman's infertility lies in her frigidity. . . . The full love experience thus has an objective meaning with respect to the child." He also spoke of pregnancy prevention as "biological suicide" and contended that "the eugenic idea" had not lost its value despite "the abuse in the Third Reich."[59] Christian physician Meta Holland in 1950 reprinted her popular *Vor dem Tore der Ehe* (Before the Gate of Marriage) – which had previously appeared in 1936 – in slightly altered form. The 1950 edition simply removed her glowing references to Hitler and the "purity of mores" in the "new Germany" along with her impassioned defense of the National Socialist sterilization program from a purportedly Christian point of view. It retained not only references to the claims of "race" and "tribe," but detailed delineations of the "eugenic" situations that made reproduction inadvisable or even immoral.[60] And Bovet, too, insisted on the need to "be concerned with the healthy inheritance of our *Volk*." He bemoaned the fact that "the less valuable elements, especially the mentally deficient, reproduce themselves approximately twice as much as healthy families. It is therefore absolutely necessary that, if we do not one day want to be completely overwhelmed by those [elements], everyone who feels himself to be healthy . . . give life to as many children as possible."[61]

But although there were certain continuities with Nazism among Christian writers, Christians could at least point to their critique of pre- and extramarital sex as *the* decisive difference between their worldview and the Nazi one. The defenders of "free love" in the postwar period had a much harder time. The overtly risqué sex-advice journal *Liebe und Ehe*, launched in Regensburg in 1949, provides a classic example of these difficulties. The journal was available by subscription and at magazine kiosks across the country, and it was important enough to attract contributions from dozens of popular medical and other publicists. It was one of the very few postwar venues in which nonmarital sex was written about repeatedly and in detail. It is hence no surprise that *Liebe und Ehe* was sharply censured as "a dirty publication" by the federal government's Committee for Youth Welfare.[62] And it is indeed striking how sensitive the (anonymous) editors were to

59 Schöllgen in *Die Kirche in der Welt* 1, no. 35 (1947–8): 160.
60 See Meta Holland, *Vor dem Tore der Ehe: Was jede junge Frau wissen muss* (Konstanz, 1936), 4–5, 91–7, and (Konstanz, 1950), 5, 87–9.
61 Theodor Bovet, *Von Mann zu Mann: Eine Einführung ins Reifealter für junge Männer* (Tübingen, 1955), 47.
62 See Karl P. Rüth, "Ist 'Liebe und Ehe' eine unzüchtige Zeitschrift?" *Liebe und Ehe* 3, no. 5 (1951): 212; see also Sven Säger, "Sind wir eigentlich prüde?" *Liebe und Ehe* 2, no. 3 (1950): 20.

antipornography sentiment. The photographs of female nudes, which had been so prevalent in the 1949 issues – replete with coy captions such as "between girl and woman" or "quiet resistance" – disappeared in the early months of 1950 (even as the celebratory photographs of happy childhood – with such captions as "mother-bliss is still the deepest bliss" – remained an ongoing feature).[63] Numerous essays in *Liebe and Ehe*'s pages strove to defend the *moral* value of the frank discussion of sex. The journal continually vacillated between assertions of the legitimacy of nonmarital sexual love and insistence on the importance of pleasurable sex to stable marriages.[64] Contributors even drew on religious language. (So here again, as with the Christians' adaptation of the language of pleasure, one can see how otherwise opposing viewpoints drew from each other's rhetorical strategies.) For example, as medical doctor Gerhard Ockel put it in a 1951 essay endorsing cunnilingus as an "actually totally natural caress": "Wherever there is true love is always sacred land, and all doing is pleasing to the Creator-power."[65] Or as Dorothee Löhe put it in 1950, defending the nude sculptures by Georg Kolbe that had been popular during the Third Reich, it was obvious that "behind these naked human beings stands a chaste Creator." Kolbe, in her view, was motivated by a "deeply humble love of God and human beings."[66] What stands out above all in *Liebe und Ehe* is a constant search to find a language with which to make sex and sexual pleasure socially appropriate goals and topics.

In that search, contributors moved back and forth between calling for greater sexual freedom and insisting that the public had already voted, as it were, with its bodies. Contributors repeatedly expressed delight at the way "morality concepts have in recent times been extraordinarily transformed."[67] Or as another author noted with pride, young girls in his day – "and by no means just the 'easy ones'" – were turning away from their parents' mores and announcing "'I have a *right* to premarital love.'"[68] Similarly, in an indicative essay in 1951 titled "On the Generational Difference in Morality," the author went on at length about the ways that women born between 1925 and 1935 were the most gratifyingly open to "objective"

---

63 See *Liebe und Ehe* 1, no. 1 (1949): 9, 21.
64 In general, the journal gave space to an eclectic and incongruous array of voices and opinions. Scientific information about the reproductive process or the newest medical treatments for impotence or venereal disease alternated with historical discussions of sexual mores in the European Middle Ages or ethnographic excursus on sex lives or beauty standards among Eskimos, Islamic Arabs, or the Ovambo of the Congo.
65 Gerhard Ockel, "Tiefenpsychologie und Sinnlichkeit," *Liebe und Ehe* 3, no. 2 (1951): 54.
66 Dorothee Löhe, "Menschenpaar," *Liebe und Ehe* 2, no. 1 (1950): 1.
67 K. Fischer, "Darf Herr X Frau Y spät abends besuchen?" *Liebe und Ehe* 2, no. 12 (1950): 15.
68 Wilhelm Schuh, "Die Eltern, die Tochter, und die Liebe," *Liebe und Ehe* 3, no. 10 (1951): 400.

discussions of the need to reform marriage law and the possible benefits of polygamy – which he saw as happy signs of a "genuinely deeper-reaching transformation" in a "progressive" direction.[69]

The Third Reich figured in contradictory ways in *Liebe und Ehe*'s pages. Among other things, the recent past was invoked both in the repeated advertisements for a sex-advice book on the grounds that it had been "forbidden in the Third Reich" *and* in a defense of the SS's *Lebensborn* program, with its homes for racially fit unwed mothers, as "above all a welfare institution."[70] At one point, the journal emphasized the repressive aspects of Nazi sexual politics and contrasted this with what it saw as more liberal popular mores: The journal noted with pride that, when the Nazis had tried to impose restrictions on pimping that also affected parents' ability to allow their daughters' fiancés to spend the night, the good common sense of the German people had rebelled and judges had been forced to interpret the law loosely.[71] But the journal also noted the inciting aspects of Nazi policy; at one point, for example, it mockingly suggested with regard to prostitution that apparently it had been "reserved for the National Socialists to strike a blow against German morality by establishing public processionals [to the brothels]. Did they want to encourage the awakening of youthful drives for population-political purposes?"[72] And in another contribution the journal noted as incontrovertible fact that the Nazi state was "morally degenerate" and had "specifically in the realm of family life championed principles that were utterly at variance with the customs and laws of the centuries-old western Christian culture."[73]

Meanwhile, as with the Christians, *Liebe und Ehe* too gave evidence of some unapologetic continuity with Nazi attitudes. And this was not just because of the uncanny resemblances to Nazi-era phrasing evident in the journal's celebrations of healthy reproduction or the remarkable similarities between the sculptures of nudes favored by the journal and Nazi-approved artwork. No one, for example, seemed to feel the need to catch or correct one contributor's matter-of-fact report that "until the Second World War the girls of the eastern states, especially the eastern Jewesses, formed the main contingent of world prostitution."[74] And the same author who had made fun of Third Reich prostitution policy also wrote an essay in which

---

69 Hans Fervers, "Vom Generationsunterschied der Moral," *Liebe und Ehe* 3, no. 6 (1951): 232.
70 See the ad for Dr. Fried, *Liebes- und Eheleben*, in *Liebe und Ehe* 1, no. 1 (1949): 44; and "Konkursmasse 'Lebensborn,' " *Liebe und Ehe* 3, no. 12 (1951): 510.
71 W. Beese, "Gibt es Kuppelei an Verlobten?" *Liebe und Ehe* 2, no. 5 (1950): 13.
72 Kurt Fiebich, "Zur Frage der Bordellisierung," *Liebe und Ehe* 2, no. 9 (1950): 11–12.
73 Helmut Meissner, "Dreiecksehe sanktioniert," *Liebe und Ehe* 3, no. 10 (1951): 413.
74 Hans Niedermeier, " 'Mein Schatz ist ein Matrose . . . ,' " *Liebe und Ehe* 2, no. 11 (1950): 19.

he criticized the Nazi regime *and* the Federal Republic for giving "child money" to "child-rich" families – *not*, as one might think, because the Federal Republic's policies constituted an offensive continuation of Nazi attitudes toward the value of reproduction, but rather on grounds that under *both* regimes such policies only ended up benefitting the "irresponsible," alcoholic, and "unbridled." Indeed, the essay's main purpose was to defend eugenic sterilization of the "less talented" in the interests of the future health of the German *Volk*, now "pressed together into the most constricted space."[75]

Far more telling, however, is the way Nazism functioned as a source of humor. It was above all the regime's racism, and its homophobia, that commentators in *Liebe und Ehe* found amusing. A good example appeared in the imaginative set of fake personal ads in cartoon form that appeared in 1950. Beginning with a sexy vestal virgin in 1500 B.C. and ending in a dystopian post–atomic war future in 1958, the author, Hans von Hohenecken, offered a "little cultural history" of sexual mores. Von Hohenecken not only managed to make fun of post–World War II women's desperation to find a mate; the tattered woman in the nuclear wreckage of 1958 looks for an "English-speaking Sibiro-Russian" and is willing to put up with being a man's "secondary wife" (*Nebenfrau*). He also treated as comedic (even as he underscored the reality of) both the persistence of racist attitudes into the post-Nazi period and the ineffectiveness of denazification when he had the unattractive, middle-aged former Nazi Party official in 1948 assure all potentially interested females that he had been cleared, that he had a home of his own and a secure pension, and that only young women "of the best race and attitude" need apply.[76]

Another prime example of *Liebe und Ehe*'s humorous side is provided by a thoroughly incoherent multipart 1951 essay on "Sexual Problems in the SS" by Martin Brustmann. A doctor of sports medicine, Brustmann gave equal attention to what he saw as the SS's heterosexual, homosexual, and homophobic proclivities. Brustmann made fun both of the "exhaustion to the point of incapacitation" induced in young SS-men by the hordes of women willingly offering themselves to them, *and* of Himmler's disorientation in the face of spreading homosexual incidents within the SS. Among other things, Brustmann was especially entertained by the way Himmler's homophobia bore resemblance to the teachings of the Old Testament, a fact

75 Kurt Fiebich, "Der Selbstmord der Intelligenz: Die Expansion der Minderbegabten," *Liebe und Ehe* 3, no. 8 (1951): 318.
76 Hans von Hohenecken, "Kleine Kulturgeschichte in Heiratsanzeigen," *Liebe und Ehe* 2, no. 8 (1950): 40.

Himmler had been "embarrassed" to have pointed out to him. Brustmann also shared with readers the news that circumcision (because of infected foreskins) was "one of the most frequently performed operations within the SS": "The lengthening of the duration of coitus due to circumcision, which made the problem of the frigid woman relatively infrequent among Jews and Mohammedans, now also benefitted the SS, and it repeatedly brought on raucous hilarity when the SS-men had to let themselves be told that they owed the advantages of this operation to that place in the Bible's Old Testament in which Jehova sealed his covenant with Israel." Distancing himself from Nazi racism by designating the circumcision story as a key example of "the paradox" and "the cunning of history," Brustmann at other points also unself-consciously repeated Nazi stereotypes (among other things declaring himself amused at how many regime-serving Germans needed to be declared "honorary Aryans" because the much-fabled Jew *Jud Süss* had managed to leave behind such "numerous traces" of his sexual activity across southern Germany).[77] In short, by constantly shifting his point of view Brustmann made it possible for readers both to identify *with* the laughing Nazis and to laugh *at* them.

Meanwhile, however, another theme evident in *Liebe und Ehe* was a diffuse but powerful sense of lamentation about a perceived general loss of eroticism and/or a sense that heterosexuality was not in a "healthy" state. For example, one physician writing in 1951 called on Germans to turn away from (what he saw as) the prevailing trend toward promiscuity and instead turn toward long-term companionship. In this context, he tried to put into words what it was about the intensity of the war years that had loosened traditional mores. In "the most recent past," he wrote, the mobilization of countless "young-blooded" bodies of both sexes, "the concentration of all forces into violence and highest achievement," and "finally the pressure of an uncertain personal and universal fate hanging over everything" led even the "previously satisfied or morally strict" to become uninhibited. "Everything we call 'love,'" he said, "came away badly." Sex itself was reduced to a "primitive act," and whatever lack of quality the participants felt they

---

77 Martin Brustmann, "Sexuelle Probleme in der SS," *Liebe und Ehe* 3/2 (1951), 63; 3, no. 3 (1951): 113; 3, no. 4 (1951): 148; 3, no. 5 (1951): 204; and 3, no. 6 (1951): 249. During the war Brustmann had been asked to evaluate members of the SS who had been charged with having committed homosexual acts, and he had sought to save two from the death penalty. In one case he argued that the man's "abnormally large sex organ" meant most women could not accommodate him; in another case, he argued that the man was not responsible for his actions because he was "feeble-minded." Himmler, furious that Brustmann was being (in his view) too easy on the men, gave instructions that Brustmann be dropped as a medical expert in cases involving homosexuality. See Geoffrey J. Giles, "The Denial of Homosexuality: Same-Sex Incidents in Himmler's SS and Police," *Journal of the History of Sexuality* 11 (2002).

simply "attempted to compensate for by the quantity of such encounters and adventures."[78]

Another physician, Dr. Gerhard Giehm, in his 1948 book on "the treatment of mental and nervous sexual disorders," excerpted in *Liebe und Ehe*, was more overtly ideological. He tried both to distance himself from what he saw as the peculiar intensity of concern with sex in postwar Germany – what he called the "temporary sickness" of "the 'sexual gospel,'" that is, "that dogma about the preeminence of the sexual in the spiritual life of human beings, which gained significance in the debacle of the postwar time, but which soon will be superceded once the atmosphere of decline has been overcome" – *and* to call for a new and healthy defense of the "great personal and social significance ... of the problem of sexuality." By declaring that the postwar period's preoccupation with sex had something to do with the totality of Germany's defeat ("The 'sexual gospel' is the bible of the sick, the conquered and abnormal. It was the faith of the defeated in the transvaluation of all values") and by announcing that the aim of the coming era must be "healthy relations of the sexes, which, strengthened through the bond of the child, pass on the inheritance of the present and past to the future, in order in this way to make eternal the existence and rights-to-recognition of a *Volk*"), Giehm also managed to displace "that dogma about the preeminence of the sexual" away from Nazism itself and onto its defeat while simultaneously denying the manifest continuities between his vision and that of Nazism. For example, Giehm engaged in antisemitic allusions, denigrating those interested in "drive-drivenness" and "the secret areas of the unconscious" (clearly references to Freud and hence to Jewishness) – these he associated with sexual "sickness." He also contended that the new age had "smashed the commandment tablets" of the previous moment and was instead "celebrating the human of antiquity," thus invoking the time-honored but Nazi-reinforced distinction between the Jew and the Greek.[79]

Seemingly much more innocent tactics were evident in Löhe's defense of Kolbe's statue of a man protectively guarding the woman walking beside him. Praising the spirituality of these nudes provided Löhe with the hook for fantasizing about the restoration of a kind of coupledom in which the man would once again be the stronger partner and in which a new race of people, a new humanity ("*ein neues Geschlecht*"), would be established by this reinvigorated couple. Her concluding hope was that these new human beings, "through their loving union," would "find their way back to the

---

78 H. Schürmann, "Promiskuität – Zeichen der Zeit," *Liebe und Ehe* 3, no. 9 (1951): 385.
79 Gerhard Giehm, "Von der Sexualität in unserer Zeit," *Liebe und Ehe* 1, no. 1 (1949): 2.

paradise we seem to have lost."[80] What is evident here, as it was in the excerpt by Giehm, is a phenomenon that might best be described as a sort of post-fascist nostalgia. Precisely the fact that what the nostalgia referred to was left unclear – was the fascist era itself the lost paradise, or was the paradise some prefascist time? and what caused the paradise to be lost? Nazism? or its defeat? or something else? – coupled with the extraordinary fervor with which the hope for regeneration was expressed, is in itself telling and unsettling.

Related claims about the generalized loss of eroticism were pervasive in mainstream scholarly and popular commentary as well. And one of the major themes pursued in mainstream venues had to do with the crisis of German masculinity. An important example is a highly regarded and oft-cited speech delivered at the founding meeting of the German Association for Sex Research in 1950 by Hans Bürger-Prinz, director of the psychiatric and neurological clinic at the University of Hamburg. Bürger-Prinz was one of the two "fathers" of postwar West German sexology (the other was Giese). Bürger-Prinz also, and crucially (although this was certainly downplayed in the wake of the war), had been a major figure in the scholarly "legitimation" of the Nazi persecution of homosexuals.[81] In his speech Bürger-Prinz claimed to find in the postwar years a weakening of masculinity, of heterosexuality, and indeed of eroticism more generally. Recasting for the new postwar climate his Nazi-era *aperçus* into how fundamentally unstable a formation heterosexual masculinity was in the first place (insights that could have been used for antihomophobic purposes but that had concretely facilitated the expansion and – murderous – radicalization of criminal prosecution for homosexuality during the Third Reich), Bürger-Prinz observed that "The *transformation of the sexual drive-dynamic* entirely into *heterosexual relations* is and always was for the man a frequently unsolved task." Without ever mentioning homosexuality, moreover, although repeatedly using the term heterosexuality, Bürger-Prinz also declared that these purported foundational problems were particularly exacerbated in the postwar period. In sexual terms, he opined, men in general tended "toward *more infantile behaviors*" and were often unable to let go of a "certain last autistic remnant." (In other words, men were having sex with women, but even as they did so they were really just having sex with themselves.) In Bürger-Prinz's expert view, however, the inclination to be concerned only with oneself and not

---

80 Löhe, "Menschenpaar," 1.
81 Peter von Rönn, "Politische und psychiatrische Homosexualitätskonstruktion im NS-Staat," pt. 2: "Die soziale Genese der Homosexualität als defizitäre Heterosexualität," *Zeitschrift für Sexualforschung* 11, no. 3 (Sept. 1998): 220–60.

with one's partner was growing in the postwar years, and "one could almost say there exists a disinclination to invest more emotional capital than necessary." As he put it in an acute tone of melancholy: "The saturation of interhuman behaviors by sexuality in the sense of the erotic is totally demolished, and only the carrying-out of the sexual activity as such is left."[82] What is evident here, on the one hand, is the beginning of a quite sophisticated, even radical, theory of sexuality – for example the decoupling of physical desires from psychic attachments or the awareness that there is nothing natural or inevitable about heterosexuality – and on the other, a deeply problematic vagueness both about his own recent past and about what exactly might be making German men so "autistic."

Bürger-Prinz had a great deal to be vague about. Other mainstream commentators were much more explicit in naming what was causing German men to be insecure and at emotional loose ends. The physician Walter Frederking, for example, when asked by the *Nordwestdeutsche Hefte* in 1947 to comment on the "crisis of marriage" observed: "The dominance of the man, which was so strongly emphasized in the Third Reich, has collapsed to a considerable degree.... In addition, the male gender is hit harder in its soul by the lost war than the female." Frederking noted that "all these confusions and shiftings now reach deep into the drive-life and the events of the body. The doctor naturally hears much about this. Again and again he is told how frequently male bodily functions are impaired, and those affected also tell me that they have heard similar things from many an acquaintance." At the same time, however, Frederking observed that "the female feeling- and drive-life are apparently not disturbed to as great an extent." Frederking alluded to German collective guilt – although he was also possibly referring to ambivalence about denazification. ("The German human being has changed more than most of us are aware. One needs only to think of the extent to which feelings and concepts of justice have become blurred and crumbled.") But his main aim was to solicit women's participation in restoring new life to "the fundamental relationship between man and woman." Sadly remarking that it was impossible at that point to know how gender relations would be configured in the future, Frederking took comfort in the knowledge that "the most important thing about the relations of the genders to each other will after all remain that they are different from each other."[83]

---

82 Hans Bürger-Prinz, "Über die männliche Sexualität," *Zeitschrift für Sexualforschung* 1, no. 2 (June–July 1950): 108–10. On the highly positive reception of this address, see the footnote to the revised reprint in *Mensch, Geschlecht*, 43.
83 Walter Frederking, "Die Krisis der Ehe: Was der Arzt meint," *Nordwestdeutsche Hefte* 2, no. 10 (1947): 33–4.

Also along related lines, as one anonymous man wrote in the "market-dominating" women's magazine *Constanze* in 1948, men were not the superb types they once had been.[84] Strategically asserting that "The men feel more or less that something is rotten in the state of man. . . . We men are finished," he proposed that the man's decline "as husband, as politician, as 'head of the household,' as lover – as man pure and simple" had multiple sources, not least of which was that "We have no more guns in our arms and we can no longer tell you heroic stories." Meanwhile, however, the author also managed both to ridicule Nazis as the ultimate male losers – people who should have been "thoroughly spanked" because "although even the stupidest must have known after Stalingrad that their looting expedition criss-cross through the world would go wrong, they nonetheless went on sacrificing millions of human beings for years in order to rescue their own pathetic lives" – *and* to blame overly rigorous denazification and the lost war for the decline in high-quality manliness. The only solution was to restore heterosexual domesticity. Calling woman "the healthier sex" with "the stronger weapons," the author enumerated those weapons as "her whole great unshakeable nature, her instinct for the practical and immediate, her dexterity" in running the household, and the "singular magic" with which, in a time of pitifully low male salaries, the woman managed daily to get lunch on the table and keep the laundry clean.[85]

Yet another intervention in *Constanze* came from the writer and psychologist Walther von Hollander, who was one of the most influential advice-givers of the postwar period. In his three-part essay on "The Man in Crisis," von Hollander acknowledged that women were experiencing a "generalized disappointment" with the men in their lives. In the most recent war women had found out for themselves that "the average man is no hero" and that apparently "also in this respect men no longer were worth unquestioning female surrender." This tragedy was experienced concretely in marriage after marriage with the "return home of the conquered man."

Yet even as he hinted at the reasons for the downfall of a certain brand of masculinity, announcing that what was corroding marriages most was "the question of guilt . . . guilt for all this catastrophe and mess" and acknowledging that "the man with his politics, his greed for power . . . his worship of violence, his cockiness when successful and his whininess in defeat" were core causes both of the most disastrous effects of Nazism and the

---

84 See "Was hat sich geändert? Die Suche nach neuen Rollenbildern: Neuansätze und Verhinderungen im Spiegel der Frauenpresse 1946–1949," in Annette Kuhn and Doris Schubert, eds., *Frauenalltag und Frauenbewegung im 20. Jahrhundert*, 4 vols. (Frankfurt am Main, 1980), 4:39.
85 H.H., "Hut ab vor unseren Frauen!" *Constanze* 2 (1948): 4–5.

disjointed state of postwar affairs, von Hollander was working to set things right.[86]

Astutely pointing out both in his essay and in response to a reader's letter that women had not exactly been guiltless under Nazism (while Germany was still undefeated, had women not "preferred the man of power, the victor?" and did women not themselves "worship power" and "love uniforms"?), von Hollander nonetheless, and simultaneously, elaborated normative notions of gender difference and trivialized – again by leaving deliberately vague – what it was about Nazism that made it so catastrophic (the crimes or the defeat?).[87] It would thus be no surprise that in the later installments of his essay von Hollander suggested that "only one thing" could lead women and men out of the current "abyss," and that was love. Criticizing what he saw as the proliferation of "casual love" in his present and insisting on women's "inextinguishable yearning for the superiority of the man," von Hollander lamented that most postwar women lacked "that pliancy and femininity, that atmosphere of the playful, the cheerful vibrancy, that the man simply needs from the woman." As von Hollander summarily observed: "That by becoming similar to the man, woman has become more empty of love as well, this seems to us to be proven. That love, the woman's true life-element, can only be re-created by the woman, seems to us clear."[88]

Lest anyone think that aside from Dorothee Löhe only men were engaging in these lines of argumentation, one need only look at the *Constanze* essay by Else Feldbinder on "He and She 1948" to find a woman making comparable claims. Feldbinder, too, decried what she saw as the loss of "spiritual tension" between the sexes and therefore of "the magic of eros." Moreover, Feldbinder lamented that "the maxim of equal rights has dissolved the maxim of chivalry." And significantly, while acknowledging long-term trends toward equality of the sexes existing since the French Revolution and simultaneously hoping that the transformation of gender relations was a temporary aberration due to the inevitable "brutalization" produced by total war, Feldbinder nonetheless singled out "the Nazi era" for ruining the "majority of men" with its "plebeian heroism" and for "trampling down every seed of a chivalrous feeling in a whole generation."[89] The implication was that Nazism's main failing was that it made for lousy men. And, as in the

---

86 Walther von Hollander, "Mann in der Krise: Anklage der Frauen," *Constanze* 1 (1948): 3, 22.
87 Ibid., 22; and "Aus Walther von Hollanders Privatkorrespondenz," *Constanze* 1 (1948): 19.
88 Walther von Hollander, "Mann in der Krise: Glanz und Elend des Intellekts," *Constanze* 2 (1948): 15; and Walther von Hollander, "Mann in der Krise: Tristan, Don Juan und der Patriarch," *Constanze* 3 (1948): 19.
89 Else Feldbinder, "Er und Sie 1948," *Constanze* 7 (1948): 3.

writings of von Hollander, so also Feldbinder, the way to cure Germany of its ills was to bring back high-quality romance.

The point that needs emphasis here is that the restoration of heterosexual domesticity as an ideal via an intensely normative rhetoric of romantic love was not an innocent apolitical enterprise. This is not just because it involved a cruel slap at those who remained involuntarily single or because it cajoled those women "lucky" enough to be married into putting up with all manner of male deficiencies (from bossiness to boorishness, to unwillingness to participate in housecleaning or child-rearing). The rhetoric of romantic love, and the injunction to women to redevelop their "cheerful" femininity and help to rebuild German men into more "chivalrous" examples of manhood, also functioned to banalize Nazism and downplay the specificities of Nazism's sexual politics, and the ways in which these had been intimately imbricated with Nazism's genocidal racism.[90] Overcoming both Nazism *and* its defeat involved the redomestication of sex.

Although the consolidation of sexual conservatism was by no means a foregone conclusion in the late 1940s and early 1950s but rather took shape over time out of the contests of the postwar decade, a close reading of the postwar discussions does reveal that the seeds for the subsequent conservativization were already being planted in the midst of the apparently more liberal discourse. However, and this is significant, the evidence from the postwar period also confronts us with the peculiar phenomenon that the conservative program succeeded not by being a coherent program at all, and not just by shutting down alternative points of view – although clearly there were strenuous efforts within the government, churches, and media working hard to impose coherence and shut down those alternatives – but rather via the proliferation of contradictory injunctions.

As Lauren Berlant and Michael Warner brilliantly put it in their summary of how "heteronormativity" works in the present-day United States, it is precisely the elasticity and incoherence of the dominant ideology, and the garbledness of the norms put forward, that make the ideological effects

---

90 As Klaus Theweleit has recently observed, one of the key points, after all, about Nazism's sexual politics is not whether it was pro- or anti-sex, but that it was about a certain *kind* of sex: "It was practically one of the war aims to liberate the country from the 'false sexuality,' with which it had been covered since at least the 1920s, in the place of the 'Jewish' to set a different form of sexuality, the German, this whole complex of up-striving world power, master race, the saturation of their bodies with lust-pumped expectation of world-domination, ennobled by the special 'pure sexuality' of the Germans." And – in one of the most original and perceptive explanations for the transition in West Germany from a culture of violence to a culture of sexual repression and conservatism – he continues: "One could also say, the coding of their sexuality with murder and death-blow, and now they are full of guilt feelings, that they pass on as fear" (Klaus Theweleit, *Ghosts: Drei leicht inkorrekte Vorträge* [Frankfurt am Main, 1998], 106).

so powerful. Heteronormativity, they observe, "consists less of norms that could be summarized as a body of doctrine than of a sense of rightness produced in contradictory manifestations." That sense of rightness, its confident banality, is facilitated not in spite of but because of the seeming mutual irreconcilability of the ways heterosexuality functions. For indeed, at one and the same time, heterosexuality can go "unmarked, as the basic idiom of the personal and the social; or marked as a natural state; or projected as an ideal or moral accomplishment."[91] This notion of "a sense of rightness produced in contradictory manifestations" is useful for understanding some of the dynamics at work in post–World War II West Germany as well. For there it was exactly the cacophony of mutually conflicting attempts to manage the postwar "sexual crisis" that ultimately *together* contributed to the normalization of the memory of Nazism.

Numerous scholars are beginning to call for a more differentiated portrait of what used to be described as the era of "amnesia" or "silence" about the Nazi past, a silence supposedly only broken by the student rebellions of the late 1960s. As the literature on sex in the postwar period suggests, there was no particular silence. It was specifically through the *talk*, the incessant insistent chatter, not the silence, that memory was managed and Nazism normalized. Among the divergent – mutually conflicting *and* overlapping – postwar constituencies of Christians, sensualists, and mainstream advice-givers there was not just a repudiation of Nazism but rather a variety of *compromise formations* that consisted of contradictory combinations of rupture and continuity, acknowledgment and disavowal, exaggeration and trivialization. Nazi racism and militarism were considered outrages by some, but for many they were jokes; eugenic ideas retained appeal among otherwise opposed constituencies. Strong masculinity was in disrepute and heterosexuality was in crisis because of Nazism *and* because of its defeat; women were both emboldened and endangered by this state of affairs; above all male egos needed boosting. Out of this incoherent jumble the sexual conservatism of the mid- to late 1950s and early 1960s emerged.

By the mid-1960s, when the sexual revolution began, young people had no idea there had been a moment in the late 1940s that had self-evidently been considered an era not just of chaos or crisis but also of "erotic freedom."[92] When the 1960s' most famous German sex reformer Oswalt Kolle announced in 1969 that the masses had "for centuries been kept from

---

91 Lauren Berlant and Michael Warner, "Sex in Public," *Critical Inquiry* 24, no. 2 (winter 1998): 548; see also 549, 552–3.
92 Walter Dittmann, "Die Krisis der Ehe: Die Ansicht des Geistlichen," *Nordwestdeutsche Hefte* 2, no. 10 (1947): 34.

the most simple, basic information," no one challenged him.[93] *Liebe und Ehe* had ceased publication at the end of 1951. The main sexological forum, the semiannual Beiträge zur Sexualforschung, became ever more conservative in the course of the 1950s, attacking Kinsey's methods and concerning itself with the elucidation of sexual pathologies and the elaboration of norms of properly reproductive familialism.[94] Already between 1955 and 1958 there were but a handful of essays in the German-speaking realm dedicated to the subjects of "marital crisis" or "marital misery," and by 1959–60 the subjects had disappeared. Meanwhile, *Constanze* became ever more a fashion magazine; by the mid-1950s, its pages were filled with advice on humoring one's husband, home decorating, and correct behavior, and there was no hint of its former liberality in sexual matters. Gone were the days when a contributor to *Constanze* could matter-of-factly write that a marriage entered into for financial maintenance was both an outdated and a "moldy arrangement," or when another could assert as self-evident the idea that "it is by no means a settled matter, whether one, if one must forgo marriage, must also forgo experience with men."[95] Christian literature came to dominate the sex-advice market, and with Family Minister Wuermeling's direction and support – and despite the emergence of some new liberal voices in the late 1950s – conservative politicians and publicists continued to set the terms of public debate about sex until well into the 1960s.[96] By the late 1960s, the young rebels could rightly complain that there was no mention of pleasure in sex-enlightenment literature; reproduction and venereal disease formed the main topics.[97] By 1963, when the survey on sexual attitudes first conducted in 1949 was repeated, the percentage of interviewees

93 Kolle quoted in Peter Knorr, "Schwierigkeiten bei der Sexualaufklärung," *Pardon* 8, no. 12 (Dec. 1969): 65.
94 See Reimut Reiche, "Kritik der gegenwärtigen Sexualwissenschaft," in Gunter Schmidt et al., eds., *Tendenzen der Sexualforschung* (Stuttgart, 1970), 2.
95 "Tut Scheiden weh?" *Constanze* 21 (1948): 3; and Luise Heise, "Unverstanden – nicht ernst genommen?" *Constanze* 10 (1948): 3.
96 For a discussion of the new Cold War liberals and their (only partially successful) efforts to depoliticize sex, see Uta G. Poiger, *Jazz, Rock and Rebels: Cold War Politics and American Culture in a Divided Germany* (Berkeley, Calif., 2000), 110–11, 205, 213, 219–20. Poiger too makes clear that although liberals from the late 1950s onward advocated making sex a private matter, liberals were more successful in the economic and political realms; they continued to have to contend with conservatives on issues related to youth and family life. An indication of the ongoing importance maintained by religious leaders in determining the terms of debate on sexual matters into the 1960s can be gleaned from the enthusiasm with which a liberal publication like *Der Spiegel* greeted the work of reformist theologians on sex. See "Freude im Haus," *Der Spiegel*, Aug. 22, 1966, 54–6, and " 'Der Sexus ist kein Sündenpfuhl,' " *Der Spiegel*, Nov. 28, 1966, 68–87.
97 See Zentralrat der sozialistischen Kinderläden West-Berlins, ed., *Für die Befreiung der kindlichen Sexualität!: Kampf den falschen Erziehern!* (Berlin, 1969), 25–45; and Ernst Busche, "Sexualpädagogik als Disziplinierungsmittel: Eine negative Dokumentation über Richtlinien, Methodik und Lehrerverhalten," *Das Argument* 56 (Feb. 1970): 28–40.

endorsing and admitting to premarital sex had dropped by more than ten points.[98]

The resolution of the postwar "sexual crisis" in a conservative direction was accompanied by the erasure of the memory of the postwar liberality *and* of the very fact of the existence of a considerable amount of pleasurable activity during the years of mass murder. Numerous statements made by members of the generation of 1968 attest to their belief that their parents' lives had been shaped by "prudery" and "taboos," and that "in the 1930s they had had communicated to them an unhappy, lifeless, pleasureless attitude."[99] The avant-garde role played by the New Left student movement within the sexual revolution of the 1960s was nurtured by intensely held convictions that the Third Reich was sex-hostile and pro-family, and that the Holocaust was the perverted product of sexual repression.[100] Yet the sexual conservatism of the mid- to late 1950s and early 1960s was not an inherited tradition, as the student movement believed, but rather a new postwar invention, not so much a continuation of Nazism's sexual politics as rather a complex reaction to and against it.

98 See "Erst die Liebe, dann die Moral? Alles über die Deutschen (15)," *Der Stern* 48 (1963): 43–52; and Elisabeth Noelle and Erich Peter Neumann, eds., *Jahrbuch der öffentlichen Meinung 1958–1964* (Allensbach, 1965), 589–90.

99 See Ulrike Heider, "Freie Liebe und Liebesreligion: Zum Sexualitätsbegriff der sechziger und achtziger Jahre," in Ulrike Heider, ed., *Sadomasochisten, Keusche und Romantiker: Vom Mythos neuer Sinnlichkeit* (Reinbek bei Hamburg, 1986), 93; Michael Schneider, "Fathers and Sons, Retrospectively: The Damaged Relationship between Two Generations," *New German Critique* 31 (winter 1984): 9; and Sabine Weissler, "Sexy Sixties," in Eckhard Siepmann et al., eds., *CheSchahShit: Die sechziger Jahre zwischen Cocktail und Molotov* (Berlin, 1984), 96.

100 See Dagmar Herzog, " 'Pleasure, Sex, and Politics Belong Together': Post-Holocaust Memory and the Sexual Revolution in West Germany," *Critical Inquiry* 24, no. 2 (winter 1998): 393–444; and Dagmar Herzog, "Sexuelle Revolution und Vergangenheitsbewältigung," *Zeitschrift für Sexualforschung* 13, no. 2 (June 2000): 87–103.

8

Family Life and "Normality" in Postwar British Culture

PAT THANE

The aim of this chapter is to offer some reflections on the experience of family life in postwar Europe from the British perspective. The relative stability of British domestic history makes it one of the deviant cases of twentieth-century European history. This has to be qualified with reference to the important exception of events in Ireland; however, these have left the culture of the remainder of the British Isles extraordinarily untouched. Through the century the boundaries of the British state have remained otherwise unchanged, though in the immediate postwar years those of the once great British Empire were to shrink dramatically, with cultural effects within Britain that have barely been explored. Twentieth-century Britain has experienced no revolution, or even a serious attempt at one, has not been occupied by another power, has not lost a major war, has experienced no mass deportations, no mass rapes. This stability has had its downside, for it has bred a certain cultural conservatism and complacency. For the purposes of this book, however, it has the advantage that it offers an opportunity, less available in countries that were more profoundly disrupted by the war, to examine what in the postwar world was a direct outcome of the experience of war and what was the outcome of other processes, both short and long term. Much was changing in Europe in the mid-twentieth century; not all of it was propelled by war.

Nevertheless, of course, Britain was profoundly affected by the war, both internally and externally. Many thousands of men and a smaller number of women (although more women than in any previous war) were members of the armed services, and many saw scenes of horror not to be expected in a placid, peacetime British life. They were injured, killed, or spent long periods away from home, often in surroundings that were strange, even terrible, such as Japanese prisoner-of-war camps. Bombing killed, injured, or displaced many who were not involved in military action. Families lost mothers, fathers, husbands, wives, daughters, and sons, although not on a scale comparable with some other European countries. The psychosocial effects of these multiple experiences on British society for decades after the war, of people who did not collapse psychologically due to their war experiences but were damaged by them to varying degrees while seeking to return to a "normal" existence, have no more been explained, or even examined, for Britain than for any other country.

Despite the growth of the influence of psychology, psychiatry, and psychoanalysis over the first half of the twentieth century, in Britain as elsewhere there was still in 1945 little awareness of the effects of wartime stress even on combatants, except when manifested as extreme breakdown, although, as we shall see, there was much interest in the effects of war. Of the armed services, the Royal Air Force went furthest in providing psychiatric care for combatants. After the war those who felt a need or desire to talk about their experiences could rarely find a professional listener, although not all might have wanted this. Nor, often, did family and friends want to hear the bad side of the war; they wanted those who returned to be normal, as they had been before, to slip back into their old lives no matter how their experiences had changed them. And some, of course, did not want to talk about the war at all. Fifty years or so later, the extent of the wartime trauma became evident to psychiatrists encountering seriously disturbed aging veterans. The effects of wartime experiences on participants in the half century that followed are extremely difficult to assess. Equally elusive are the effects on the widowed partners and children of those killed in the war.

Historians face serious methodological problems in seeking to reconstruct these hidden but profoundly important effects of war. Oral historians encounter problems of ethics as well of as of method in probing painful and possibly damaging past experiences. Interpretations of the effects of World War I on British culture signal caution in the use of other types of sources. For example, literary historians have argued, on the basis of a limited canon of texts mainly produced by noncombatants, that the experience of the "great" war so threatened masculine self-confidence that men reasserted masculine authority both within their families and in society more generally, with conservative cultural effects. But examination of a wider range of texts, including those by combatants, and increasing understanding of British society in the 1920s and 1930s gives rise to serious doubt that this phenomenon was so widespread or so simple.[1] Literary and autobiographical

---

1 Susan Kingsley Kent, *Making Peace: The Reconstruction of Gender in Interwar Britain* (Princeton, N.J., 1993); Sandra M. Gilbert, "Soldier's Heart: Literary Men, Literary Women, and the Great War," in M. R. Higonnet et al., *Behind the Lines: Gender and the Two World Wars* (New Haven, Conn., 1987), 197–226. This interpretation has been ably criticized in Stephen M. Cullen, "Gender and

texts tell us much about the experience of both world wars, but only if used with care.

The re-creation of a family life, of a real or imagined normality after the war, was as important in Britain as it was in countries that had been far more severely disrupted. But what was "normal"? Even before the war, families in much of Europe underwent a process of change that continued through the war. Most dramatically, birth and death rates had fallen, apparently permanently. British birthrates fell steadily from the later nineteenth century and reached the exceptionally low point of 14.4 per 1,000 population in 1933, the lowest level of any European nation between the wars. There were significant but less dramatic declines in Germany, France, and other European countries.[2] Low birthrates were a cause for concern in many countries in the 1930s and 1940s, and created an international discourse around fertility, infertility, and motherhood, sometimes but not invariably with eugenic overtones. Falling birthrates were everywhere seen as symbolic of national weakness and decline, as William Beveridge (twenty years later to be hailed as the father of the British welfare state) signaled with reference to Britain as early as 1924:

The questions now facing us are how far the fall will go; whether it will bring about a stationary white population after or long before the white man's world is full; how the varying incidence of restriction among social classes and creeds will affect the Stock; how far the unequal adoption of birth control in different races will leave one race at the mercy of another's growing numbers or drive it to armaments or permanent aggression in self-defence.[3]

The efforts of Hitler and Mussolini to raise birthrates are well known. So also is the longer established French concern with its low birthrate.[4]

Similar concerns were evident in Britain in the 1930s and 1940s, but no official measures were introduced to attempt to raise birthrates. It was recognized that women would not readily return to bearing uncontrolled numbers of children, that a historic revolution in birth control was taking place. However, the belief that the falling birthrate was damaging and should be reversed remained widespread and influential.[5]

the Great War: British Combatants, Maculinity and Perceptions of Women," Ph.D. diss.. Oxford University, 1999.

2 Brian R. Mitchell, *European Historical Statistics, 1750–1970* (London, 1978), 27–32.

3 Sir William Beveridge, "Population and Unemployment," in R. L. Smyth, ed., *Essays in the Economics of Socialism and Capitalism: Selected Papers Read to Section F. The British Association for the Advancement of Science, 1886–1932* (London, 1964), 270.

4 Maria Sophia Quine, *Population Politics in Twentieth-Century Europe: Fascist Dictatorships and Liberal Democracies* (London, 1996).

5 E.g., George Orwell, "The English People" (1944), in George Orwell, *The Collected Essays, Journalism, and Letters*, 3 vols. (London, 1970).

At the same time, death rates were falling in all age groups. It became increasingly probable that all babies would live to adulthood; fewer marriages were broken by widowhood; and more people lived to old age. In Britain in the 1930s, although less obviously in other major European countries, rates of marriage were rising; fewer people remained single, and marriage was on the way to becoming almost universal, as it had not been in Britain since the mid-nineteenth century. The outcome of these demographic trends was that in Britain in the 1930s a new family pattern, indeed a new and historically unprecedented normal life-course, was established that survived the war. Almost everyone married; they had and seem generally to have planned for small families, averaging two children, both of whom survived, compared with an average of about five (and a wider range around the average, from zero to fourteen)[6] at the beginning of the century, several of whom might have died; and marriages were long-lasting because they no longer were broken by death with the frequency that had been common throughout history. Divorce became easier to obtain as a result of a succession of legislative changes in the interwar years, but it remained expensive, socially abhorrent, and relatively rare. It became possible for everyone to expect to grow old, to imagine and to plan for a different and longer life-course. In addition to being an important change in personal life, this meant in terms of family life that three generations or more of the family would be alive together for a considerable time and, despite an ever-present myth to the contrary, more often than not be in regular contact and exchanging mutual affection and support, although rarely occupying the same household. Fear of the ill effects of this aging of the population caused disquiet, even panic, in Britain, as in France, at this time.[7] There were broadly similar, although by no means identical patterns of change throughout northwestern Europe in the 1930s. In Italy, by contrast, around 1930 the average middle-class couple had three children, a factory worker on average had 5.9 children, and an agricultural laborer 6.5; 14 percent of all Italian families had at least seven children. However, infant mortality rates in Italy remained high until after World War I, and standards of health, nutrition, and housing were poor compared with northern Europe, especially in agricultural districts, where 48 percent of the population lived, compared with 20 percent in Britain.[8]

6 Michael Anderson, "The Social Implications of Demographic Change," in F.M.L. Thompson, ed., *The Cambridge Social History of Britain, 1750–1950*, 3 vols. (Cambridge, 1990), 2:1–70.
7 A. Sauvy, "Social and Economic Consequences of the Aging of Western European Populations," *Population Studies* 2, no. 1 (June 1948): 115–24; P. M. Thane, "The Debate on the Declining Birth-Rate in Britain: The 'Menace' of an Ageing Population, 1920s–1950s," *Continuity and Change* 5, no. 2 (1990): 283–305.
8 Quine, *Population*, 21–2.

In Italy, against the European trend, it was only after the war that the birthrate, and also the infant mortality rate, fell, although it remained higher in rural than in urban areas. In Britain, the new family pattern that was emerging before the war was disrupted by wartime separation and death, but underlying trends were unchanged. The birthrate rose somewhat in the later 1930s and more strongly from the middle of the war before stabilizing in the 1950s, although at a significantly lower level than the norm prevailing before the 1920s. Throughout Europe, the widely expressed prewar pessimism about an irreversible future decline in the birthrate and a failure of populations to replace themselves was confounded after the war by a general reversal of the decline in fertility, a "baby boom" that lasted until the late 1960s, accompanied by sustained falls in death rates. European demographics tended to converge in the postwar decades, although slowest to change were the conservative and economically backward societies of Spain, Portugal, and Ireland, all of which had been neutral in the war and were relatively isolated from its direct effects.

The pattern was not identical everywhere. The Federal Republic of Germany experienced a sharp fall in the birthrate during the difficult years up to 1950, then a steady rise; Denmark experienced a similar fall, then a flattening out. In Greece, which did not experience the general increase in prosperity, the birthrate fell steadily until the 1960s, when the economy improved. In Belgium, it rose steadily from the end of the war until the 1960s; in France, a sharp rise, 1945–50, was followed by a more gradual increase. In the late 1940s, the average French woman had three children, and France experienced the highest marriage rates ever recorded. The rise in the birthrate was sustained for too long to be a short-term consequence of the war. In France in particular, the state provided more generous incentives to couples to have children than ever before. In March 1945, De Gaulle told the French people that twelve million babies were needed in the next decade. Larger family allowances were provided, including housing allowances for those unable to afford accommodations and financial support to enable families to go on holiday together or to send their children to holiday camps. It is unclear whether such incentives stimulated French fertility, which they had failed to do in the past, or if they had the equally desirable effect of improving the living standards and survival rates of poorer French families. The international character of the trend in fertility suggests that it was only marginally affected by state policies and had more to do with rising living standards and greater optimism about the future than had prevailed in the interwar years, although everywhere there were divergences due to local factors. By 1960, there was a broad Western European convergence in average family size. The percentage of births that was the third or higher was 27.4 in Greece, 28.2 in the Federal Republic of Germany, 33.2 in the United Kingdom, 34.8 in Italy, 38.8 in France and, exceptionally, 60.9 in the Republic of Ireland.[9]

The 1930s to 1950s was the golden age, indeed the only age, of the near universal, stable, long-lasting marriage, often considered the normality from which we have since departed. In all developed countries, an image of the small, contented, "normal" family was much reproduced and celebrated in the proliferating, widely available new forms of visual imagery that also characterize the period, particularly in film and advertising. In Britain as elsewhere, it was a norm in which there was considerable social investment, and great efforts were made to preserve it in the form of marriage and child-care manuals, marriage guidance and child counseling agencies, all to some degree and increasingly informed by psychology and psychoanalysis.[10] Their prevalence suggests that the other side of this family "norm" was awareness of its fragility. Indeed, its survival was short-lived and reality was often less stable than nostalgic retrospect suggests. The average annual number of divorce petitions in England and Wales was 4,785 between 1931 and 1935; 16,075 between 1941 and 1945; 38,382 in 1951; 31,905 in 1961. These statistics suggest some of the difficulties in assessing the cultural impact of war. The wartime rise in divorce is likely to have been due in part to wartime separations and new experiences, but they may also have owed something to the effects of a further liberalization of the divorce law in 1937. The steep rise until 1951 also may have been due to the effects of wartime disruptions to relationships, but it is hard to distinguish these from the effects of the introduction of Legal Aid by the Labour government in 1948, which enabled poorer people to use the divorce courts free of charge or at low cost. The slight fall by 1961 may be explained by the removal of a logjam of delayed divorces in the course of the 1950s. The level of divorce nevertheless remained significantly higher than before the war. To what extent this was due less to cultural or legal factors than to the fact that more people were surviving into middle life can only be guessed.

The "normal" family life to which many people in Britain aspired after the war and which was promoted through a range of communications media was therefore a new rather than "traditional" model of the family, although it quickly came to be represented as traditional and desirable. It was not wholly

9 Deborah Sporton, "Fertility: The Lowest Level in the World," in Daniel Noin and Robert Woods, eds., *The Changing Population of Europe* (Oxford, 1993), 49–61; Claire Duchen, *Women's Rights and Women's Lives in France, 1944–1968* (London, 1994), 97–105.
10 On France, see Duchen, *Women's Rights*, 96–125.

conservative in any obvious sense, and in respect to the relatively high divorce rate, decidedly not so. Personal relationships at their most intimate were often represented in later decades as being especially conservative and prudish in the 1950s, but, although Britain almost certainly was a more sexually constrained society after the war than many of its European neighbors, it is not obvious that it was more so than before the war. Britain in the 1930s has been described as a repressed society, and it is hard to disagree with this.[11] If anything, there are signs of a certain, relative loosening up in sexual relations in Britain in the 1950s. "Illegitimate" births (per 1,000 unmarried woman aged 15–44) rose from an average of about 6 per year through the 1920s and 1930s in England and Wales to 11.4 between 1941 and 1945. They fell only slightly, to 10.7, between 1951 and 1955 and rose significantly to 19.1 between 1961 and 1965. Scotland, which is and has long been culturally and institutionally different from England in many respects, had a different pattern, averaging 13 per year from 1902 to 1919, to 9.6 from 1931 to 1935, a figure to which it reverted in the 1950s, following a rise to 11.8 during the war. By 1966, it had risen to 16.5. Comparable figures for France were 7.6 for 1950–5, rising to only 6–6.5 through the 1950s and 1960s.[12] The "swinging sixties" can be said to have grown out of, rather than to represent, a reaction to the 1950s, although even then Britain was a long way from mass abandonment of sexual restraint.[13]

Another sense in which the "normality" of postwar Britain was historically abnormal, with its wide-ranging effects on cultural and family life, was that the period from 1945 to c. 1973 was the only period of full employment during peacetime in at least two hundred years. This was in part an outcome of the war, due to the determination of the Allied powers to prevent a recurrence of the economic instability of the prewar years, which had contributed to the outbreak of war, and the resulting international institutions such as the General Agreement on Tariffs and Trade (GATT), and to some degree to the effects of the Marshall Plan. But the postwar "golden age," as historians have come recently, and ruefully, to call it, can only partly be explained by such institutional change.[14] The "golden" years came more slowly to the countries most ravaged by the war, although they

11 S. Szreter, "Victorian Britain, 1837–1963: Towards a History of Sexuality," *Journal of Victorian Culture* 1 (1996): 136–49.
12 A. H. Halsey, ed., *Trends in British Society Since 1900: A Guide to the Changing Social Structure of Britain* (London, 1974; reprint, 1988), 49; Duchen, *Women's Rights*, 97.
13 Bill Osgerby, *Youth in Britain Since 1945* (London, 1998), 46–7; Hera Cook, "The Long Sexual Revolution: British Women, Sex, and Contraception in the Twentieth Century," Ph.D. diss., University of Sussex, 1999.
14 A. K. Cairncross, *Years of Recovery: British Economic Policy, 1945–51* (London, 1985).

then moved rapidly ahead. In France, levels of unemployment remained high until the mid-1950s, then fell. The pattern in Germany was similar, while Italy still had 8 percent unemployment in 1955, when the equivalent figure for Britain was 1 percent.[15]

The outcome in Britain, and eventually elsewhere, was that although pockets of unemployment remained and poverty had certainly not been eradicated in the 1950s, it is hard to exaggerate the extent to which full employment made possible a new stability in the lives of the mass of the British working class. Many families knew for the first time that, unlike their parents and grandparents, they could expect and could plan for a regular weekly income and generally a higher income all the year around, even a paid vacation. One week's vacation with pay each year became common among British manual workers only in the late 1930s. In 1948, 3.1 million manual workers in Britain had two weeks paid vacation a year; by the mid-1950s, 12.3 million did so, almost the entire manual workforce. This new stability contrasted with the insecurity of the period of mass unemployment before the war, a feeling shared by those with work, and with the pervasive insecurity of manual employment in the nineteenth century and up to the First World War. Full employment and rising living standards did not, however, put a stop to strikes in Britain; rather, it may have encouraged them by increasing both workers' expectations and their bargaining power. The number of strikes was consistently high between 1945 and 1960, as it was in Germany and Italy, though not in France. Trade union membership among men and women also rose in most of Western Europe, although in France it shrank.[16]

The new sense of personal security derived from the labor market was reinforced by postwar changes in social welfare policies. Most of these built on prewar antecedents and proposals,[17] and had many shortcomings, but they went far beyond anything available before. In Britain, what they owed to the war was that the desire of politicians to sustain popular morale had led to the production of a series of wartime proposals for reform, which sped up the pace of change. The desire for an improved postwar world brought about the election in 1945 of the first Labour government to win a clear and large majority, which went further to implement wartime promises of welfare reforms than could have been expected from a Conservative government. From 1946 onward, all British people knew that they would have a regular pension when they retired from paid work, indeed that retirement

15 Mitchell, *Statistics*, 64–76.   16 Halsey, *Trends*, 123–8.
17 Pat Thane, *Foundations of the Welfare State*, 2d ed. (London, 1996); Rodney Lowe, *The Welfare State in Britain since 1945*, 2d ed. (London, 1998).

at about age sixty-five was now a realistic alternative to the previous fate of older working-class people of laboring until physical weakness forced them to stop; that they had access to free health care of reasonable quality; and that children had access to free education through the university level.

Generally, social policies took for granted, and sought to support, the normal family headed by a male worker whose wife's paid work was a secondary and intermittent activity, if she engaged in it at all. This was a realistic assumption in most countries in the late 1940s, although state policy in France tended to treat women as independent workers and mothers as it long had, due largely to the salience of increasing the birthrate in all its social-policy thinking.

Again, there were broad similarities in the growth of state welfare activity across Western Europe after the war: Growth was fastest in Britain and the Nordic countries, which initially at least drew on the British model. Britain is sometimes regarded as the paradigmatic postwar welfare state. However, even by 1950 Britain's spending on social security was lower as a percentage of gross domestic product than that of the Federal Republic of Germany, Austria, and Belgium; by 1952, it was lower than that of France and Denmark; by 1954, Italy had pulled ahead, Sweden by 1955, and the Netherlands in 1957.[18] In all of these countries, changes in demography, in the labor market, and in welfare provision, taken together, created a sense of security and stability in the postwar world for working-class and lower-middle-class people that was qualitatively new on such a mass scale.

This was reinforced by improvements in the environment in which families lived. In Britain, the quality of working-class housing improved slowly but significantly under the Labour governments of 1945–51. Contrary to some interpretations, Labour gave priority to reconstruction of the economy over social expenditure[19] and chose to build relatively few new working-class houses. Labour was responsible for planning and building a cluster of "New Towns," away from the crowded older cities, which provided homes, leisure facilities, and jobs. The Conservative Party in the 1950s cleared the backlog of dilapidated housing with a more extensive, if lower quality, house-building program. The need to build was partly an outcome of the war because much housing had been destroyed by bombing, but this had just exacerbated a housing problem inherited from the rapid urbanization

18 Jose Harris, "Enterprise and the Welfare State," in T. R. Gourvish and A. O'Day, eds., *Britain Since 1945* (Basingstoke, U.K., 1988), 43.
19 Correlli Barnett, *The Audit of War: Illusion and Reality of Britain as a Great Nation* (London, 1986); Harris, "Enterprise," 39–58.

of the nineteenth century and which successive governments in the 1920s and 1930s had begun to tackle. The result was that increasing numbers of working-class families after the war had relatively comfortable new homes with modern conveniences. In 1951, 48 percent of households in England and Wales did not have exclusive use of piped water, toilet, or bath; by 1961, this had fallen to 30 percent.[20] This suggests both the extent of change and how much still remained to be changed. Again, patterns were similar elsewhere in Europe, but were influenced by the fact that Britain was the most highly urbanized country in Europe at the beginning of the war, whereas other countries, such as Italy, experienced rapid urbanization after the war.

For working-class women almost everywhere, improved housing, combined with stable incomes and smaller families, meant that housework gradually ceased to be the unremitting heavy labor it had always been, the more so due to the increased availability of, and their increased capacity to buy, consumer goods, including household appliances. In the late 1940s in Britain, vacuum cleaners were rare in working-class homes; in 1963, 72 percent of all homes possessed one. Nationally, 3.6 percent of families had washing machines in 1942, 29 percent in 1958, 64 percent in 1969.[21] Credit became more readily available for such purchases, and more people availed themselves of it. The Conservative governments of the 1950s encouraged private consumption as vigorously as Labour in the 1940s had sought to hold it back in order to strengthen the economy in the long term, a strategy that weakened Labour politically and contributed to their losing ground to the Conservatives. Other forms of acquisition also expanded in the late 1940s, 1950s, and 1960s as recorded rates of crime, especially of theft, rose rapidly. The statistics, however, were influenced by improved methods of detection and of recording.[22]

For many, although by no means all working-class individuals and families, homes became more comfortable places. Creating an attractive home itself became an important pastime for many women and men whose previous dwellings had offered no such creative possibilities. Gardening and "do-it-yourself" home handiwork absorbed more male leisure time in the 1950s. For many women, work in the home became, sometimes at least, pleasurable rather than the endless struggle to fetch water, to combat dirt and bugs, and to haul heavy washing, all of which women remember as the

20 Halsey, *Trends*, 305.
21 Elizabeth Roberts, *Women and Families: An Oral History, 1940–1970* (Oxford, 1995), 29.
22 Halsey, *Trends*, 533.

experience of the 1930s and 1940s.[23] One woman described her mother's washing day at that time:

Monday was a dreadful day. Mother had basins and buckets all over the kitchen floor when we got home from school . . . there was the tile floor and water everywhere. She had a boiler lit with gas and a mangle you worked by hand . . . it was such a big job, you know. It was a horrible day.

As for herself: "Funny thing is, I love washing, it's my favourite job. I don't do it now, the automatic washing machine does it."[24] Yet this new life for working-class women created further work for them: They had still to work and save to make a more comfortable family life possible. The average number of hours spent by British women on housework did not fall. As facilities improved, expectations of standards of housekeeping rose. But the class distribution of household labor did change: The minutes per day worked in the home by working-class women, who benefited most from the changes, averaged 480 in 1937, 500 in 1950, 440 in 1961, and 354 in 1975. Middle-class women, no longer supported by domestic servants after the war, worked for 235 minutes per day in 1937, 440 in 1961, and 370 in 1975.[25] But all women who had access to better homes and new technology gained a potential capacity to choose how much time to devote to housework, now that a lesser proportion of it was unavoidable for family decency and survival. For many, it was a new kind of domesticity, not necessarily imposed, unpleasurable or uncreative, and their lives were not necessarily bounded by it; indeed, as we shall see, increasing numbers of married women entered the paid labor force during the 1950s.

At the same time, the range of leisure activities for families and individuals increased. Televisions were owned by 0.2 percent of British adults in 1947, 4.3 percent in 1950, 39.8 percent in 1955, and 81.8 percent in 1960. Partly in consequence, cinema attendance fell from 1,635,000 admissions in 1946 to 1,396,000 in 1950, and to 515,000 in 1960. Attendance at spectator sports such as football and cricket fell, whereas participation in sports increased, from the popular table tennis and badminton, via rugby and sailing, to the more esoteric fencing. Increasing numbers of books were borrowed from public libraries, and increasing numbers of people attended adult education

---

23 Joanna Bourke, *Working Class Cultures in Britain, 1890–1960: Gender, Class, and Ethnicity* (London, 1994).
24 Elizabeth Roberts, *A Woman's Place: An Oral History of Working-Class Women, 1890–1940* (Oxford, 1984), 29–30.
25 Paul Johnson, ed., *Twentieth Century Britain: Economic, Social, and Cultural Change* (London, 1994), 401.

classes, which might be oriented toward leisure or to practical or intellectual training.[26] Formal membership of religious denominations fell and was low in England, Wales, and Scotland (though highest in the latter): 8.2 percent of the population were members of the Church of England in 1939, 6.7 percent in 1950, and 6.2 percent in 1970. Comparable figures for the Church of Scotland were 26.2, 24.9, and 25.1, respectively. Much larger proportions of the population informed opinion pollsters that they had some religious belief.[27] Only in Northern Ireland did formal religious affiliation, both Catholic and Protestant, rise over the postwar decades.[28]

The lives of many working-class families and individuals were transformed after the war from an old to a new "normality." Many of the prewar better-off elite in Britain experienced the postwar world as abnormal and disturbing. They were less likely than some of their counterparts elsewhere in Europe to have suffered privation in either of the world wars or the interwar period. They resented the austerity, shortages, and continued rationing of the later 1940s and wished to return to the comfort and freedom to consume, which had been their normality before the war. Rationing of foodstuffs in fact increased in the later 1940s because the government sought to restrict imports and personal consumption in order to boost exports and production of capital goods for export. Postwar austerity disturbed working-class people much less because they had rarely known lives free from austerity. Many middle-class people also accepted that restrictions were necessary in the national interest. Eighty percent of middle-class housewives interviewed in London in 1949 did so, although a noisy minority formed the British Housewives League in 1945 to complain of being "under-fed, under-washed and over-controlled." They almost certainly had some influence in encouraging middle-class women to vote Conservative in the elections of 1950 and 1951. That working-class women voters appear to have swung toward Labour in the late 1940s, whereas middle-class women swung against the government, indicates the different experiences and responses of different social groups at this time.[29]

The middle and upper classes faced a postwar world without servants, which was new and alarming. The servant population already was dwindling in Britain before the war; postwar full employment meant that fewer women needed or were willing to enter the constraints of full-time private domestic service, although unknown numbers worked casually in other

---

26 Halsey, *Trends*, 558–73.   27 Johnson, *Twentieth Century*, 427–41.
28 Halsey, *Trends*, 414.
29 Ina Zweiniger-Bargielowska, *Austerity in Britain. Rationing, Controls, and Consumption, 1939–1955* (Oxford, 2000); James Hinton "Housewives in Action: The Housewives' League and the Attlee Government," *History Workshop* 38 (autumn 1994): 128–56.

peoples' homes as daily cleaners. Many of the elite also felt threatened by what they saw as the increased power of the masses and of socialism, even in its moderate Labour Party and trade union form, especially as the Cold War gathered pace. This parallel increase in feelings of insecurity among the higher classes and in the security of the mass of the population diminished in the thirteen years of Conservative government and growing prosperity between 1951 and 1964.

Feelings of insecurity did not disappear. They were generated externally by the Cold War and by fears about nuclear annihilation. In Britain, the Campaign for Nuclear Disarmament was formed in 1958 and through the 1960s attracted large numbers to its annual Easter March.[30] Domestically, young people caused alarm with their apparent rejection of the peaceable domesticity in which their parents were investing so much. Fears were widely expressed shortly after the war that "war babies" would grow into "juvenile delinquents" due to the disruptive effects of the wartime absence of fathers and the long working hours of mothers. Indeed, rates of recorded offenses committed by young people were markedly higher in 1950 than in the 1930s, and they rose steadily through the 1950s and 1960s, although this was partly due to changes in the scope and organization of law enforcement. Films and other media expressed a general cultural unease concerning the younger generation. For example, *The Blue Lamp* (1949) starred Dirk Bogarde as a reckless young killer, and a voice-over warned of "restless and ill-adjusted youngsters" suffering "the effects of a childhood spent in a home broken and demoralized by war." In 1954, newspapers first identified Teddy Boys distinguished by their "flashy" and unfamiliar dress as a social danger. They made much of the relatively tame "riots" that accompanied the showing of the American film *Rock Around the Clock* in 1956. A young generation, many of its members enjoying full employment and regular wages as much as their parents did but with fewer commitments, less cautious and more hedonistic in their spending, and apparently much attracted by American style, was disturbing to 1950s Britain. Some blamed the war. A Home Office report, *Delinquent Generations*, warned in 1960 that children born between 1935 and 1942, the youth of the 1950s, were especially prone to delinquency due to their wartime experiences, although it was frequently emphasized that this was an international and not just a British problem. Fear about the impact of "Americanization," which hit Britain sooner than much of the rest of Europe, was probably at least as influential in fueling these fears as concern about the effects of the war.[31]

---

30 Paul Byrne, *The Campaign for Nuclear Disarmament* (London, 1988).
31 Osgérby, *Youth*, 10–13, 32–6.

In 1958, the first "race riots" occured in London, expressing another aspect of cultural change and, for some, discomfort and insecurity. Immigration from the Caribbean and from South Asia of people from what had been the British Empire seeking work, and encouraged by the government to do so in full-employment Britain, rose from the end of the 1940s in parallel with the decline of the Empire, as steadily growing numbers of colonies obtained their independence. Migration was another general feature of Western European society, even when the movement of people displaced by the war itself was over. Poor rural areas of Italy and Ireland exported people as they long had. Countries where there was full employment, particularly Britain, France, and Germany, experienced mass immigration. Another profound way in which the war changed Europe was though the process of decolonization, which it precipitated, the effect of which was to profoundly change the cultural composition of many societies over the next half-century.

Another sphere central to family life in which the influence of the war experience intersected with longer term change concerned the roles and experiences of women. A women's movement had existed in most European countries before the 1940s. Gradually women gained the vote on the same terms as men (although not until 1944 in France), and in many countries the 1920s and 1930s can be seen as a period in which women gained in political influence and experienced greater freedom in employment and social life.[32] There was no revolution in gender roles and relationships, but there was change, gradual and uneven though it was. Changes in gender roles were promoted in part by the demographic changes discussed above, particularly the decline in the birthrate and the growing practice of birth control. From the 1930s to the 1950s, the first generations of young women grew up who took for granted the knowledge that they could control their fertility, that they would probably have no more than two or at most three children early in life, normally in their twenties, and that a substantial part of their life-course would remain when child-bearing and child-rearing were over. They could grow up imagining very different lives for themselves than their mothers and grandmothers had known. For working-class women, this new thinking intersected with another reality that had more substance after the war than before: For the first time in history, working-class parents could hope with some degree of realism that their children could achieve

---

32 M. Pugh, *Women and the Women's Movement in Britain, 1914–59* (Basingstoke, U.K., 1992); Duchen, *Women's Rights*; Pat Thane, "What Difference Did the Vote Make? Women and British Politics, 1918–50," in Amanda Vickery, ed., *Women, Privilege, and Power: British Politics, 1750 to the Present* (Stanford, Calif., 2001).

better lives than their own, materially and perhaps also in terms of status and education, because new opportunities had opened up for them.

Women interviewed in Britain by the social research organization Mass Observation just after the war showed acute awareness of these changes and their importance. A thirty-nine-year-old woman from Willesden, London, described as coming from a skilled working-class background, said: "I think two is a nice family ... nobody wants to raise a family of sickly children. I don't think I'm selfish in not wanting more, but I've got other ideas for the children. I want them to have every opportunity so that we can be proud of them."[33] A twenty-five-year-old woman in Bermondsey, described as coming from an unskilled, working-class background, said: "Well, I know the one'll be enough for me, if I get any say in it. I reckon we all feel more responsible for our kids than they did when they had those big families – we don't want more than we can give a fair chance to."[34] Her neighbor, aged forty, said: "[We] could never have done what we did for our boy if we'd had more children. He's had the best of education and we let him go right through the secondary school, he won his matriculation and had just started work in a bank when the war broke out."[35] Growing up with such expectations invested in them is likely to have affected the lives of their children.

Middle-class women were more likely to comment on the transforming impact of demographic changes on their own lives rather than those of their children, whose already satisfactory lives were much less influenced by mid-twentieth century changes. A twenty-seven-year-old university-educated woman said that she "would like to have more leisure to follow up special studies, read more and attend concerts."[36] A middle-class thirty-four-year-old said: "I'd like to have one more child. Two doesn't seem a family somehow, but on the other hand I don't want to go on having children all my life. I want to be free for part of my time and have time to do other things." She was unclear, though, about what other things, saying: "Well, at first I should just like to relax and put my feet up. There's no telling afterwards – let me have my rest first."[37]

Changes in women's roles – much less in those of men – and in family life had clearly taken place before the war. The war itself unavoidably changed the roles of men and women, and changed family patterns in the short term. It has become conventional to see the postwar period as a time of

33 Mass Observation Archive, University of Sussex, Topic Collection: "Family Planning," 1944–9, box 3, file A: F 30 C Willesden.
34 Ibid., Bermondsey F 25 D.   35 Ibid., F 46 C.
36 Ibid., box 1.   37 Ibid.

reimposition of traditional gender roles, but in Britain at least the reality was more complicated. The "Report of the Royal Commission on Population of 1949" suggests that even in official discourse it was recognized that traditional "normality" could not be reimposed. The Royal Commission had been established during the war to examine the implications of the falling birthrate and, if possible, to propose means to reverse it. By the time the report was published the birthrate was again on the rise, but the commissioners were unaware of this. The report stated: "It is clear that women today are not prepared to accept, as most women in Victorian times accepted, a married life of continuous preoccupation with housework and care of children and that the more independent status and wider interests of women today, which are part of the ideals of the community as a whole, are not compatible with repeated and excessive childbearing."[38] The report went on to recommend family allowances and improved social services to enable women to combine child care with lives of greater independence. It continued, in language clearly influenced by the war:

Concern over the trend of population has led to attempts in some countries, e.g., Germany and Italy in recent times, to narrow the range of women's interests and to "bring women back into the home." Such a policy not only runs against the democratic conception of individual freedom, but in Great Britain it would be a rebuking of the tide. It ignores the repercussions which the fall in the size of the family itself has had upon the place of women in modern society. . . . The modern woman is not only more conscious of the need for outside interests but has more freedom to engage them; and it would be harmful all round, to the woman, the family and the community to attempt any restriction of the contribution woman can make to the cultural and economic life of the nation. It is true that there is often a real conflict between motherhood and a whole-time "career." Part of this conflict is inherent in the biological function of women, but part of it is artificial . . . we therefore welcome the removal of the marriage bar[39] in such employments as teaching and the civil service and we think that a deliberate effort should be made to devise adjustments that would render it easier for women to combine motherhood and the care of a home with outside activities.[40]

The report did not describe or advocate a revolution in gender roles. There was no suggestion that women did not have prime responsibility for children, no matter what else they might do, nor did the commissioners advocate reimposition of traditional cultural norms. It is often asserted that in practice after the war "women" were pushed into domesticity and out of such limited inroads as they had made into the public sphere during the war.

38 *Report of the Royal Commission on Population*, 1949, 148.
39 The rule that women should resign from certain occupations on marriage.
40 *Report of the Royal Commission on Population*, 150.

But the postwar experience of women in Britain and elsewhere in Europe varied by age and social class as well as in myriad individual ways. From as early as 1943, the government in fact encouraged women to stay in the labor market after the war because ministers anticipated a labor shortage. This encouragement increased after the war, when the labor shortage was real, and reached a peak in 1947. But not all women were targeted equally. Younger women were encouraged to stay at home, to boost the birthrate and nurture the new generation, while older women, whose children were grown, were urged to take paid work. By contrast, in France after the war the government urged even mothers of young children to take up paid work and provided child care to assist them, but it faced resistance particularly from Catholic pro-family organizations. At the end of the war, younger women in Britain tended to leave the labor market, often thankfully after the stress of wartime work or because the limited opportunities open to them were less attractive than home and family. Many older women either stayed in the labor market or entered it if they had spent the war years raising children. The work they did had changed little since before the war and suggested that paid work in itself did not guarantee more equal status between the sexes: Women's work tended to be low-status, low-paid, and often part-time.

Once more there were significant class differences. Working-class women had always taken paid work when their families needed it. In the 1930s, there were still, as there had long been, strong social barriers to middle-class married women working for pay after marriage, even where there were no formal prohibitions in the form of a marriage bar; and working-class women often also aspired to liberation from the heavy double burden of arduous unpaid housework and arduous paid work. Upper-class women did not work for pay at any stage in their lives. After the war, the double load was gradually eased for many working-class women by the lightening of domestic work. Also, from the late 1940s onward, significant numbers of middle-class married women began to enter the labor market in later life, when their children had grown. This did not become a norm until at least the 1970s, and few of them entered high-status jobs, but the long-established cultural barrier to their paid employment had apparently been lifted following the experience of war combined with the postwar demand for labor.

An associated change was that in the 1940s it was normal, among couples who could afford it, for the wife to give up paid work upon marriage to care for her husband and home. By the late 1950s, most working- and middle-class women stayed in the labor market until their first pregnancy. Married couples opted for a longer period of accumulation of savings and goods before the wife gave up paid work, at a time when such accumulation was becoming more accessible. This development also suggests a change in the meaning of marriage and family life: Women no longer were routinely expected to make home and husband the center of their lives, but the care of young children was expected to take primacy over paid work. There were similar changes in all but the most conservative Western European countries, but some – such as Sweden and France – gave women more material support (such as child-care stipends) to enable them to choose between paid or unpaid work, in or out of the home.

The war in many European societies seemed indeed to bring about a new emphasis on maternal responsibility for child care, and especially on child care as the prime responsibility of the mother of young children. In Britain this was expressed in the 1940s and 1950s in radio programs, guidance texts for parents, mass-selling paperback books on social psychology, and in the training of medical, psychiatric, and social workers. A belief that all mothers should give their young children almost uninterrupted care or risk severe psychic damage to the child was mainly derived from wartime studies of the behavior of children wholly and sometimes traumatically separated from their parents. However, it was widely promoted as essential in all families for successful *Child Care and the Growth of Love*, the title of an especially influential, wide-selling book by John Bowlby, published in 1953.[41] Such ideas were powerfully expressive of cultural unease in postwar Europe about a past, present, and future in which rapid change prevented a return to "normality" and indeed called its very meaning into question.

41 Denise Riley, *War in the Nursery: Theories of the Child and the Mother* (London, 1983).

9

Continuities and Discontinuities of Consumer Mentality in West Germany in the 1950s

MICHAEL WILDT

I

On May 2, 1954, the following cigarette advertisement was published in the German weekly *Stern*:

Life is worth living again. Behind us lie years that seem like a bad dream today. Sorrow was knocking on everyone's door and many hearts were in the grip of despair and hopelessness. We were in such dire straits that we did not hold life in high esteem anymore – life almost had lost its meaning! The natural conse- quence was the loss of even the most basic moral standards, in accordance with which we otherwise arrange our thoughts and lives. For us, even an everyday re- quirement such as eating got a completely excessive value; everyone was obsessed with the idea of somehow getting something to eat. Likewise we lusted after al- cohol and nicotine. We indulged in the pleasures of life without moderation and restraint, and barely gave a thought to the fact that at some point we would have to pay for this mindless undertaking, that one day our organism would cease to cooperate and would confront us with a hefty bill. In the meantime, many things have changed entirely. Life is worth living again, and we again regard health as the supreme good. We have returned to accepting those limits of pleasure that Goethe called the hallmark of the master. We no longer live without thinking of tomorrow.

This text is striking not only because it advertises cigarettes in an unusual way but also because it acknowledges the end of the postwar era nine years after the war. The currency reform had marked the decisive change from the years of hardship and scarcity, and therefore was elevated in the collec- tive memory of West Germans to the "myth of the origin of the golden age" (Lutz Niethammer). However, the state of emergency, now no longer characterized by hunger and privation but by greed, came to a close – so the message of the text – in the mid-1950s. Since then normality had returned;

Translated by Richard Bessel and Dirk Schumann.

211

instead of living exclusively in the present, it had become possible to direct one's thoughts to the future and to return to enjoying life in the moderate manner that characterized a people of poets and thinkers.

To be sure, it was not only Theodor W. Adorno who felt that such a return would be both impossible and presumptuous. "The notion that after the war life could go on 'normally' or that culture could be 'rebuilt' – as if the rebuilding of culture were itself not negating it – is idiotic," he wrote in 1944. "Millions of Jews have been murdered, and that is supposed to be an interlude and not the catastrophe itself?"[1] The Holocaust as a "break with civilization" (Dan Diner), the tangible and intangible shocks of wartime had wrecked German society so thoroughly that it was hardly possible simply to pick up the threads of life before the war. Some years ago Hans-Peter Schwarz described the crucial question of West German history as why the catastrophe did not happen: "The political psychology of the ruling elites and the population at large, foreign policy and domestic order, expectations abroad and the self-perception of West Germans, the founding and the early history of the Federal Republic, as well as the traumatic fixations which continue up to now – all of this only becomes understandable as a reaction to that psychological, political, economic, and moral chaos from which the Bonn republic and West German society built themselves up."[2]

Looking at the German scene in 1945 would hardly have encouraged one to forecast a stable future for this landscape of ruins. The Germans had experienced the end of the war less as a liberation than as marking their survival. Their main concern was not to shed their guilt but to make their way in a "society under rubble." While learning their role as consumers, West Germans were burdened with the lasting experience of shortages and even hunger. For them, the last years of the war and its immediate aftermath were a period of a state of emergency. While Germans were pursuing the extermination of the European Jews, the war reached their own towns. Thousands died or lost their homes in bombing raids. Thousands fled from the front and became refugees. In this shattered society, not only houses but also the familiar structures of everyday life had fallen to pieces. Men who as members of the "master race" had ravaged Eastern Europe and the Soviet Union, women who were forced to devote all their energies to feeding their families, youngsters who learned to survive as thieves and black marketeers – all

---

1 Theodor W. Adorno, *Minima Moralia: Reflexionen aus dem beschädigten Leben* (Frankfurt am Main, 1985).

2 Hans-Peter Schwarz, "Die ausgebliebene Katastrophe. Eine Problemskizze zur Geschichte der Bundesrepublik," in Hermann Rudolph, ed., *Den Staat denken: Theodor Eschenburg zum Fünfundachtzigsten* (Berlin, 1990), 151–74, quotation 152.

had undergone extreme experiences and now longed for "normality" and "security."

When reading speeches or articles of this period, even those formulated by representatives of the German authorities, one is left with the impression that this period of misery, hunger, cold, and torn families was accepted as if it were a penance after which the country and the people would be purged of guilt. The first postwar mayor of Hamburg, Dr. Rudolf Petersen, wrote in 1947: "Two years after the collapse of the Third Reich, the German people has effaced with patience and unspeakable suffering a good deal of the guilt that burdened it by its government during these twelve years of cruel dictatorship. It is high time to forget the past."[3] By no means had the political culture of the Third Reich fallen to pieces with the surrender. In 1946, 37 percent of those questioned in an opinion poll in the American Zone of Occupation maintained that exterminating Jews, Poles, and "non-Aryans" had been necessary for the security of Germany. A third were unwilling to accept that "Jews" should have the same rights as "Aryans," and 30 percent looked down on "Negroes" as an inferior race.[4] Even in the mid-1950s, 42 percent – the relative majority – of those questioned considered Hitler one of the greatest German statesmen, had he not started the war.[5]

Fear of new wars and crises did not vanish from the horizon of the 1950s. A vague fear of the next war, a constant anxiety and uncertainty remained during the next decade. According to surveys conducted by U.S. institutions and West German research institutes, 57 percent of the people interviewed in West Germany in 1950 expected a third world war within the next ten years. At the beginning of the Korean War, many households bought stocks of flour, sugar, and other foods that could be stored. Food retailers noted a rapid increase in sales during those weeks. This pessimistic mood receded after the end of the Korean War, but in 1956, at the time of the Suez Crisis and the Soviet invasion of Hungary, the percentage of those who thought a world war possible within the next three years rose from 5 to 13 percent. Conversely, those who considered such a scenario rather unlikely declined dramatically, from 60 to 32 percent.[6]

---

3 Quoted in Michael Wildt, "Zweierlei Neubeginn: Die Politik der Bürgermeister Rudolf Petersen und Max Brauer im Vergleich," in Ursula Büttner and Bernd Nellesen, eds., *Die zweite Chance: Der Übergang von der Diktatur zur Demokratie in Hamburg 1945–1949* (Hamburg, 1997), 57.
4 Felix P. Lutz, "Empirisches Datenmaterial zum historisch-politischen Bewusstsein," in Bundeszentrale für politische Bildung, ed., *Bundesrepublik Deutschland: Geschichte – Bewusstsein* (Bonn, 1989), 150–69.
5 Elisabeth Noelle and Erich Peter Neumann, eds., *Jahrbuch der öffentlichen Meinung 1957* (Allensbach, 1957), 278.
6 Axel Schildt, *Moderne Zeiten: Freizeit, Massenmedien und "Zeitgeist" in der Bundesrepublik der 50er Jahre* (Hamburg, 1995), 308.

It was not until the beginning of the 1960s that this fear of war vanished. In the spring of 1960, 5 percent of Germans polled thought a new world war was probable, 39 percent considered it possible, and 56 percent believed that it was improbable. In the autumn of 1962, over one-third of all the households questioned declared that they kept food in storage for times of crisis.[7] Even in 1967, most people interviewed for an Allensbach survey agreed that one should withdraw one's funds from the bank as fast as possible if the economic situation suddenly took a turn for the worse.[8] The fear of an inflation that would rapidly and irrevocably destroy one's savings, something that Germans had experienced repeatedly during this century, was apparently deep-seated. So, when we look at the years of prosperity in the 1950s and 1960s, we should not forget this underlying mentality of fear, anxiety, and uncertainty.

II

In view of these "burdens of the past," Hans-Peter Schwarz's question asking why West German history did not lead to catastrophe seems to be absolutely right. It is usually answered with reference to the experience of affluence. The currency reform in June 1948 represented a break both in the history of experience and in the history of consumption in West Germany. From one day to the next, shops offered all the goods that had been unobtainable for years. In the public-opinion surveys that U.S. authorities had carried out previously, people had claimed that their greatest worries were food, clothing, and missing relatives. With the currency reform, however, all their worries focused on one thing: money. Now money had its value restored after times of scarcity and hunger, and "normality" should return to households. After years of rationing, people now could afford delicacies they had long missed – things like butter, cream, coffee, or white flour. The significance of the currency reform in 1948 thus cannot be analyzed in economic categories alone; it must be considered as a symbolic turning point that marked the end of the distress.

Growing prosperity and increasing consumption, so it is said, cemented the loyalty of West Germans to their new republic. The phrase "Bonn is not Weimar" was based to a great extent on the hope that by experiencing

---

7 Institut für Demoskopie, Allensbach, "Die Verbreitung von Krisenvorräten in den Haushalten der Bundesrepublik, November 1962," Bundesarchiv Koblenz, ZSg 132–1008.
8 Elisabeth Noelle and Erich Peter Neumann, eds., *Jahrbuch der öffentlichen Meinung 1965–1967* (Allensbach, 1967), 279.

a modern, democratically structured "normal" Western society its citizens would become "normalized" as well. The everyday practice of a "consumer society" that developed along Western lines doubtless contributed, at least in the West, to a normalization of German society, which had been disrupted by war and Nazi crimes. "Modernization" and "democratization" appeared to have been realized harmoniously. "The history of the modernization of the Federal Republic of Germany is a success story," as Wolfgang Zapf remarked succinctly,[9] but, as Axel Schildt added, its course was not self-evident.[10]

At the same time, this optimistic interpretation was viewed with skepticism. Helmut Schelsky voiced a profoundly conservative mistrust as to whether modern mass consumer society would not bring "leveling" and "uniformity" rather than democracy. Conservative critics, fearing that all natural and social differences could be evened out and that the individual would be subsumed in the mass, resembled the sorcerer's apprentice who no longer was able to control those spirits he had unleashed. The double strategy of fostering economic and industrial modernity while at the same time trying vehemently to ward off social and cultural modernity – which Daniel Bell shrewdly described as "disjunction"[11] – formed the intellectual backdrop for the criticism of those economists who, while defending free entrepreneurship and the market economy, deeply mistrusted the sovereignty of the individual. They doubted that individuality and sovereignty, that multiplicity of consumption and freedom of choice, could be equated. *Homo consumens*, who had just been enthroned as "king customer," did not know, so their criticism, how to properly use the power that he had only recently acquired. "The consumer," wrote Erich Egner, the doyen of household economists, "stands in the market like a reed in the wind, driven to and fro. It was the consumer lacking orientation, not the sovereign of the market, which is the reality of the twentieth century."[12] In a book widely discussed at the time, David Riesman roundly criticized modern consumer society. He subdivided modern history into three phases: the tradition-directed, the

---

9 Wolfgang Zapf, "Zum Verhältnis von sozialstrukturellem Wandel und politischem Wandel: Die Bundesrepublik 1949–89," in Bernhard Blanke and Hellmut Wollmann, eds., *Die alte Bundesrepublik: Kontinuität und Wandel*, Leviathan Sonderheft 12 (Opladen, 1991), 130–9.
10 Axel Schildt, *Ankunft im Westen: Ein Essay zur Erfolgsgeschichte der Bundesrepublik* (Frankfurt am Main, 1999), 10–11. The whole sentence reads: "Die Bundesrepublik ist im grossen und ganzen – bisher – eine Erfolgsgeschichte, aber selbstverständlich war dieser Verlauf nicht" ("The Federal Republic – by and large – is a success story but this course was not self-evident").
11 Daniel Bell, *Die nachindustrielle Gesellschaft* (Frankfurt am Main, 1976).
12 Erich Egner, "Die Marktstellung des Konsumenten," *Jahrbücher für Nationalökonomie und Statistik* 165 (1953): 21–49, quotation 33. Original emphasis.

inward-directed, and the other-directed human being.[13] The decline of the population, the reduction of work time, and the accompanying enormous expansion of the possibilities for leisure and consumption, especially in the second half of the twentieth century, had, in his view, repressed the "need to save and the 'consciousness of scarcity' of many inward-directed people" and created a "drive to consume and a lasting 'consciousness of affluence'" that made people capable of indulging in "wasteful luxury and use of free time and of surplus production." This "enabled man to indulge in luxury and leisure and to use the production overflow."

III

On the ground, West German reality still looked gray and bleak. This can be seen in the housekeeping books kept by more than two hundred families, typical four-person households who recorded their incomes and outlays and whose data served (and still serve) as the basis for the calculations of the Federal Office of Statistics.[14] Expenditure on food was the dominant household expense for these families. In 1950, they spent DM 132.54 monthly on food, which was 46.4 percent of all household expenditure. In 1963, this expenditure had risen to DM 192.75 and amounted to 34.6 percent, and it still consumed the largest single portion of the budget.[15] Expenditure on clothing took second place. In the early 1950s, this covered the extra needs resulting from the shortages of the war and its aftermath, including replacement of the improvised pieces of clothing such as the legendary coats made of soldiers' uniforms or worn-out shoes. If one divides these expenses into those for "fixed" needs, which were unavoidable, and those for "elastic" needs, the remaining free disposable portion, then, according to the calculations of the Federal Office of Statistics, the fixed portion in these employee households was the larger far into the 1950s. It was only in 1957 that the households spent somewhat more, 50.2 percent, on their elastic needs than on their fixed ones.

13 "What is common to all the other-directed people is that their contemporaries are the source of direction for the individual – either known to him or those with whom he is indirectly acquainted, through friends and through the mass media" (David Riesman, Reuel Denney, and Nathan Glazar, *The Lonely Crowd: A Study of the Changing American Character* [New York, 1950], 37).

14 Statistisches Bundesamt, Fachserie M (Preise, Löhne, Wirtschaftsrechnungen), Reihe 13 Wirtschaftsrechnungen, Stuttgart 1949ff; see Hannelore Reddies, "Das Verfahren der laufenden Wirtschaftsrechungen von 1950 bis 1964 und ab 1965," *Wirtschaft und Statistik*, n.s. 17 (1965): 496–500. The respective statistical offices of the German *Länder* analyzed these books and sent the resulting data to the Federal Office of Statistics, which published the aggregated findings.

15 For a detailed account, see Michael Wildt, *Am Beginn der "Konsumgesellschaft": Mangelerfahrung, Lebenshaltung, Wohlstandshoffnung in Westdeutschland in den fünfziger Jahren* (Hamburg, 1994), 59–115.

One of these families, Family Z, from Kiel, serves well here as a source of information on the possibilities and limits of everyday consumption. The husband, born in 1924, worked as a machine fitter in the Kiel gas works; his wife, a housewife, was one year older; they had two children, born in 1946 and 1947.[16] In 1949, Family Z was living in a one-room apartment. The husband alone provided the income, most of which was paid weekly, the remainder during the following month after a final calculation; to that were added special payments for vacation and Christmas. The monthly income of Family Z in July 1949 totaled DM 300, which just covered the necessary everyday expenses. Buying larger consumer goods involved extraordinary financial efforts. In April 1949, Herr Z entered in the housekeeping book the reason for borrowing DM 7 from his mother-in-law: "The last weekly pay was used to buy a spring coat and one dress, therefore we are short of housekeeping money." At the end of May Herr Z again noted a loan of DM 24: "The borrowed money is needed for buying a kitchen table." In June, the income was insufficient to buy coal: "There is a deadline for buying coke as payment in kind. Due to the payments for the kitchen furniture the wage is not sufficient for this." In June, DM 25 again had to be borrowed and was returned when a large wage payment was given out in the same month. In July 1950, for the first time the family borrowed DM 80 from a credit institution, the Waren-Kredit-Gesellschaft (Goods Credit Association) in Kiel, repayable in monthly installments of DM 20. In addition to that, they withdrew money from their savings account in order to buy a leather purse and a men's suit, spending DM 108 altogether. Vacation in August, which they spent at home, again required a loan, in addition to a wage advance. Despite this, Herr Z had to enter into the housekeeping book on September 4: "Due to vacation, extraordinary expenses during the preceding month, therefore ran up debts." The amount the family lacked was only DM 3.50!

In 1949, weekday expenditures were limited to basic foodstuffs, such as milk, bread, and fat, and it was only shopping for the weekend that made the list in the housekeeping book significantly longer. On Sundays, the family also had meat and seems to have liked goulash in particular, with chocolate pudding and vanilla sauce as a dessert. Tropical fruit was a rare treat at this time. For holidays such as Easter, there was much more on the shopping list: In addition to bread, butter, and milk, Frau Z also bought apples, lentils, onions, leeks, noodles, and, for the holiday dinner, a roast. The couple even

---

16 The household accounts of Family Z from 1949 to 1960 are in the Schleswig-Holsteinischen Landesarchiv Schleswig under the call number: Abt. 616 (Stat.Landesamt), nos. 131–40.

allowed themselves some real coffee: "50 [grams] real coffee" was entered on April 14, 1949. Otherwise, they drank only coffee substitute.

Exceptions such as these, which clearly differentiated shopping for holidays such as Easter or Christmas from shopping for workdays, show that during the lean years at the end of the 1940s and the beginning of the 1950s consumption was limited but not monotonous. Bread rolls on the weekend and goulash and chocolate pudding for Sunday dinner were both a change and a contrast to food on workdays. Sunday embodied the exceptional – this is what Family Z held on to even in these "gray" times when they had to count every penny.

This was not only true for Family Z in Kiel. When the Allensbach Institute for Opinion Research asked in a 1955 survey on "social reality" about, among other things, Sunday dinner, 83 percent of those questioned responded that they had had meat on the preceding Sunday.[17] On workdays, a third of them would eat soup and dessert, on Sundays more than half. Although almost half rated meals on workdays either as "simple" or as *gut bürgerlich* (plain cooking), more than two-thirds agreed that their last Sunday dinner deserved being called *gut bürgerlich*. The contrast between workdays and Sundays, which also showed in the length of the meals or in the place where they were taken – kitchen or living room – remained a salient feature of eating habits in the 1950s.

However, minor details reveal how the consumption of Family Z began to improve in subtle degrees. In 1950, coffee substitute still was always on the shopping list, as were egg powder and artificial honey. But although the couple had indulged in 30 grams of real coffee only for Easter and Christmas the year before, in 1950 they bought more than double that amount, 62.5 grams, for each weekend in May, September, and November.

The first year to appear in the housekeeping books of Family Z during which, after the lean wartime and postwar years, they could afford considerably more than satisfying only basic everyday needs was 1953. They bought much more fat than before, drank coffee more often, and had oranges in numbers unrivaled even later on. They also purchased much more clothing and without the financial strains of previous years; they were able to have their sofa reupholstered for DM 64; and, last but not least, they went to the cinema much more often than in previous years.

Borrowing money for a short period in order to cover special purchases became a common practice in 1954. In April, a DM 100 loan from the

---

17 Institut für Demoskopie, Allensbach, "Die soziale Wirklichkeit" (1955), Bundesarchiv Koblenz, ZSg 132–449. Part of the findings of this survey have been published in Otto Lenz, *Die soziale Wirklichkeit* (Allensbach, 1956).

Waren-Kredit-Gesellschaft was used to buy shoes for the whole family. In July, DM 100 were obtained for a lady's bathrobe and for trousers; in October a men's suit and children's boots were purchased on credit. On December 12, 1954, right in time for Christmas, Family Z acquired their first major consumer item: a vacuum cleaner, the Rapid model by Siemens. With the help of acquaintances, they were able to take advantage of a particularly favorable offer and save 30 percent off the list price of DM 144.

The vacuum cleaner actually was among those consumer goods that were being purchased in the first half of the 1950s. According to a survey by the Institute for Opinion Research in 1955, 39 percent of West German households owned a vacuum cleaner.[18] When asked what they yet had to acquire in order to be able to say that they were doing well, the interviewees put the vacuum cleaner in third place, after the refrigerator and the washing machine. It is interesting to note the different ways of acquiring these items, as the case of Family Z demonstrates. Whereas electric stoves and washing machines were purchased primarily in specialty stores and refrigerators and kitchen machinery mainly were obtained directly from the producers or bought wholesale, most vacuum cleaners were ordered when the proverbial vacuum cleaner salesman came to visit.[19] The reason for using this direct method was price. Discounts of 30 percent, such as the one that Family Z had received, were not rare. In return, however, the items had to be paid for in cash right away. One may see – in the case of Family Z as well – how strongly the principle of saving first and spending later still prevailed, which in the economic context of the 1950s had the advantage of discounts, and how limited the extent was to which buying habits were characterized by a willingness to possess a given article and pay it off in the future.

Four years later, at Christmas 1958, Family Z had – for the time being – reached the peak of their consumption. Herr Z wrote on the expenditures page of the housekeeping book: "1 TV set 53 cm type Weltblick, total price DM 885, down payment DM 295, in installments." No other consumer item was placed in the housekeeping books of Family Z in so symbolic a manner as was the television. That this expensive piece of equipment was paid for in installments was not called into question. Neither could the television, the

---

18 Institut für Demoskopie, Allensbach, "Die soziale Wirklichkeit" (1955) (typescript), Bundesarchiv Koblenz ZSg 132–449. In a sample referring to income and consumption of the Federal Statistical Office, 74 percent of the households asked stated that they owned a vacuum cleaner, more than 50 percent had bought it between 1949 and 1957. Statistisches Bundesamt, Fachserie M, Reihe 18: "Ausstattung der privaten Haushalte mit ausgewählten langlebigen Gebrauchsgütern 1962/63" (Stuttgart, 1964).

19 "Die Beschaffungswege der Konsumenten bei Grossartikeln des Hausrats," special issue no. 4 of *Mitteilungen des Instituts für Handelsforschung an der Universität Köln* (Cologne, 1954).

price of which equaled two months' salary for Herr Z, be purchased out
of current income, nor did the family have sufficient funds in their account
to pay for it from their savings. For Family Z, the television set was the
most expensive consumer item acquired between 1949 and 1960. Due to
this purchase, the Kiel family was among the earliest owners of a television
set in the Federal Republic. According to a survey taken by the Institute
of Opinion Research in July 1958, only 9 percent of all private households
owned television sets, but 34 percent desired them.[20] Social differences
played only a minor role: Households of white-collar workers, civil servants,
and skilled workers each had the same proportion of television owners; and
even households with net incomes of DM 400 per month on the one hand
and DM 1,000 per month on the other did not differ very much from one
another in this regard.[21] Only households with incomes of over DM 1,000
in 1958 owned a significantly higher number of television sets. Thus, the
television set proved to be a consumer item that spread quickly, and its spread
was much less dependent on social class and income than its price would
suggest.[22]

IV

"Catching up" is the key phrase of the early 1950s, not least for the seven
million refugees and expellees who had arrived in West Germany with
only a few belongings and who now had to equip their own households.
But even the most immediate needs of the postwar years could hardly be
met from current income, as the example of Family Z demonstrates. This
is why, after the currency reform, credit associations emerged, of which
the Kiel family also took advantage. The amount of credit did not surpass
DM 300 as a rule, and interest rates were between 7 and 12 percent. The
credit associations were funded by the savings institutions and, above all, by
the retail trade, which gave loans to consumers in the form of checks for

---

20 Institut für Demoskopie, Allensbach, "Wunsch und Besitz" (1958) (typescript), Bundesarchiv
    Koblenz ZSg 132–707. A poll taken at the same time by the Frankfurt-based DIVO Institute found
    that 11 percent of the West German population owned a TV set; DIVO Institut, ed., *Der westdeutsche
    Markt in Zahlen: Ein Handbuch für Forschung, Werbung und Verkauf* (Frankfurt am Main, 1958).
21 At the beginning of the 1960s, there was a television set in almost 49 percent of the workers'
    households with an income between DM 600 and 800, half of which had been purchased before
    1960; Statistisches Bundesamt, Fachserie M, Reihe 18: "Ausstattung der privaten Haushalte mit
    ausgewählten langlebigen Gebrauchsgütern 1962/63" (Stuttgart, 1964).
22 See Schildt, *Moderne Zeiten*, 262–300; Knut Hickethier, "Der Fernseher: Zwischen Teilhabe und
    Medienkonsum," in Wolfgang Ruppert, ed., *Fahrrad, Auto, Fernsehschrank: Zur Kulturgeschichte der
    Alltagsdinge* (Frankfurt am Main, 1993), 162–87.

goods that could be redeemed in specific shops.[23] In fact, furniture, stoves, and clothing were at the top of the lists of the credit associations in the early 1950s, whereas radios, bicycles, cameras, and even washing machines and refrigerators appeared at the bottom. As for the social composition of the customers, blue-collar workers predominated (50–60 percent), followed by white-collar workers (18–25 percent), and civil servants (16 percent); the self-employed hardly figured in the purchase of goods in installments.

However, the break in patterns of private consumption toward the end of the 1950s should not be overlooked. From 1957 to 1958, the expenditures of a four-person workers' household rose rapidly in important areas such as transportation, vacation, cinema/television, electrical household appliances, and personal hygiene. Here was an unmistakable turning point that separated the two stages of postwar consumption from one another. This break was most obvious with respect to the ownership of durable consumer goods: The overwhelming majority of households in the Federal Republic were, according to a survey by the Federal Office of Statistics on incomes and consumption at the beginning of the 1960s, able to afford refrigerators, television sets, or electrical kitchen appliances only after 1958. Whereas in the early 1950s it had been most important for these households to meet basic family needs (with the cost of food a major portion) and to make up for the furniture and clothing damaged or lost due to the war, from the end of the 1950s it became possible to purchase not just the basics but more and new consumer goods and thus to begin sharing in affluence.

The feeling that a boom was under way raised expectations for the future. Based on the feeling that things were constantly "getting better," there was a burgeoning confidence in a crisis-proof development of affluence. The assertion "Now it's our turn!" meant looking ahead, but at the same time it was rooted in the experiences of the preceding years of scarcity. Whereas from today's perspective the 1950s are marked above all by the deficits of consumption – the "yet-to-come" possession of all those consumer goods that were to be offered during the years ahead and that we now take for granted – the experience of contemporaries was characterized by the increase, by the possession "already achieved" of all those goods already on offer. It is this change of perspective that enables us to understand how during the 1960s the mentality of striding forward, the expectation of perpetual growth that characterized consumer society, could emerge. In this respect, the late 1950s and early 1960s marked a turning point separating the two

---

23 See Waldemar Koch, *Die Entwicklung der deutschen Teilzahlungswirtschaft seit 1945 und ihre Problematik* (Berlin, 1955), 14–31.

phases of consumption in the postwar years: the lean years, in which one
had to "scrape" and count every penny, and the beginning of a new form of
consumption in which, to quote Ernest Zahn, consumers no longer looked
at "what they had missed, but at what they desired."[24]

V

The refrigerator topped the list of items that people wanted to buy in the
1950s: In a 1955 opinion survey by the Allensbach Institute, it ranked first,
above the washing machine, the vacuum cleaner, and the television set.[25] In
the follow-up survey in 1958, the desire for a refrigerator again occupied first
place.[26] Even in low-income households, which earned less than DM 250
a month and of which only 5 percent owned a refrigerator, 35 percent
wanted one. In 1955, only 10 percent of all West German households
owned a refrigerator;[27] in 1958 it was 21 percent;[28] and in 1962–3 there
was a refrigerator in 51.8 percent of all private households in the Federal
Republic.[29]

Frau H., born in 1923, lived in a working-class village near Bremerhaven
in the 1950s. Her father worked in the nearby shipyard, and her mother was
a housewife. "We bought our refrigerator in late '58–'59," she describes.
"It was more than 500 marks. I felt pressed because the quantities became
larger, one could buy cheaper, there were sales but they all went down the
drain because I could not store them. And then in summer – '59 was a
terribly warm summer – we all were at the dike, all Bremerhaven was at
the dike. I still remember, it was such a hot day, and we all ran home and
were all dried out. At home I had the big Coca-Cola bottles, and there
was ice in the fridge. Father got his bottle of beer, cold, the children cola
and ice. And home-made ice cream. Each had their own big glass, and the
children could slurp it up."[30]

The refrigerator brought some relief from daily shopping. For Frau H. the
period "pre-refrigerator" meant having to shop several times a day. "Then

24 Ernest Zahn, *Soziologie der Prosperität* (Cologne, 1960), 22.
25 The electric food processor ranked ninth; Institut für Demoskopie, Allensbach, "Die soziale Wirklichkeit" (1955), Bundesarchiv Koblenz ZSg 132–449.
26 In the meantime, the food processor had moved to fourth rank behind the washing machine and the
   TV set; Institut für Demoskopie, Allensbach, "Wunsch und Besitz" (1958), Bundesarchiv Koblenz
   ZSg 132–707.
27 Institut für Demoskopie, Allensbach, "Die soziale Wirklichkeit" (1955).
28 Institut für Demoskopie, Allensbach, "Wunsch und Besitz" (1958).
29 Statistisches Bundesamt, Fachserie M, Reihe 18: "Ausstattung der privaten Haushalte mit
   ausgewählten langlebigen Gebrauchsgütern 1962/63" (Stuttgart, 1964).
30 Interview with Frau H. on Jan. 12, 1990, quoted in Wildt, *Am Beginn der "Konsumgesellschaft,"* 145.

we did not yet have a refrigerator. We really had to go shopping every day. There was a shop at every corner. In the morning, there was milk and bread at the door, in the afternoon I did the shopping for supper and for the next morning so as not to have to get up too early." Now perishable goods could remain fresh longer. But over and above the economic argument that with a refrigerator one could save money, the main point for Frau H. was the ice and ice cream in the refrigerator, the pleasure to be able to make her own ice cream or to drink ice-cold drinks on a hot summer day.

Where did the money for the new consumer goods come from? Although the nominal incomes of workers in West Germany doubled between 1950 and 1963, from DM 212 to DM 489 a month,[31] this alone was not sufficient to purchase the new, expensive consumer goods. It was not least the wish to be able to satisfy such consumer desires that led the number of wives taking up additional work to rise considerably in the 1950s. Whereas in 1939 the share of gainfully employed wives was 23.6 percent in the German Reich, in the Federal Republic it was 19.7 percent in 1950 and 35.7 percent in 1961 (57 percent in 1980).[32]

One way they could be purchased was patiently to save every disposable mark until the amount needed for the purchase was reached. That people saved more in the Federal Republic during the 1950s can be seen in the growth of the proportion of income that was saved in private households: It increased from 3.2 percent in 1950 to 8.7 percent in 1960.[33] In a broad opinion survey in May 1953, the Nuremberg Society for Consumer Research (Nürnberger Gesellschaft für Konsumforschung, or GfK) analyzed the "structure of needs of the consumer market" (Bedarfsstruktur des Käufermarktes). Altogether, 4,470 households answered questions on their incomes and expenditures.[34] According to the survey, about 30 percent of all households questioned had to pay installments, DM 15 per month on

31 Rainer Skiba, Das westdeutsche Lohnniveau zwischen den beiden Weltkriegen und nach der Währungsreform (Cologne, 1974); Erich Wiegand, "Zur historischen Entwicklung der Löhne und Lebenshaltungskosten in Deutschland," in Erich Wiegand and Wolfgang Zapf, eds., Wandel der Lebensbedingungen in Deutschland (Frankfurt am Main, 1982), 65–153.

32 Walter Müller, Angelika Willms, and Johann Handl, Strukturwandel der Frauenarbeit 1880–1980 (Frankfurt am Main, 1983), 35; see now also Christine von Oertzen, Teilzeitarbeit und die Lust am Zuverdienen: Geschlechterpolitik und gesellschaftlicher Wandel in Westdeutschland 1948–1969 (Göttingen, 1999).

33 Reinhold Exo, Die Entwicklung der sozialen und ökonomischen Struktur der Ersparnisbildung (Berlin, 1967), 335, table 57. See also Karl M. Maier, Der Sparprozess in der Bundesrepublik Deutschland: Eine empirische Analyse des Sparverhaltens der privaten Haushalte seit 1950 (Frankfurt am Main, 1983).

34 Gesellschaft für Konsumforschung e.V., Die Bedarfsstruktur im Käufermarkt, Nürnberg 1953, Archiv der GfK, U 174. Partial results of the survey have been published: "Die Bedarfsstruktur im Käufermarkt," Jahrbuch der Absatz- und Verbrauchsforschung 2 (1956): 5–37, and Paul W. Meyer, "Wie sieht der Konsument das Teilzahlungsgeschäft: Ergebnisse einer wissenschaftlichen Basis-Untersuchung," Die Teilzahlungswirtschaft 2 (1954): 48.

average, which equaled only 3.5 percent of their average monthly net income. Broken down into groups of goods (more than one answer possible), 60 percent of the payments were used for purchasing furniture, about 21 percent for transportation,[35] 18 percent for clothing, and 15 percent for household and kitchen expenditures. Almost 60 percent of the households were saving, with 70 percent of them saving only for short-term purchases such as clothing and furniture. For the majority of households interviewed, buying on installment still carried the stigma of not being "respectable" and admitting that one did not have sufficient funds of one's own. In addition, there was the fear that the installments could not be met and that the purchased goods would have to be returned.

The GfK always asked its interviewers to send in their own observations and judgments with the statistical surveys, which makes the GfK market analyses of the 1950s particularly vivid. A correspondent from Oberhausen (Ruhr) wrote: "As expected, one could determine in the course of this survey that people wish to have a lot of necessary consumer items and that nowhere is money sufficient." A correspondent from Ratzeburg (Schleswig-Holstein): "Everywhere the same impression: The purse is too small and the needs too large." Another from Eschweiler (Rhineland): "Due to the imported higher standard of living (American GIs) and the deprivations during the war, the demand for all sorts of consumer goods, even luxury items, is so great that producers would barely be able to meet it if everyone earned according to one's needs and if, most of all, daily costs of living were lower." A correspondent in Langquaid (Lower Bavaria): "In general, it can be said that planning does not play a large role in the households. Planning is only possible when one is saving; there is not much saving, so there is not much planning, either. Apart from that, buying on installments renders planning unnecessary." And a correspondent in Seesen (Lower Saxony): "Everyone believes that what does not come at once will never come. People are reckoning in days, weeks, months, but not in years."

Four years later, the situation still had not changed much. In a survey in the autumn of 1957 to ascertain the purchasing plans of private households, one of the questions asked how the most expensive purchase of the preceding year had been financed. Thirty-one percent of the interviewees answered that they had made "extra savings," 15.4 percent had resorted to

---

35 However, as for this part of the expenses there were huge differences according to household income. While families with an income up to DM 300 a month had made only 9.9 percent of all purchases of vehicles on installments, families earning more than DM 500 accounted for 25 percent of these purchases.

existing savings, 19.1 percent had financed the item from their current income, and 26.6 percent had paid in installments. Broken down according to occupation, the findings showed that workers took the lead with purchases in installments. Asked how they wanted to pay for their next large purchase, 46.3 percent responded that they wanted to make extra savings, whereas only 14.9 percent wanted to pay in installments.[36]

VI

The consumer society, and paying in installments as the way to get there, did carry a negative image in the Germany of the 1950s. Frau G. had bought her refrigerator in installments, but the pressure exerted by the payments was notoriously great: "We had a luxury item, even then: a large Bosch refrigerator. That was the only thing we had bought, everything else I had been given as a dowry. We really wanted to have a refrigerator, for I was used to it from home – my mother must have bought one of the first refrigerators. So we have paid this refrigerator in installments. Since then I have never ever done anything in installments! So awful – I don't know, for five years or so.... You couldn't get rid of it."[37]

The expectation that one would be paying things off for years to come and the suspicion that one might be living beyond one's means obviously burdened this form of purchasing in West Germany. In Frau G.'s account the contradiction becomes evident: on the one hand, wanting to fulfill one's desire for a refrigerator, on the other, being able to accomplish this only by taking up a loan. On balance, the refrigerator was bought with a bad conscience – a feeling that still was far removed from the consumer's mentality of first enjoying the product and paying for it later.

A broad survey of the Allensbach Institute for Opinion Research in 1959 on the use of money in private households confirmed that traditional values were still held in high esteem.[38] Eighty-two percent of those asked agreed that thrift was an important quality that absolutely was part of a good character. Sixty-six percent preferred waiting two hours for a bus to taking a taxi, and 60 percent would rather abstain from going to the movies than pay for an expensive place in a box seat. Fifty-one percent of the households asked

---

36 Karl G. Specht, "Der Haushalt als Stätte des Verbrauchs," *Hauswirtschaft und Wissenschaft*, no. 1 (1958): 23–8.

37 Interview with Frau G. on February 28, 1990, quoted in Wildt, *Am Beginn der "Konsumgesellschaft,"* 148.

38 Institut für Demoskopie, Allensbach, "Umgang mit Geld" (1960) (typescript), Bundesarchiv Koblenz ZSg 132–829; most of it published in Günter Schmölders, Gerhard Scherhorn, and Gerhard Schmidtchen, *Der Umgang mit Geld im privaten Haushalt* (Berlin, 1969), 61.

were ranked by the Allensbach Institute as having definite saving principles. These maxims appeared internalized to such an extent that − as the case of Frau G. vividly demonstrates − the conscience would immediately make itself felt if these principles were violated. Accordingly, the "thrifty" ones showed considerable reluctance when asked whether they would borrow money from an acquaintance if, through no fault of their own, they got into financial difficulties. They preferred reducing their expenses to asking others for money. In this respect, it is not unimportant that a third of the households interviewed in a 1953 survey by the Society for Consumer Research said that they placed their savings under the proverbial mattress.[39] The Allensbach question about installment purchases yielded a familiar result. Almost a third of the households questioned had taken out a loan in 1959, 21 percent on installments, 7 percent as credit with a bank or savings institution.[40] Even in December 1962, only 29 percent of those interviewed in a survey by the DIVO Institute on purchases on installments approved, whereas 71 percent rejected them.[41] The economist Günter Schmölders even speaks of a "taboo against purchases on installments prevailing in Germany."[42]

Whereas in the United States, expanding the horizon of consumption and steadily increasing the standard of living became a mentality, and the satisfaction with what had been achieved engendered new needs and desires for new consumer goods, in Germany the values of solidity and durability were still in place. In 1956, for example, 90 percent of the Germans interviewed intended to buy furniture or radio equipment that was more expensive and of a better quality in order to be able to use it as long as possible instead of buying something cheaper that would have to be replaced once it had gone out of fashion. It is interesting to note that by far the majority of Germans in the same survey voiced the opinion that Americans paid less attention to quality and went for what was more modern.[43] "The average American consumer, who has internalized the secular trend of income development, adapts his level of consumption in advance to the expected rise of income," concluded social researchers Georg Katona, Burkhard Strümpel, and Ernest Zahn. "He believes that the favorable trend will continue; the present

---

39 Gesellschaft für Konsumforschung e.V., *Die Bedarfsstruktur im Käufermarkt* (Nuremberg, 1953). Among the households with an income of up to DM 300 a month, the "mattress savers" in 1953 even made up the majority. Forty-four percent of all households asked saved their money in savings accounts.

40 Schmölders, *Umgang mit Geld*, 130–1. 41 Ibid., 133.

42 Ibid.

43 Umfrage des DIVO-Instituts vom September 1956, quoted in Schildt, *Moderne Zeiten*, 418–19.

situation is the self-evident minimum. Optimism is related to improving what has been achieved; pessimism to its continuation. In contrast, Germans refuse to project the remarkable recent increase of their standard of living into the future. In times of relative optimism they believe that the status quo will continue; if they are pessimistic they fear for the maintenance of what they have achieved. Whereas Americans thought about spending tomorrow's income, Germans occupied themselves with planning to spend yesterday's savings."[44]

VII

The differences between the United States and Germany are evident; the "Americanization" of consumption behavior and the spread of paying on credit as a way to a consumer society were not simply a matter of imitation or of a time lag. Deep-rooted fears, attitudes, and mentalities first had to change before economic optimism and expectations for the future could determine even everyday consumer behavior. But despite these clear differences, processes were under way that set changes in motion.

It was evident from opinion surveys that paying in installments was looked down on – to maintain a thrifty household meant not to live beyond one's means. However, the survey by the Allensbach Institute in 1959 on the use of money, for example, showed that the average amount of installments in those households that had taken up debts stood at the considerable sum of DM 70 monthly and came to between 15 and 17 percent of monthly income. And a breakdown into age groups showed significant differences: Whereas those over sixty almost without exception had made no purchases on credit, the percentage of those under forty who had done so was above average. And whereas civil servants and white-collar workers, as the Allensbach Institute noted, were "particularly disinclined to run up debts," urban blue-collar workers were at the top of the list of those "prone to run up debts."[45]

Buying on installments, as the authors of the study emphasized, "was now for urban workers obviously an adequate and hardly a disreputable method for dealing with the difference between the standard of consumption and income."[46] The high percentage of low-income workers' households among those buying in installments shows that for them this form of purchasing served as a means to acquire specific, expensive consumer goods. Although

44 George Katona, Burkhard Strümpel, and Ernest Zahn, *Zwei Wege zur Prosperität: Konsumverhalten, Leistungsmentalität und Bildungsbereitschaft in Amerika und Europa* (Düsseldorf, 1971), 110.
45 Schmölders, *Umgang mit Geld*, 135–6.   46 Ibid., 136.

they viewed saving as a special virtue, they were the least able to afford to do so. Among the minority of those buying on installments at the end of the 1950s and the beginning of the 1960s, most were far removed from a supposedly "modern" orientation toward consumption. And it was the youth whose loyalty to the traditional canon of values diminished and who did not consider running up debts to be a sin against the principles of good housekeeping.[47] The authors of the Allensbach study cautiously raised the question of whether the ways in which the younger generation approached consumption demonstrated an increased rationality in economic matters or whether it may just have been the typical carefree attitude of the young. In the 1960s, however, it became unmistakably clear that there had been a change, that West Germans had come to embrace the pursuit of happiness and that, in the words of sociologist Ralf Dahrendorf, "pursuit of personal success, orientation toward consumption and individualism, marked rejection of any form of military discipline, matter-of-factness, and materialism" had become part of their mentality.[48]

Although the principles of thrift coexisted with the practice of participating in the consumer society by purchasing on installments, it is evident that the dichotomy posited by Katona, Strümpel, and Zahn described only part of the social reality. Rather, in the 1950s, particularly toward the end of the decade, a transition in consumer behavior can be observed that tried to reconcile traditional principles with a changing practice. It was a "modernization" of practice of sorts that, while drawing its legitimation from tradition, consolidated trust in everyday behavior, thus paving the way for changes in the legitimation of the practice itself.

The new societal ideal was oriented toward individual achievement, pursuit of private success, and participation in mass consumption. In becoming acquainted with market practices, with consumer society, West Germans were taking lessons in plurality. Mass consumption meant not only an increasing number of goods, it also meant a change of practice, the development of new experiences. Customers who made purchases in self-service stores had to learn to find their way through this consumer's world, and they had to learn a new language to decipher the various semiotic codes associated with the goods. In becoming part of "consumer society," everyone

---

47 The extent of the break in attitudes toward cultural lifestyles between the generations is stressed by Kaspar Maase, *BRAVO Amerika: Erkundungen zur Jugendkultur der Bundesrepublik in den 50er Jahren* (Hamburg, 1992).

48 Ralf Dahrendorf, *Gesellschaft und Freiheit: Zur soziologischen Analyse der Gegenwart* (Munich, 1961), 315.

had, in the words of Pierre Bourdieau, to take care "not to differ from the ordinary, but to differ differently."[49]

By turning around the macro perspective of "modernization" – a process which neither its left-wing nor right-wing critics could evade – the notion of plurality aims not so much at the increase of goods offered but at the practice of the consumers. In such a changing perspective, modern mass consumption, which has been referred to as the cornerstone of the "modernization" of West German society, becomes a complex network of practices of using, buying, preparing, serving, and finally eating, all of which have their own dynamic, their own context, their own meaning. "In fact there is, as opposed to the rationalized, expansionist, centralized, spectacular, and noisy production," so the French historian Michel de Certeau, "another production of a completely different type, which is called 'consumption' and which is characterized by its richness of cunning, its crumbling away according to the occasion, its poaching, its clandestine nature, and its continuous murmuring – all in all a quasi-invisibility because it hardly stands out by its own products (where would be space for them?) but by the art of using those products that have been imposed on it."[50] Developing a distinctive style out of the multitude of options became the main task for consumers: The consumer had to learn how to make choices. The practice of consumption, which far into the 1950s had consisted of making much out of little, now became the art of producing something individual out of much.

---

49 Pierre Bourdieu, "Klassenstellung und Klassenlage," in Pierre Bourdieu, *Zur Soziologie der symbolischen Formen* (Frankfurt am Main, 1975), 42–74, quotation 70.
50 Michel de Certeau, *Kunst des Handelns* (Berlin, 1988), 81. Original French ed.: *L'invention du quotidien 1, Arts des faire* (Paris, 1980).

10

"Strengthened and Purified Through Ordeal by Fire"

Ecclesiastical Triumphalism in the Ruins of Europe

DAMIAN VAN MELIS

"If they have died as the children of God with remorse for their sins, then...the gassed have in a moment found that which we, for all our searching and groping, cannot find: the truth, the light."[1] After 1945, from the Catholic Church's point of view, there was nothing to add to what it had always propounded about modern societies, about wars, and about violence: Wars are bad because they cause death and suffering, but they are legitimated as "just wars"[2] when they serve against aggressors, unjust regimes, and dictatorships. These regimes are the result of people and societies failing to subordinate themselves to the Church. The Church's main opponent was not war, suffering, or violence, but the Modern Age itself with the waning of ecclesiastical power as a result of secularization. As the agent of God's will, the Church alone knew how to build a peaceful society. The destruction and devastation of the time drastically confirmed this conviction. Churchmen simply did not perceive the very specific nature of the violence of this period. It was not so much a case of mundane disinterest in experiences of violence (which was particularly evident in West Germany) but of a particularly stubborn insistence on old political, ideological, and religious stereotypes. As a result of this self-confidence and of the massive Allied support in West Germany and the support of many postwar governments in Western Europe for the Catholic

---

Translated by Laila Friese and Richard Bessel.

1 *Katholisches Sonntagsblatt: Bistumsblatt der Diözese Rottenburg* 94, no. 44 (1946): 261.

2 See Anselm Doering-Manteuffel, *Katholizismus und Wiederbewaffnung: Die Haltung der deutschen Katholiken gegenüber der Wehrfrage 1948–1955* (Mainz, 1981), 9–13; Wilhelm Janssen, Joachim Krause, Otto Kimminich, and Ernst Nagl, "Krieg," in Görres-Gesellschaft, ed., *Staatslexikon: Recht, Wirtschaft, Gesellschaft*, 7 vols., 7th ed. (Freiburg im Breisgau, 1995), 3:703–19, esp. 715–16; Richard Hauser, "Krieg," in Josef Höfer and Karl Rahner, eds., *Lexikon für Theologie und Kirche*, 14 vols. (Freiburg im Breisgau, 1961), 640–3.

Church, in 1945 the Church appeared to be the victor among the ruins.[3]

When we speak about the Catholic Church we have a relatively clearly defined object and an easily comprehensible institution in mind: It is the worldwide institution organized under the leadership of Pope Pius XII (1939–58), which closely cooperated with the international, national, and regional Church hierarchies. The bishops and clerics in turn supported other Catholic institutions such as universities, associations, and parishes.[4] There has been little research into the history of the Church's grassroots, for example of individual parishes and cloisters, or ordinary priests and the laity. Research has concentrated on the higher echelons of the Church, on the Catholic or Christian political parties, and more recently on the "milieu."[5] After 1945, a considerable number of Catholics indeed did continue to oppose the official line of the Church leadership in political and ideological questions, but they acted in the first instance not as Catholics or representatives of Catholicism but rather as politically committed citizens. In this regard, at least into the 1960s, they comprised a minority relative to supporters of the official institutions and doctrine.

Since 1945, the members of the Church's hierarchy and its spokesmen have followed an astonishingly unified sociopolitical line of argument in all countries of Europe. One has to use the word "astonishing," because up to 1945 the experiences of the Catholic Church in different countries had in fact been very different. Whereas, on the one hand, there were examples of the Catholic Church actively cooperating with right-wing leaders, as in Italy and Spain, we know, on the other, of the unclear relationship between the dictators and the Church in Germany and Austria, falling somewhere

---

3 See the introduction to Joachim Köhler and Damian van Melis, eds., *Siegerin in Trümmern: Die Rolle der katholischen Kirche in der deutschen Nachkriegsgesellschaft* (Stuttgart, 1998), 10–17.

4 On the categories: (Catholic) Church, political Catholicism, associational Catholicism, official Church, and Catholic milieu, which frequently are elided in popular speech, see the already somewhat dated article by Michael Klöcker, "Der Politische Katholizismus: Versuch einer Neudefinierung," *Zeitschrift für Politik* 18 (1971): 130; as well as Karl Rahner, "Katholizismus," in Höfer and Rahner, eds., *Lexikon für Theologie und Kirche* 6:89; Oskar von Nell-Breuning, "Katholizismus," in Karl Gabriel and Franz-Syver Kaufmann, eds., *Zur Soziologie des Katholizismus* (Mainz, 1980), 24; Doris Kaufmann, *Katholisches Milieu in Münster 1928–1933* (Düsseldorf, 1984), 11–15; Gerhard Kraiker, "Politischer Katholizismus in der BRD: Eine ideologiekritische Analyse," Ph.D. diss., University of Stuttgart, 1972, 10–11; Kark Gabriel, "Die neuzeitliche Gesellschaftsentwicklung und der Katholizismus als Sozialform der Christentumsgeschichte," in Gabriel and Kaufmann, *Zur Soziologie des Katholizismus*, 201–25; Ute Schmidt, *Zentrum oder CDU: Politischer Katholizismus zwischen Tradition und Anpassung* (Opladen, 1987), 16–22; as well as more recently Wilhelm Damberg, *Abschied vom Milieu? Katholizismus im Bistum Münster und in den Niederlanden 1945–1980* (Paderborn, 1997), 17–36. On the definition of theological terms, see the relevant dictionaries and ecclesiastical manuals.

5 A recent overview of the research on this theme is offered by Wilhelm Damberg, *Abschied vom Milieu?* 17–36.

between accommodation and resistance. Furthermore, there were churches for whom the time was one of martyrdom. This is particularly true in Poland. Despite these differences, it is possible to discern a strong and unified line of argument on the subject of violence in all countries. For this reason, it is appropriate to concentrate on the Church leaders and their ideas and patterns of interpretation, ideas that dominated the Church's actions. Nevertheless, the thesis presented here needs to be tested by further research. This is particularly true with regard to the influence of the official line at the grassroots of the Church and to those countries where the church stood on the side of the losers and the persecuted.

GERMANY

How did the Catholic Church respond after 1945 to the period of fascism and the Second World War? The Germanophile Pope Pius XII viewed the experiences of the Nazi dictatorship thus: Nazism was an "ordeal by fire" from which, despite some losses, the Church had emerged "strengthened and purified."[6] Just as the Church had already fought against other secular states, so, too, had it defended itself against National Socialism. The only important dividing line was that between the Church and its opponents, the National Socialist dictatorship was equated with other state and social systems – for example with parliamentary democracies, or socialist or liberal blueprints for society. This was of course equally applicable to Stalinism, about which the Church worried little, however. The Soviet Union was seen as absolutely evil and thus almost required no further comment.[7]

This attitude, so common to Catholicism as a whole, is memorably captured by the reformist Catholic Romano Guardini, who was himself little liked by the Vatican: "Without a religious element life is like an engine

---

6 Pope Pius XII to the German bishops, Jan. 18, 1947, in Bruno Wuestenberg and Joseph Zabkar, eds., *Der Papst an die Deutschen: Pius XII. als Apostolischer Nuntius und als Papst in seinen deutschsprachigen Reden und Sendschreiben von 1917–1956* (Frankfurt am Main, 1956), 127.

7 This can be read from, among other things, the Papal Encyclical 'Quadragesimo Anno' of 1931, which indeed did deal comprehensively with socialism but despatched communism in but a single paragraph. The stereotypical fomulations about socialism and communism can be found easily with the indexes of the relevant source collections such as Wuestenberg and Zabkar, eds., *Der Papst an die Deutschen*; Wolfgang Löhr, ed., *Dokumente deutscher Bischöfe 1945–1949*, vol. 1: *Hirtenbriefe und Ansprachen zu Gesellschaft und Politik 1945–1949* (Würzburg, 1985); Bernhard Stasiewski and Ludwig Volk, eds., *Akten deutscher Bischöfe über die Lage der Kirche 1933–1945*, 6 vols. (Mainz, 1968–85); Ludwig Volk, ed., *Akten Kardinal Michael von Faulhabers 1917–1945*, 2 vols. (Mainz, 1978). A concise overview of the research and literature on the numerous historical and theological studies of Catholic anticommunism recently has been presented by Andreas Lienkamp, *Ein vergessener Brückenschlag: Theodor Steinbüchels Sozialismusrezeption im kirchlichen, theolgischen und politischen Kontext* (Paderborn, 1999), sec. B.

which has run out of oil.... Existence becomes disorganized – and then rash actions that have been taking place in increasing measure for thirty years suddenly reach their peak, and violence is the result."[8] However, along with the entire official Church, Guardini sought the opposite, namely, an authority that had precedence over all spheres and aspects of society. He expressly demanded that science not be only scientific, economics not only economic, and politics not only political.[9] It was not functional differentiation and the autonomous laws of social subsystems that were needed, but an old form of integralism – that of a society embraced and steered by *one* power, *one* idea, *one* goal. This one power was of course the Church. The goal was the "Christian West," the *Abendland*, because all the mistakes of the time – the liberalization of sexuality in the same way as the mass murder in the concentration camps, the war as well as the loss of importance of confession – were due to the renunciation of God and to secularization.

The Church continued to claim that it alone could be effective in shaping society by virtue of its privileged knowledge of God and His revelation. Given the establishment of parliamentary systems in almost all of Europe, this claim was utopian. Influential Catholic social theorists nevertheless continued to pursue this idea even into the 1960s. Consequently, a social theory that reduced all questions to a single one resulted in a considerable lack of interest in *real* problems. The antisecularist interpretation reduced the capability of most churchmen to understand society, so that they considered only those aspects of reality that they could integrate into their interpretation of society. This is demonstrated above all in the fact that the innumerable church positions with regard to all areas of societal life – whether traffic, nutrition, abortion, the fixing of borders, the book trade, expulsion and flight, reparations, holidays, former forced laborers, prisoners of war, political parties, the Nuremberg Trials, economic policy, and many others – almost always culminated in religious or ideological stereotyping formulae, which demanded a Christian society, a return of the Christian West, in the final analysis a position of power for the Catholic Church leadership at the center of society. The specific consequences of this perceptual difficulty, combined with massive social-political interests, may be illustrated in a West German context, namely, the attempts to deal with National Socialist violence through denazification and other political stratagems for dealing with the past.

8 Romano Guardini, *Ende der Neuzeit: Ein Versuch zur Orientierung* (Würzburg, 1950), 106.
9 Ibid., 100.

Unlike the Protestant Church, the Catholic Church officially considered denazification to be legitimate. Among other things, this was based on the fact that unlike the Protestants, almost no Catholic clerics had joined the National Socialist Party (NSDAP). Nonetheless, the bishops soon engaged in vehement criticism of denazification. They wanted as few Catholics as possible to lose their positions in the economy, administration, and judiciary. Moreover, criticism of the Allies increased the popularity of the Church in the eyes of the public. Both the protection of Catholics from dismissal and the search for approval among the population allowed the Church to close ranks and become more politically effective.[10] At the same time, the Church helped countless Nazi criminals to escape or hide their past. This was not a matter of a few individual cases but of a systematic "care of the culprits": The Church intervened at the political level, formed networks, paid lawyers, and so on.[11]

These activities were all aimed at obtaining decisive influence in the new (and old) personal and political networks. The Church thereby not only gained political influence but also used its resources within the ecclesiastical infrastructure to help Nazis escape to Latin America via the Vatican, and even provided the greatest possible forgiveness in the form of the confessional.[12] The certainty of the Church that it possessed the ultimate truth with regard to National Socialism and the question of guilt, as well as the tradition of the official Church pronouncement of God's forgiveness, allowed the leaders of the Church this specific religious contribution to the politics of dealing with the past. Because the cause of fascism was seen in the act of turning away from God, the return to Christ and his Church was regarded as the real reversal – and absolute *re-education* – and re-admission into the Church was judged as the publicly visible and, in religious terms, relevant rejection of the "forces of Satan." The Church thereby declared itself the medium and the subject of forgiveness, without mentioning or mourning the majority of the victims of National Socialism (most of whom were not

---

10 Damian van Melis, "Der katholische Episkopat und die Entnazifizierung," in Köhler and van Melis, eds., *Siegerin in Trümmern*, 43–72.

11 Karen Riechert has recently written an account of these ecclesiastical networks and machinations ("Der Umgang der katholischen Kirche mit historischer und juristischer Schuld anlässlich der Nürnberger Hauptkriegsverbrecherprozesse" in Köhler and van Melis, eds., *Siegerin in Trümmern*, 18–42), whose significance also has been stressed by Norbert Frei, *Vergangenheitspolitik: Die Anfänge der Bundesrepublik und die NS-Vergangenheit* (München 1996), and Ulrich Herbert, *Best: Biographische Studien über Radikalismus, Weltanschauung und Vernunft 1903–1989* (Bonn, 1996).

12 Vera Bücker, "Die katholische Publizistik zwischen Vergangenheitsbewältigung und Neubeginn," *Zeitschrift für Geschichtswissenschaft* 46 (1998): 891ff; Damian van Melis, " 'Ganz Deutschland war ein einziges grosses Konzentrationslager': Die katholische Kirche und die Frage der deutschen Kollektivschuld," in Gary Schaal and Andreas Wöll, eds., *Vergangenheitsbewältigung: Modelle der politischen und sozialen Integration in der Bundesrepublik Deutschland* (Baden-Baden, 1997), 129–46.

of the Catholic faith) and without asking the survivors their opinion. The political and legal tracking down of Nazi criminals was thereby reduced to something unimportant or "extrinsic."

The Church's efforts in this regard were considerable. In fact, they were so great that in the process the Church forgot the victims, including its own members, such as the many priests executed in Dachau or interned elsewhere. They hardly merited a mention. When the survivors were mentioned and acknowledged, it was only as witnesses for the purposes of the Church in its battle with the Modern Age. When National Socialism and its victims were mentioned, it was only as a means by which to demand an even stronger commitment against secularization and for Christianity. The Nazi past and the brutality of the war were not matters for the Church.[13] They were either forgotten or simply used as a vehicle for the Church's current struggle.

SPAIN

There are many reasons for considering Germany of great significance within the Catholic Church: It produced many influential theologians, it provided the Vatican with great material assistance, and Pius XII was a Germanophile. But there were other nations that were "more Catholic" than Germany – if the grammatical comparative makes any sense with regard to this adjective – because their societies were monoconfessional.

One of the countries that was not directly affected by World War II and the Shoah yet played an important role in European Catholicism nonetheless was Spain.[14] Here particular value was placed on reciprocity: Franco's Spain

13 Despite the occasional clear proximity of some individual representatives of the Catholic Church to the Nazi state and to some Nazi organizations, in almost no cases was there a concern to deny the crimes of members of the Church or to cover up the indirect responsibility of the Church. The massive degree to which the Church distanced itself from the only recently collapsed dictatorship and directed its gaze toward the future is shown by one subject relating to this official Church strategy which, unfortunately, up to now has not been investigated: the Munich suffragan bishop Johannes Neuhäusler, who himself was interned in the Dachau concentration camp and who from 1945 on his own and with political vehemence campaigned for the rights of former Nazis – something which led to considerable annoyance not only among the British and Americans. See Johann Neuhäusler, *Kreuz und Hakenkreuz: Der Kampf des Nationalsozialismus gegen die Katholische Kirche und der kirchliche Widerstand* (Munich, 1946); *Keesings Archiv der Gegenwart*, Mar. 18, 1948 (p. 1424), May 21, 1948 (p. 1504), and Oct. 15, 1948 (p. 1665).

14 There were notable exceptions to the Spanish abstinence with regard to World War II, such as the involvement of German and Italian armed forces during the Civil War and the "Blue Division," with which Franco could send especially enthusiastic Falangists off to the Russian Front. On the conduct of Spain with regard to persecuted Jews, see Bernd Rother, "Franco und die deutsche Judenverfolgung," *Vierteljahrshefte für Zeitgeschichte* 46, no. 2 (1998): 189–220.

cultivated its Catholicism and the Vatican supported Franco's dictatorship, which had long been isolated by the international community. Spain had also experienced shocking violence from the 1930s onward: the Civil War and the persecution of the defeated Republicans. Death, imprisonment, torture, and emigration left their marks on the lives of hundreds of thousands of people and families.

How did the Church react to the experiences of the civil war and to the anticommunist repression mercilessly continued up to the 1970s? Reading the pastoral letters of the Spanish episcopacy of that time, one comes across many remarks from the standard repertory of official Catholic pronouncements – on schools, the family, sexual morality, and so forth. Time and again there were respectful letters to the "Caudillo-por-la-Gracia-de-Dios." Because there were no political parties and few institutions of civil society that could have played an important role in political and societal life, the influence of the Church on the government and its administrative apparatus was relatively large, whereby the spectrum of themes dealt with by the bishops in Spain was broader than in more secularized states. Nevertheless, one searches in vain for statements on the violence and monstrous brutality of the civil war.

There is of course one important exception: The brutality of the Republicans and the suffering of the Church in Republican Spain. Although the violence in Spain could not be compared to that of Nazi Germany, the lines of argumentation were similar: The violence was a consequence of the Modern Age, disrespect for the Church, and the resulting terrible sin of the Modern Age that did not kowtow to the Church. In contrast to the German context, this antisecularist interpretation does have some plausibility when applied to Spain. The conflicts of the civil war were in fact part of the violent tradition of the "two Spains," of the division of the nation into two camps, characterized by – among other things – anticlericalism versus loyalty to the Church.[15] Nonetheless, like their German counterparts the Spanish clergy did not look at the real social conflicts and the accompanying violence, but concerned themselves primarily with ideological quarrels through which they interpretatively categorized the orgies of violence of the 1930s and 1940s.

When Francoism was in crisis after the defeat of Germany, when even the Vatican kept a safe distance from the Franco regime, the Bishop Plá I Daniel felt it necessary to "say very clearly" in a pastoral letter that "the European and World War had nothing to do with the Spanish civil

15 Walther L. Bernecker, *Spaniens Geschichte seit dem Bürgerkrieg* (Munich, 1984), 13–14.

war. . . . All Catholics must recognize the Spanish Civil War as a genuine crusade for God and Spain."[16] In July 1945, after the Second World War and because of the international isolation of his dictatorship, Franco used Catholic activists in a "whitewashing exercise of the regime."[17] They reinforced the Catholic character of the political system and thereby regained the support of the Vatican. With the help of a concordat, the Pope reintegrated Spain into the international community. In the 1950s, Spain's Catholic regime somehow had to manage the balancing act of, on the one hand, winning the support of the defenders of the old Republic, who were among the most important founders of the United Nations and NATO, and, on the other, of legitimizing the civil war and the continued right-wing repression and violence that followed it.

EUROPE

Mainly because of the hierarchical structure of the Church and because of its fixed ideological and theological system, spread throughout Europe and strengthened by Vatican activities in the nineteenth century, the interpretation of most recent events was similar in the Catholic Churches of the different European countries. Reading the account by Wim Damberg on the history of the Catholic Church in the Netherlands,[18] one gets the impression that the clergy and the laity employed by the Church after 1945 had nothing more important to do than to occupy themselves with their own administrative system. The only reference to the war appears to be the question of whether or not they should reverse the changes to the organization of the Church, which they had been forced to make during the occupation.[19] The subject of violence or questions about their own collaboration, resistance, or the fate of the many who were persecuted or murdered are of marginal importance. As far as Italy is concerned, Paola Pomeni and Karl-Egon Lönne have written of the various breaches in Catholicism but

---

16 Guy Hermet, *Los catolicos en la España franquista* (Madrid, 1986), 203. At a gathering of cardinals in Rome in February 1946, Bishop Plá I Daniel repeated the comparison, stereotypical in Catholic propaganda, with the crusades of the Middle Ages. See Stanley G. Payne, *El catalicismo español* (Barcelona, 1984), 233.
17 Hermet, *Los catolicos en la España franquista*, 207.
18 Damberg, *Abschied vom Milieu?* 554.
19 Broad sections of the Church hierarchy did not at all welcome these revisions as they strengthened the influence of the laity, which had been pushed back with the aid of the internationally coordinated organizational framework of the "action catolica" only during the 1930s and 1940s. For more details, see Wim Damberg, " 'Radikale katholische Laien an die Front!' Beobachtungen zur Idee und Wirkungsgeschichte der Katholischen Aktion," in Köhler and van Melis, eds., *Siegerin in Trümmern*, 142–60; Antonio Murcia Santos, *Obreros y obispos en el franquismo: estudio sobre el signifcado eclesiológico de la crisis de la Acción Española* (Madrid, 1995).

not of conflicts about the long-lasting support for Mussolini.[20] There are further examples of the ecclesiastical criticism of secularization from France, the United States, England, and other European and North American countries.[21]

A critical examination of the orgies of the violence of the preceding decades, which would have abandoned the old paths of the Church's interpretation of society and taken account of the new quality of industrially organized mass murder, did not take place. Another example demonstrates how strongly the representatives of the Catholic Church remained wedded to their old concepts, namely, that of Europe and West European Unity. This matter is meaningful because here the Church apparently was not so introspective as with regard to the questions of violence and suffering in contemporary history. The Church became more actively involved, so much so that the Catholics of Western Europe became the most important supporters of West European Unity.[22] Criticism of secularization nonetheless continued to play a role here as well.

From the 1940s until today, the Catholic Church has made many statements in favor of European unity. It supported the unifying policies of Konrad Adenauer, Robert Schuman, and Alcide de Gasperi, among others, and supported the creation of the *secular* Europe of the European Coal and Steel Community, cultural cooperation, and the European Community. Although the main driving force for the pro-European engagement within Catholic internationalism lay, especially in Italy and Germany, in deeply rooted Catholic mistrust of recently established nation-states and in the hope of having a stable majority over the Protestant churches in Western Europe, churchmen played a somewhat involuntary part in the dynamics of secular Western European unity through their coalition with bourgeois modernizers such as Adenauer. While these dynamics could integrate the ecclesiastical rhetoric about the "Christian West" unproblematically, at the same time the social, economical, and political development crushed the ideological frame of the Catholic aims. Here, too, the particular blindness of

---

20 Paolo Pomeni, "Zur Rolle des Katholizismus in der italienischen Nachkriegspolitik," in *Kirchen in der Nachkriegszeit: Vier Zeitgeschichtliche Beiträge von Armin Boysens, Martin Greschat, Rudolf von Thadden und Paolo Pombeni* (Göttingen, 1979), 139–57; Karl-Egon Lönne, *Politischer Katholizismus im 19. und 20. Jahrhundert* (Frankfurt am Main, 1986), 295–306.

21 They may be found, for example, in Martin Greschat, " 'Rechristianisierung' und 'Säkularisierung': Anmerkungen zu einem europäischen konfessionellen Interpretationsmodell," in Jochen-Christoph Kaiser and Anselm Doering-Manteuffel, eds., *Christentum und politische Verantwortung: Kirchen im Nachkriegsdeutschland* (Stuttgart, 1990), 1–24.

22 The suggestion by Lönne (*Politischer Katholizismus*, 291, 283) that Catholics were the strongest proponents of Western European unification can be illustrated with the examples of the three politicians: Konrad Adenauer in Bonn, Robert Schuman in Paris, and Alcide de Gasperi in Rome.

the functionaries in the clergy is very evident. One can summarize the problem thus: Although the Catholic Church propagated the idea of a united Europe, it only understood this in terms of a Christian West.

What do Europe and the Christian West have to do with violence? As far as the recent history of the Second World War is concerned, the Church completely blocked out the fact that European unity had brought together the bitter enemies of the war. It promoted the cause of unity because it liked the idea of a Christian West, but at the same time it either forgot or repressed Europe's all too recent history. There are several examples to the contrary, such as that of the Catholic peace movement "Pax Christi," but they had little influence on the official church until the end of the era of Pius XII. An example from the Europe-friendly, Francophile, and academic Dominican newspaper *Die Neue Ordnung* (The New Order) demonstrates the Catholic mainstream. In 1953, the editor criticized the Oradour trial against the soldiers of the Wehrmacht as an "assault on the Christian West," which was likely to get in the way of European unity. "And so the process of calling people to account continues; and those Christians who are trying to create a new order, and are striving with all their might to build a dam against the flood of passions, hate, and desire for revenge, who want to be the guardians of the Western *Humana Civilitas* and of its Christian values, they have to come to terms with the fact that whoever wants to destroy their work need only ask: 'And what about the Oradour trial?' This puts them in a deeply embarrassing position."[23]

CONCLUSION

How did the Church react to the experiences of violence during the Second World War? There are many indications that after 1945 it saw itself as a victor in the ruins of violence. The old, Church-oriented interpretation of history and society had apparently triumphed: The Modern Age and all those who did not subordinate themselves to the Church's directives were to blame. The Catholic spokesmen were caught in the web of their criticism of secularization, making no serious effort to analyze the real social and political issues of the time. Pope Pius XII preached that the main lesson of the war was that all politicians should return to the Church: "What hard lesson and warning do we get from the recent years? May this be understood and be healing to other peoples! . . . 'Learn your lesson, you rulers of the earth' (Psalms 2, 10). This must surely be the greatest desire of everybody who

23 *Neue Ordnung* 7 (1953): 111–12.

sincerely loves mankind."[24] These views not only referred to the past but also marked the political engagement of the Church and many Catholics during the 1950s and 1960s.

A glaring light on the distance between these theological interpretations of society that formed in the nineteenth century and the problems of the present raise the discussions about military-political affairs, which also were conducted by Catholics during the 1950s and 1960s. This is demonstrated by the position taken by the moral theologian Johannes B. Hirschmann on the moral justification of "atomic defense." With reference to Francis of Assisi, one of the main representatives of the nature-loving and peace-loving traditions within Christianity, the loyal Jesuit demanded the "courage, in view of the destruction of millions of lives, to affirm the sacrifice of atomic armament in the present-day situation." This stood closer to "the spirit of the theology of the cross than a notion that prematurely sacrifices principles of natural law to an unthought-through theological premise, as Protestant clergy and theologians do today on a broad front. What they sacrifice is a good piece of common Christian substance."[25] The coalition of the Church with the West, which was motivated not least by anticommunism, secured it a privileged place in politics and society for a short period after 1945. The general orientation of the Church dignitaries toward the past, which became visible in their understanding of state power, is only one example of their inability to comprehend the recent past and present on the basis of the religiously obtained categories they employed to analyze society. Although the Church was able to establish itself in the heart of society both materially and politically, its own ideas clearly failed. Once Church pronouncements were taken increasingly less seriously and were criticized increasingly heavily both inside and outside the Church, even the hierarchy dispensed with its fragments of nineteenth-century ideology that had passed into stereotypes. By the late 1960s, it stood among the ruins of its own ideas about society. It was Pope John XXIII (1958–63) and the Second Vatican Council (1962–5) who recognized the narrowness of the Church's leadership. Only then was there a break with tradition that allowed an explicit consideration of the violence of the 1930s and 1940s.

---

24 Pius XII to the College of Cardinals, June 2, 1945; in Wuestenberg and Zabkar, eds., *Der Papst an die Deutschen.*

25 Johannes B. Hirschmann, "Kann atomare Verteidigung sittlich gerechtfertigt sein?" *Stimmen der Zeit* 162 (1957–58): 293. The political and intellectual proximity of this position to the Church's approach to World War II is illustrated by the comment from the *Katholischen Sonntagsblatt der Diözese Rottenburg-Stuttgart,* no. 96 (1948): 147, in which the "dropping of the atomic bomb on Hiroshima" was described as a "source of great grace . . . because the assistance given by some [Catholic] priests moved many pagan Japanese to be baptized."

11

The Nationalization of Victimhood

Selective Violence and National Grief in Western Europe, 1940–1960

PIETER LAGROU

The concept of this book seems to start from an implicit but inescapable acknowledgment. Compared to the over-specialization, the fragmentation, the technicality, and finally the undeniable overproduction of the historiography on World War II, the history writing on World War I is remarkably advanced in producing an integrated, intellectually ambitious analysis of the experience of the war and its impact on post-1918 Europe. This historiography attained a comparative European scale, and it reached into the realms of social and cultural history.[1] Mechanized warfare during four long years had brought violence on an unprecedented scale. Mass-mobilization, massive casualties, and an entire generation traumatized by mutilation, shell-shock, and the experience of daily horror had profoundly impregnated European societies with the experience of this war, including a home front of mourning widows and orphans, of depleted villages, factories, and neighborhoods. The experience, moreover, had been fundamentally identical for all belligerents, and it had thereby unified the European continent through a common fratricidal cataclysm. The widow and the soldier, the German and the British, had all, somehow, lived the same war. Even if these European societies chose in the two decades following the war very different paths – aggressive fascism or *pacifisme municheois* – victors and vanquished initially had to cope with a very similar legacy of mass death, mutilation, and war trauma. The social and cultural impact of the violence of this war on what followed it have been captured by George Mosse, Jay Winter, Paul Fussel,

---

1 See, e.g., some recent comparative publications: Annette Becker and Stéphane Audouin-Rouzeau, *Guerres et cultures: vers une histoire comparée de la première guerre mondiale* (Paris, 1994); Jean-Jacques Becker and Stéphane Audouin-Rouseau, eds., *Les sociétés Européennes et la guerre de 1914–1918* (Nanterre, 1990); Jay Winter, *Sites of Memory, Sites of Mourning: The Great War in European Cultural History* (Cambridge, 1995); Jay Winter and Jean-Louis Robert, eds., *Capital Cities at War: London, Paris, Berlin, 1914–1919* (Cambridge, 1997); Aviel Roshwald and Richard Stites, *European Culture in the Great War: The Arts, Entertainment, and Propaganda, 1914–1918* (Cambridge, 1999).

Antoine Prost, Annette Becker, and Stéphane Audouin-Rouzeau in a way
that can only be admired by historians of World War II and its aftermath as
a model to follow. In that regard and despite – partly because of – the sheer
volume of literature, the historiography on World War II and its impact on
twentieth-century European history is still in its infancy.

No single period in European history has been studied in such absolute chronological isolation as World War II. There were technical reasons to do so, especially in the occupied countries of Europe. Wartime
archives are classified separately, and access to them was subject to specific
rules and regulations for a long time. Historians of the period had special
skills – familiarity with the German language and German archives, with
the intricate functioning of the occupation apparatus – and they more often
than not belonged to specialized institutions and official commissions created to study this exceptional subject.[2] There also were moral and political
reasons to do so. To suppose there could be any link at all between Hitler's
and Adenauer's Germany, between Vichy France and the Fourth Republic,
or between *Grossraum Europa* and the European Economic Community
(EEC) was an unacceptable form of political slander or communist propaganda, not a hypothesis of historical examination. Until the early 1980s,
European historians of World War II enjoyed a great social legitimacy as
commemorators, educators, legal advisers, and consciences of the nation,
and they accordingly enjoyed only a modest scholarly legitimacy in the
community of historians.

Whence this difference in treatment? More than a half-century and several
generations of historians have passed since the end of the war and the old,
convenient arguments of a lack of distance or of political taboo no longer
hold. Nor is it simply a matter of magnitude or of new extremes reached on
the scale of human horror. The central problem, in my opinion, is that it is
very problematic to transpose an approach inspired by the First World War
and its homogeneous experience of the violence of war to World War II
and its consequences. After 1918, it was clear to everyone what "violence"
had concretely meant during the war: shell-shock, mutilation, artillery, and
infantry attacks on enemy trenches. Moreover, this violence is not only
comprehensively qualifiable but also quantifiable in impressive detail, thus
concretely establishing that it was part of the individual experience of a vast
majority of members of wartime societies.

---

2 See Pieter Lagrou, "Historiographie de guerre et historiographie du temps présent: cadres institu-
  tionnels en Europe occidentale, 1945–2000," *Bulletin du Comité international d'histoire de la deuxième
  guerre mondiale* 30–1 (1999–2000): 191–215.

This was most directly so for the mobilized servicemen and indirectly for each and every family, neighborhood, and village that had sons, fathers, brothers, and neighbors to weep for, fallen on the battlefield or dead as a consequence of war injuries. The Great War produced eight million casualties, half of them British, French, or German, of a total of sixty-five million mobilized soldiers. In France alone, almost eight million men had been mobilized, which represents 80 percent of all men of military age; almost one and a half million, one out of every six mobilized soldiers died; more than one million returned from the war as invalids; six hundred thousand women were widowed and seven hundred sixty thousand children orphaned.[3] Detailed demographic studies have since demonstrated that these massive consequences of war did indeed affect the whole of the population in a more or less proportional distribution.[4] The expression of "a lost generation" and a *génération du feu* statistically has, after 1918, a tragically concrete reality, as have, as a consequence, the expressions of a society plunged in collective mourning and grief.

After 1945, the concept of "violence of war" becomes so plural as to lose its conceptual clarity. The Australian soldier ripped apart by German bullets on Omaha Beach, the Jewish child gassed in Auschwitz, or the housewife buried under the debris of the Dresden bombing all evidently suffered violent deaths, but, unlike the violent deaths of the Great War, it is very much questionable whether this fact alone suffices to state that they lived or died through a comparable experience. The multiple faces of violence during World War II are also translated in a very unequal distribution of the burden of this violence over different European countries and within each country for different groups of the population. I will illustrate the problematic implications of this plurality through the concrete example of the legacy of the war in the occupied countries of Western Europe.

A summary presentation of the violence of war during the years 1939–45 on the model of the general introductions of the Great War as given above, that is, through its most obvious consequence, namely, casualty figures, gives a contrasting picture. In a history of mass death, World War II in the European theatre was primarily a conflict between Nazi Germany and the Soviet Union. The military confrontation on the eastern front was exceptionally murderous, especially for the Soviet Union, whose military losses between 1941 and 1945 equal those of all belligerents during the Great War

3 See Antoine Prost, *Les Anciens Combattants et la Société Française 1914–1939*, vol. 2 *Sociologie* (Paris, 1977), 1–27.
4 See Adrian Gregory, "Lost Generations: The Impact of Military Casualties on Paris, London, and Berlin," in Winter and Robert, eds., *Capital Cities at War*, 57–103.

combined. Nazi Germany lost less than half as many soldiers on the eastern front as did its enemy, a difference that can be explained mainly by the systematic murder of the massive numbers of Soviet prisoners of war (POWs) by execution or starvation. Military losses on the eastern front are dwarfed, however, by the numbers of civilian casualties. In the Soviet Union – primarily in Belorussia and Ukraine – and in Poland, twelve million civilians died as victims of genocide, massacre, population displacement, and famine. The civilian population of Germany was, in comparison, exceptionally spared from the violence of war. Three hundred thousand German civilians were killed by their own regime, and most civilian casualties occurred among German communities living outside the German borders of 1938, who were expelled after 1945. Allied bombing of German cities caused fewer deaths than the German assaults on the cities of Leningrad or Warsaw. The mass death of civilians on the eastern front was not an accident of war but one of the central aims of Nazi warfare, namely, to vacate vast territories by decimating the local Slav populations and thus make room – *Lebensraum* – for German colonization. As a result, the Soviet Union and Poland suffered more casualties than all other countries combined. Violence, terror, and death were direct experiences for every single individual in these societies. Other parts of Eastern Europe and the Balkans in particular also suffered heavy death rates and were left in total social and demographic turmoil by the ethnic character of the violence and by population displacements.

This picture is a terrifying illustration of the effectiveness of Nazi warfare, which had attained its two major war aims: the destruction of Eastern Europe and the assumption of the role of *Herrenvolk* for the German population. Indeed, the experience of privilege and domination, and the habituation to colonial relationships through occupation and the importation of eight million migrant workers, characterizes the German war experience no less than the experience of violence – administered by German soldiers and marginally undergone by German civilian victims of Allied bombings.[5] It is the obvious explanation of the unfaltering support of the German population for the Nazi war effort, the absence of any form of popular insurrection or even disobedience until the very end of the war, that contrasts so strikingly with the situation on the German home front in 1918.

In a history of World War II casualties, the war on the western front is a minor affair. Of the 3,250,000 German military casualties, only 128,000

---

5 See esp. Ulrich Herbert, *Fremdarbeiter: Politik und Praxis des "Ausländer-Einsatzes" in der Kriegwirtschaft des Dritten Reiches* (Berlin, 1985), and Ulrich Herbert, *Geschichte der Ausländer-Beschäftigung in Deutschland, 1880 bis 1980: Saisonarbeiter, Zwangsarbeiter, Gastarbeiter* (Berlin, 1986).

died on the western front between September 1939 and December 31, 1944.[6] This proportionally small number of losses gives an indication of the intensity of the military battles on a continental scale. Because the military confrontation was limited to a few weeks during the invasion in May–June 1940 and a few months during the summer and fall of 1944, the impact of the war was primarily the impact of occupation policies. These resulted from very different war aims in the west than in the east. Rather than decimation and massive transfers of population, which constitute a tremendous upheaval, war aims in the west were economic exploitation and pacification, that is, occupation at the smallest military cost in order to liberate troops for the crucial confrontation on the eastern front. Western Europe was somehow the reverse side of racist war, because Nazis' intentions in the west were entirely different from their war of attrition in the east. The numbers and the nature of violent deaths during World War II in the occupied countries of Western Europe were also entirely incomparable to the ones they suffered during World War I.

Official French figures estimate war-related casualties at 600,000, subdivided into three categories: 170,000 military casualties, 150,000 civilians on national territory, and 280,000 outside national boundaries who were among the populations displaced by the enemy.[7] These figures not only seem inflated by about one-third compared to the actual losses; they also fail to represent the actual composition of French losses and the disparities among different groups of the population. The French losses are concentrated in two murderous phases of the war, each lasting only a few weeks. First of all, in France, the six weeks between the German invasion in May 1940 and the surrender by Marshal Philippe Pétain in June were the single

6 John Ellis, *The World War II Databook: The Essential Facts and Figures for All the Combatants* (London, 1993), 256. For a detailed discussion of German military losses, see Rüdiger Overmans, *Deutsche militärische Verluste im Zweiten Weltkrieg* (Munich, 2000), 228, and Overmans, "Die Toten des Zweiten Weltkriegs in Deutschland. Bilanz der Forschung unter besonderer Berücksichtigung der Wehrmacht- und Vertreibungsverluste," in Wolfgang Michalka, ed., *Der Zweite Weltkrieg: Analysen, Grundzüge, Forschungsbilanz* (Munich, 1989), 858–73. Overmans calculates that 3,550,000 Germans living in the area corresponding to the present borders of the German Federal Republic died while in military service. Total losses of German military formations include 910,000 dead from the former eastern regions, 210,000 from the annexed regions and 260,000 from Austria (total for the Reich: 3,550,000 + 1,380,000 = 4,900,000), plus almost 400,000 dead among conscripts and volunteers from occupied regions, primarily the Soviet Union.

7 Commission Consultative des Dommages et des Réparations, *Monographie D.P.2 Dommages aux Personnes* (Paris, 1948), 6. This figure is cited, among others, in Christian Bachelier, "Bilan et coût de la Guerre Mondiale," in Jean-Pierre Azéma et François Bédarida, *1938–1948: Les années de tourmente: Dictionnaire Critique* (Paris, 1995), 164; John Keegan, *The Second World War* (London, 1989); Ellis, *World War II Databook*, 253. On the official statistics, see esp. Serge Barcellini, "La gestion du deuil par l'Etat français au lendemain de la Seconde Guerre Mondiale" in Francine-Dominique Liechtenhan, ed., *Europe 1946: Entre le deuil et l'espoir* (Brussels, 1996), 121–40.

most violent episodes of the war, with 100,000 French casualties. The next peak in mortality occurred during the summer of 1942, with the deportation from France and, with only few exceptions, the subsequent murder of about 50,000 Jews, two-thirds of the total of 75,000 victims of the genocide for the whole period of the war in France.

When broken down properly, the distribution of war losses in France presents a much more fragmented picture than official figures suggest. For the military casualties, apart from the largest aforementioned group, figures are amalgamated from different campaigns and military formations. The war on the western front, from the landing in Normandy on June 6, 1944, until the German surrender on May 8, 1945, claimed 15,200 French military casualties.[8] The limited size of "Free French Forces" engaged on the Allied side is translated in limited total numbers of losses: 8,000 in the African campaign and 8,500 in Italy.[9] In the latter campaigns, about 60 percent of French troops were colonial troops, which means that if these losses are, quite legitimately, included in the figures of French losses, any calculation of death rates should nevertheless take the total population of metropolitan France plus its colonies as a basis for its calculations. More important, French soldiers who engaged the Wehrmacht on the eastern front who were levied in the annexed departments of Alsace and Lorraine are not included in the figures of military losses but in the third category of "displaced populations." The 40,000 soldiers listed as dead or missing on the eastern front from a total of 130,000 French citizens in German uniform indeed outnumber French losses on the Allied side, with the exception of the battle of May–June 1940.[10]

Civilian losses on French territory are probably closer to 100,000 than the official 150,000: 60,000 victims of air raids (the same number as in Great Britain), fewer than 10,000 victims of execution, and 26,000 civilian victims of land-based military operations.[11] Among the figures for displaced populations, the number for French victims of the genocide is closest to revised statistics: 100,000 instead of 75,000. The official figure of dead among the other victims of deportation to German concentration camps is 60,000, whereas the most reliable figures available of the total number, both those

8 *Le Monde*, June 8, 1945, 2a, courtesy of Jean Astruc.

9 *Guerre 1939–1945: Les Grandes Unités Françaises: Historiques Succints. Campagnes de Tunésie et d'Italie. Opérations de Corse et de l'Ile d'Elbe (1942–1944)* (Paris, 1970), 416 and 990–1, resp.

10 Commission Consultative des Dommages et des Réparations, *Dommages subis par la France et l'Union française du fait de la guerre et de l'occupation ennemie (1939–1945): Part Imputable à l'Allemagne* (Paris, 1950), 86.

11 See revised figures in *Journal Officiel*, May 26, 1948, 2.938, quoted in Henri Amouroux, *La grande histoire des Français après l'occupation IX Les réglements de comptes* (Paris, 1991), 73–6.

killed and those who survived, stands at 63,000.[12] Sixty percent survived their deportation, leaving 26,000 dead. The two largest groups of displaced persons from France suffered relatively low death rates: 21,000 deaths from a total of 950,000 POWs held captive till the end of the war (for Soviet POWs the numbers stand at 3.3 million deaths from a total of 5.7 million captives), and a most probably lower figure still for the 840,000 civilian workers.[13] Taken together, my calculations total approximately 140,000 dead among displaced populations, half of the official figure of 280,000.

Compared to the precise recording of military casualties during World War I, figures on war-related losses during World War II in France are a complicated amalgamation of very different categories of victims. If, due to these difficulties, it is impossible with the current state of historical knowledge to advance a precise total, one conclusion is obvious: Unlike World War I, during World War II death struck the French population in very uneven measures. This applies particularly to the Jewish population but also to other victims of persecution, such as communists. More surprising, this conclusion is even valid for military casualties: Some communities, in Alsace and Lorraine, in Senegal and Morocco, had many more fallen soldiers to mourn than did the average French village or neighborhood.

The French case is no exception among the occupied countries of Western Europe. The picture is rather more extreme in other countries because of an even weaker proportion of military casualties. This can be explained by the violence of the battle of France in May–June 1940 and the relative importance – that is, compared to other occupied countries of Western Europe – of France's subsequent military efforts. The Western European losses during the German invasion of 1940 represent 2.3 percent of the four million mobilized soldiers in France; 7,500, or 1.15 percent of 650,000 mobilized soldiers in Belgium; 2,900 or 0.72 percent of 400,000 mobilized soldiers in the Netherlands; and 2,000 casualties of the 25,000 soldiers of the Norwegian army.[14] The Danish case – in the absence of military resistance – was more akin to *Anschluss* than invasion. The Dutch example gives the most contrasting picture.[15] War-related mortality was

---

12 See *Statistique de la déportation*, Mar. 12, 1975. The report, resulting from a detailed inquiry by the local correspondents of the official *Comité d'histoire de la deuxième Guerre Mondiale*, was never published, due to protests from the organizations of camp survivors that such a publication would belittle their martyrdom and Nazi crimes. See file ARC 075.6, Institut d'Histoire du Temps Présent, Paris.

13 See Yves Durand, *La captivité: Histoire des prisonniers de guerre français 1939–1945* (Paris, 1980), 21.

14 See Ellis, *World War II Databook*, 253.

15 Figures established by the Dutch Institute for War Documentation, dd. 08/1986. Courtesy of Dick van Galen Last.

very low in the Netherlands, except for one group: the Jewish population. One hundred and two thousand Jews from the Netherlands were murdered between the summer of 1942 and the end of the war. They represent 55 percent of all war-related deaths in the Netherlands. Twenty-three thousand Dutch died in the war against Japan, civilians included, and in the merchant and military navy. In Europe, the war caused more than 60,000 Dutch deaths – other than genocide – among them 23,000 civilian victims of air raids and land-based military operations, 15,000 victims of the famine of the winter of 1944–5, 8,000 workers sent to Germany, 6,750 victims of German repression, 5,000 volunteers for the Wehrmacht, and 350 POWs. Even the Italian losses – the official figure is 440,000 – are comparable to French losses, in spite of the involvement of Italian troops on the eastern front (85,000 deaths) and in the Balkans (39,000 deaths).[16] In a different context: British losses stand at 240,000 soldiers and 60,000 victims of air raids, plus 100,000 soldiers levied in the Commonwealth.[17] If the extraordinary victims of genocide are included, French and British losses are numerically comparable. American losses in this war – all military – are comparable in total numbers only (292,000).[18]

The obvious conclusion of these summary statistics is that the occupied countries of Western Europe formed an exception in a continent bled white by millions of casualties. In these societies, violent death was not part of the individual experience of the overwhelming majority of the population. Specific groups were decimated – the Jewish population of the Netherlands reached the brink of total extinction – but their experience was exceptional, outside the average realm of collective war experiences. For the majority of the population, seen from a continental perspective, it is no exaggeration to state that these countries were fortunate. Another conclusion is that there is no "postwar generation" similar to the ones in Poland, the Soviet Union, Yugoslavia, or even Germany, that is, a generation marked by a collective experience of war. After that dramatic moment of the unification of society by war in the trenches, World War II brought a dispersion of society along the lines of incommensurably different war experiences. In France, the vita of François Mitterand is often referred to as prototypical for his generation, which came of age during the occupation: He embodies an improbable combination of a priori incompatible experiences because he was a POW in Germany, a government official in Vichy, a resister in France,

---

16 See Ellis, *World War II Databook*, 253.
17 Keegan, *Second World War*, and Central Statistical Office, *Statistical Digest of the War* (London, 1951), 13.
18 See Ellis, *World War II Databook*, 256.

and a politician in London and Algiers.[19] The World War II generation in France is clearly an intermediate one – a generation of missing solidarities, of divergent experiences, and of alienation and suspicion. As such, it falls between two other generations unified by war: the glorious generation of the *poilus* of the Great War and the forgotten generation of the conscripts of the Algerian War.[20] This situation is exemplified by the French Ministry for War Veterans, where, even today, the agenda is set, on the one hand, by that first paradigmatic generation of war veterans who created the institution, the legislation, the rituals, the organizations, and the discourses, a generation that has all but disappeared, and, on the other hand, by that second generation that is reaching retirement age and looking back to that dirty colonial war. The World War II generation is an unhappy and utterly fragmented generation in this institution, continually trying to conform to models that are impossible to emulate due to the simple fact that the French army of 1940 was defeated in six weeks' time.

The observation that violence, or at least war-related mass death, was not the collective experience of the societies on the western front of the European continent in the years between 1939 and 1945, does not mean that World War II was an insignificant intermezzo in their twentieth-century history. In order to fully acknowledge the specificity of the war experience in these countries – which is hardly ever done – two admissions must be made. First, the impact of war has to be traced to other spheres of history than that of warfare, that is, of combat, military confrontation, casualties, and so forth. The active involvement of these countries in warfare during World War II – and this is more painful an admission than it seems – was limited. War – that is, foreign occupation – affected society in very different and highly subversive ways.[21] It implied a generalized crisis of the established order and a delegitimization of national and local authorities. It dramatically increased social and geographical mobility through massive population displacements, deeply disrupting the traditional settings of social life. The accompanying loss of social control created a generalized atmosphere of insecurity, mounting to acute panic in the period of the liberation. Its political translations, with the phantom of communist-inspired revolution, were the most transitory expression of this. The moral panic and the religious crisis were, in the long run, of much greater significance for the subject that concerns us here.

---

19 See, e.g., Pierre Péan, *Une jeunesse française: François Mitterand, 1934–1947* (Paris, 1994).
20 See, e.g., Antoine Prost, "The Algerian War in French Collective Memory," in Jay Winter and Emmanuel Sivan, eds., *War and Remembrance in the Twentieth Century* (Cambridge, 1999), 161–76.
21 See Pieter Lagrou, *The Legacy of Nazi Occupation: Patriotic Memory and National Recovery in Western Europe, 1945–1965* (Cambridge, 1999).

A second observation is of crucial importance to understand the difference between the impact of the war years and their representation. In Western Europe, a violence that was not, in fact, "collective," that is, striking the population in an equally diffused measure, was to a great extent "collectivized" in memory.[22] Mass death and the metaphor of the front was the dominant way of remembering, even to some degree in a country such as the Netherlands, which had not participated in the First World War. Contrary to 1918, French and Belgian society, for example, were not a community in mourning in 1945: Communities had many members to mourn for, but others had been little affected. The challenge for postwar society was not the scale of the violence it underwent but its highly selective nature. The central question was how to reconstitute a community, how to invent a common experience to substitute for this disrupted past. The answer of commemorators to this very selective violence would be a highly selective commemoration, whereby certain experiences, certain groups, and certain symbols come to be seen as common to all, as characteristic of a "national" experience. This metaphoric memory – the *pars pro toto* – propagated common symbols of what had been an anything but common suffering.

The basic concept of this chapter is a schematic opposition between "the 1940s" and "the 1950s," and the analysis of the articulation of the commemoration of the war *grosso modo* confirms this opposition. At the end of the war, Western European societies presented an image of *éclatement*, of dispersion, rivalry, and alienation between different groups with different experiences. The most visible, vociferous opposition was the one between collaboration and resistance. A consensual, national commemoration of resistance was almost immediately put into place. Rituals stemming from a military context – banners, parades, monuments to the unknown soldier – and celebrating victory through combat were hardly convincing in the post-1945 context, and in a matter of months, resistance formations lost much of their capacity to function as national *milieu de mémoire*, as standard-bearers of a national memory by proxy.

In the course of the second half of the 1940s and continuing into the 1950s, a different memory was in the ascendancy that better mirrors the multiplicity of the war experience: "the memory of the camps." The profiles of the displaced populations returning in 1945 presented a disturbing plurality to postwar societies. Between 3.5 and over 5 percent of the population of Western European countries had been displaced to Germany during the war (not counting internal displacements): POWs, workers, Jews, political prisoners, collaborationist refugees. Their return brought home a

22 Ibid.

cacophony of experiences: genocide and political persecution, political and military collaboration, war-related economic migration. They also constituted a natural *milieu de mémoire*, highly visible as a group through their belated and collective return, requiring the intervention of the state and of private charities to overcome the problems of re-integration and recovery. As a social phenomenon, population displacement was the only directly visible consequence of war that could match death and mutilation during World War I by proportion.

The immediate reactions to this peculiar trauma of war-related population displacement were varied. National authorities screened repatriates to weed out suspicious elements. More important, they endeavored to re-educate the returning POWs and turn them into new citizens of new, combative nations and to redress the perverse influences of five years of collaborationist and German propaganda. Social organizations – employment agencies, trade unions, institutions of public health – and religious organizations were very concerned about the moral and physical condition of returning workers. Displacement to Germany might have eroded their work ethic, weakened their faith, loosened their mores, and contaminated their bodies with typhus, tuberculosis and, especially, venereal diseases. Their reintegration and rehabilitation required recognition of the peculiar circumstances of their German journey in the face of criticism and denigration. The army of 1940 had not been a spineless and humorless *troupe de capitulards*; the workers had not been traitors or enthusiasts for the Nazi New Order, but victims of a merciless enemy as well as saboteurs and militants of the Allied cause. The social organization of the national recovery and the accompanying commemoration held some recognition for the diversity of the war experience. A discourse of national martyrdom developed that had more resonance than the bellicose commemoration of the resistance, which was too much out of phase with the direct experience of the population. The displaced populations embodied this martydom better than any other group. Prisoners of war and victims of the genocide, survivors of concentration camps and returning workers had all been "deported" as victims of a cruel enemy with the guilty complicity of national traitors. All "deportees" had suffered in varying degrees and all had, also in varying degrees, defended the honor of their fatherland from which they had been so painfully separated.

One group among them stood out and caught public attention: the survivors of German concentration camps.[23] Not only did the shock of the carnage and the image of the skeleton-like survivors provoke a reaction

---

23 See also Pieter Lagrou, "Victims of Genocide and National Memory: Belgium, France, and the Netherlands, 1945–1965," *Past and Present* 154 (1997): 181–222.

comparable to that toward the slaughter of the war in the trenches, it also allowed for a patriotic commemoration. Among the returning survivors of concentration camps, the arrested resistance fighters and political opponents represented a new generation of *poilus* of a new war of unimaginable cruelty and heroism. Symbols of their extreme experiences – barbed wire, camp barracks, human beings packed in freight cars, prison uniforms, shaved heads, SS prison guards, dogs, and watchtowers – constituted a powerful language representing the war experience *tout court* – including the experience of groups whose individual trajectory had never included any of it. The first to assimilate the symbolism of the *univers concentrationnaire* were POWs and workers. They aspired to be included in the aura of incomparable suffering and patriotism that surrounded the hero-survivors of the camps. Commemorations establishing a direct link between the horror of the "deportation" and the horror of the Great War were at least as influential as the ones establishing a link between the victory of 1918 and the "victory" of the resistance in 1945. In France, the commemoration of Compiègne in 1946 combined the return of the stone ledger of the armistice of November 11, 1918, with a commemoration of the transit camp for "deportees" sent to Nazi camps, thereby including POWs and workers in the event. In Belgium, the Ysertower, a monument to the war in the trenches, and Breendonk, the Nazi torture camp on Belgian territory, were united in a single commemorative event.

The language and the symbolism of "deportation" gradually supplanted earlier commemorations centered around the resistance. Political controversy and popular skepticism had devalued the heroic aura of the resistance. The memory of resistance and deportation in fact underwent a fusion in their public representation. On the one hand, undisputed resistance heroes were the ones who had proven and paid for their heroism with deportation to Nazi camps. On the other hand, all survivors of the camps were represented as resistance heroes whose deportation had been the consequence of their patriotic or at least antifascist opinions and activities. This implied the marginalization of "lesser martyrs" who had earlier claimed to be part of the *univers de la déportation*: POWs and particularly workers. In the Netherlands, this had been the case from 1946 onward. In France, this process took years, including a long legal battle between labor conscripts and the organization of camp survivors that had issued a formal interdiction for the former to call themselves "deportees" as they had insistently done since 1943. This also implied the exclusion, in the Netherlands and in Gaullist organizations, and the assimilation with antifascists and patriots, in Belgium and in left-wing French organizations, of all other victims of Nazi persecution, particularly Jewish survivors of the genocide. By the early 1950s, organizations of "deportees," representing themselves as the personifications of both heroism through national resistance and martyrdom through victimization by the Nazi persecutors, were the only officially accredited, generally respected *milieu de mémoire* of World War II in the Netherlands, in Belgium, in France, and internationally.

During the 1950s, "deportation" became a cultural icon with a codified symbolism in monuments, rituals, expositions, and publications. Most concentration camp sites were organized as places of remembrance according to this "icon" in the late 1950s and in the course of the 1960s, both in the German Democratic Republic (Buchenwald, Sachsenhausen, Ravensbrück) and in the Federal Republic of Germany (Dachau), as were national sites of remembrance of persecution (the Breendonk camp, the *journée nationale de la déportation*). They were an awkward historical construction creating a confused image of national heroes who were victims of the supreme horror perpetrated by Nazi henchmen. Workers and POWs were explicitly excluded from this extraordinary *univers concentrationnaire*, Jews, for whom the gas chambers were essentially designed, more implicitly so. The metaphor, the *pars pro toto*, was reduced to a narrow construction of national martyrdom, to the smallest common denominator of the multiplicity of national experiences during the war. This applied to the different categories of war victims and heroes who had previously claimed their part in the national remembrance, but it also constituted a minimum compromise for the different political forces. The remembrance of the "deportation" in France was the feat of the commemorative policies of the governments of the *troisième force* throughout the existence of the Fourth Republic. The *journée de la déportation* constituted an alternative to commemorations of June 18, private property of the General, and of November 11, when *milieux de mémoire* of World War II only occupied a modest place behind the glorious *poilus*. It also expropriated the communist party of its main commemorative strategy. The return of De Gaulle and his personal conception of commemoration under the Fifth Republic would of course affect this after 1958. In Belgium, the belated solution to the Royal Question, when King Leopold III finally abdicated in 1950 in favor of his son after six years of crippling controversies over his war record, raised hopes for a national reconciliation on the theme of national martyrdom and deportation. These hopes would be thoroughly ruined by the end of the decade by the increasing militarism of an unrepentant Flemish nationalism.

In that regard, the 1950s absolutely were a period of forced conformity in the commemoration of the war. The axiomatic profession that the war had been a collective ordeal had found its most narrow expression in the formalized symbolism of "deportation," whereby the best of the nation had suffered most. The threatening multiplicity of experiences had been singularly reduced to some sort of symbolic common denominator. The occupied countries of Western Europe were mourning their dead in a way that was reminiscent of the post-1918 period, with the difference that their experience was not part of the recognizable personal experiences of the overwhelming majority of the population. Constructed as it was as a peculiar combination of inexpressible horror and fathomless heroism, the *univers concentrationnaire* was a remote abstraction in which almost none of the contemporaries, including most victims of Nazi persecution, could recognize their personal experience. The effect of this gross inadequacy of collective ways of remembering the war was some form of alienation between private memory and public discourse. Public remembrance, at the level of monuments, organizations, and discourse, often contradicted private memories to the point of inauthenticity. Contrary to the collective mourning after 1918, which helped individuals in the process of surviving and overcoming, the heroized remembrance after 1945 often rendered this process more difficult. This also explains why this particular kind of remembrance was so short-lived – contrary again to many of the timeless rituals inaugurated after 1918.

The cramped, artificially unanimous, singularly singular icon of war memory of the 1950s is indeed often presented as the norm, as a period of calm and consensus, whereas it is totally abnormal when placed in the perspective of the controversies and confrontations that preceded it and that would soon follow. The "admission" of the memory of the genocide in particular shattered the very idea of a "common experience," of a nationally shared destiny from the early 1960s onward. No, not all citizens had lived through the same war, but this admission had so long seemed incompatible with the requirements of national recovery. In the long run, an experience as shattered and fragmented as World War II could only generate a shattered and fragmented memory.

It is a common shortcut in general histories of contemporary Europe to see whatever followed the end of World War II as a consequence of it. By an inverse reasoning, one is tempted to conclude that because there is such a striking and unprecedented convergence in Western Europe after the war, the experience that caused this convergence must have been very similar for the different countries that participated in this war. (Europe discovered through this fratricidal war that it had to unite to avoid new wars, whence the EEC; Europe discovered how evil totalitarianism was and decided to combat all its new appearances, whence NATO.) The shortcut is entirely unwarranted. As the transient convulsions of the *Wiedergutmachung* or the failing of the European Defense Community seem to suggest, Western European destinies converged after 1945 in spite of fundamentally diverging experiences of the war. It is not the least of the paradoxes of twentieth-century European history to observe how the relatively homogeneous experience of the First World War was followed by total divergence in the decades that followed it, whereas the totally dispersed experience of World War II was followed by unprecedented convergence. The commemoration of World War II in the 1950s had at least this in common with many other processes taking place simultaneously, such as European integration: It was designed as an answer to the acute need for unity in European society after 1945, and this very much in spite of what had characterized the experience of World War II.

12

Italy after Fascism

The Predicament of Dominant Narratives

DONALD SASSOON

INTRODUCTION

National collectivities – like all collectivities – cannot exist without some shared sense of their past. They tell and consume stories about themselves. They explain who "we" are, what "our" history is. As in fairy tales, they establish who the villains and the heroes are. These narratives are formed, evolve, and are challenged by other narratives. Some are dominant, hegemonic, and manifest; others are subordinate, dormant, and hidden. Groups within nations – parties, regions, ethnicities, churches – elaborate their own stories, confirming or denying the dominant narrative, or simply coexisting with it. The conflict is continuous, part of the life of modern nations.

These struggles are fought with unequal means. The dominant historical narratives achieve their status because they are produced and promoted by dominant groups and by those entrusted with the task of diffusing them. Politics and economics play a preponderant role because the construction of these narratives requires a disproportionate access to the means of circulating ideas. Politicians, journalists, press magnates, those in charge of the mass media, but also educators, prestigious intellectuals, textbook writers, publishers, filmmakers, songwriters, and, occasionally, historians have a considerable advantage over those with reduced access. Unlike the myths of antiquity, the historical narratives of the post-traditional age are not necessarily taken on trust but must conform to some well-known and established facts. They cannot be made up out of thin air and cannot totally contradict the actual experience of those to whom they are addressed.

Narratives are the shape and form we give to "reality." "Real" life is often disorderly and messy; it is a conglomeration of events; it never unfolds like

259

a story.[1] When we tell, as truthfully as we can, the stories of our lives or of what happened yesterday, we select elements of reality, call them facts, link them together, erase those that do not "fit" in the narrative, decide on what is relevant and what is not on the basis of the story we wish to tell – what Hayden White calls "emplotment." This storytelling is a fundamental aspect of social interaction. We shape stories so that others can understand them. In so doing, we bear in mind what they might expect, understand, and believe. We are thus constrained by a pre-existing common field of understanding. It is easier to interact with groups and communities who share our culture than with those whose field of understanding is different from our own.

The designated consumers of national narratives are the members of the nation. However, they too have their own "private" stories, their own sense of the past, often but not always shaped or filtered by the dominant narratives. Because they have restricted means of distributing their own stories, they are uncertain whether these are merely their own (and their families' and friends') or whether they coincide with those of others. It is only by projecting one's own story outside one's immediate community that the story can enter into a wider circuit, compete with dominant narratives, have a chance of establishing itself, and make its mark. Communication is the essence of this game.

Belief does not necessarily make a narrative dominant. Dominance is not achieved by ensuring that everyone believes in its truth. It is not a question of "brainwashing" by constant propaganda. Dominance is acquired by preventing the emergence of other rival narratives or by discrediting them. Your story becomes truly dominant when it is "the only story in town."

This is analogous to how monopolies and oligopolies are formed. Here domination consists in controlling an extensive share of the market for particular products. This is achieved by defeating existing competitors and by preventing the emergence of others. Various strategies are devised to erect barriers to entry: low prices, massive advertising, high quality, merging with potential competitors, state help. Here, too, the potential monopolist faces constraints such as legislation and consumer resistance.

Historical narratives can be regarded as products to be marketed. Power rather than profits are the reward. A position of dominance, however, must constantly be defended; victories are never final. The ruling ideas, as the Marxists remind us, may well be the ideas of the ruling classes. However, in

1 For a theoretical treatment of these themes, see Hayden White, "The Historical Text as Literary Artifact," in Hayden White, *Tropics of Discourse: Essays in Cultural Criticism* (Baltimore, 1978), and the introduction to his *Metahistory: The Historical Imagination in Nineteenth-Century Europe* (Baltimore, 1973).

order to rule, a class or group must become adept not only at defending its ideas but also at the delicate art of discarding some of its old ideas whenever they are seriously challenged and adopting new ones. Thus, modern narratives are in a perpetual state of flux and are constantly reshaped. This is their predicament.

The purpose of this essay is to examine some of the historical narratives about Fascism, the Resistance, and the Second World War as they emerged in Italy during the 1950s, and the problems they encountered.

SKELETONS IN THE CLOSET

Revelations of the shameful role played by various European countries, institutions, and individuals during the Second World War have multiplied since the 1980s, although the hunt for skeletons in the closet had been under way sometime before. Throughout the 1950s, however, the closets were well sealed and the skeletons quite invisible. One should distinguish countries according to their past experiences: those which had experienced fascism or authoritarian regimes before the war, such as Germany and Italy; those whose governments sided with Germany at some stage during the war (for example, Romania and Hungary); those under occupation (for example, the Netherlands, France, and Greece); those that stayed out of the war but had governments resembling those of fascism and that lasted throughout the 1950s and beyond (Portugal and Spain); and, finally, democratic countries that stayed out of the war but cooperated with Germany and appeared to contemplate a future coexistence with fascism in Europe with a certain degree of equanimity (Sweden and Switzerland). Britain, as the only belligerent European country that was not occupied, was spared such problems – the only skeletons to be uncovered were provided by the few Nazi sympathizers and the many appeasers.

In all these instances, the known past represented a source of embarrassment, and silence appeared to be the best strategy. Of course, there were often technical reasons for such procrastinated disclosures. In Germany, for instance, it was only in the late 1950s that the United States began to return the surviving archival material on the Nazi years it had confiscated. Everywhere the delayed opening of archives is often cited as an explanation, but this is unlikely to be the primary cause of reticence. After all, there also are technical reasons why finding the truth is more difficult after fifty years. Memories fade, witnesses die. Besides, although recent discoveries may have unearthed specific new facts or more solid evidence, there have been few earth-shaking revelations. Was anyone surprised when it emerged – albeit late in the day – that German banks and businesses had supported Nazism and sought to benefit from it? Or that Swiss banks did not go out of their way to trace the heirs of depositors who disappeared? Or that many academics, artists, journalists, functionaries, and civil servants tried to protect (or to acquire) their privileges and prestige by being deferential toward authority, any authority, including that of the Third Reich? Ingratiating oneself with one's superiors often is an indispensable prerequisite to one's advancement.

If so many revelations have become manifest so recently, it is because the damage they cause is relatively inconsequential. German businesses or Swiss banks may find the whole thing a little embarrassing, but they can and will buy their way out of it quite easily. Their "clean" competitors will gloat on the sidelines – but not for long. It was quite different just after the war, when West Germany had to be reconstructed as a powerful bastion against communism and when "punishing" all Nazi sympathizers would have involved putting a great many German entrepreneurs behind bars. Similarly, in the 1950s and 1960s, when German scientists, former servants of the Reich, helped the United States in rocketry and space research, there was no broad indignant campaign to have them dismissed. The recent spate of denunciation of complicity in war crimes is promoted by a new generation, innocent of crimes. Those accused are now either elderly and powerless individuals or organizations currently managed by those who could not have been directly responsible for any harm or crime in the past. Embarrassing as it may be to find skeletons in the family closet, and to realize that one's criminal parents put them there, it is not quite as bad as being caught, red-handed, putting them there in the first place.

The end of the Cold War has permitted the revival of a narrative – the history of collaboration with fascism and Nazism – that, in the 1950s, had been propagated mainly by minorities on the Left, especially the communist Left. Their purpose was to discredit conservatives who then dominated most West European societies. These, in turn, owed their reprieve to the fact that they were regarded as a trustworthy force in the containment of communism.

In the 1960s, the situation began to change. At a different pace, in different countries, historical revisionism became fashionable. Its purpose, conscious or unconscious, and regardless of what the specific targets were – for these vary from country to country – was to challenge the traditional role of historians in constructing a national consciousness, a role that developed in the nineteenth century and became entrenched in the twentieth.

A new generation of left-leaning young intellectuals came to the fore relishing the prospect of ransacking the past and pillorying their elders. By the 1970s and 1980s, they had positions of power in the universities and the media. They themselves provided a captive market for the consumption of revisionist history, for history had become the main site of a struggle against the older 1950s narratives.

The main site of this revisionism was contemporary or very recent history, what the French call *l'histoire du temps présent* and the Germans *Zeitgeschichte*. This acquired legitimacy in school and university curricula, and as a field of scholarship only after the 1960s, if at all, when it coincided with the development of historical revisionism in all its varying manifestations. In 1978, the Institut d'Histoire du Temps Présent was established in Paris. Only in 1982 was contemporary history (that is, post-1939 history) introduced in the senior classes of the French *lycée*.[2]

Another factor that helped the flowering of contemporary history was the rapid expansion of the historical profession and the concurrent enlargement of higher education. This quantitative development altered the fundamental rules of intraprofessional competition. In circumstances in which many younger, not-yet-established historians competed among themselves, innovation and originality, rather than cautious deference toward the powers that be, became the preferred strategy for prestige and recognition. Revisionism paid off, especially in countries – such as the United States and Great Britain – that had relatively few Second World War skeletons in their closets and that were able to build on a well-established tradition of writing the history of other countries. Furthermore, it was far easier to obtain access to the media and the press if one could present one's research as a novelty subverting existing preconceptions. Thus, one of the chief determinants of the expansion of contemporary historical studies was to be found outside the profession, at the point of connection between historians and the system of mass communication. A historical debate has greater chances of achieving national coverage if it raises issues concerning national identity and enters into disputes with clear political overtones.

The growth of this historical revisionism has led to a multiplicity of narratives, so that it is far more difficult for any of these to become dominant. Even in countries with a national curriculum in history, the emphasis is on the span of time to be studied and the themes to be covered rather than on the actual content.

This greater pluralism has had the paradoxical effect of making historians even less able to control the dissemination of their narratives. The situation can be compared, once again, to that of a market with a diversity of

2 François Bédarida, "France," in Anthony Seldon, ed., *Contemporary History: Practice and Method* (Oxford, 1988), 129–32.

products: historians write different histories, whereas politicians, the media, journalists, popularizers, and filmmakers pick and choose the most suitable narratives, according to diverse criteria (potential popular concern, political self-interest, etc.). Historians can influence popular views of the past only by using the mass media. The traditions of their profession may make them reluctant to simplify and pander to the *demos*. Their craving for wider fame and recognition, although tempered by the difficulty of explaining complex issues in simple language, makes them eager to accept the mediation of the press.

In Italy (and in Germany), the utilization of the press to present one's history as a challenge to the dominant narrative was not the work of leftist historians but of conservatives who became the intellectual representatives of hitherto suppressed narratives widely held by the population. These conservatives were able to achieve a double feat: They spoke up for those who did not dare to (out of fear they could be accused of being soft on fascism) and challenged a "leftist" narrative that appeared to dominate the academic world.

The case of the Italian historian Renzo De Felice, author of a multivolume biography of Mussolini started in 1965 and left uncompleted, is emblematic. For more than thirty years, he was acclaimed by the conservative press as the archenemy of the left-wing historiography and culture that, he claimed, had dominated Italy since the war and hindered all debates. His numerous interviews (some of which were published as books) provided journalists with assertions and statements that could be marketed as cultural scoops.[3] His famous *Intervista sul fascismo* – a book-length interview, which is a popular genre in Italy – became a best-seller when it was published in 1975.[4] In it, he explained that there was very little common ground between Nazism and Italian Fascism,[5] that Italian Fascism had been relatively mild, that it ran the economy efficiently, that Fascists were modernizers,[6] that most Italians were quite happy under Fascism, that Mussolini had positive attitudes toward education but was let down by the teachers,[7] that antifascist historians are biased, ideological, and keen to demonize Mussolini rather than follow objective historians like De Felice himself,[8] that antisemitism was largely a German imposition, that Fascist Italy was essentially peace-seeking at least

---

3 Gianpasquale Santomassimo, "Il ruolo di Renzo De Felice," *Italia Contemporanea*, no. 212 (Sept. 1998): 556.

4 Renzo De Felice, *Intervista sul fascismo*, ed. Michael A. Ledeen (Rome, 1975). Twenty years later another polemical tract caused, as planned, an even more vociferous public debate; see his *Rosso e Nero* (Milan, 1995).

5 *Intervista sul fascismo*, 24, 42, passim.   6 Ibid., 62.

7 Ibid., 57, 66.   8 Ibid., 111–14.

until 1934,[9] that Mussolini was dragged into the war because he wanted to protect Italy from the Germans,[10] and that, nonetheless, he had been forced into an alliance with Hitler by the French and the British.[11] The popularization of De Felice ensured his enormous renown, whereas his massive unfinished biography of Mussolini, well over six thousand pages in eight volumes, was read only by specialists willing and able to plough through a morass of deadening prose. As Richard Bosworth lamented: "A De Felice sentence could run to a page and a half ... a chapter rarely fell short of 100 pages."[12] Another, MacGregor Knox, speaks of "amorphous chapters, sometimes over 200 pages long," convoluted sentences, ambiguous words.[13] The practical function of De Felice's academic work was to give authority to his views and provide legitimacy for his ascent as the chief popularizer of the conservative view of Fascism.

THE COMMUNIST STORY OF THE RESISTANCE

Throughout the 1950s, the story of the Italian resistance against Fascism and Nazism was by and large constructed by the Italian Communist Party (PCI). Many noncommunist scholars and researchers, especially those connected to the small Action Party, concurred in this construction. However, without the active encouragement and efforts of Communists (including Communist scholars and historians), it is unlikely that this story of the Resistance would have achieved such prominence.

A significant proportion of the limited amount written on the Resistance in the 1950s had been the work of those who had taken part in it. It was published by left-wing publishing houses, did not comply with established academic conventions and procedures, and was often written in a celebratory style. The cultural industry made very limited use of such material. Whereas Britain and the United States produced an endless stream of war films, the stories of the Italian Resistance, equally susceptible to being transposed into exciting fictional accounts, did not find a place in the enormous output of Italy's cinema industry (the largest in Europe in the 1950s), except during the brief season of neorealism and then mostly in the form of "art" films. Popular entertainment kept well away from the war, the Resistance, and

---

9 Ibid., 51.   10 Ibid., 72–3.
11 Ibid., 71.
12 Richard Bosworth, *The Italian Dictatorship: Problems and Perspectives in the Interpretation of Mussolini and Fascism* (London, 1998), 116n. This is one of the best, and certainly the clearest, collection of historiographical essays on Italian Fascism.
13 MacGregor Knox, "In the Duce's Defence," *Times Literary Supplement*, Feb. 26, 1999, 3.

Fascism, as did television and radio, which were state-owned and a fiefdom of the ruling Christian Democrats.

The aim of the Communists was to establish the Resistance as the foundation myth of the Italian Republic and hence as the dominant historical narrative. Institutes for the history of the Resistance were set up, mainly by left-wing historians (including many amateur historians who had taken part in the Resistance). Memoirs and canned histories, mainly of a celebratory kind, were promoted, as were novels and films. The PCI used the Resistance in its numerous rituals, celebrations, fêtes, meetings, and extensive publications.[14] Every April 25, the "Day of Liberation" and a public holiday, the Communists and, to a lesser extent, the Socialists held vast rallies commemorating the event, whereas the ruling political parties celebrated it in a rather perfunctory manner.

The Resistance itself was not taught in universities or in schools. Few scholarly texts on the subject appeared.[15] In part, this was simply a reflection of the widespread prejudice of schoolteachers and academics to the teaching of recent history. The first chair of contemporary history in an Italian university was established in 1961.

It was argued that contemporary history made the necessary scholarly detachment difficult if not impossible. The archives were not open, not properly catalogued, or had been destroyed during the war, or the relevant ministry had not provided the necessary funds. This, argued the Left, was because "they" did not want the history of the Resistance to be written and because "they" had something to hide.

Furthermore, it was almost impossible for history teachers to "cover" the twentieth century in the 1950s because the national curriculum in history stopped in 1918. In the 1960s, it was extended to 1945, but because pupils in the last three years of secondary schooling were supposed to be taught the "whole of history" since the Greeks and Romans, it would have taken unusual determination for a teacher to complete the syllabus. Thus, an entire generation of school pupils had, as sources for Fascism and the Resistance, the recalcitrant recollections of parents who preferred to forget and the timid accounts provided by an overwhelmingly conservative media. The Communist narrative of the Resistance remained enclosed in the subculture of the Left.

14 For an analysis of these, see David Kertzer, *Politics and Symbol: The Italian Communist Party and the Fall of Communism* (New Haven, Conn., 1996).

15 One of the few serious texts of the 1950s was Roberto Battaglia, *Storia della Resistenza italiana* (Turin, 1953).

The obstacles were almost certainly enhanced by the fact that professional historians were constantly confronted with competing histories told by the large number of survivors and participants, including many politicians and journalists, who "were there" and "knew what really happened." The Crusades may not provoke as much interest as recent wars, but at least specialists do not encounter people claiming to have superior knowledge because they took part in them.

A further obstacle to the diffusion of contemporary Italian history (that is, post-1914) was that, apart from the largely Communist-led Resistance, Italy's recent past had been less than glorious: The country, a late entrant into the First World War, had a peripheral role in it; it had been humiliated and treated like a second-rate power at the subsequent peace conference; it had then endured, more or less passively, twenty years of Fascism; then it entered the Second World War on the wrong side (once again late and mainly because it looked as if Germany would win); after a succession of military disasters (Greece, Africa, and Russia) and when it became apparent that Germany was not going to win, Italy switched sides. Since the Risorgimento and Italian unification (1861), the country had had no national heroes, certainly none comparable to Garibaldi, Cavour, and Mazzini. Even the Resistance had not produced any national heroic figure of the caliber of Churchill, Roosevelt, de Gaulle, and Stalin.

In the 1950s, the historians' reluctance to deal with the near past was enhanced by the fact that their own past, and that of the academic community as a whole, had been less than valorous. There was no exodus of non-Jewish academics comparable to that which took place in Germany during Nazism.[16] In 1929, only eleven tenured professors refused to sign an oath of allegiance to Fascism. The others complied, and most did so enthusiastically, including many historians. Many of these still held their chairs in the 1950s; some had been helped in securing these positions by the exclusion of Jewish academics after 1938.

The dominance of the PCI in shaping the Resistance narrative was not seriously challenged by other parties, including the Church-aligned Christian Democratic Party (DC). Unable to construct a credible alternative version, they opted to ignore the issue altogether. The freedom to construct history is more limited than postmodernists imagine. It was simply not possible to present an account of the Resistance that ignored the role the Communists played. It would have been difficult to remind people that Communists had

---

16 Gabriele Turi, "Fascismo e cultura ieri e oggi," in A. Del Boca, M. Legnani, and M. G. Rossi, eds., *Il regime fascista* (Rome, 1995), 544.

fought for freedom and democracy while at the same time propounding the main DC story that they had saved Italian families from the Communists, the Italian representative of totalitarian Bolshevism, the enemies of God and the Church. Moreover, a significant part of the electorate of the DC was made up of those who had either accepted Fascism and believed in it or who had been apathetic and indifferent to it. In addition, there were potentially rich electoral pickings on the far right, where 5–6 percent of the electorate still clung tenaciously and nostalgically to the ideas of Fascism or the traditional values embodied by the monarchy. Thus, the best strategy for the DC was to distance itself from the Resistance.

The Communists themselves faced a dilemma, having to choose between two possible yet contradictory accounts of the Resistance. The first represented it as the effort of a heroic elite, overwhelmingly Communist, who took to the hills and the mountains, and fought for two long winters in dramatic circumstances before coming down to liberate the main cities of northern Italy on April 25, 1945, just before the arrival of the Allies. This "elite" version of the Resistance story clashed with a second, alternative version that represented the Resistance as the accomplishment of the entire people, of workers, peasants, and intellectuals united against fascism and led not only by Communists but also by Socialists and Catholics.[17]

The first, or "elite" version highlighted the isolation of those who fought the Resistance from the mass of the Italian people and distinguished the Communists from others who fought against the Fascists and the Nazis in order to underline their outstanding contribution.[18] Understandably enough, this version was particularly emphasized by former partisans, an important lobby within the parties of the Left because they represented a significant section of the Communist leadership and of the more active members. These partisans could be more easily exalted in the elite version. Their story conformed more closely to the well-established epic trope of the hero who leaves family and home to right a wrong and fight for his country, noble ideals, and a better world.

As a narrative, however, it was unlikely to yield substantial political dividends and did not fit well with the PCI's grand strategy, which was to govern the country in coalition with the other main forces. This conformed to the coalitionist strategy advanced by Communists throughout Europe.[19] The

---

17 Battaglia's book, cited above, falls into this second category, especially in overemphasizing the help given by the local rural population to the resistance fighters.

18 Guido Quazza, who was not a Communist, contributed much to this narrative. See his *Resistenza e storia d'Italia: Problemi e ipotesi di ricerca* (Milan, 1976).

19 I discuss the coalitionist strategy of the Communists in my *One Hundred Years of Socialism* (London, 1997), chap. 4.

aim was to be accepted as a legitimate and democratic force in a broad coalition government. At first (1944–7), this strategy was successful, but the Cold War put an end to it. Although Communists took over power throughout Eastern and Central Europe, suppressing opposition and merging, often forcibly, with the Socialists, they were expelled from governments in western countries, including France and Italy, where they had made significant gains.

With the outbreak of the Cold War, the chances for the PCI to return to power had become negligible. Nevertheless, the search for legitimacy continued. The party persevered in its efforts to establish antifascism as the ideological foundation of the young republic. It hoped that, although in opposition, it would be recognized as a constitutional and legitimate force, unlike the neofascist party, which would later be treated as a pariah. If antifascism could become a national value, accepted by all legitimate forces, it would delegitimize anticommunism. The two positions, antifascism and anticommunism, would become reciprocally incompatible.

It was obvious to Palmiro Togliatti, the leader of the PCI, that this could be accomplished only if the Resistance was seen as the mass struggle of all Italians against a minority of unpatriotic Fascists, Hitler's stooges. There was no room, in this story, for the partisans' more restricted Resistance and their embarrassing reminiscences, redolent of Leninist overtones of military struggle and insurrection.

In the new version of the story, on the contrary, one could underline the contribution of Christian Democrats and others as the erstwhile partners of the Communists in the Resistance and in the short-lived postwar governments of national unity. The political motivations behind Togliatti's project become even more evident if we bear in mind how the significant contribution of the small progressive Action Party to the Resistance was usually downplayed, probably because, after the war, it had proved electorally insignificant.

Throughout the 1950s and the early 1960s, the two conflicting versions of the Communist story coexisted uneasily. However centralist the PCI and however strong Togliatti's authority, this account could not gain absolute dominance, not even within the party. The former partisans kept alive their own version with the support of senior leaders such as Pietro Secchia, who headed the party organization office, and Luigi Longo, who was Togliatti's designated successor.

Party discipline forced Secchia and Longo to pay lip service to the wider narrative, but as the years went by they put their records and those of their comrades before political expediency. Secchia, in a 1949 speech to the Senate, energetically denied that the Communists wanted to have a "monopoly" on the Resistance and stressed the participation of other parties.[20] Twenty years later, a bitter man, marginalized within his own party, he resumed the other narrative:

In Italy, the struggle of the partisans was important and heroic, but it was not the struggle of an *entire* people in arms. We were always dissatisfied with how few we were. . . . It is true that we were able, with the support of the people, to liberate a number of cities, but these insurrections preceded the arrival of the Allies by only two or three days; in the case of Bologna it was a matter of only a few hours.[21]

Luigi Longo, the foremost commander of the Resistance in the North, sharply denounced, on October 15, 1950, "official Italy, the authorities, and the press who want to erase our glorious national past . . . but this Italian people will not forget because the deeds of our partisans are engraved in their homes, their flesh and their hearts . . . the Resistance was a people's war against a cruel enemy who ignored all laws."[22] But on April 25, 1968, he was moved to remind his (Communist) audience:

The facts speak for themselves: the commitment of the communists in the war of liberation was absolute and essential to its success; out of 256,000 fighting partisans the *garibaldini* were 153,600. . . . Without the Communists the Resistance would never have become such a glorious epic. They prepared for it during the hard years of fascist dictatorship. We are thus tempted to ask our critics: where were you in the dramatic days and nights of the Republic of Salò and of Nazi occupation? We did not see you in the prisons, in the camps, in the battlefields of the mountains and the valleys, in the cities and the factories where we, communists, were present in such large numbers.[23]

Under these circumstances, it is not surprising that Togliatti's own version fared even worse outside the ranks of the Left. Catholics and liberals found it far more politically profitable to dwell on anticommunism, forget the Resistance, or suggest that the partisans had been guilty of "excesses." It is often in the interest of the party or parties in power to stress the differences separating them from the opposition. If such contrasts can be expanded to a major conflict between rival and incompatible ideologies, so much the better. It is thus understandable that those in power did not wish to be reminded, or to remind anyone, of the days when they stood shoulder to shoulder with the Communists.

20 Speech of Oct. 28, 1949, in Pietro Secchia, *La Resistenza accusa* (Milan, 1973), 68.
21 Article in *Rinascita* of Feb. 9, 1971, republished in ibid., 549–50.
22 Luigi Longo, *Chi ha tradito la Resistenza* (Rome, 1975), 194.
23 Ibid., 293–6.

The Communist narratives encountered further obstacles. Italy had been liberated by the armed forces of the United States and its Western allies, who now confronted the Soviet bloc. It was, in the 1950s, difficult to denounce American "imperialism" when, a few years previously, the Americans had liberated the country and been welcomed with open arms by all and sundry. The Communists could downplay the role played by the Americans, but not ignore it. Their anti-Americanism had to face the fact that Italians were (and are) far less culturally prejudiced against the United States than the French or even the British. Decades of Italian migration to the United States and the constant influx of American songs and films, in spite of Fascist cultural protectionism, had enhanced a positive image of America as the land of modernity and prosperity, and was a further obstacle to the Left's intention to bolster a left-wing version of patriotism by idealizing the Resistance.

Novels and the few films that attempted to celebrate the Resistance almost always embraced the elite or heroic version. In fiction that was unquestionably the better story. Narratives, including most popular modern narratives, favor situations in which individuals face an agonizing choice, such as whether or not to fight. When the enemy is recognizably evil, the nobler alternative is always to fight. Resistance songs, far more frequently performed after than during the events they celebrate, followed the same pattern. The famous *Ciao, Bella Ciao* (new lyrics on an old folk tune) is a song about a (male) partisan who (a little too cheerfully) waves goodbye to his girlfriend as he joins the Resistance to fight for socialism and freedom. *Fischia il vento* (*The Wind Blows* on the tune of the Russian folk song *Katiuschka*) is a more mournful ballad but the message of personal sacrifice for the greater good is the same: "The wind blows/ our shoes are torn/ and yet we must go on/ towards our Red Spring."

The Left often pilloried the few who departed from this prescribed script. Beppe Fenoglio's (1922–63) now celebrated Resistance novel, *I ventitre giorni della città di Alba* (Einaudi, 1952), disenchanted in tone and irreverent in content, was criticized in the Communist daily *l'Unità*. The critics may have been swayed by the fact that Fenoglio had not been a "comrade" but had fought with the monarchist brigades.[24] But Italo Calvino's (1923–85) *I sentieri dei nidi di ragno* also irritated the official Left even though Calvino was, until the invasion of Hungary in 1956, a loyal and active member of the Communist Party. His Resistance heroes, however, instead of being bona fide factory workers and progressive intellectuals, were too close to the

---

24 Recent work suggests that, in fact, Fenoglio provided a relatively accurate description of the rural population of the area where his Resistance novels take place. See Philip Cooke, "*Il partigiano Johnny*: Resistenza e mondo contadino nelle Langhe," *Italia Contemporanea*, no. 198 (Mar. 1995): 63–76.

despised *lumpenproletariat*: petty thieves, former *carabinieri*, black-marketeers, misfits – all described by Calvino with sympathy and without moralism. Their motivations for joining in the fighting were unclear, varied and, in any case, not sufficiently ideological.[25]

However, the main difficulty facing the Communist narratives was that most Italians had taken no part in the Resistance. They could not recognize it as their story. Southerners were even more alienated from it because the Resistance had occurred in northern and central Italy. Most of the south had been liberated by the Allies before the Resistance had even started. Even in the north, it is unlikely that many more than 200,000 partisans could have been directly involved in the fighting, except in the final weeks. It is difficult to compute how many more helped and materially supported the partisans, but there is little doubt that most people remained passive. They probably hoped that the Anglo-American forces would win the war and that peace would return quickly. They waited patiently, enduring the conflict as noncombatants usually do. Nevertheless, they could not insert themselves into either of the two Communist narratives, and even many among those who celebrated the Resistance had to do so vicariously, as an experience they had not undergone.

The stories of nonparticipation in major events are difficult to tell. Although part of a shared past, they seldom have their own historians. Passivity is rarely described, let alone celebrated. Waiting out the outcome of a struggle between Good and Evil may be understandable, but it is hardly commendable – although some Catholic writers attempted to celebrate such passivity as another form of Resistance, ethically superior to that so much more "militarist" of the Communists.[26]

THE OTHER SIDE(S) OF THE STORY

It is almost a tautology to say that it is difficult to unearth the stories hidden below the cacophony of dominant narratives. If they surface, it is because other hitherto dominant narratives are in difficulty. Or perhaps they were never so hidden after all, although it is true to say that in the 1950s most Italians must have felt an obligation to subscribe to a version of the past they did not really believe in, namely, that they were all antifascist. This made

25 Fulvio Senardi, "Pollicino e il sottosuolo, ovvero Il sentiero dei nidi di ragno," *Problemi*, no. 105 (May–Aug. 1996): 163.

26 An example of such recent mythmaking is Pietro Scoppola, *La Repubblica dei partiti* (Bologna, 1991), 109; for a discussion of the passive Resistance, see Gian Enrico Rusconi, *Se cessiamo di essere una nazione* (Bologna, 1993), 45–91.

them unable to formulate a position in which their own passivity during the war was something other than a form of complicity with Fascism.

Narratives about the Resistance and life under fascism different from those of mainstream left-wing historiography were never hidden. They found a way to surface not through historical analyses or publicly held rituals – how can one celebrate inaction and passivity? – but through the constant encouragement of the ruling political parties, the media operators, the journalists, and conservative and liberal intellectuals.

One such version can be summarized thus: Fascism was imposed on the Italian people, who accepted it passively, without opposition and without enthusiasm. Fascism did some good things and some bad things; the worst was to drag Italy into the Second World War, a war the Italians fought without enthusiasm or fanaticism because they loathe wars. Fascism introduced antisemitic legislation, but the Italians never lost their humanity; they did not apply these laws, or they circumvented them as they circumvent laws they do not like because they do not have a sense of the state, they are not fanatics, they are not like the Germans. Fascism conquered Ethiopia because it wanted to transform Italy into a colonial power. Once again the Italians went along with it, but, unlike the British and the French, they were not real colonialists, treated the natives well and with humanity, and are fondly remembered. During the war, as the American and British troops advanced, Mussolini and the Fascists regrouped in the North and formed the Salò Republic where, admittedly, atrocities were committed, but mainly by the Germans or by Italians who were puppets in the hands of the Germans.

This "passive" narrative recognizes that the Communists played a major part in the Resistance, but only to demonstrate that the Communists, after all, were not ordinary Italians; they were, in fact, somewhat "Russian," their strong political passion underlining their "un-Italianness"; and in any case, so the story goes, they did not really fight against the Germans but kept the weapons they received for an eventual Communist insurrection that, fortunately, never occurred.

This passive narrative could be labeled a narrative of survival. It does not tell the story of how one fought for justice and defeated evil, but of how one survived events that defy understanding. The resulting disparaging self-portrait may appear a caricature because it conforms strongly to the well-established stereotype of Italians as fundamentally unheroic. Yet it is entirely believable because, just like the more epic narratives, it corresponds to a range of accepted or plausible historical facts and constitutes an instance of what Gramsci called *senso comune*. This narrative can be called "the myth of the Good Italian."[27] Epitomized by the standard cliché of Italians as *brava gente*, that is, decent and good-hearted folk, this story is not an exclusive prerogative of the Italians. Similar, not always flattering but self-justifying national stereotypes are available elsewhere. Germans invoke an almost biological *Untertanengeist* or "spirit of submission" to authority responsible for their acceptance of all the catastrophes of the past.[28] The British, notwithstanding the antics of drunken, shaven-headed football hooligans, hold on to the belief that they are tolerant, that they "play fair" and "play by the rules" while the others do not. Americans like to think of themselves as clean-cut, honest, and naive, perhaps ill-equipped to deal with the dastardly plots of foreigners. The myth of the Good Italian is particularly useful in dealing with accusations of complicity in or tolerance of criminal behavior. This way of distancing oneself from evildoers, however, requires an equivalent distancing from those who fight them. After all, the existence of heroes indicates that passivity was not the only course of action and that resistance to evil was possible.

The myth of the Good Italian is not just a construction from below, not just the self-justification of those who felt left out by the dominant story of heroic Resistance or who did not recognize themselves in the ideals and ethics that it embodies. It should not be seen as a dormant, hidden story, a story deprived of a public voice, articulated only in families or among friends. It was given considerable legitimacy by the press, films, the media, and the intellectuals. Benedetto Croce, Italy's leading Liberal philosopher, famously argued that Fascism had been a "parenthesis" in Italian history, a fleeting aberration, an illness that had temporarily afflicted an otherwise healthy body, and that, in any case, it had been a European phenomenon not limited to Italy.

Journalists who had supported Fascism but repented, such as Indro Montanelli, the most influential and famous newspaperman of postwar Italy, contributed to this general whitewashing even at the cost of denigrating Italians. The technique used, consciously or otherwise, varied, but it usually consisted of depicting the Italians as inefficient, provincial, ignorant, conformist, and unused to the ways of democracy. Because newspaper readership was very low, it is evident that such an unflattering portrait was not aimed at the readers but at the others, the "common people" who of course remained quite silent. Yet this silence was confirmed by the images of the Italian past purveyed by television. Fascism was seldom if ever justified or defended in

---

27 For a perceptive account of this in connection to Italian antisemitism, see David Bidussa, *Il mito del bravo italiano* (Milan, 1994).
28 See Richard J. Evans, *Rethinking German History* (London, 1987), chap. 5.

television documentaries, but it was usually portrayed as something that was external to Italians, a strange and alien phenomenon. It was not a product of Italy's past; it mysteriously arrived out of nowhere, hoodwinked a gullible people, led them to war, and brought about the country's ruin. The central aspects of this populist narrative (bad leaders, good people) are almost classically those of the fairy tale: A malign spirit arrives and plagues the land until *an external force*, a dragon-slayer, arrives to rid the land of the nightmare.

This story, of course, rings true to many people. Far from being peculiar to Fascism, it springs out of the chasm that exists everywhere between the leaders and the led, between those who command and those whose life's condition is to obey. This chasm is always magnified in societies in transition between tradition and modernity. It is thus not surprising that the myth of the Good Italian should become almost paradigmatic of what Gramsci called common sense: a set of almost unquestioningly espoused assumptions held to be natural and everlasting when they are, in reality, historically determined and hence transient.[29]

The myth of the Italians as fundamentally "good guys" lasts to this day. On May 11, 1999, a leading article on the front page of Italy's most important and most widely read daily, the *Corriere della Sera*, by the best-selling journalist Enzo Biagi, was entitled "Gli Italiani, brava gente" and opened with those words. A nauseatingly self-congratulatory and sentimental set of ill-connected sentences (the trademark of this popular writer) celebrated the loving affection with which the good Italian folks welcomed the Albanian refugees from Kosovo: "We have not yet found accommodations for all the victims of the Umbrian earthquake, but a little girl from Pristina will receive a tent, a bowl of soup, a hug, and perhaps also a doll."[30] According to the United Nations High Commission on Refugees, by May 12, 1999, Italy had taken in 1,183 refugees from Kosovo and thus ranked eleventh in the league of recipient countries, well behind Germany (10,380), Turkey (6,898), Norway (3,215), France (3,137), as well as Canada, Austria, the Netherlands, the United States, Sweden, and Belgium.[31]

But some things do change. Many of the old narratives have somewhat outlived their political usefulness. The Communist Party no longer exists. A "postcommunist," Massimo D'Alema, was prime minister between 1998 and 2000. The neo-fascists have become respectable post-fascists and were in

---

29 The key passages on *senso comune* are in Antonio Gramsci, *Selections from the Prison Notebooks* (London, 1971), 324–31.
30 Enzo Biagi, "Gli Italiani brava gente," *Corriere della Sera*, May 11, 1999.
31 See *Financial Times*, May 14, 1999, p. 2. Italy, however, was well ahead of Great Britain, which ranked 15th, with only 782 refugees.

government between 1994 and 1996. Nearly all the former partisan leaders are dead. The old narratives can now be challenged more easily not only because there are more and arguably better historians but because politicians and their parties are less implicated in them.

The research conducted in the last decade or so has brought to the surface voices and themes seldom heard before. It has illuminated new aspects of the clash of narratives about Fascism and the war. Rather than providing a lengthy and inevitably perfunctory wide-ranging survey, I have chosen here to concentrate on a few instances to illustrate the conflicts between various narratives and how the emergence of some was prevented by the dominance of others.

The first case dealt with, that of Nazi massacres, exemplifies the contrast between the heroic depiction of the Resistance and the alienation from it of part of the local population. The case of the fate of the body of Mussolini is an example of a historical fact that does not fit any of the available narratives. The account of how women's roles in the war were represented illustrates how the sentimentalization of family relations has stifled other avenues of research. The cases of the Allied bombing of cities and other forms of violence against civilians illustrates the difficulty of expressing outrage when the perpetrators are friends and liberators. The silence over Italian colonialism is an example of the conflict between the myth of the Good Italian and the reality of colonial wars. Another significant memory "lapse" concerns Italian antisemitism under Fascism; this is all the more remarkable because the academic community itself, the self-defined protector of historical memory, had not until recently written the history of how it excluded Jewish students and teachers from the education system.

CONTRADICTORY NARRATIVES

The Case of Nazi Massacres

There are several recorded instances of Nazi massacres of civilians. In most cases, these were reprisals for the activities of partisans. At Guardistallo, near Pisa, on June 29, 1944, after a partisan clash with German patrols the Germans shot fifty Italian civilians. Similar events occurred at Sant'Anna di Stazzema, near Lucca, and at Civitella Val di Chiana, near Arezzo.[32] The official version of these events, naturally enough, blamed the Germans for retaliating against unarmed civilians. Memorials were erected. Annual

32 See "La strage di Civitella," in Romano Bilenchi, *Cronache degli anni neri* (Rome, 1984), and Giovanni Contini, *La memoria divisa* (Milan, 1997).

commemorative rituals were staged. Remembrance plaques were affixed at the approach of the villages. The local population, it was assumed, accepted the official view, all the more so because many of these villages regularly returned large Communist majorities at all postwar elections. Yet, recent research has produced a different view. The inhabitants of Guardistallo, in particular, remain sharply divided.[33] Many of them blame the partisans more than the Germans. In Piedmont, Nuto Revelli, a former partisan turned oral historian, revealed that many peasants regarded the war as none of their business ("War? Just people shooting at each other" – was not an uncommon response) and partisans as troublemakers and that, although they were more than willing to talk about the Great War of 1915–18 (fought by their fathers and grandfathers), they disliked reminiscing about Fascism and the Resistance.[34] When pressed by Revelli, the peasants revealed that, as far as they were concerned, the Resistance comprised a conflict among forces equally alien: the Germans, the Fascists, and the partisans.[35]

None of those interviewed in Tuscany and Piedmont, and who were critical of the partisans, held a positive view of the Germans or in any way attempted to justify their deeds. On the contrary, they accepted the common perception of the Germans as inhuman and worse than beasts, but this fueled their criticisms of the partisans. They pointed out that, precisely because the Germans could not be expected to behave in a civilized and humane way, the partisans should have been more prudent; they should have realized that they were unleashing a devilish retaliation; they should have taken measures to protect the local population before engaging in combat. That they did not do so was because they did not have an appropriate regard for the village as a collectivity. They had separated themselves from it; they had chosen to be different. They had acquired a reputation of valor and fearlessness at the expense of others.

For years this story, so different from the official version that celebrates the heroic solidarity of the villagers with the partisans and their shared contribution to the common struggle, had remained concealed from outsiders. Some aspects of it were probably constructed gradually, after the event. In 1944, the idea that Germans were somewhat predisposed to commit atrocities and acts of barbarism had not yet become established. The inhabitants of small Tuscan villages and towns could not have known of the extermination of

33 See Paolo Pezzino, *Anatomia di un massacro: Controversia sopra una strage tedesca* (Bologna, 1997), and also Franco De Felice, 'I massacri di civili nelle carte di polizia dell'Archivio centrale dello Stato,' *Studi Storici*, no. 3 (1997): 599–638.
34 Nuto Revelli, *Il mondo dei vinti* (Turin, 1977).
35 See the discussion in Mario Isnenghi, *Intellettuali militanti e intellettuali funzionari* (Turin, 1979), 285–90.

the Jews in concentration camps. They were unlikely to have been aware of it even in the 1950s. The Holocaust was seldom mentioned by Italian radio or even by the Communist press. The leading Tuscan daily, the conservative *La nazione*, preferred to concentrate on Soviet atrocities. Primo Levi's now justly famous *Se questo é un uomo* (*If This Is a Man*), printed in 1947 by a small publishing house (after having been turned down by the prestigious, and left-wing, Einaudi publishers), attracted very little attention.[36]

The reaction of some of the inhabitants to the Tuscan massacres can be contrasted to that of those few villages in the south that underwent a similar fate. In these southern instances – the most important of these massacres occurred in Caiazzo, in the province of Caserta not far from Naples – the reprisal was directed against apolitical civilians acting in self-defense or anger against the behavior of German troops.[37] For instance, in Bellona a young man killed a German soldier as revenge for the rape of his sister. The Germans retaliated by executing fifty-four people and devastating four-fifths of the village. The surviving villagers did not blame the young man. His action had not been dictated by politics but by his love for his sister and his sense of family honor. He would have done the same against an Italian soldier and so would have most of the men in the village. He had behaved in perfect harmony with the ethics of the village: From the villagers' point of view, his action was understandable, almost unavoidable. He could not be blamed. It had been a private act.

This is why the villagers had no wish to commemorate it in a public way. In 1945, the authorities put up only a small slab of marble with an inscription. In 1968 – a period of revival of antifascism – a monument was erected. The local population had not even demanded that the German military, responsible for the atrocity, be tried. They regarded the terrible fate they had suffered almost in the same light as a natural disaster, to be endured. In still relatively premodern rural communities, wars are lived as if they are natural calamities: Their causes are unknown and baffling, their outcome a matter of chance, and their consequences irrelevant; the only sensible course of action was to find a way of surviving. Those lucky enough to survive the violence that inevitably accompanies wars put the past behind them as soon as possible and got on with their lives.

In the wider world, however, such an apolitical mentality could not surface until changed political circumstances enabled it to do so. The crisis

---

36 It was only in 1958, when the second edition came out, this time by the prestigious publishers Einaudi, that it started being widely read.
37 See the account in Gloria Chianese, "I massacri nazisti nel Mezzogiorno d'Italia," *Italia Contemporanea*, nos. 209–10 (Dec. 1997–Mar. 1998).

of communism culminating in the collapse of the Berlin Wall coincided with the crisis of the Italian political system and the transformation of the Italian Communist Party into the Democratic Party of the Left. To have been a Communist no longer was a matter of pride in a heroic past, but rather a political embarrassment. Far from abating, the politicization of historical debates was given a new lease on life. Anticommunist pundits took up the disparagement of the Resistance with enthusiasm. A spate of books and articles on postwar revenge killings by partisans against former fascists helped to revive the passive reading of the Resistance and give it a new twist.[38] Those who stood by the sidelines during the war – it now appears – were not wrong; Fascists and antifascists were equally to blame, equally bloodthirsty. The Communist dominance of the Resistance, far from being challenged, was accepted as further evidence that Italians faced a clash between two totalitarianisms, both equally despicable.[39]

The Death of Mussolini

It would be interesting to have a comparative study of the "execution of the tyrant" as the foundation myth of a new social order. Before the era of mass politics, that is, before the nineteenth century, execution was preceded by a solemn trial, a vote was taken, and the public execution followed. The tyrant's guilt was established collectively by representatives of the people. An assembly that conferred legitimacy and the semblance of legality to the proceedings tried Louis XVI and Charles II. The execution by decapitation was public, the head showed to the crowd "standing in" for the people as a whole.

Things proceeded differently in the twentieth century. The "tyrant" was executed swiftly by shadowy figures. Responsibility is unclear. The people remain innocent and uncontaminated. The cases of Tzar Nicholas and his family in 1918 and Nicolae Ceausescu and his wife in 1989 – the dawn and the demise of communism, respectively – are exemplary of this furtive elimination.[40]

---

38 See, in particular, Pietro Di Loreto, *Togliatti e la 'doppiezza": Il PCI tra democrazia e insurrezione 1944–48* (Bologna, 1991), and also Scoppola, *La Repubblica dei partiti*, whose sources – local Christian Democrats and an unpurged police force – are evidently unreliable.

39 These views have also become widespread in France thanks to François Furet and others. See François Furet, *Le passé d'une illusion* (Paris, 1995); in Germany similar positions had been adopted by Ernst Nolte, and in Italy by Renzo De Felice.

40 Hitler's suicide prevented the definition of the Nuremberg Trials as a "trial of the tyrant." Eventually Nuremberg became constructed as the source for a new system of universal rights deemed more important than national sovereignty.

The end of Mussolini resembles this modern pattern. On April 28, 1945, having donned a Luftwaffe coat to pass as a German officer, Mussolini attempted to escape into Switzerland with his mistress, Clara Petacci. At Dongo, near Lake Como, both were captured by members of the Fifty-Second Garibaldi Brigade (Communist partisans) and executed. Their bodies were subsequently taken to Piazzale Loreto in Milan and strung up by the heels to be derided and defiled by a mob.

There have been dozens of books, memoirs, pamphlets, and newspaper articles on the arrest and execution of Mussolini.[41] Most of these are journalistic accounts promising, but not delivering, novel revelations.[42] Until 1998, when Sergio Luzzato published his work, what was missing was a detailed reconstruction of the defilement of the corpses.[43] An undefinable reticence enveloped this dark episode that "fits" neither the Communist Resistance narratives nor the image of the Good Italian.

The execution of Mussolini was a source of embarrassment to the Communists. It could never become a founding myth of Republican Italy: The deed was performed almost surreptitiously, like some gangland murder, and the fact that he was executed by a single man, a Communist partisan, and without a trial could not be used by the Left. The execution contradicted their view of the Resistance as a mass phenomenon. It could be used more easily by anticommunists: Mussolini had been killed in cold blood by the Reds, efficient killers and hence not really Italians. What actually occurred in Piazzale Loreto, although generally known, conflicted not only with the Communist story of the popular resistance but also with the myth of the Good Italian. The Milan crowd jeering at the bodies and throwing garbage at corpses could embody neither the heroic and honorable Italian people nor the decent and kind-hearted folk who dislike violence. They appeared to be little better than a miserable mob, lacking in dignity, cowardly defiling the corpse of a man they had so recently feared, admired, and revered.

It is thus not surprising that this episode was never used for any sort of commemoration. There is, to this day, no plaque in Piazzale Loreto to remind passersby that this is where the man who had ruled Italy for twenty years had died. The Communist Party kept the identity of the executioner, Walter Audisio, well hidden – it was later revealed by profascist activists. There was no attempt to turn Audisio into a hero.

---

41 See the survey in Marino Viganò, "Arresto e esecuzione di Mussolini nei rapporti della Guardia di finanza," *Italia Contemporanea*, no. 202 (Mar. 1996): 113–38.
42 An exception is Candiano Falaschi, *Gli ultimi giorni del fascismo: Come furono giustiziati Mussolini e i gerarchi. Le testimonianze dei protagonisti dell'ultimo atto della Resistenza* (Rome, 1973).
43 Sergio Luzzato, *Il corpo del Duce* (Turin, 1998).

That the bodies of Mussolini and Petacci had been displayed upside down was generally known. As a historical "fact" it was in the public domain, but it was not researched, documented, or reconstructed, and never found a proper place in any of the major popular narratives. It did not fit in, it was disturbing, and the fate of disconcerting narratives is to be passed over in silence.

Bombed and Raped by the Liberators

Being bombed is one of the most dramatic and terrible experiences civilians can undergo during wartime. In the fall of 1942, a massive Allied bombing campaign began in major Italian cities and towns (from Malta first, then from Libya and Tunisia), mainly at night. It should be added that the bombing of civilians after 1943 served no purpose whatsoever because the population was already demoralized and no longer supported the war effort. The daytime bombing of Milan on October 20, 1943, by the Royal Air Force also hit a primary school and led to the deaths of 174 children and their teachers. The Fascists used this to denounce the cruelty of the British. The overall losses caused by the bombing campaign were among the most serious Italy suffered during the war in terms of human lives lost and destruction of buildings and materiel.[44] In Britain, the German blitz over London in the spring and summer of 1940 has been celebrated in endless films and documentaries. Visitors to London's Imperial War Museum can even, for a small extra charge, savor the pleasures of the "blitz experience." In Italy, no such commemoration was possible. Those responsible had been Italy's liberators and later contributed to its rebirth. It was not possible to commemorate the victims, if only by implication, criticizing the Allies and acknowledging those who were still nostalgic about Fascism. Where no narrative is possible, denial and forgetfulness ensue, and the story of the bombing of cities and civilians remained untold and unstudied for nearly fifty years.[45]

A similar silence concealed for years the history of the rapes of Italian women by Allied troops.[46] Here, once again, novelists stepped in where historians feared to tread. Alberto Moravia's famous novel *La Ciociara* (Two Women) filmed by De Sica in 1960 with Sophia Loren in the title role, tells

44 Achille Rastelli, 'I bombardamenti aerei nella seconda guerra mondiale Milano e provincia," *Italia Contemporanea*, no. 195 (June 1994): 309–42.

45 One of the first is the article by Rastelli cited above and dated 1994; on the bombing over Rome, see also Cesare De Simone, *Venti angeli sopra Roma: I bombardamenti aerei sulla Città Eterna 19 luglio e 13 agosto 1843* (Milan, 1993).

46 See the useful survey by Gloria Chianese, "Rappresaglie naziste, saccheggi e violenze alleate nel Sud," *Italia Contemporanea*, no. 202 (Mar. 1996): 71–84.

the story of a displaced mother and her young daughter, who was raped by Moroccan troops serving in the French forces.[47] This entrenched the image of Moroccan soldiers as rapists and had the added – and useful – effect of drawing attention away from American soldiers, whose dominant image, thanks to endless films, is the archetypal liberator. The contributions of other forces, be they British, French, Polish, Australian, Canadian, Indian, or Moroccan, have been ignored.

Violence toward women by advancing armies fighting away from home is a common occurrence in wars, but one had to wait until the 1990s and articles in the feminist journal *DWF: donna, woman, femme* to find research on it.[48] Research on the mass rapes by the Moroccan troops in the village of Esperia near Frosinone in central Italy revealed that some Italian men, including the local priest, had been raped too. Their rape was passed over in silence, for the sexual abuse of a man is too disturbing to find a proper place in conventional war narratives. Equally disturbing was the subsequent fate of many of the women who had been raped. It turns out that their distress continued after the war: Few of the young women who had been raped were able to find husbands, whereas husbands who returned home after the war showed anger and contempt toward their raped wives.[49]

The rapes by Moroccan troops are the best known acts of violence committed by Allied troops, probably because of Moravia's novel and the film it inspired. Indeed, the term *marocchinaggio* was often used, especially in the 1950s, as synonymous for rape. The racist undertones are inescapable, yet the widespread use of the term abetted the refusal to recognize that white U.S. soldiers, too, had raped women and were also responsible for acts of violence and theft against the local population, especially in Naples – as evidenced by the reports of the Military Police filed in the National Archives in Washington, D.C.[50] The most frequent representation is that of friendly GIs distributing chocolates to children for the benefit of the film units of the armed forces.

It is easier to write the history of the victims of Fascism and Nazism than that of the victims of those who had liberated Italy from Fascism and Nazism.

---

47 This was one of the four highest earning Italian films of the year, presumably thanks to the reknown of Sophia Loren. See Gian Piero Brunetta, *Storia del cinema italiano dal 1945 agli anni ottanta* (Rome, 1982), 525.

48 See the special issue of *DWF: donna, woman, femme*, no. 17, 1993, containing studies using a diversity of oral sources.

49 Gioacchino Gianmaria, Luigi Gulia, and Costantino Iadecola, *Guerra, liberazione, dopoguerra in Ciociaria 1943–47* (Frosinone, 1995).

50 Chianese, "Rappresaglie naziste," 78–9.

In war narratives, the "ideal" pathetic victims are women, although occasionally they can be represented as exemplary heroines, following a well-established trope in Western culture. It was assumed that hardly any women took part in armed combat. Their contribution was, at most, one of support, the courier or *staffetta* who provided communication, gathered information and did other intelligence work, distributed resources such as money and food, provided shelter and hiding places.[51] In fact, some 70,000 women joined the Women's Defense Groups, 35,000 women were combatants, 4,600 were arrested and tortured, and 623 were executed or killed on the battlefield.[52] However, in popular representations such as films and novels, what prevails is an image of women as innocent victims of the war concerned mainly with their own roles as caregivers and nurturers.[53] When women are portrayed as brave and heroic, their motivations are usually ascribed not to "manly" causes such as ideology or patriotism but to their attachment to lovers or relatives – as is the Anna Magnani character in Roberto Rossellini's film *Roma città aperta* (1945). Men fight for the home-land or for an ideal. Women fight for their husband, their children, or their parents. They are not ideologues, have no national consciousness. They are mothers, wives, and daughters, in other words "real" human beings, closer to the myth of the Good Italian than the men. When they act, it is usually in order to trace their husbands or their loved ones among displaced people and refugees.

In fictionalized accounts, the motivation behind this is almost always love and affection. However, this disguises other possibilities, such as the legitimate calculation that a woman would be safer with a man, especially in time of war. The presence of a man would reduce a woman's chances of being raped, he would help her in the fields when the crops needed harvesting, or he would be able to support her and their children financially.[54] Little sympathy is shown toward women who developed relationships with other men while their husbands were away at war or in prisoner-of-war camps.[55]

51 Even this image is being challenged. See the account of the conference on women and Resistance in occupied Europe held in Milan, January 14–15, 1995, in Roberta Fossati, "Donne guerra e Resistenza tra scelta politica e vita quotidiana," *Italia Contemporanea*, no. 199 (June 1995): 343–47.

52 Victoria De Grazia, *How Fascism Ruled Women: Italy, 1922–1945* (Berkeley, Calif., 1992), 274. There are no agreed-on Resistance statistics: Jane Slaughter writes that 55,000 women were active; see her *Women and the Italian Resistance, 1943–45* (Denver, 1997), 33.

53 Ibid., 274.

54 Anna Bravo, "Guerre e mutamenti nelle strutture di genere," *Italia Contemporanea*, no. 195 (June 1994): 367–74.

55 Roger Absalom, "Per una storia di sopravvivenze: contadini italiani e prigionieri evasi britannici," *Italia Contemporanea*, no. 140 (1980): 105–22; and his longer work *A Strange Alliance: Aspects of Escape and Survival in Italy 1943–45* (Florence, 1991).

In the 1950s, not surprisingly, the few accounts of the fate of women during the war tended – like all such accounts – to romanticize and sentimentalize their roles and ignore the economic basis of the modern family. Calculations based on need were seen as mercenary or unworthy, and narratives have preferred the stereotype of the woman who always acts out of emotion. The militant feminist literature of the 1970s also contributed to this by privileging research into the contribution of women to the Resistance. Only recently have historians begun to piece together how women might have perceived the war rather than how they *ought* to have perceived it.[56]

The Myth of the Gentle Colonialist

Denis Mack Smith, in *Mussolini's Roman Empire*, stressed that Italian colonial policy was deeply marred by corruption, incompetence, and cruelty. In Ethiopia, the Italians showed no magnanimity in victory but behaved brutally and arrogantly. Mussolini ordered prisoners to be executed. Poison gas was used as part of a systematic policy of terror; hundreds of villages were burnt down and the surviving inhabitants executed.[57] In Africa, Italian colonialists behaved no better than those of other countries.[58]

Well-established journalists, such as Indro Montanelli, have long peddled the view that Italian imperialist policy in Africa was soft, humane, and tolerant. This view was identical to the image cultivated by Fascism in the 1930s. Among ordinary people it is still the prevailing view, although, in fact, Italian colonialism has simply been forgotten: no films, no novels. The Fascist monuments erected in Rome and elsewhere celebrating the Italian empire do not jog anyone's memory. They have simply become part of the landscape, their original purpose erased by collective amnesia. The Right did not wish to be reminded of Italian colonialism, and the Left and the Christian Democrats blamed Mussolini and Fascism and absolved the Italians from collective guilt.

56 See, e.g., Anna Bravo, ed., *Donne e uomini nelle guerre mondiali* (Rome, 1991); F. Koch, "Lo sfollamento nella memoria femminile: Proposte di lettura di alcuni testi dell'Archivio diaristico nazionale," *L'Impegno*, no. 1 (1993); for a British-based study, see Penny Summerfield, *Reconstructing Women's Wartime Lives: Discourses, Subjectivity in Oral Histories of the Second World War* (Manchester, U.K., 1998).

57 Denis Mack Smith, *Mussolini's Roman Empire* (Harmondsworth, U.K., 1979), 78–9.

58 One should avoid generalizing, however: Nicholas Doumanis's account of the Italian occupation of the Dodecanese contrasts the islanders' relatively positive memories of Italian occupation to the official Greek patriotic narrative which stressed the oppressive nature of the occupation, another instance of the divergence between dominant and subaltern narratives; see Nicholas Doumanis, *Myth and Memory in the Mediterranean* (Basingstoke, U.K., 1997). More work on the Greek response to the Italian occupation during World War II is needed.

Little of note was written on Italian colonial policy until 1973, when Giorgio Rochat's pioneering book, *Il colonialismo italiano*, was published.[59] Over the years, the Ministry of Foreign Affairs had published selected documentation of nearly fifty volumes on Italian colonization in Africa. The purpose was to demonstrate that Italian colonialism was quite different from that of other countries and that the good works achieved greatly outweighed the misdeeds. It is an unsurprising result if one considers that fifteen of the twenty-four members of the editorial committee had been either governors of Italian colonies or senior civil servants in the (Fascist) Ministry for African Affairs.[60] Most of what we know about the Italians in Ethiopia is due to the pioneering efforts of Angelo Del Boca and Giorgio Rochat, whose work has undermined the credibility of the complacent view of Italian colonialism.[61]

In 1988, Rochat revealed the extent to which Italians had used gas in Ethiopia well after it had been prohibited by an international agreement (and was never used in military operations in the Second World War).[62] Later, Angelo Del Boca cited twenty-seven cables wherein Mussolini ordered his generals in Ethiopia to use gas.[63] There were controversies and denials, especially by leading proponents of the myth of the Good Italian. Finally, in 1996, the Italian government accepted that gas had been deliberately used in Ethiopia. Later, in 1997, the then-president of the republic, Oscar Scalfaro, apologized during an official visit to Addis Ababa and promised to return the Axum obelisk looted by the Fascists during the 1936–41 occupation. It had been kept illegally by the Italian government for over fifty years in spite of the terms agreed to at the end of the Second World War. As Bosworth points out, "official" Italy was as late as official Japan in acknowledging its murky past, including the existence of concentration camps in Italy.[64]

The myth of the Good Italian was far from dead, even in the late 1980s. Those responsible for Italian colonial atrocities were never punished, and there was never a major public debate. Thus, the vast majority of Italians are barely aware of the history of Italian colonialism; many ignore its very

---

59 Giorgio Rochat, *Il colonialismo italiano* (Turin, 1973).
60 Angelo Del Boca, "Il colonialismo italiano tra miti, rimozioni, negazioni e inadempienze," *Italia Contemporanea*, no. 212 (Sept. 1998): 589–603.
61 See the following books by Angelo Del Boca, all published in Rome: *Gli italiani in Libia* (1986); *Le guerre coloniali del fascismo* (1991); *L'Africa nella coscienza degli Italiani: miti, memorie, errori, sconfitte* (1992); and *Gli italiani in Africa Orientale* (1984); see also by Giorgio Rochat, *Guerre italiane in Libia e in Etiopia. Studi militari 1921–1939* (Treviso, 1991).
62 See Giorgio Rochat, "L'impiego dei gas nella guerra d'Etiopia 1935–36," *Rivista di storia contemporanea* 17, no. 1 (1988): 74–109.
63 See his *I gas di Mussolini, il fascismo e la guerra d'Etiopia* (Rome, 1996).
64 Bosworth, *Italian Dictatorship*, 180–1.

existence – something quite inconceivable in other European former colonial powers: Britain, France, Holland, and Portugal.

Antisemitism and the Universities

At the end of 1943, at the height of the German occupation, the then-rector of the University of Padua, Concetto Marchesi, a classics scholar and a Communist, called on students to join in the armed struggle against Fascism. The appeal subsequently became consecrated as one of "the most noble documents of the Resistance."[65] In 1945, Padua became the only Italian university to be presented with the Gold Medal of the Resistance. In 1995, it was chosen as the venue for a conference on the fiftieth anniversary of the liberation of Italian universities. By then, the climate of opinion had changed. Rather than engaging in another round of self-congratulation, the university decided to examine its own past and, in particular, the eager participation of the academic community in the expulsion of Jewish students and teachers from the universities. The opening paper, by Roberto Finzi, noted that in 1938 there were 1,368 tenured university professors, distributed in twenty-seven universities; ninety-six were expelled for "racial" reasons, that is, 7 percent (Jews then constituted 0.075 percent of the Italian population). This does not include the numerous university assistants and, of course, the students.[66] In the context of the subsequent fate of European Jewry, the loss of employment by ninety-six Jewish academics may appear rather insignificant. It is, however, symptomatic of a wider problem, namely, the self-identification, at the time, of most of the Italian intelligentsia and particularly of the academic community with the political establishment. Solidarity with colleagues and ésprit de corps, so strong in other circumstances, seemed to have mattered little. Equally forgotten were the lofty academic ideals of dispassionate research, pursuit of truth, and the transmission of knowledge. Their counterparts in Vichy France had behaved equally shamefully, but in Belgium the Université Libre of Brussels protested energetically to the German authorities.[67] Some Jews were spared, and the Université Libre upheld its principles, all the more remarkable because

---

65 The words are those of the then doyen of Communist historiography, the late Paolo Spriano, in his fifth volume of *Storia del Partito comunista italiano: La Resistenza, Togliatti e il partito nuovo* (Turin, 1975), 201.

66 Roberto Finzi, *L'università italiana e le leggi antiebraiche* (Rome, 1997), 42n., 51; but see also David Bidussa, *Il mito del bravo italiano*, and Angelo Ventura, "La persecuzione fascista contro gli ebrei nell'Università italiana," *Rivista storica italiana*, no. 1 (1997): 121–97. Ventura teaches at the University of Padua and was the main organizer of the conference.

67 Claude Singer, *Vichy, l'Université et les Juifs: Les silences et la mémoire* (Paris, 1992).

Belgium was occupied by the Nazis, while Italy, in 1938, was not. The lives of dissenting academics were not at risk; imprisonment was very unlikely. They probably did not even run the risk of losing their jobs, although they certainly risked missing opportunities of advancement and promotion. The few who protested, like the futurist poet Filippo Tommaso Marinetti (an early supporter of Fascism), did not suffer.[68] It is clear from the diaries of Giuseppe Bottai, the then-minister of education, that Mussolini himself had hesitated before signing the Race Decree, unsure of what the reaction would be to such onslaught against an almost invisible minority.[69] The race laws were not suddenly introduced. Discreet pressures from university rectors might have made a difference. Instead, the only real battle the universities fought with the government was aimed at ensuring that all the newly vacated chairs would be filled. The only internal conflict was an undignified competition to establish who would fill them.

Some of the significant facts about Italian antisemitism did not have to be unearthed from obscure archives. The basic facts were known all along. Throughout the 1950s, 1960s, and 1970s, the story was not told. Historians, whose fundamental task is to remind people of what they have collectively forgotten, remained silent. Some became apologists for the architects of the antisemitic legislation and for Education Minister Giuseppe Bottai, generally described as an intelligent and "critical" Fascist – almost, I am tempted to add, an antifascist Fascist. Thus, Giordano Bruno Guerri, in his reverential biography of Bottai published in 1976, stated that "the real racists in Italy were very few and Bottai was certainly not one of them," that "his speeches against the Jews are much less harsh than his legislation might lead one to expect," that "all the scholars who have looked into the matter agree that Bottai was not really a racist, in the sense that he did not believe in biological racism," which he had "only" accepted "politically."[70] By 1996, Bottai's rehabilitation was almost complete, and the center-left mayor of Rome, Francesco Rutelli, later the Left candidate for Prime Ministerial office, attempted unsuccessfully to name a street in the capital after him.

None of the Jews expelled from Italian universities and who had emigrated were ever formally offered their old posts. They had to petition and to submit themselves to a lengthy bureaucratic process. No compensation was ever paid.

---

68 Renzo De Felice, *Storia degli ebrei italiani sotto il fascismo* (Milan, 1977), 465–7; this is a two-volume expanded edition, the original was published in 1961 by Einaudi.
69 Cited in Finzi, *L'università italiana*, 39–40.
70 Giordano Bruno Guerri, *Giuseppe Bottai un fascista critico* (Milan, 1976), 168–9.

Whereas Finzi and Ventura were the first to deal specifically with academic complicity in Fascist antisemitism, the first serious work on the history of the Italian Jews under Fascism was De Felice's *Storia degli ebrei italiani* (1961). Although he concentrated on the documentation available on official antisemitism, De Felice did not hesitate to make wider claims he did not substantiate, namely, that "anti-Semitic legislation found no support at all in the majority of Italians";[71] that the ferocious anti-Jewish press campaign "failed to convince the majority of Italians";[72] that, on the contrary, "...the bulk of public opinion reacted negatively to racist policies."[73] Some hundred pages later the tone changes somewhat: It turns out that "important segments" of Italian society, particularly intellectuals, must accept some share of responsibility for having allowed antisemitism to develop, although they did so by "passively" acquiescing to it.[74] The Italian people, once again, are just good folks, forever innocent.[75]

CONCLUSION

In the 1950s, the field of contemporary history was not nearly as developed in Italy as it was elsewhere. The high level of politicization of historical debates forced historians into an adherence to narratives established by political parties, political activists, and politicians. Then as now, historical journals were divided along political lines. In these circumstances, it was particularly difficult to conduct a dispassionate debate about disturbing issues of the recent past. Historians who were less connected to politics eschewed recent history altogether. Academics were content to speak to each other and allowed nonhistorians to remain in charge of popularization by adopting what Stuart Woolf has called a posture of "supercilious condescension towards *divulgazione*."[76] They defended the hallowed Italian tradition of writing with verbose complexity, an attitude that maintained the distance between professionals and the wider public. By contrast, British historians endowed with enviable literary skills, such as Denis Mack Smith and Eric Hobsbawm, enjoyed well-deserved popular acclaim.

In these circumstances, political parties have set the terms of the debate on the recent past. Their narratives dominated the field. I have tried to explain

---

71 De Felice, *Storia degli ebrei italiani*, 368.   72 Ibid., 368.
73 Ibid., 370.   74 Ibid., 462–3ff.
75 De Felice simply reflected the widely held views of all those who wrote about Italian antisemitism after the war; see the survey by Enzo Collotti, "Il razzismo negato," *Italia Contemporanea*, no. 212 (Sept. 1998): 577–87.
76 Stuart Woolf, "Primo Levi's Sense of History," *Journal of Modern Italian Studies* 3, no. 3 (fall 1998): 283.

why this was so, and delineate the obstacles encountered by the Communist and Communist-inspired narratives of Fascism and the Resistance. I have also tried to show that, as a result, an alternative reading of the past emerged – the myth of the Good Italian. Far from shedding light on events, this has merely provided a degree of comfort for those, presumably the majority, who wished not to remember. I have offered a number of examples showing how historical amnesia was an unconscious but coherent response to the dominance of narratives of the Left, which many ordinary people could not share. This combination of collective forgetfulness and popular myth, constantly encouraged by the media and the parties in power, constituted the main challenge to the dominant narratives on fascism and the Resistance.

In the 1950s, historians were still the servants of the political parties. In the 1960s, they gradually began to emancipate themselves. By the 1990s, they had become relatively independent – at least by the not very exacting standards of the past. This was due to the end of communism, which facilitated the transformation of the PCI into a social democratic party, and to the collapse of the ruling political parties following the great corruption scandals of the early 1990s. Finally able to escape the political ghetto they had been confined to since 1945, the neo-fascists promptly resurfaced as respectable post-fascists. But it was not in the interests of post-communists or post-fascists to fight old historical battles. Historians, who do not have the option of forgetting about history, were as far away as ever from making any real impact on the formation of new memories. The new parties – such as the separatist Northern League and Silvio Berlusconi's neoconservatives – found that the past could be invented on the spot as a string of soundbites that did not require any academic legitimization. This was manifest in the case of the League. No shred of evidence acceptable to historians could ever be found to substantiate the romantic and mythic vision of a past Northern Italian identity.

Berlusconi adopted a different approach. With communism gone and no one left to defend it, it was politically advantageous to warn all and sundry that the new post-communists were really old communists in modern clothes. The past left-wing narratives on Fascism and the Resistance could be challenged all the more readily because their dominance was never undisputed. In addition, Berlusconi was a media tycoon in control of half of Italian broadcasting. This accelerated a process where the shaping of a collective sense of the past has become, more than ever, dominated by the mass media. Those in charge of contemporary history are now nonhistorians, journalists, pundits, and gurus who fill the cultural pages of the Italian press and participate in endless television chat shows. They fearlessly denounce the politicians of the past, the old mythmakers whose myths no longer are fashionable, but in so doing they pander to their audience and provide them with a reassuring message: To have no beliefs, no party, and no political values is the right thing to do. Thus, in the end, the most enduring narrative has turned out to be that of the Good Italian, the cowardly, incompetent, but kind-hearted character celebrated in endless film comedies.

13

The Politics of Post-Fascist Aesthetics

1950s West and East German Industrial Design

PAUL BETTS

The history of postwar European culture is undergoing major reconstruction. Not only did the events of 1989 irreversibly alter the face of European politics and society, it has also radically reshuffled the relationship between past and present. The last decade has witnessed an explosion of new scholarship challenging what were once firmly held Cold War orthodoxies. Favorite topics of late include the subterranean force of European nationalisms, the roles of culture and religion as agents of Cold War complicity or subversion, as well as the lasting significance of the wartime legacy of mass death and destruction long after 1945. What distinguishes this post–Cold War historiography is the way it has placed the question of cultural continuity squarely at the center of discussion. Whereas Cold War scholarship on fascism, World War II, and the Holocaust generally concentrated on their multiple causes, the new trend inclines toward investigating its manifold effects.[1] Of growing interest to many cultural historians these days is the extent to which the legacy of what is significantly called "fascist modernism" – whether it be narrative tropes, visual codes, and/or political mythologies – continued to influence the reorganization of postwar life and culture.[2] In so doing,

---

1 Useful broad-based examples include Graham Bartram et al., eds., *Reconstructing the Past: Representations of the Fascist Era in Post-War European Culture* (Keele, 1996); and Nicholas Hewitt, ed., *The Culture of Reconstruction: European Literature, Thought and Film* (New York, 1989).
2 Recent titles include Erin Carlston, *Thinking Fascism: Sapphic Modernism and Fascist Modernity* (Stanford, Calif., 1998); Marla Stone, *The Patron State: Culture and Politics in Fascist Italy* (Princeton, N.J., 1998); Suzanne Pagé, ed., *Années 30 en Europe: Le Temps menacant 1929–1939* (Paris, 1997); Mabel Berezin, *Making the Fascist Self* (Ithaca, N.Y., 1997); Simonetta Falasca, *Fascist Spectacle: The Aesthetic Power of Mussolini's Italy* (Berkeley, Calif., 1997); Wendy Kaplan, ed., *Designing Modernity: The Arts of Reform and Persuasion, 1885–1945* (New York, 1995); Jan Tabor, ed., *Kunst und Diktatur: Architektur, Bildhauerei und Malerei in Österreich, Deutschland, Italien und der Sowjetunion 1922–1956* (Baden, 1994); Andrew Hewitt, *Fascist Modernism: Aesthetics, Politics and the Avant-Garde* (Stanford, Calif., 1993); Richard Golsan, ed., *Fascism, Aesthetics and Culture* (Hanover, N.H., 1992); John Milfull, ed., *The Attractions of Fascism* (New York, 1990); and Alice Kaplan, *Reproductions of Banality: Fascism, Literature, and French Intellectual Life* (Minneapolis, 1987). Note too the special issues on "Fascism and Culture,"

scholars are moving away from older interpretations of how European culture was irreversibly "Americanized" or "Sovietized" to suit overarching Cold War imperatives. This essay explores some of these new issues by looking at the comparative reworking of West and East German culture in the shadow of Nazism. But instead of offering general comments about their hothouse cultural production, I am interested in addressing why industrial design serves as a revealing case study for reconsidering the double cultural construction of post-fascist aesthetics.

Choosing industrial design may seem somewhat odd at first, particularly since postwar culture is largely associated with the revival of literature, painting, film, architecture, music, and theater. Even the most cursory glance through the vast historiography on post-1945 German culture proves the extent to which design – not unlike kindred second-class subdisciplines such as fashion, television, pop music, and advertising – has been routinely ignored. Only recently have scholars begun to realize that if the 1950s and 1960s marked the genuine emergence of broad-based consumer cultures, then the history of the so-called "low arts" as both cause and effect of this wider phenomenon may afford fresh perspectives on postwar life and society. Excluding design from mainstream postwar cultural studies is all the more unfortunate given its unprecedented authority in both countries after 1945. At a time when the more traditional cultural branches of West and East German culture – with the arguable exception of fiction – were struggling unsuccessfully to regain their interwar international audiences, design helped them establish lasting reputations as vibrant centers of industrial modernism.

The attraction of design was partly due to economics. By the early 1950s, both Germanys realized that economic recovery strongly depended on generating export revenues as quickly as possible. The early postwar windfall resulting from increased American and West European demand for Braun toasters and Bosch refrigerators on the one hand, and the success of Zeiss glass and East German industrial machinery in the Soviet Union on the other, was an often-cited indication of the pivotal role of industrial goods exports within each country's immediate economic forecast.[3] In West Germany, the most ardent advocate of this view was none other than

---

Modernism/Modernity 3, no. 1 (Jan. 1996), "The Aesthetics of Fascism," *Journal of Contemporary History* 31, no. 2 (Apr. 1996), and "Fascism and Culture," *Stanford Italian Review* 8, nos. 1–2 (1990).

3 Werner Abelshauser, *Die Langen Fünfziger Jahre: Wirtschaft und Gesellschaft der Bundesrepublik Deutschland 1949–1966* (Düsseldorf, 1987); and Jeffrey Kopstein, *The Politics of Economic Despair* (Chapel Hill, N.C., 1996).

the Federal Republic's legendary minister of economics, Ludwig Erhard. Whereas it is well known that his "social market economy" was based on the trinity of consumer satisfaction, social welfare, and political stability, much of which was shaped by his wartime experience as a fellow at Germany's leading consumer research agency, the Nuremberg Institute,[4] it is often forgotten that industrial design occupied a central position in his economic philosophy. In one 1952 speech delivered before the powerful German Federation of Industry (BDI), for example, Erhard insisted that new industrial design was instrumental in helping recoup the country's former pre-eminence in the field and winning back the edge from foreigners who "have further cultivated our former successes." Only by producing "beautifully designed manufactured equipment" both at home and abroad, so he continued, could West Germany overcome this "design gap" and in turn strengthen its fledgling economy.[5] The subsequent export boom in West Germany's plastics and consumer electronics industries in the wake of the Korean War only confirmed the centrality of design within a rapidly expanding capital goods sector.[6] What is so interesting is that a similar attitude prevailed in East Germany, too. Granted, the German Democratic Republic was hardly able to keep pace with its western neighbor's takeoff during the 1950s. Wartime destruction, postwar reparation payments, food rationing, and back-breaking production quotas forced the German Democratic Republic (GDR) to channel most of its economic activity into heavy industry and machine production at the expense of consumer durables.[7] Nonetheless, industrial design was widely recognized as vital to East German economic growth. Whereas it was not really until the New Economic Policy of the Socialist Unity Party (Sozialistische Einheitspartei Deutschlands, or SED) in 1962 that the GDR began to direct overdue attention

---

4 See Erhard's articles, "Werbung und Konsumforschung," *Die Deutsche Fertigware* 2A (1936): 41–8, and "Einfluss der Preisbildung und Preisbindung auf die Qualität und Quantität des Angebots und der Nachfrage," in Georg Bergler and Ludwig Erhard, eds., *Marktwirtschaft und Wirtschaftswissenschaft* (Berlin, 1939), 47–100. For background, see Dieter Mühle, *Ludwig Erhard: Eine Biographie* (Berlin, 1965), 54–62.

5 Ludwig Erhard, "Abschrift: Bildung des Rates für Formentwicklung," May 24, 1952, B102/34496, Bundesarchiv Koblenz.

6 Dieter Mertins, "Veränderungen der industriellen Branchenstruktur in der Bundesrepublik 1950–1960," in Heinz König, ed., *Wandlungen der Wirtschaftsstruktur in der Bundesrepublik Deutschland* (Berlin, 1962), 439–68. More generally, see Werner Abelshauser, *Wirtschaftsgeschichte der Bundesrepublik Deutschland, 1945–1980* (Frankfurt am Main, 1983).

7 André Steiner, "Dissolution over the 'Dictatorship of Needs?' Consumer Behavior and Economic Reform in East Germany in the 1960s," in Susan Strasser, Charles McGovern, and Matthias Judt, eds., *Getting and Spending: European and American Consumer Societies in the Twentieth Century* (New York, 1998), 167–84.

toward addressing pent-up domestic consumer demand, the sphere of design commanded powerful economic presence from the early 1950s.[8] Their respective institutional design networks were surprisingly similar in this regard, as both created new "design cultures" composed of government officials and industrialists, designers and publicists, together with educators and museum curators, who all identified design as a vital means of constructing a post-fascist industrial culture. Included here were not only new design schools, journals, museums, and trade fairs, but also new state-level organizations. Whereas Bonn's Ministry of Economics created the German Design Council (Rat für Formgebung) in 1951 as a new government agency charged with promoting West German industrial design both at home and abroad, East Germany followed a few years later by establishing an Office of Industrial Design (Zentralinstitut für industrielle Formgestaltung, later changed to Amt für industrielle Formgestaltung) within the Ministry of Economic Development to support and sell modern GDR commodities and equipment.

The primacy of design was also related to postwar cultural idealism. Like other postwar reformers, modernist architects and designers hoped to redeem the ruins of Nazism and the war by transforming the wreckage into a brave new world of post-fascist German modernity. In the immediate postwar years, the refounded German Werkbund – whose regional branches were equally active in Düsseldorf and Dresden, East and West Berlin – emerged as a forceful agent in this broad reform movement. Originally founded in 1907 as a pioneering association of artists and industrialists dedicated to engineering economic and cultural reform through the modernization of German architecture and design, the Werkbund had been one of the most successful German cultural organs – together with the Bauhaus – in leading the crusade for industrial modernism through the 1920s and early 1930s. Although many of its leading lights had emigrated after 1933, those remaining Werkbund members in Germany in 1945 were convinced that their long campaign to introduce mass-produced, high-quality, and affordable housing and everyday wares was more pressing than ever. For them, the seemingly limitless physical and moral destruction resulting from Nazism and the war occasioned a momentous historic opportunity to fulfill their old dream of design as radical reform. The well-known architect and longtime Werkbund member Otto Bartning captured this

---

8 Katherine Pence, "Schaufenster des sozialistischen Konsums: Texte der ostdeutschen 'consumer culture,' " in Alf Lüdtke and Peter Becker, eds., *Akten Eingaben Schaufenster: Erkundungen zu Herrschaft und Alltag* (Berlin, 1997), 91–118.

unreserved Werkbund enthusiasm with starting over in a 1946 *Frankfurter Hefte* article:

The force of the bombs was strong enough not only to destroy the luxury facades and architectural ornamentation, but also the foundations of the buildings themselves. No doubt we will build them anew (not "rebuild"), but without the former facades. Simple, economic, purposeful, functional – that is, to build honestly. Here our material want can prove to be a virtue. Certainly the idea is not new, but has only been heightened by the disenchantment process (*Entzauberungsprozess*) of the war. Yet the Werkbund has been preaching this same message since 1907. Has its hour finally arrived? . . . What a chance we have now, since not only houses, schools, churches, and theaters must be built, but also bowls and plates, clocks, furniture, clothes, and tools must be totally reconstructed![9]

Underlying this common idealism in all zones was the shared belief that 1945 was a decisive moment of liberation, a beatific tabula rasa affording the possibility of creating what another architect and publicist called "a new world of noble and useful forms arising from the destruction and ruin . . . a redesigned social world [*neue Ordnung des Gestaltens*] steeped in the values of economy, honesty and good form, which are the very witnesses of spiritual order."[10] What was quite clear, however, is that they were less interested in trying to forge a new design aesthetic than in recuperating the pre-1933 *Neue Sachlichkeit* principles of rational urban planning, architecture, and product design.[11] To this end, the immediate postwar period witnessed an impressive number of small, makeshift exhibitions amid the rubble – many of which were organized by the regional Werkbunds – aimed at rehabilitating Weimar modernism as a sorely needed compass of postwar renewal and repair.[12] Even the virtual evaporation of the early postwar utopianism informing architecture and city planning by the early 1950s did not derail this impassioned project; rather, its reform zeal was effectively transferred into the sphere of design as the last bastion of this postwar reconstruction idealism.[13]

Such sentiment took on additional gravity given that design was one of the few German cultural spheres that remained practically free of superpower control. Indeed, it acted as a unique crucible for engineering new

9 Otto Bartning, "Stunde des Werkbundes," *Frankfurter Hefte: Zeitschrift für Kultur und Politik* 1, no. 2 (May 1946): 88.
10 Alfons Leitl, "Anmerkungen zur Zeit," *Baukunst und Werkform* 1 (1947): 6, 8.
11 See Heinz König's typed manuscript of Aug. 24, 1945, "Über Aufgaben des Deutschen Werkbundes," DWB 1945–1949/1, Werkbund-Archiv, Berlin.
12 Eckhard Siepmann, *Blasse Dinge: Werkbund und Waren 1945–1949: Eine Ausstellung des Werkbund-Archivs im Martin-Gropius-Bau [1989]* (Berlin, 1990).
13 For background, Werner Durth and Niels Gutschow, *Träume in Trümmern: Stadtplanung 1940–1950* (Munich, 1993).

German cultural identities. Unlike most West German cultural branches – above all painting, cinema, education, and pop music – which were subject to heavy American influence,[14] West German designers patently rejected American streamlined styling. True, various American design figures, such as Charles Eames and Florence Knoll, garnered consistent praise.[15] But this in no way curbed the outpouring of West German polemics, which judged the more general American philosophy of streamlining products in the name of streamlining sales curves to be both dishonest and irresponsible.[16] Typically, they viewed America's "Detroit Baroque" as essentially a child of the Depression, where business recruited designers to help stimulate flagging consumerism after the 1929 Crash.[17] Condemned as wasteful, deceitful, and even overly militaristic, American streamline design was subjected to the same animus once reserved for nineteenth-century European historicism.[18] The 1952 German translation of French-born American streamliner Raymond Loewy's 1950 autobiography, *Never Leave Well Enough Alone*, became a favorite reference for pointing out the corrosive cultural effects of American civilization.[19] The very vocabulary used to define West German design reflected this cultural attitude. The more traditional German concept of *Formgebung* (form-giving) and *Formgestaltung* (form-shaping) was commonly retained in the Federal Republic – the (West) German Design Council was tellingly christened as the *Rat für Formgebung* – as a defense against the putative Anglo-American conflation of design with cosmetic styling.[20] So in clear contrast to other cultural fields, this species of American culture was neither admired nor emulated as a beacon of progressive modernity. The fact that the Nazis had openly exploited this 1930s American streamline aesthetic for their own "futurist" political propaganda

14 For painting, Jost Hermand, "Modernism Restored: West German Painting in the 1950s," in *New German Critique* 32 (spring–summer 1984): 23–41, and Hermann Raum, *Die bildende Kunst der BRD und West-Berlins* (Leipzig, 1977); David Posner, "The Idea of American Education in West Germany during the 1950s," *German Politics and Society* 14, no. 2 (summer 1996): 54–74, and Ralph Willett, *The Americanization of Germany, 1945–1949* (London, 1989).

15 See, e.g., the cover story on Knoll, "Im Haut- und Knochen-Stil," *Der Spiegel*, Aug. 13, 1960, 64–75.

16 Wilhelm Braun-Feldweg, *Normen und Formen* (Ravensburg, 1954), esp. the introduction.

17 This view was neatly articulated by Tomas Maldonado, "New Developments in Industry and the Training of the Designer," *Ulm* 2 (Oct. 1958): 25–40. For the history of American design, see Terry Smith, *Making the Modern: Industry, Art and Design in America* (Chicago, 1993), and Arthur Pulos, *American Design Ethic: A History of Industrial Design to 1940* (Cambridge, Mass., 1983).

18 That most German designers – unlike their American counterparts – did not come from the domain of advertising and commercial design, but rather were trained as artists and architects, was a cherished distinction in the 1950s literature.

19 The reception of Loewy in West Germany is discussed in the exhibition catalog, Angela Schönberger, ed., *Raymond Loewy: Pionier des Industrie-Design* (Munich, 1984).

20 Heinrich König, "Industrielle Formgebung," *Sonderdruck aus Handwörterbuch der Betriebswirtschaft* (Stuttgart, 1957), 1988–92.

also helped establish cultural distance from both the Nazi past and American present.[21] Demonizing the aesthetics of Nazi militarism and American commercialism thus enabled West German designers to clear some political space in which to reclaim their own pre-1933 modernist traditions.[22]

East German design also possessed unusual cultural latitude. Much of this had to do with the fact that the Soviet Union – dominant in so many other aspects of East Bloc Modernism from the late 1940s on – offered nothing in terms of design guidance and/or imitation. Not that the SED's official condemnation of international modernism as insidious Western "formalism" and rootless "cosmopolitanism" during the famed "Formalism Debate" at the Third Party Conference in 1952 did not exert a profound influence on East German industrial culture. Just as East German architects thereafter looked to Moscow or nineteenth-century German classicism as cultural models, GDR designers now "rediscovered" Biedermeier arts and crafts as historical inspiration in shaping a genuinely socialist *Volkskultur*. Yet it is wrong to say that GDR industrial design turned its back on 1920s modernism altogether; in fact, the sphere of technical design (including machinery, hair dryers, and toasters) was never really Stalinized precisely because there was no relevant nineteenth-century tradition on which to draw.[23] It was therefore the undeniably modern dimension of industrial design – to say nothing of its export value – that accounted for its relative independence from the socialist realist dictates imposed on most other East German cultural fields.[24] The recovery of the Wilhelmine Hellerau furniture style as well as Bauhaus prototypes through the ideologically charged 1950s and 1960s underscored design's special role in mediating East German modernism. So despite propaganda to the contrary, modern design occupied a central place at the Leipzig trade fairs and in the state's official annual compendium of select East German products, *Form und Dekor*, from 1955 onward. Further proof of design's unique status in GDR culture could be found in East Germany's premier design journal, *Form und Zweck* (Form and Purpose), whose articles often contained thinly veiled critiques of SED economic and cultural policies. In this way, design enjoyed unparalleled cultural autonomy in both Germanys in negotiating modernist pasts and presents.

21 Hans-Dieter Schäfer, "Amerikanismus im Dritten Reich," in Michael Prinz and Rainer Zitelmann, eds., *Nationalsozialismus und Modernisierung* (Darmstadt, 1991), 199–215.
22 This argument is elaborated in Paul Betts, *The Pathos of Everyday Objects: A Cultural History of West German Industrial Design, 1945–1965* (Berkeley, Calif., forthcoming), chaps. 3, 4.
23 Georg Bertsch and Ernst Hedler, *SED: Schönes Einheit Design* (Cologne, 1994), 22.
24 Often such delicate cultural politicking meant that those reissued 1920s prototypes appeared with quotations from Goethe in catalogs and exhibitions. Heinz Hirdina, *Gestalten für die Serie: Design in der DDR* (Dresden, 1988), 13.

The Bauhaus legacy proved to be of great service in this context. This was especially true given that the quest to resuscitate German antifascist culture after 1945 was continually bedeviled by the fact that virtually all German cultural spheres, whether they be architecture, painting, film, music, philosophy, literature, or history-writing, had been badly contaminated by fascist association.[25] The postwar rehabilitation of the Bauhaus thus had as much to do with its Nazi victimhood as its 1920s reputation as a mecca of avant-garde culture. That the Bauhaus was constantly attacked by the Nazi press as the supreme symptom of "cultural bolshevism" and "cultural degeneration," dramatically closed a few weeks after Hitler seized power, and then savagely ridiculed in the famed 1937 "Degenerate Art" exposition in Munich, effectively sealed its postwar standing as a polestar of post-fascist culture across the occupational zones. Although (or perhaps precisely because) many of its most famous figures had long quit Germany for more hospitable environs abroad, it hardly deterred the celebration of the Bauhaus as what East Germany's leading design historian rightly called a symbol of "peace, progress, antifascism, and democracy."[26] Granted, efforts to re-open the Bauhaus in both Dessau and Weimar failed to materialize; nevertheless, mainstream art and cultural magazines – like *Aufbau* and *Bildende Kunst* – did their part in hailing the Bauhaus as badly needed postwar cultural medicine.[27] Former Bauhaus teachers and students also readily assumed key posts at West and East German art and design schools; those Bauhaus designers still in Germany (for example, Wilhelm Wagenfeld, Mart Stam, Marianne Brandt, Gustav Hassenpflug, Herbert Hirche, and Peter Keler) quickly resumed their design work after the war. One of the most striking long-term effects of this "transzonal" revival of the Bauhaus legacy immediately after 1945 was that there was remarkably little Cold War hostility between German design cultures. Even the short-lived and loosely enforced anti-West propaganda blitz following the Formalism Debate did not alter that. Although East German design enjoyed positive coverage in West German design journals, the reverse was also true, for the GDR design journal *Form und Zweck* always gave high marks to West German design and its explicitly anti-American ethos. Another good example was the first issue of the state's official design compendium, *Form*

25 Jost Hermand, *Kultur im Wiederaufbau: Die Bundesrepublic Deutschland 1945–1965* (Frankfurt am Main, 1989), 89–108, and Hermann Glaser, ed., *Die Kulturgeschichte der Bundesrepublik Deutschland*, vol. 1: *Zwischen Kapitulation und Währungsreform 1945–1948* (Frankfurt am Main, 1985), 91–111.
26 Hirdina, *Gestalten für die Serie*, 11.
27 A particularly good example is Gustav Hassenpflug, "Kunst im Menschlichen verankert: Geist und Geschichte des Bauhauses," *Bildende Kunst* 1, no. 7 (1947): 24.

und Dekor. Although it mouthed the conventional clichés against capitalist decadence and exploitation, it concluded by saying that it would be keen on including well-designed wares from the Federal Republic of Germany (FRG) in future editions.[28] But perhaps the best testimony was the career of former Bauhaus student and postwar star designer Wilhelm Wagenfeld, who was universally lauded as the paragon of design quality and integrity in both West and East Germany. Not only did his 1948 collection of essays on design, *Wesen und Gestalt* (Essence and Form), serve as the uncontested standard work for both design cultures, his design objects were always featured in exhibitions and catalogs (among them *Form und Dekor* and West Germany's own updated and reissued *Deutsche Warenkunde*, or German Goods Catalog) in both republics throughout the 1950s and 1960s. Even more compelling was that he shuttled back and forth between West and East German design firms (for example, Arzberg Porcelain, WMF, and Jena Glassworks) until the 1961 erection of the Berlin Wall. One would be hard pressed to cite such German-German exchange and goodwill in any other cultural branch.

By the mid-1950s, the Bauhaus legacy became particularly valuable diplomatic capital for West Germany. That design was used to broadcast positive national images was hardly unique to the postwar period, especially in light of the long tradition of linking design with the state ever since the London Crystal Palace Exposition of 1851. But design acquired unprecedented political power during the Cold War, if for no other reason than that it was often used – along with consumerism itself – to measure the differences between East and West. The infamous "kitchen debate" between Nikita Khrushchev and then–U.S. Vice President Richard M. Nixon in the American pavilion at the 1959 Moscow Fair, where they sparred over the ideological meaning of hi-tech American kitchens and consumer appliances, signaled a watershed moment in the Cold War politicization of material culture.[29] Yet the postwar rehabilitation of modern design carried special symbolic weight in West Germany's broad campaign to distance itself from Nazi culture. For this the Bauhaus story was used to help reclaim (an albeit sanitized) Weimar Modernism as its new affirmative cultural heritage.[30] The GDR's official condemnation of Bauhaus Modernism in 1950 as sinister bourgeois formalism and American cultural imperialism made it all the easier for

28 "Vorwort," *Form und Dekor* (Berlin, 1955), ii.
29 Walter Hixson, *Parting the Curtain: Propaganda, Culture, and the Cold War, 1945–1961* (New York, 1997), 151–83.
30 Paul Betts, "The Bauhaus as Cold War Legend: West German Modernism Revisited," *German Politics and Society* 14, no. 2 (summer 1996): 75–100.

West Germany to don the Bauhaus mantle as its own.[31] West Germany's high-culture celebration of Bauhaus master painters Paul Klee and Wassily Kandinsky, the institutionalization of Bauhaus pedagogy at postwar art and design schools, and above all its popularization in middle-class life (for example, domestic interiors, furniture styling, and graphic design) registered the Bauhaus's accrued Cold War significance in helping create a liberal West German culture.[32] And even though the International Style most definitely did not dominate West German architecture in the 1950s and 1960s, it was noticeably invoked for the Federal Republic's more representative buildings, such as the Bundeshaus in Bonn, the West German Embassy in Washington, D.C., and the famed Berlin INTERBAU showcase project.[33] In no way should this be construed to suggest, however, that the Bauhaus legacy was fixed and uniform. Consider West Germany's lesser-known organic design culture, the so-called *Nierentischkultur*, which set out to recover a different Bauhaus heritage. In contrast to the more austere functionalist dimension of Bauhaus modernism championed by the German Werkbund, the Ulm Institute of Design, and the German Design Council, this other design culture – which generally flourished in department stores – applied the abstract organic motifs found in the paintings of Klee and Kandinsky to common household objects. The brash colors and wild asymmetrical shapes of 1950s lamps, vases, ashtrays, and tapestries were part of an effort to foreground lively individual spirit and painterly innovations as the Bauhaus's true patrimony.[34] Nonetheless, the conflict indirectly underlined the Bauhaus's cultural authority in the creation of postwar progressive culture.

31 Thomas Hoscislawski, *Bauen zwischen Macht und Ohnmacht: Architektur und Städtebau in der DDR* (Berlin, 1991), 38–43, 101–11, 297–310. A documentary history of the official East German debates on the Bauhaus and modernism in general can be found in Andreas Schätzke, ed., *Zwischen Bauhaus und Stalinallee: Architekturdebatte im östlichen Deutschland 1945–1955* (Braunschweig, 1991).

32 Christine Hopfengart, *Klee: Von Sonderfall zum Publikumsliebling* (Mainz, 1989); Christian Gröhn, *Die Bauhaus-Idee* (Berlin, 1991); Andreas Schwarz, "Design, Graphic Design, Werbung," in Wolfgang Benz, ed., *Die Geschichte der Bundesrepublik Deutschland*, vol. 4: *Kultur* (Frankfurt am Main, 1989), 290–369; and Michael Kriegeskorte, *Werbung in Deutschland 1945–1965* (Cologne, 1992).

33 This is not to say that the West German celebration of the Bauhaus went unchallenged. In 1953, West German architect Rudolf Schwarz provoked a wide controversy in West Germany when he charged that the Bauhaus was less a symbol of liberal humanism than a band of communist "terrorists" who propagated the "jargon of the Comintern." Nonetheless, the severity of the West German counterattack marked the extent to which Bauhaus criticism was virtually rendered taboo in West Germany until the late 1960s. Winfried Nerdinger, "Das Bauhaus zwischen Mythisierung und Kritik," in Ulrich Conrads et al., eds., *Die Bauhaus-Debatte 1953: Dokumente einer verdrängten Kontroverse* (Braunschweig, 1994), 7–19.

34 Thomas Zaumschirm, *Die Fünfziger Jahre* (Munich, 1980); Christian Borngräber, "Nierentisch und Schrippendale: Hinweise auf Architektur und Design," in Dieter Bänsch, ed., *Die Fünfziger Jahre: Beiträge zu Politik und Kultur* (Tübingen, 1985), 210–41; and Albert Bangert, *Der Stil der 50er Jahre: Design und Kunsthandwerk* (Munich, 1983).

But doubtless the most decisive element in the Cold War reworking of the Bauhaus legacy was its remarkably successful transplantation in the United States. With this the Bauhaus story afforded the added advantage of bridging a German modernist past with a modernist American present. Nowhere was its blue-chip Cold War stock more visible than in the 1955 founding of the Ulm Institute of Design as the "New Bauhaus." Initially inspired by Inge Scholl, who wanted to found a new school of democratic education in honor of her two siblings, both of whom were killed as members of the "White Rose" antifascist resistance group, the Ulm Design School dramatized the perceived connections among antifascism, modern design, and social reform. That the American High Command of Germany and the West German government jointly underwrote the Ulm project indicated the extent to which rebaptizing the Bauhaus served as indispensable Cold War diplomacy. Not only did the director of the American High Command of Germany, John J. McCloy, extol Scholl's "crusade to enlighten the German people" as integral to the Allied effort to "help the German people take a democratic road" and "find a close association with the peoples of Western Europe";[35] the inauguration ceremony itself, punctuated by Walter Gropius's keynote address, also functioned as a spectacle of a reformed West Germany, because such notables as Henry van der Velde, Albert Einstein, Carl Zuckmayer, Theodor Heuss, and even Ludwig Erhard all lent their public support. Journalists on hand roundly applauded what one observer called "the Bauhaus idea come home" as a boon for an enlightened West German culture.[36] Given West Germany's campaign to distance itself from its fascist past and to establish closer cultural relations with the United States, the Ulm Institute's privileged pedigree of both anti-Nazi resistance and Bauhaus modernism provided timely testimony to this cause. Not for nothing did one West German cultural historian ironically describe the school as a sort of "coming to terms with the past with American assistance."[37]

35 John McCloy, untitled speech (IO/433), Stadtarchiv, Ulm. Similar sentiment could be found in the 1957 special issue of *Atlantic Monthly* dedicated to "The New Germany," where the Ulm school was described as a vital means by which West Germans could "lead their country back into the main line of European cultural development." Clemens Fiedler, "The New Bauhaus in Ulm," *Atlantic Monthly*, Mar. 1957, 144. Background on McCloy's decisive importance in shaping West German cultural policies can be found in Thomas A. Schwartz, *America's Germany: John J. McCloy and the Federal Republic of Germany* (Cambridge, Mass., 1991), esp. 156–84.
36 Eva von Seckendorff, *Die Hochschule für Gestaltung in Ulm: Gründung 1949–1953* (Marburg, 1989), 89ff. Note as well Walter Dirks, "Das Bauhaus und die Weisse Rose," *Frankfurter Hefte* 10, no. 11 (1955): 769–73, and Manfred George, "Eine Helferin des 'anderen Deutschlands'," *Aufbau*, Nov. 25, 1956.
37 Christian Borngräber, *Stil Novo: Design in den fünfziger Jahren* (Berlin, 1978), 23.

All the same, the elevated cultural value attributed to postwar design was equally linked to the larger cultural effects of fascism. In part, this had to do with the curious fact that it was precisely those ex-fascist countries – West and East Germany, Italy, and Japan – that rose after 1945 as the undisputed world leaders in industrial design.[38] Although design heritage and export pressures partly explain this phenomenon, an integral dimension resides in the peculiar cultural legacy of fascism itself. To better understand this, it pays to recall Walter Benjamin's famous characterization of fascism as the "aestheticization of politics." By this, he was referring to well-known fascist techniques, such as mass political rallies, monumentalist architecture, propaganda films, and the cult of leadership. According to Benjamin, the fascists had specifically deployed these in an attempt to intensify the identification of the people with the government and to dissolve all political resistance, cultural distance, and – in the German case – racial difference in an aesthetic spectacle of unified purpose and nationalist mission.[39] What is particularly useful about his analysis is that it deftly sidesteps the tedious secondary discussion about isolating any supposedly "fascist style" in order to address the larger issue at hand, namely, the explosion of aesthetics under the fascists. Although no one would deny that urban mass cultures had substantially reordered European everyday life after World War I,[40] the crucial difference rested in the fascist fusion of state and aesthetics.[41] Not only was this evident in Hitler's and – to a lesser extent – Mussolini's coordination of culture, the media, and the arts in the name of new nationalist ideologies, it was also manifest in the fascist obsession with rendering politics visible and spectacular. Countless historical pageants, *Volk* festivals, military parades, propaganda films, art exhibitions, death cults, and grandiose buildings exemplified the fascist desire to invent mythic imperial pasts and futures, all the while mobilizing the passions of the present for imminent

38 Hans Wichmann, *Italien: Design 1945 bis Heute* (Basel, 1988); Sherman Lee, *The Genius of Japanese Design* (New York, 1981); and Regine Halter, ed., *Vom Bauhaus bis Bitterfeld: 41 Jahre DDR-Design* (Giessen, 1991). Not to say these countries were peerless in the field; Swiss and Scandinavian design, for example, exerted considerable influence on European design during the first two decades after the war. But they never commanded the same international stature as the post-fascist polities, nor did they generate any of the same intensity of discussion.

39 Walter Benjamin, "The Work of Art in the Age of Mechanical Reproduction," in Walter Benjamin, *Illuminations*, trans. Harry Zohn (New York, 1969), 217–52. For historical background, see George Mosse, *The Nationalization of the Masses: Political Symbolism and Mass Movements in Germany from the Napoleonic Wars through the Third Reich* (Ithaca, N.Y., 1975).

40 For Germany, see John Willett, *The New Sobriety, 1917–1933: Art and Politics in the Weimar Period* (London, 1978), and *Wem gehört die Welt: Kunst und Gesellschaft in der Weimarer Republik* (Berlin, 1977).

41 George Mosse, "Fascist Aesthetics and Society: Some Considerations," *Journal of Contemporary History* 31, no. 2 (Apr. 1996): 245–52.

war-making.[42] The Nazis were even more extreme in this visualization of politics, denouncing all loyalty to liberal political texts (for example, the Versailles Treaty and Weimar Constitution) in favor of decisive political action based on fatal aesthetic criteria – beautiful versus ugly, healthy versus degenerate, German versus Jew.[43] Leaving aside specific fascist motivations and policies, the point is that it was precisely the visual mediation of all politics that forever earmarked fascist culture.

It thus was no coincidence that this particular fascist legacy was strictly prohibited after 1945. In West Germany and Italy, for example, antifascist culture in many ways began with divorcing state and aesthetics. But this went far beyond the endgame frenzy to tear down the visual trappings of fascism at the conclusion of the war. The termination of the fascist era's massive production of nationalist kitsch and "cult of leadership" memorabilia, the rejection of monumentalist architecture, the demilitarization of industrial design, the demystified cultural representation of post-fascist political statesmanship, and – in the case of the FRG – the decentralization of state, education, and culture all testified to the radical break from fascist political aesthetics.[44] By the same token, the state's disinclination toward converting city squares and streets into venues for political demonstrations together with the fact that their most important state ceremonies – and this is particularly true in West Germany – generally took place indoors before relatively small audiences (to say nothing of the way in which these leaders were photographed) also signaled a studied departure from the fascist ritualization of social space.[45] Even the virtual postwar disappearance of large-scale urban spaces, the workspace, and the "laboring community" as sites of aesthetic idealism was part of this dramatic cultural denazification of public life.[46]

---

42 Important contributions on this subject also include Peter Reichel, *Der schöne Schein des Dritten Reiches: Faszination und Gewalt* (Munich, 1991); Klaus Behnken and Frank Wagner, eds., *Inszenierung der Macht: Ästhetische Faszination im Faschismus* (Berlin, 1987); and Berthold Hinz, ed., *Die Dekoration der Gewalt: Kunst und Medien im Faschismus* (Giessen, 1979).

43 Eric Michaud, *Un Arte de l'Eternité* (Paris, 1996).

44 Much of the Fascist Era cultural glorification of leadership was effectively transferred to the visual representation of the pope after 1945. I thank Emilio Gentile for pointing this out to me.

45 Herfried Münkler, "Das kollektive Gedächtnis der DDR," in Dieter Vorsteher, ed., *Parteiauftrag: Ein neues Deutschland* (Berlin, 1997), 458–68. Another interesting example is the changed cultural perception of the German Autobahns, whose initial image as a fascist object of motorized mass desire and military mobility gave way to its postwar reincarnation as a common symbol of post-fascist freedom and individual travel. Kurt Möser, "World War I and the Creation of Desire for Automobiles in Germany," in Strasser, McGovern, and Judt, eds., *Getting and Spending*, 195–222.

46 Otl Aicher, "Planung in Misskredit," in Hans Werner Richter, ed., *Bestandsaufnahme* (Munich, 1962), 398–420; Joan Campbell, *Joy in Work, German Work* (Princeton, N.J., 1989), esp. the conclusion.

For all of these reasons, the defeat of fascism was no ordinary change of government. What had happened was that the Industrial Age's first full-blown audiovisual regimes had violently imploded, effectively leaving the new West German and Italian states denuded of any real cultural representation or mass media presence. Not to say that these new postwar states remained absent from postwar public life; obviously the nervous campaign by the regional West German and Italian governments (often in cooperation with the churches) to regulate mass media – notably film, radio, and later television – in the name of postwar propriety and Christian decorum represented a forceful intervention in post-fascist cultural affairs.[47] But these initiatives, I would argue, were in large measure fueled by the fact that these fragile liberal polities lacked sufficient cultural legitimacy and positive images with which to combat what clearly was a crisis of cultural representation regarding post-fascist society. The controversy surrounding the 1951 West German film *Die Sünderin* (The Female Sinner) and Italian neo-realist cinema as subversive cultural scourges are good cases in point.[48] In fact, it was precisely the absence of affirmative, binding images of post-fascist political community – whose belonging was instead articulated in the form of liberal constitutions – that best marked this rupture with fascist political culture. But this not only entailed a rejection of fascist visual politics and a return to liberalism's penchant for text-based political community and commitment; the problem of articulating post-fascist community found other expressions as well. One particularly instructive example rested in the difficulty West German historians had in invoking positive shared pasts and futures as a means of explaining the present, not least because their former masterplots of social solidarity (nationalism, socialism, National Socialism) had either been destroyed by the Nazis or been sacrificed to Cold War imperatives.[49] The expressly postnationalist language of the West German Basic Law and the marginalization of older affective tropes of "people's history" (*Volksgeschichte*) and "national community" (*Volksgemeinschaft*) as heuristic and political guidance dramatically demonstrated that the nineteenth-century concept of the

47 Heide Fehrenbach, *Cinema in Democratizing Germany: Reconstructing National Identity After Hitler* (Chapel Hill, N.C., 1995); Axel Schildt, *Moderne Zeiten: Freizeit, Massenmedien und "Zeitgeist" in der Bunderepublik der 50er Jahre* (Hamburg, 1995); and Paul Ginsborg, *A History of Contemporary Italy: Society and Politics, 1943–1988* (London, 1990), 239ff.

48 Fehrenbach, *Cinema in Democratizing Germany*, chap. 3; and Christopher Wagstaff, "The Place of Neo-Realism in Italian Cinema from 1945–1954," in Nicholas Hewitt, ed., *Culture of Reconstruction*, 67–87.

49 Peter Alter, "Nationalism and German Politics after 1945," in John Brueilly, ed., *The State of Germany* (London: Longman, 1992), 154–76; and Eric Santner, *Stranded Objects: Mourning, Memory, and Film in Postwar Germany* (Ithaca, N.Y., 1990), esp. 1–31.

nation as narration did not survive the war.[50] That (West) German history was rewritten by historians and social scientists after 1945 as the sociology of *Sonderweg* deviance only underscored the extent to which history had been severed from *Heimat*.[51] This meant that the post-fascist absence of any real visual expression of collective space was accompanied by the lack of any aesthetics of collective time.[52] So whatever one might say about the scandalous cultural continuities between the 1940s and 1950s, the fascist campaign to aestheticize the relationship between people (really, ruler and ruled) was effectively destroyed by the liberalization of West Germany and Italy.

It was no surprise, then, that the home and the restored nuclear family served as West Germany's new romanticized sphere of post-Nazi moral and aesthetic idealism. To be sure, the desire to build a new liberal state on the twin pillars of home and family became the guiding principle of West German social policy through the 1960s. Whereas it conventionally has been associated with the conservative agenda of Christian Democratic politics, most notably that of Chancellor Konrad Adenauer's family minister, Franz-Josef Wuermerling, one should remember that the policy to shore up FRG families enlisted wide support among the churches, conservative women's groups like the German Housewives Association, and even the Social Democrats. Common to all was the belief that the stable family was the best defense against the profound psychological and social dislocation resulting from both the war and its subsequent "hunger years." It was also construed as a necessary deterrent against state socialism insofar as it provided a "healthy division" of state and society, public and private, work and leisure, along with segregated gender roles and activities.[53] But what is often forgotten is that design also played a decisive role in this Cold War project.

---

50 Leonard Krieger, *The German Idea of Freedom: History of a Political Tradition* (Chicago, 1957), 458–71; and Winfried Schulze, *Deutsche Geschichtswissenschaft nach 1945* (Munich, 1989). The situation was different for Italy, where the strong presence of the Italian Communist Party and its mass-produced myth of the Resistance meant that its linkage to a salutary past remained partly intact.

51 Michael Geyer, "Looking Back at the International Style: Some Reflections on the Current State of German History," *German Studies Review* 13, no. 1 (Feb. 1990): 112–27.

52 Additional proof of the cultural rupture from any romantic historical destiny or imagined collective time resided in the conspicuous absence of any West German cult of the dead; nor were there, in stark contrast to the first postwar period, rashes of public commemorations and memorials honoring the fallen soldiers of the Second World War. Even the official homage to the famed martyred resisters – such as the Scholl siblings and the July 20 conspirators – was mainly treated as virtuous moments from a safely distant past. Sabine Behrenbeck, *Der Kult um die toten Helden: Nationalsozialistische Mythen, Riten und Symbole 1923 bis 1945* (Vierow, 1996), esp. the conclusion.

53 Robert G. Moeller, *Protecting Motherhood: Women and the Family in the Politics of Postwar West Germany* (Berkeley, Calif., 1993), esp. chap. 4; Ingrid Langer, "Die Mohrinnen hatten ihre Schuldigkeit getan . . . Staatliche-moralische Aufrüstung der Familien," in Bänsch, ed., *Die Fünfziger Jahre*, 108–30; and Sybille Meyer and Eva Schulze, *Auswirkungen des II. Weltkriegs auf Familien* (Berlin, 1989).

Specifically, the crusade to strengthen the family was complemented by the widespread postwar campaign to modernize the German home as a symbol of denazification and cultural progress.[54] It was precisely this linkage of the family and modern goods that gave the Cold War construction of West German modernity its particular flavor. Once again, American materialism was treated as the chief bugaboo. Just as West Germany's design culture had condemned Raymond Loewy and American streamline design as both dishonest and culturally corrosive, these reformers worried about the deleterious cultural effects of Americanized material egoism.[55] What prevailed, however, was not an ideological separation of the family and the market but rather a new rhetoric devoted to reconciling consumerism and family values. Here Erhard himself fittingly led the charge. In numerous speeches and writings, he maintained that this very coupling would help counter the perceived pitfalls of American-style cultural liberalism.[56] Illustrative of this logic was a 1955 government venture by Wuermeling and Erhard aptly named "Operation People's Washing Machine" in which families could deduct new consumer appliances from their taxes in the name of strengthening the Cold War trinity of the home, the family, and modern goods.[57] Postwar aesthetics followed suit. Not only did postwar housing tend to expand the area of the living room as a means of strengthening the social bonds of the family, the home itself served as a new battleground of West German "petit modernizers" convinced of the necessary connections among family, modern goods, and progressive culture. It was no accident that the 1950s gave rise to a robust flowering of interior decoration, household advice literature, and lifestyle magazines that strove to modernize postwar private life and commodity culture, much of which mass-produced idealized images of the model West German bourgeois family surrounded by modern design objects and the latest consumer appliances.[58] The newfound

54 Michael Wildt, *Vom kleinen Wohlstand: Eine Konsumgeschichte der fünfziger Jahre* (Frankfurt am Main, 1996).

55 To be sure, the Americans also worked to mitigate the social dangers of material individualism by filtering consumerism through the family. Elaine Tyler May, *Homeward Bound: American Families in the Cold War Era* (New York, 1988), chaps. 3–5. Nonetheless, West Germans invariably invoked the stereotyped image of American consumerism as a rhetorical foil against which to forge a more "moral" West German industrial culture.

56 Ludwig Erhard, *Prosperity through Competition*, trans. John B. Wood and Edith Temple Roberts (London, 1958), 169.

57 While it is true that the importance of this initiative paled in comparison to the introduction of installment purchasing and extended consumer credit as key factors behind the modernization of West German domestic life, the point is that even the state saw these modern appliances as less household luxuries than agents of domestic national stability. Jennifer A. Loehlin, *From Rugs to Riches: Housework, Consumption, and Modernity in Germany* (Oxford, 2000), 68.

58 Angela Seeler, "Ehe, Familie und andere Lebensformen in den Nachkriegsjahren im Spiegel der Frauenzeitschriften," in Anna-Elisabeth Freier and Annette Kuhn, eds., *"Das Schicksal Deutschlands*

meaning of postwar design, interior decoration, and "lifestyle" was thus in-separable from this more general West German reorganization of aesthetics as a category of political liberalism and family-based materialism, one which was supposed to shield West German modernity from the perils of a Nazi past, an American present, and a potentially communist future.

The East German case naturally was quite different. Like West Germany and Italy, the GDR was dedicated to constructing a new, modern state cleansed of the legacy of fascism, but it did not feel compelled to divorce the state from culture and ceremonial space; on the contrary, it simply per-petuated what some have called Stalin's grandiose *Gesamtkunstwerk* project to subordinate culture and aesthetics to state ends.[59] The intricate relation-ship between Soviet and GDR culture cannot be adequately treated here,[60] but the relevant point is that East Germany did not break from the 1930s aestheticization of politics. The revival of monumentalist architecture, the regularity of state pageantry, the politicization of public space and the work-place, the celebration of martyred heroes, the state policing of literature and the arts, the religious iconography and pop culture memorabilia glorify-ing the SED, as well as the cultural elevation of the united "community of workers" all underscored these visual continuities with both Soviet and Nazi culture.[61] And just as the SED easily reinvented the pageantry of col-lectivity, so too was there little problem in constructing a new aesthetics of collective time based on the historical triumph of the German working class over centuries of reaction and resistance.

However, this hardly meant that the design of everyday consumer durables was relegated to minor significance there. In fact, it attracted great interest from the very beginning. East Germany devoted considerable energy to remaking everyday things as shiny emblems of a victorious socialist culture, one that was to act as a defense against Western "fascist imperial culture" and "cultural decadence."[62] Such policy assumed great urgency in the wake of the 1953 uprising, whereafter the SED directed growing attention to both

liegt in der Hand seiner Frauen": *Frauen in der deutschen Nachkriegsgeschichte*, vol. 5 of *Frauen in der Geschichte*, Geschichtsdidaktik 20 (Düsseldorf, 1984), 91–121; and Maria Hohn, "Frau im Haus and Girl im Spiegel: Discourse on Women in the Interregnum Period of 1945–1949 and the Question of German Identity," *Central European History* 26, no. 1 (1993): 57–91.

59 Boris Grojs, *Gesamtkunstwerk Stalin: Die gespaltene Kultur in der Sowjetunion* (Munich, 1988).

60 Norman M. Naimark, *The Russians in Germany: A History of the Soviet Zone of Occupation, 1945–1949* (Cambridge, Mass., 1995); and David Pike, *The Politics of Culture in Soviet-Occupied Germany, 1945–1949* (Stanford, Calif., 1992).

61 Gert-Joachim Glaessner, "Selbstinszenierung von Partei und Staat," in Dieter Vorsteher, ed., *Parteiauf-trag*, 20–39.

62 Simone Barck, "Das Dekadenz-Verdikt: Zur Konjunktur eines kulturpolitischen 'Kampfkonzepts' Ende der 1950er bis Mitte der 1960er Jahre," in Jürgen Kocka, ed., *Historische DDR-Forschung: Aufsätze und Studien* (Berlin, 1993), 327–44.

satisfying consumer demand and assuring a wary public that the future – despite present problems – still belonged to socialism. For this, the GDR broadcast its own modernized domestic culture as the proud fulfillment of its "socialist humanity." As in West Germany, the picture of the modern social-ist family relaxing together amid the latest goods and consumer technology became a mass-produced symbol of normality, security, and prosperity in GDR lifestyles journals like *Die Kultur im Heim* (Culture in the Home). Although it is true that the home also served as a preserve of East German arts and crafts, the emphasis on modern design wares (including radios and televisions) became more evident in the 1960s.[63] What is so striking are the similarities between both German domestic cultures in terms of the cultural representations of happiness and prosperity. Admittedly, the favorite West German image of the modern middle-class home complete with elegantly dressed (that is, nonworking) housewives and high-tech kitchens was a dis-tinguishing self-image of the leisured West. But even here the 1950s ideals of East German home life – despite party rhetoric about the full equality of the sexes – betrayed its own myth of the "new woman in socialism" based to a large degree on old bourgeois assumptions of proper female behavior and duties.[64] Here they shared a common perception about the elective affinity of traditional family and modern design as a key expression of post-fascist culture.

One area where they parted company was on the relationship between art and design. Here their respective positions were quite ironic and unexpected. West German high-design culture generally objected to the mass culture elision of art and design, and in turn often tried to ground critical design in science. The emphasis on the ornamental and purely aesthetic dimension was not only denounced as irresponsible (American) design practice but also as only perpetuating the irrationalism and diversionary cultural politics of the Nazi period.[65] What is so odd is that the GDR moved in precisely the opposite direction. This was all the more perplexing given that hard-headed functionalism was once viewed as uniquely well-suited to socialism. After all, functionalism was supposedly a post-bourgeois aesthetic in which class-based decorative styling was rejected in the name of economic rationalization and

---

63 Christiane Keisch, "Die fünfziger in der DDR," in Barbara Mundt, ed., *Interieur + Design in Deutsch-land 1945–1960* (Berlin, 1993), 44–9; and Marion Godau, "Die Innenraumgestaltung in der DDR," in Kerstin Dörhöfer, ed., *Wohnkultur und Plattenbau: Beispiel aus Berlin und Budapest* (Berlin, 1994), 105–19.

64 Jörg Petruschat, "Take Me Plastics," in Halter, ed., *Vom Bauhaus bis Bitterfeld*, 111–12. More generally, Ina Merkel, . . . *und Du, Frau an der Werkbank: Die DDR in den 50er Jahren* (Berlin, 1990), esp. 76–105.

65 See Herbert Lindinger's comments in Herbert Lindinger, ed., *Ulm Design: The Morality of Objects* (Cambridge, Mass., 1987), 77–8.

social utility. Its stress on austerity, rationality, and use–value was seen as the perfect aesthetic expression of the larger GDR effort to create a controlled socialist consumer culture ("each according to his needs") that did not fall victim to capitalist decadence and fetishism.[66]

It was in this context that unitary forms, standardized models, material longevity, and product affordability were enshrined as the early hallmarks of an "enlightened" (that is, needs–based) socialist culture.[67] But during the economic take–off period of the 1960s the state changed course by introducing more zip and color into socialist product design. Its new design tack was largely the result of the SED's fear that functionalist socialist goods looked too ascetic and cheap.[68] The sudden explosion of colorful plastics at that time in GDR material culture (like the FRG a few years before) marked the shift. Now plastics were championed as a vital element in modernizing and beautifying GDR everyday life, what SED leader Walter Ulbricht called "an essential element of the socialist cultural revolution,"[69] especially insofar as plastics promised to help alleviate the perennial shortage of consumer durables.[70] In the sphere of design, the emphasis moved away from preserving the German arts and crafts tradition toward stylizing socialist goods with a distinctly modern face. This is where industrial design and the designers assumed such great cultural authority in the GDR, for they were entrusted with helping engineer a new visual vocabulary of socialist prosperity and progress. Design was then called on to modernize the surfaces of everyday life, to reconcile the antinomies of socialist *Volkskultur* and industrial civilization.

There was another crucial factor at play, however, that went beyond the political marriage of style and state, for the GDR's initial rejection and subsequent endorsement of functionalism was not merely a Cold War reaction to Western "cold functionalism"; it also pivoted on the thorny

66 This was also linked to social control. Note for example the state's worry during the 1950s about the potential dangerous effects of modular furniture: "If the user is free to do what he wants with them [the components], free to arrange the constitutive parts as he pleases, the proportions of the assembled pieces will change in an uncontrollable and artistically unacceptable manner and the underlying intellectual idea will become unclear and elude social control" (Gerhard Hillnhagen, *Anbaubaumöbel: Anbau- , Aufbau- , Baukasten- und Montagemöbel* [Berlin, 1953], quoted in Bertsch and Hedler, *SED: Schönes Einheit Design*, 2).

67 Ina Merkel, "Der aufhaltsame Aufbruch" and Jochen Fetzer, "Gut verpackt . . . ," in Nene Gesellschaft für bildende Kunst, *Wunderwirtschaft: DDR-Konsumkultur in den 60er Jahren* (Cologne, 1996), 11–15, 104–11, respectively.

68 Merkel, "Consumer Culture in the GDR; or How the Struggle for Antimodernity Was Lost on the Battlefield of Consumer Culture," in Strasser, McGovern, and Judt, eds., *Getting and Spending*, 290.

69 Quoted in Horst Redeker, *Chemie gibt Schönheit* (Berlin, 1959), 14.

70 Raymond Stokes, "Plastics and the New Society: The German Democratic Republic in the 1950s and 1960s," in Susan E. Reid and David Crowley, eds., *Style and Socialism: Modernity and Material Culture in Postwar Eastern Europe* (Oxford, 2000), 65–80.

problem of affect. Even if the discussion first began in the 1950s, it was not until the 1961 construction of the Berlin Wall that the debate about the pathos of functionalist objects began in earnest. Having closed off its society from the West as a precondition to the development of a new socialist modernity, the SED now sought vehicles of positive identification to help bridge the gap between people and government, economy, and culture. One of the key landmarks in the SED's effort to integrate life and *Kultur* was the Bitterfeld Conference. Here, GDR artists and writers were asked to bring the world of culture (and themselves) closer to the lives of everyday people by providing cultural inspiration and solidarity so as to better bind citizen and state. Although initially limited to the traditional spheres of cultural affectivity, namely, literature and painting, the scope of the campaign was enlarged in the early 1960s. The debate at the Fifth German Art Exposition in 1962 made it plain that the SED now wished design to be included in the crusade to modernize socialist culture. For was not design, so the SED reasoned, an "applied art" endowed with the "spiritual qualities" that could move and win its subjects?[71] What is so compelling is that the state hoped to do this by strengthening the relationship between people and things. Designers were now summoned alongside writers and artists to provide new sources of affective identification with the state. As noted by East German Design Council director Martin Kelm, the new socialist designer's chief task was to "contribute to the development of the socialist lifestyle and character."[72] This crusade was aimed at transforming less ritualized social places: the workplace and the home. Design then took its place within the SED's broader project to collectivize aesthetics, visualize progress, and mobilize consumer passions.[73] This was all the more decisive if we recall that the GDR's early project to foreground the importance of housing, architecture, and urban planning as the preferred sites of socialist cultural identity shifted markedly toward commodities and domestic spaces by the late 1950s. The deterioration of GDR cities as well as the ever-waning effect of the SED's instrumentalization of urban space reinforced this collapse of public aesthetics. It was in this context that design was to exert its visual power to "humanize the world of work," modernize the home, and in turn buy emotional loyalties.

But no matter how much industrial design was used by both Germanys to broadcast positive new images of antifascist culture and post-Nazi progress,

---

71 An early articulation of these views can be read in Horst Redeker, *Über das Wesen der Form* (Berlin: Inst. für angewandte Kunst, 1958).
72 Martin Kelm, *Produktgestaltung im Sozialismus* (Berlin, 1971), 81.
73 Münkler, "Das kollektive Gedächtnis der DDR," 458–68.

there were still irrepressible continuities with the past. In the main, this has to do with the former marriage of fascism and modernism. That Italian Fascists had exploited avant-garde culture for their own purposes has long been common knowledge; less well known is that the Nazis enthusiastically embraced industrial modernism as well. Alongside the widely circulated images of Speer-esque monumentalism, Teutonic kitsch, and pastoral romanticism there flourished a widespread Nazi fascination with automobiles, airplanes, and mass media. This is not to suggest that the Third Reich's infamous "blood and soil" ideology was somehow unreal or powerless; no doubt much of German culture was violently purged of Weimar Modernism during the first few years of the regime. Yet it is worth recalling that such reactionary Nazi cultural policy was largely confined to the fields of painting, statuary, crafts, and representative architecture.[74] Design offers a unique view of Nazi industrial culture if for no other reason than modern design enjoyed a remarkable career during the Third Reich. For one thing, it performed a vital role in the Nazi economy. At first this may seem puzzling, given the conventional view that Nazi economics was primarily based on military buildup, weapons production, and consumer rationing. True as this was, there also were a handful of leading German design firms – among them Rasch Tapestries, Pott Silverware, Rosenthal Porcelain, and Arzberg Porcelain – that had established worldwide reputations and export markets by 1933. Not surprisingly, the Nazis in no way wished to jeopardize such a lucrative source of profit and international goodwill, with the result that there was no violent "coordination" of the design world because most of these firms were simply encouraged to continue their design production as before. Such policy found broad support among Nazi economists at the time, who shared the opinion that improved export sales would go a long way toward overcoming the recession of the early 1930s.[75] Thanks in large measure to the state's patronage and promotion of modern design, Nazi Germany posted impressive numbers in the export of finished consumer goods.[76]

74 Recent scholarship has shown that even these spheres were more receptive to modernism than once believed. Jonathan Petropoulos, *Art as Politics in the Third Reich* (Chapel Hill, N.C., 1996); and Glenn R. Cuomo, ed., *National Socialist Cultural Policy* (New York, 1995).

75 See the 1933 "Bericht über die Tätigkeit des Leipziger Messeamts," R55/318, Bundesarchiv Koblenz.

76 A 1935 report remarked that the dividends from the Leipzig spring trade fair had increased from RM 250.4 million to RM 291.4 million in the course of one year. Kurt Pröpper, "Leipziger Herbstmesse im Zeichen der Leistung," *Die Deutsche Volkswirtschaft*, Aug. 3, 1935. See also "Leipziger Messe: Gebrauchsgüter in Front," *Berliner Tageblatt*, Aug. 31, 1936. The 1937 Leipzig spring trade fair attracted over 260,000 visitors and tallied RM 495 million, RM 65 million of which was made in the export sales of household consumer durables. "Eine halbe Milliarde Messeumsatz," *Berliner Börsen-Zeitung*, May 4, 1937. The Nazi seizure of power in 1933 did not greatly affect the importance of the trade fair, as representatives from the United States, Great Britain, and France continued to frequent the fair until the war.

The 1936 introduction of the Four-Year Plan only added to its significance. Given the country's increasing diversion of metal, concrete, and wood into weapons production and building construction, the consumer-goods sectors of porcelain, glass, and synthetics became vital to German economic strength.[77] In fact, these modern glass and porcelain manufacturers enjoyed continued stylistic latitude and cultural prestige throughout the Nazi period precisely because of design's export value and its use of nonmilitary materials.[78] The 1939 declaration of war and the resulting Allied blockade again highlighted the value of modern goods. Joseph Goebbels himself waxed about the necessity of maintaining high export standards and production levels during his inaugural addresses at the opening of the 1939, 1940, and 1941 Leipzig fairs, now renamed the "war fair" (*Kriegsmesse*).[79] He and others insisted that the established international reputation of German design firms was a badly needed source of revenue in helping German business recoup its general losses during the war.[80]

The Nazi promotion of modern design also was linked to politics. Even if it never reached the same high-profile ideological stature as the plastic arts and architecture, industrial design was commonly used to convey winsome images of Nazi modernity. This was certainly true for the major international exhibitions of the 1930s. For instance, the Nazis wasted little time in dispatching crates of contemporary religious paintings (including works by expressionists Emil Nolde and Ernst Berlach) and avant-garde design to outfit the German section of the 1933 Chicago "Century of Progress" exposition. Its objective was not only to prove that the regime was sympathetic to new trends but to show a skeptical American audience that Nazi Germany

77 Franz Schmitz, "Leipziger Messe und Vierjahresplan," *Stahl und Eisen* 57, no. 8 (Feb. 25, 1937): 193–6.
78 Wilhelm Wagenfeld, former Bauhaus member and chief designer at the Vereinigte Lausitzer Glaswerke in Weisswasser, went so far as to say that he enjoyed more creative freedom under the Nazis than at anytime before or after. Wilhelm Wagenfeld, "Bericht aus der Werkstatt," in Wilhelm Wagenfeld, *Wesen und Gestalt: Der Dinge um uns* (1948; reprint, Berlin, 1990), 57. For the wartime history of the cutlery works of C. Hugo Pott, see Antoinette Lepper-Binnewerg, "Die Bestecke der Firma C. Hugo Pott, Solingen 1930–1987," Ph.D diss., University of Bonn, 1991, esp. 54–71.
79 "Reichsminister Dr. Goebbels zur Eröffnung der Leipziger Frühjahrsmesse," *Deutsche Bergwerkzeitung*, Mar. 7, 1939.
80 One wartime report went so far as to claim that the German glass, porcelain, and ceramics industries actually doubled production from 1938 to 1940. Erich Schäfer and Richard Knauf, *Der Absatzgrosshandel in der Kriegswirtschaft: Bericht des Seminars für Gross- und Aussenhandel an der Handels-Hochschule, Leipzig* (Berlin, 1941). Another 1939 report claimed that the fair grossed around RM 840 million, 57 percent better than the previous year; exports tallied RM 160 million as opposed to RM 174 million the year before. Moreover, 55 percent of those exhibiting goods concerning *Hausrat* and *Wohnbedarf* reported that they had made the same or more sales than 1938. Karlrobert Ringel, "Analyse des Auslandsgeschäfts auf der Leipziger Frühjahrsmesse 1939 nach dem Bericht des Werberats der Deutschen Wirtschaft," *Rhein-Mainische Wirtschaftszeitung*, June 20, 1939.

truly was a home of cultural modernism tempered by Christian ideals.[81]
Modern industrial design also was foregrounded in the German sections of
the famed Milan Triennales in 1933, 1937, and 1940, where the work of
Weimar designers such as Wagenfeld, Hermann Gretsch, Trude Petri, and
Otto Hindig was proudly displayed as the very best from Nazi Germany.[82]
Most revealing of all was the German Pavilion at the 1937 World Exposition in Paris: Over the years this show has received wide coverage from
cultural historians who have treated Speer's daunting exhibition edifice –
a columned, monumentalist tower and hall adorned with oversize Prussian
eagles and surrounding Arno Breker statuary – as one of Nazi Germany's
premier cultural self-representations to an international audience. What is
invariably overlooked, though, is that the pavilion interior of this Nazi
show of force was awash with modern design objects (including Porsche's
racing car, Wagenfeld glassware, Gretsch tableware, and even newly developed television sets) as new emblems of the Third Reich's distinctly modern
culture.

Such displays of Nazi Modernism were not limited to foreign venues,
however. They were equally as intensive on the home front, despite early
Nazi propaganda. The Nazi closure of the Bauhaus and "coordination" of
the Werkbund hardly deterred continued state support of modern design
throughout Germany. Recall the spate of modern design exhibitions organized by the long-forgotten *Kunst-Dienst*, or "Art Service." Originally
founded in the late 1920s as a Protestant religious art organization, the
Kunst-Dienst was transformed under the Nazis into a kind of makeshift
Werkbund (a good number of key Werkbund members were Kunst-Dienst
affiliates after 1934) that advanced the cause of modern design. Another
example was the Third Reich's home decoration books and journals, which
routinely featured well-known modernist design artifacts through the late
1930s – such as Marcel Breuer's steel-tube chairs, Wagenfeld lamps, and
Bauhaus tea kettles – as manifestations of what one contemporary writer
called "good German interior decoration."[83] Additional testimony appeared

---

81 For the self-congratulatory version, see T. V. Roelof-Lanner, ed., *Der deutsche Führer durch die
Weltausstellung 1934* (Chicago, 1934); Barbara Miller Lane, *Architecture and Politics in Germany,
1918–1945* (Cambridge, Mass., 1968; reprint, 1985), 177.

82 The Germans received over two hundred design prizes at the 1940 Milan Triennale alone. Mag-
dalena Droste, "Bauhaus-Designer zwischen Handwerk und Moderne," in Winfried Nerdinger,
ed., *Bauhaus-Moderne im Nationalsozialismus: Zwischen Anbiederung und Verfolgung* (Munich, 1993),
85–101.

83 Carl Borchard, *Gutes und Böses in der Wohnung in Bild und Gegenbild* (Leipzig, 1933). As late as 1939,
metal furniture was still recommended in the Nazi advice books for its "federnde Schönheit." Marion
Godau, "Anti-Moderne?" in Sabine Weissler, ed., *Design in Deutschland, 1933–1945: Ästhetik und
Organisation des Deutschen Werkbundes im "Dritten Reich"* (Giessen, 1990), 74–87.

in the 1939 publication of German *Warenkunde*, a three-hundred-page loose-leaf compilation of select goods that the state distributed to German industrialists as standard bearers of German industrial culture. Included in it were many classic pieces of Weimar design, whereas the more *völkisch* arts and crafts were appended to the back. But perhaps the most striking illustration of Nazi Modernism remains the extraordinary six-year career of Speer's "Beauty of Labor" Office, an ancillary organization of the infamous German Labor Front. Created in 1934 to help make "German everyday life more beautiful" as well as to restore the "dignity of labor" and "joy of work" supposedly absent from modern industrial life, this bureau oversaw the modernization of literally tens of thousands of German factories and workspaces.[84] In so doing, Beauty of Labor shamelessly plagiarized – as Speer admitted in a 1978 interview – the hated "cultural Bolsheviks" in reorganizing German work life along the principles of *Neue Sachlichkeit* architecture and design.[85] To top it off, modern cutlery, tableware, and furniture designed by Bauhaus followers Wagenfeld and Gretsch were made standard in all of these new worker canteens and recreation areas, as well as on board the celebrated "Strength Through Joy" vacation cruiseliners.

Unavoidably, this raises a number of thorny questions about influence and continuity. Quite arresting is the fact that those design objects singled out and advertised after 1945 as symbols of "cultural denazification" were often the very same ones showcased in Nazi design exhibitions and Beauty of Labor canteens just a few years before. In the GDR, the design wares featured in its design journals, exhibitions, and especially its annual catalog of exemplary industrial objects, *Form und Dekor*, as vessels of antifascist "democratic humanism" were often only reproductions of prototypes manufactured by Beauty of Labor. Similar continuities abounded in West Germany, too. Here again, many of those celebrated items shown in West German exhibitions, journals, home decoration literature, and its own updated 1955 *Warenkunde* were already present in its 1939 forerunner. Close inspection of the Werkbund's highly touted first major postwar exhibition, the 1949 "New Living" show in Cologne, undermines the validity of its advertised break from the past. Most revealing of all, though, was the West German pavilion at the 1958 Brussels World Exposition. Doubtless it was a highly charged event for West Germany, not least because Germany's last showing at a major international venue had been Speer's Nazi Pavilion at

---

84 Anson Rabinbach, "The Aesthetics of Production in the Third Reich," *Journal of Contemporary History* 11, no. 4 (Oct. 1976): 43–74.

85 "Interview mit Albert Speer am 16.11.1978 in München," in Sabine Weissler, ed., *Die Zwanziger Jahre des Deutschen Werkbunds* (Giessen, 1982), 292–309.

the 1937 Paris World Exposition. This time the message was radically different because Bonn entrusted its organization to the new Werkbund and German Design Council. To make clear that 1958 was not 1937, International Style modernism was studiously showcased as proof of West German cultural regeneration and political change. Just the architectural styles told the story: Flat, unimposing *Neue Sachlichkeit* buildings with large windows were chosen (not unlike Bonn's *Bundeshaus*) as the visual antithesis to Speer's overpowering vertical pseudoclassicism (to say nothing of the Prussian eagles and surrounding statuary) a generation before. Even the pavilion's theme – *Bescheidenheit*, or humility – was intended both to counter former Nazi megalomania and to play down the emergent West German pride in its improbable "economic miracle."[86] Yet this seemingly resolved FRG oedipal drama hid one repressed issue: Many of those modern things presented as part of this new everyday reality of post-fascist culture were ironically the very same ones featured at the 1937 Paris show. To be sure, certain techno-objects of 1930s desire, most notably Porsche's racing car, were nowhere to be seen here; nor was it insignificant that the emphasis shifted from massive displays of the symbiosis of German workers and modern things in 1937 toward instructive display rooms and quiet living room interiors in 1958. Notable, too, was the presence of undeniably pioneering new design objects (for example, the phonographs and kitchen equipment produced by the design team at Braun) along with various items from other countries (like Charles Eames chairs and Olivetti typewriters) as tributes to West Germany's new internationally oriented industrial culture. Nonetheless, the inclusion of these older things cannot but question the broadcast affinity between the Bauhaus and Bonn, modernist styling and the liberal state.

To argue that 1950s design was nothing but a shameless restoration of Nazi Modernism widely misses the mark, however.[87] The relevant point is that the Third Reich contributed precious little in terms of design innovation, devoting its energies instead to reflagging classic Weimar modernism for its own purposes. Roughly put, German industrial design did not change very much from 1925 to 1965; and this goes for both West and East Germany. What did change of course was its cultural meaning and representation, because the very same objects were embraced by dramatically incongruous political regimes as visual markers of their specific political projects. It is little wonder, then, that after 1945 all Nazi racist rhetoric concerning

---

86 G. B. von Hartmann and Wend Fischer, ed., *Deutschlands Beitrag zur Weltausstellung Brüssel 1958: Ein Bericht* (Düsseldorf, 1958).

87 Typical is Bernd Meurer and Harmut Vinçon, *Industrielle Ästhetik: Zur Geschichte und Theorie der Gestaltung* (Giessen, 1983).

design as _Dasein_ was systematically dropped by both German cultures, much in the way that the Nazis themselves had expunged the socialist language suffusing Weimar design a generation earlier. But the "re-education" of this design legacy remained quite limited. A surprising number of texts published in both West and East Germany in the first decade after the war simply deleted the offensive passages from their 1930s editions before reprinting them as postwar cultural counsel. Purging toxic Nazi rhetoric was not enough, however. A new, positive language of modern design needed to be invented, especially because most of its objects (at least until the mid-1950s) were essentially the same. This was why both design cultures insisted on grounding design in humanist morality, inasmuch as this was apparently the one ideology that the Nazis disdainfully ignored.

This was no easy task, however, mainly because the Nazis had openly appropriated the rhetoric and styling of industrial modernism (including the German Werkbund's long-standing idealist language about the "spiritualization" of things and technology, "quality work," and of course the "joy of work") for their own purposes. Against this, both West and East Germany worked to build their new design identities on the moralization of material, what was often called "good form." Indeed, "good form" functionalism was praised in both countries precisely because it allegedly combined ethics and aesthetics. No better example existed than West German President Theodor Heuss's call for design as social reform. His foray into design politics makes more sense if we recall that Heuss himself was a former Werkbund secretary during the 1920s, a Kunst-Dienst member in the 1930s, and a long-time advocate – he helped create the German Design Council – of modern design. In a 1951 speech entitled "What is Quality? On the History and Mission of the German Werkbund," Heuss strove to retrieve the concept of German "quality work" and even "joy of work" from its ideological perversion under Nazism and finished by saying that proper design – again, "good form" – was synonymous with what he called _das Anständige_, or moral decency.[88] So even if the objects were often the same as before, there was a surprisingly energetic campaign by all camps to salvage modern design as ethical compass and inspiration.

To be sure, this post-fascist ideology of the humanist artifact was used as a means of decontaminating design after 1945. It "normalized" modern design by ideologically cleansing it of its unsavory historical associations. But what probably normalized design more than anything else (especially

---

88 Theodor Heuss, _Was ist Qualität? Zur Geschichte und zur Aufgabe des Deutschen Werkbundes_ (Tübingen, 1951), 35–39, 80. Note that Heuss used the term "job pride" (_Berufsstolz_) to dodge the Nazi association with _Arbeitsfreude_.

in West Germany) was the actual consumption of these products in the 1950s and 1960s. The wartime mass desire for these largely unavailable consumer design items found fulfillment during the 1950s in the form of physical acquisition, as the pathos of everyday objects shifted from collective sacrifice to personalized satisfaction and social status. Nevertheless, the material promises and expectations from the 1930s helped give form to consumer desires after 1945. In the end, it was the social experience of relative affluence – measured first by food consumption, then by the purchase of consumer durables – that forever shaped the popular understanding and memory of post-fascist normality.[89] Design therefore took its place alongside consumption as the real mediating agent of a new aesthetics of postwar prosperity. But this went far beyond simply transforming modern art's ideology of individual freedom and post-fascist personality into mass-produced commodities.[90] It was also crucial – together with advertising – in converting the political language of post-fascist progress and well-being into explicitly material terms. In so doing, it helped produce new social distinctions and stylized consumer subcultures in a country in which the traditional markers of social class – above all property and education – were badly disrupted during the war. No less significant was that design and consumerism played a decisive role in mediating the relationship between citizen and state after 1945. Michael Wildt's sharp analysis of 1950s poll results is quite persuasive on this question. What he shows in particular is that West Germans were hardly enamored with democracy through the early 1950s; many even valued Hitler as "one of the greatest German leaders" as late as 1953. Wildt's point is that it was not any love for liberalism that ultimately turned Germans into democrats, but rather that "West Germans became democrats through consumption." Political legitimacy, so he concludes, was won in the sphere of consumer objects and commodity design.[91] The Federal Republic's celebrated banalization of virtue – one that effectively broke with the earlier Nazi banalization of evil – was really bought with the visible signs of economic affluence. Economic historian Werner Abelshauser was then quite correct in saying that

---

89 Wildt, *Vom kleinen Wohlstand*, passim. See also Ulrich Herbert, "Good Times, Bad Times: Memories of the Third Reich," in Richard Bessel, ed., *Life in the Third Reich* (Oxford, 1987), 97–110; and Lutz Niethammer, "'Normalisierung' im Westen: Erinnerungen in die 50er Jahre," in Gerhard Brunn, ed., *Neuland: Nordrhein-Westfalen und seine Anfänge nach 1945/1946* (Essen, 1986), 175–207.

90 This sort of cultural production touched off a wide discussion in West Germany about the real possibility of any adversarial avant-garde. Essential here is Hans Magnus Enzensberger, "Die Aporien der Avantgarde," *Einzelheiten II* (Frankfurt am Main, 1963), 50–79.

91 Michael Wildt, "Changes in Consumption as Social Practice in West Germany During the 1950s," in Strasser, McGovern, and Judt, eds., *Getting and Spending*, 301–16.

"the history of the Federal Republic is above all its economic history"[92] because it was the feverish consumer sector that bound citizen and state by fulfilling newly demilitarized, decentralized, and privatized dreams of the good life.[93] Hence, the postwar reconstitution of West German industrial culture perhaps found its most salient expression here: The fascist aestheticization of politics had been replaced by a post-fascist aestheticization of economics.

Or had it? At this point it pays to reconsider the underestimated role of design itself in normalizing everyday Nazi life and politics. In part, this could be seen in the Third Reich's campaign to inscribe its modernist ideology on the face of commonplace objects, particularly to the extent that they supposedly embodied Nazi cultural achievement and "racial genius." But it is wrong to reduce such rhetoric to crude ideological window-dressing. As Alf Lüdtke has shown, the Nazi exploitation of the old romantic concepts of "German quality work," "work value," and even "joy of work" were remarkably effective in winning over workers to the regime by appealing to their psychosensual identification with "re-enchanted" industrial labor. Design played no small role here, especially in the way that it furnished material evidence of new policies. Beauty of Labor's extremely successful campaign to modernize German factories convinced many workers that the Third Reich was serious about improving the lives of the vaunted *Volksgemeinschaft*; modern canteens, swimming pools, and new worker housing further cultivated loyalty to the regime. What is more, high-quality design objects – celebrated as the very fruit of this new industrial work ethos – helped forge vital links between pride and production, work and culture.[94] That these things were made standard in all new factory canteens for daily worker use strengthened these connections even more so.

But if design performed a stabilizing function in the sphere of production, it also did so in the realm of consumption. At first, this may strike the reader as peculiar, not least because the Third Reich can scarcely be described as a resplendent consumer paradise. That the Nazis never produced one single Volkswagen for private use or that they ultimately built far fewer so-called "people's homes" than their hated Weimar successor are two often-cited examples of their failed consumer policies. True enough, but we ought to bear in mind that our judgments of fascist (and for that

---

92 Abelshauser, *Wirtschaftgeschichte*, 8.
93 Arne Andersen, *Der Traum vom guten Leben: Alltags- und Konsumgeschichte vom Wirtschaftswunder bis heute* (Frankfurt am Main, 1997).
94 Alf Lüdtke, *Eigen-Sinn: Fabrik-Alltag, Arbeitererfahrungen und Politik vom Kaiserreich bis in den Faschimus* (Hamburg, 1993), esp. 318ff.

matter, communist) economics remain colored by the Cold War success of Keynesian theory, which always presumed an elective affinity between general material satisfaction and liberal government.[95] It is worth recalling here that it was not during the great economic takeoff of the 1950s when the West effectively erased the distinction between economics and politics. As recent scholarship has shown, the political theology of collective material prosperity – in which the disgruntled consumer emerged as a formidable voice of political reckoning – was really a child of the Depression. It was first during this systemic crisis that political legitimacy was forever wedded to economic wealth. Certainly this was the case in the United States, France, Great Britain, and later West Germany, but I would hazard that it found echoes in Nazi Germany as well.[96] Although no one would deny that the fascist governments departed from their liberal enemies in their wholesale application of violence and terror to reorganize socioeconomic life, it does not follow that they had no use for the magical power of modern design to manufacture fetching images of future prosperity. After all, is it not true that it was the Depression itself that gave birth to the Golden Age of industrial design, whose heightened economic and cultural value was equally manifest in liberal and fascist countries alike?[97] The objection that the fascists never really delivered these promised goods to the consumer is not as indefensible as first presumed, however. Industrial design enabled them to mass-produce new material dreams of deferred gratification and popularized postwar affluence (for example, the Volkswagen), which became even more precious amid consumer rationing and wartime sacrifice. In fact, it could be argued that the stepped-up campaign to advertise these goods after 1936 directly corresponded with the dimming prospect that these objects could ever be realistically provisioned *en masse*. Is it only coincidental, for instance, that the Kunst-Dienst's most active period in organizing design exhibitions was after the outbreak of war? In a context in which extended free time, material goods, and rights were not distributed as rewards for demanded

---

95 Perhaps Erhard himself said it best when he argued that "[d]emocracy and a free market economy are as logically linked as dictatorship and state-controlled economies"; consumer happiness, so he continued, served as the very foundation of economic stability and political democracy. Erhard, *Prosperity Through Competition*, 6, 171 (translation modified).

96 James Livingston, *Pragmatism and the Political Economy of Cultural Revolution, 1850–1940* (Chapel Hill, N.C., 1994); Charles McGovern, "Consumption and Citizenship in the United States 1900–1940"; Victoria DeGrazia, "Changing Consumption Regimes in Europe, 1930–1970: Comparative Perspectives on the Distribution Problem"; and Lizabeth Cohen, "The New Deal State and the Making of Citizen Consumers," all in Strasser, McGovern, and Judt, eds., *Getting and Spending*, 37–58, 59–84, 111–25, respectively. A good study on West Germany is Erica Carter, *How German Is She?* (Ann Arbor, Mich., 1997).

97 Donald J. Bush, *The Streamlined Decade* (New York, 1975); and Klaus-Jürgen Sembach, *Into the Thirties: Style and Design, 1927–1934*, trans. Judith Filson (London, 1986).

sacrifice and service, was it not aesthetics all along – as Benjamin had seen – that fused fascist subject and state? Design thus played a key role for many Germans in giving form to private dreams of normality and prosperity beyond the travails and suffering of war. This signals an ironic reversal: Where Hitler and Goebbels borrowed heavily from advertising techniques in selling politics like commodities, now commodities (particularly after 1939) were increasingly being sold as politics. For this reason it is misleading to say that the fascist campaign to aestheticize the relations between people (including the violent removal and annihilation of those deemed "unfit" to live) had been simply supplanted by a post-fascist impulse to aestheticize the relation between people and things, for the literal commodification of political transcendence was already present in the Third Reich as well. Leaving aside the hazy and largely still unknown reception of these objects, it can at least be safely said that the wartime invention of postwar bonanza and the good life was by no means the monopoly of the Allies.

On this score, design successfully brokered an abiding iconography of normality and prosperity both during and after the war. If nothing else, this comparative German-German story of postwar design revealed the extent to which the Nazi promises of material affluence (cars, homes, more leisure time, and consumer comfort) had eventually come true for many West and East Germans by the mid-1960s, even if the original promissory political regime was long dead. To this, one might venture to add that it was the Third Reich's massive introduction of industrial modernism to common workers (whether encountered in Beauty of Labor canteens, numerous exhibitions, or subsidized design wares from the 1939 *Warenkunde*) that effectively popularized modern design and its material theology of the good life for postwar consumption.[98] In so doing, design was unique in mediating past and present, change and continuity, citizen and state. This was especially true for West Germany, where a fragile state and the absence of any real affective language of secular solidarity (Jürgen Habermas's *Verfassungspatriotismus* notwithstanding) meant that political loyalty was forged in the marketplace. And even if the SED had no trouble fabricating images and rituals of political collectivity, the uprising of 1953 – and for that matter 1989 – made it plain that the political aspects of material happiness were of grave importance there as well, so much so that the government was ultimately sued for false advertising.

---

98 The same could be said about the postwar legacy of tourism as the continuation of the Third Reich's remarkably successful "Strength Through Joy" mass leisure program. Kaspar Maase, *Grenzloses Vergnügen: Der Aufstieg der Massenkultur 1850–1970* (Frankfurt am Main, 1997), 196–234.

Naturally, there were crucial differences: Whereas West German design was used to differentiate consumers, East German design was intended to unite them. What is more, the elevation of design as a visual shorthand for distinguishing between East and West arguably represented the real secularization of culture after 1945, whereafter beauty, freedom, and difference became distinctly material categories. The same held true for cultural memory. The late 1970s and early 1980s nostalgia wave for the "Golden 50s" together with East Germany's continuing post-1990 *Ostalgie* (GDR-nostalgia) for the GDR's 1960s experiment in "consumer socialism" underlined the extent to which everyday goods served and continue to serve as vehicles of national myth, cultural identity, and private history.[99] This is to say that despite two generations of division and hostility, the commodity form rested at the heart of German-German social life. Socialism, for all of its social engineering, never altered that. So even if these post-fascist German republics ultimately transferred their dreams of a mythic future from the political to the economic sphere after 1945, their hopes and loyalties still remained products of industrial aesthetics.

99 *Die Pubertät der Republik: Die 50er Jahre der Deutschen* (Frankfurt am Main, 1978); Eckhard Siepmann, ed., *Bikini: Die Fünfziger Jahre. Kalter Krieg und Capri-Sonne. Fotos, Texte, Comics, Analysen* (Berlin, 1981); and "Mit Pepita voll im Trend: Der neue Kult um die 50er Jahre," *Der Spiegel* 14 (1984): 230–9. Aside from the excellent *Wunderwirtschaft* catalogue cited earlier (note 67), two additional examples of recent ex-GDR reminiscences are Andreas Ludwig, ed., *Alltagskultur der DDR: Begleitbuch zur Ausstellung "Tempolinsen und P2"* (Berlin, 1996); and Volker Handloik and Harald Hauswald, eds., *Die DDR wird 50: Texte und Fotografien* (Berlin, 1998). An analysis of the relationship between "Ostalgie" and GDR material culture can be found in Paul Betts, "The Twilight of the Idols: East German Memory and Material Culture," *Journal of Modern History* 72 (Sept. 2000): 731–65.

14

Dissonance, Normality, and the Historical Method

Why Did Some Germans Think of Tourism after May 8, 1945?

ALON CONFINO

Every historical period offers its dissonances: that which actually happened but seems totally incongruent with the conditions of the time and which therefore tests to the limit the interpretative ability of the historian. I would like to present such a dissonance: Germans thinking of tourism following Germany's May 1945 defeat, in the midst of rubble, hunger, and occupation. We think about this period in many terms, but tourism is not one of them. And by denoting the period after May 1945 I do not mean the following years leading to the 1950s, but the following days and weeks. Who dared to think of tourism after May 8, 1945? Is the historian fantasizing? Or is history fantastically unpredictable?

On September 1, 1945, in the city of Emden, a group of tourist activists, soon to be organized into the Regional Tourist Union of East Friesland (Landesverkehrsverband Ostfriesland), asked the Allied occupation authorities for permission to resume activities.[1] Was this a case of Germans who, following the years of war, had become mentally imbalanced? The reverse seems true. On July 20, 1945, five weeks before the Emden case and merely six weeks after Germany's defeat, a meeting took place at Braunschweig's Ministry of State between a senior government official, Dr. Voigt, and the

Earlier versions of this essay were delivered in 1999–2000 at the École des Hautes Études en Sciences Sociales in Paris, the Humboldt University in Berlin, Cambridge University, and the 1999 German Studies Association meeting in Atlanta. I should thank Michael Werner, Wolfgang Hardtwig, and Richard Evans. I am grateful for Kristiane Klemm and Hasso Spode for making the research for this essay possible at the Institut für Tourismus in Berlin. I should also like to thank Omer Bartov and Francesca Fiorani for their critical comments. About the place of National Socialism in history, my discussions with my father, Michael Confino, about this essay and over the years, were the most insightful for me.

1 "Ein Dezenium Verbandsarbeit: Berichte der deutschen Fremdenverkehrsverbände," *Der Fremdenverkehr* 11, no. 5 (1959): 26. The permission was received on September 1, then revoked; the association had its first meeting in February 1946.

director of a local spa, Mr. Fick, who also was a high official at the Regional Tourist Union of the Harz (Landesfremdenverkehrsverband Harz). On the agenda was the immediate reconstruction of Lower Saxony's tourism industry. The two men asked the British occupying forces for permission to found a tourist association; this was denied, with the argument that the state had more urgent tasks. Tourism activists continued to push their cause through meetings, speeches, and pamphlets. Finally, the British gave up. On March 28, 1946, tourism activists founded the Working Group of Spas and Health Resorts in the Harz (Arbeitsgemeinschaft Harzer Heilbäder und Kurorte).[2]

Obviously, what I term "dissonance" was perceived by some Germans as nothing of the sort.[3] Why did tourism activists revive tourism so quickly after the defeat? This question demands an explanation, for it is simply inconceivable to think that the people who in the summer of 1945 founded the Regional Tourist Union of East Friesland thought only of having fun. There is a familiar historical narrative in the 1950s of West Germany and of travel as an inevitable and rather predictable progress of economic improvement, leading to the development of mass media and consumer culture, and resulting finally in mass tourism. This narrative is true, but it is only half the truth. It can describe the social and economic structures of West Germany and of tourism, but it cannot explain their meanings. And it cannot account for, much less explain, a tourism revival in a devastated society where economic improvement, mass media, and consumer culture belonged to the realm of fantasy more than to the realm of actuality. After all, how many people in Emden could seriously plan and complete a trip in September 1945? Just what, exactly, did these tourism activists think they were doing?

---

2 *Jubiläumsschrift des Harzer Verkehrsverband e.V. zu seinem fünfzigjährigen Bestehen* (Braunschweig, 1954), 31–2.

3 The remarkable revival of tourist activities and organizations after the defeat confirms that this dissonance was not that exceptional. The first postwar tourist association was founded in Baden in December 1945. In the same month, the old tourist association in Dortmund resumed its activities. And the preparatory meeting for the foundation of the German League of Tourist Associations and Spas (Bund deutscher Verkehrsverbände und Bäder) took place in June 1946. Overall, by February 1947, thirteen tourist associations were active in the Western occupation zone in Württemberg, the Rhineland, Westphalia, Bavaria, and other regions. For Baden, see "Ein Dezenium Verbandsarbeit," 60. For Dortmund, "50 Jahre Landesverkehrsverband Westfalen," *Der Fremdenverkehr* 10, no. 2 (1958): 15; "Ein Dezenium Verbandsarbeit," 41. On the German League of Tourist Associations and Spas, see *Abschrift: Referat des Verbandsdirektor Stadtrat a.D. Ochs . . . am 6.9.1946 auf der Hohensyburg betreffend Vorbereitung der Gründung des Bundes deutscher Verkehrsverbände und Bäder*, Noncataloged material, Institute für Tourismus, Berlin (hereafter Ncm, IfT). On the newly founded associations, see *Neugegründete Fremdenverkehrsverbände in Deutschland: Stand vom 10.2.1947*, in Ncm IfT.

    Moreover, lively discussions on tourist issues took place in the associations' newspapers and journals, as well as in conferences and meetings. The German Central Office of Tourism (Deutsche Zentrale für Fremdenverkehr) was founded in 1948 as West Germany's national tourist organization. The *Deutsche Zeitschrift für Fremdenverkehr* was first published in July 1949.

Their evaluations are simultaneously revealing and in need of interpretation. Why did tourism activists use tourism as a medium to evaluate the Third Reich in terms of progress? What did journalist Anton Luft mean when, following a trip organized by the Nordmark Regional Tourist Union (Landesfremden-Verkehrsverband Nordmark), he said: "It was in June 1948 when we, with DM 40 in our pockets, again began a normal life: We took for the first time [since the war] a press trip to the North Sea."[4] At first blush there is nothing particularly striking about this statement, but on closer reading one realizes that it leaves much to be interpreted. Why did Luft think of tourism as the beginning again of "a normal life"? When exactly was life "normal"? When did it change, and why? What past events or periods did Germans perceive as being not normal?

For the historian, the tourism dissonance is a stroke of luck: First, it enables us to have a glance into a society that often kept its emotions about the recent past under a tight lid. After the defeat, and in some cases already in anticipation of it, there emerged in West Germany a formulaic response as to one's role in and sentiments about National Socialism. Open expression of political and ideological belief in National Socialism was forbidden and, given the denazification policies of the occupying forces, unwise. But it seems improbable that Germans obliterated all traces of the past from public and private life. Traces of the past, certainly of one like National Socialism, remained. The question is, where and how to find them? Exploring the tourism dissonance provides a look beyond what seems at times an impenetrable façade.

Second, the tourism dissonance sharpens our awareness of the procedures by which we attempt to understand the past. There is a gap between our preconceived assumptions of how Germans should have behaved after May 8, 1945, on the one hand, and how some of them actually did behave, on the other. This should make us conscious and critical of our hidden presuppositions, of the attempts to read the past not in its own terms but from the viewpoint of our concerns in the present, for what I call a dissonance was perceived differently by some Germans. Tourism activists were levelheaded, bourgeois professionals who were aware of the gap between talking about traveling, which associated adventures and exotic places, and the miserable conditions around them. Still, they and many others, as we shall see, continued to think and talk about tourism. Why? A hidden meaning eludes us. In fact, thinking about tourism in this period in terms of a

---

4 Anton Luft, "Erfahrungen mit Pressefahrten," *Der Fremdenverkehr* 8, nos. 3–4 (1956): 10.

dissonance makes us aware of its limits as an explanatory device. It brings to the fore, paradoxically, the question: Was there really a dissonance? Or better, what, exactly, constituted this dissonance? Rather than basing our investigation on the expectation that tourism was not congruent with the period, I suggest that we leave our expectations behind and take seriously Luft's remarks, and to think of the problem not only in terms of dissonance but also in terms of its opposite – normal life and normality.

It is clear to us what is the dissonance in the tourism case, but how should we define *normality*? By "normality" I mean a set of practices and beliefs that constitute a typical and legitimized pattern of life and code of behavior, for there is, as we know, nothing normative about normality. What seems a normal behavior to one society is rejected as self-evidently absurd or completely wrong by another. There exists, in a sense, not one single, unified notion of normality but multiple notions of normalities, for not only among nations but also within societies there are different ways to conceive of the normal. The normal is not an appraisal of reality; rather, it is an appraisal of value. It is based on a process of comparison and analogy with previous experiences as well as with future expectations. For the historian of normality, one criterion in the selection and interpretation of evidence is the subjective experience and beliefs of contemporaries. It is this approach that I pursue in this chapter, exploring the meaning of tourism in West Germany between 1945 and 1960 as a culture of normalities, as a way for Germans to relate to the Nazi period, and to the prewar years (1933–9) in particular, in multiple ways.

I view tourism as the "the exceptional normal," to use the notion of the late Italian microhistorian Edoardo Grendi, when "the smallest dissonances prove to be indicators of meaning that can potentially assume general dimensions."[5] By exploring the dissonance we can get to that which was perceived as normal. This chapter is conceived as a thought experiment. Normality and dissonance are taken as experimental variables. These are slippery concepts, but I prefer to try and use them consciously as explanatory devices rather than only as embellished metaphors.

My work is based on an analysis of tourist rhetoric as well as of the tourists' behavior. The methodological problems of getting to the tourist experience are significant. There are many sources on tourist activities, but most are not by tourists. Think about yourself: When you travel, you

---

5 Edoardo Grendi, "Microanalisi e storia sociale," *Quaderni Storici* 7 (1972): 506–20. The citation is from Giovanni Levi, "On Microhistory," in Peter Burke, ed., *New Perspectives on Historical Writing* (University Park, Pa., 1992), 109. I am indebted to microhistory for thinking about the problematics of the essay and the period.

experience a multitude of emotions, motivations, and fantasies, but you rarely leave behind a trail of written documents. In exploring the tourist experience, the emphasis is on a sensibility that came to be expressed in public action; it calls for a certain mixture of imagination and speculation.

I

After the war, tourism, as discourse and practice, became a medium with which to think about Germany's recent turbulent past, about that which was normal and exceptional in one's everyday life as well as about national experience. Even before there had been significant actual traveling, there had already been significant tourist rhetoric in the Third Reich and the postwar period. And the rhetoric of tourism after 1945, as an image of national belonging, represented several overlapping and at times contrasting attitudes toward National Socialism. The rhetoric was produced by activists in tourist associations and the tourist trade, mostly middle-class men, liberal professionals (writers, lawyers, journalists) and businessmen, who had been connected to the tourist industry for decades, including during the Nazi period. The social composition of German tourism remained unchanged from the 1920s to the 1950s: Most tourists were from the upper and middle classes; some workers traveled, but overall, workers remained underrepresented. By the mid-1950s, tourism reached the peak levels of the interwar years; the end of the 1950s is considered the beginning of mass tourism in Germany.

Tourist rhetoric depicted the prewar Nazi years as overwhelmingly positive.[6] The fiftieth anniversary of the Harz Tourist Union (Harzer Verkehrsverband) in 1954 provided a suitable occasion to draw a historical balance sheet. A special commemorative booklet was published in which members of the tourist union remembered the Nazi period as one of great improvements: "Overall German tourism, and with it the tourism in the Harz, experienced strong growth through the decline of unemployment, the general economic activity, and the rapid increase of motor vehicles."[7] The visible symbol of progress was the "Harz highway" project: "In terms of landscape, the highway is one of the most beautiful in North and Central Germany, and will be a particular attraction for motor vehicle tourism in the Harz."[8] The booklet especially mentioned Dr. Fritz Todt, "whose unfailing

---

6 The following discussion is partly based on a section of my essay "Traveling as a Culture of Remembrance: Traces of National Socialism in West Germany, 1945–1960," *History and Memory* 12, no. 2 (fall–winter 2000): 92–121.
7 *Jubiläumsschrift des Harzer Verkehrsverband e.V. zu seinem fünfzigjährigen Bestehen*, 29.
8 Ibid., 28.

interest and energy" was invaluable for tourism development.[9] Todt was
appointed by Hitler in 1933 as general inspector for German roads and
charged with building a new network of motorways, the famous *Autobahnen*.
But Todt was not exactly an innocent transportation expert. He joined
the Nazi Party as early as 1923 and was Hitler's personal friend. In 1940,
he became minister of armaments, becoming the leading force behind
the war economy. (Albert Speer replaced him when he died in a plane
crash in 1942.) None of this appeared in the Harz association's booklet. The reason lies not, one has the impression, in a premeditated plan
to deceive but rather in the perception that there was nothing especially
wrong with the *Autobahn* program and, by extension, the regime that
supported it.

Indeed, postwar descriptions of tourism in the Third Reich were painted
either in the professional language of the trade, which had been in place
since the beginning of modern tourism in the nineteenth century, or in a
poetic language that is part of tourism discourse everywhere. Either way, the
language of tourism was selective and disclosed nothing of several dramatic
patterns of German society in those years: accommodation with a murderous system, striving for world domination, and persecution of Jews. For
traveling in the Third Reich, similar to every other sphere of life, was an
integral part of the period's systematic racial terror. The 1935 Nuremberg
Laws forbade most hotels from accommodating Jewish guests.[10] A decree
by the Ministry of the Interior from July 24, 1937, set extreme restrictions on the presence of Jews in spas; an additional decree from June 16,
1939, made participation impossible. Given what we know of Nazi ideology, this information is quite predictable. More significant is the evidence of
grassroots activity, before the Nazi legislation, to remove Jews from tourist
sites and hotels. Massive discrimination started in the fall of 1934. The
case of Neustrelitz stood for many communities in Germany during that
period: The owners of the town's hotels and guesthouses together with
the local tourist and transportation bureau agreed "to post everywhere the
inscription: Jews are unwelcome." In contrast to the silence over this past,
descriptions of the conditions of tourism under Allied occupation were dramatic, often expressing self-pity. Thus, one writer in 1954 tells us, conditions
for the revival of tourism in the Harz after 1945 were terrible: First, all beds
were confiscated by the occupation forces. Then, "the occupying army disposed of 480 percent more than the annual, normal timber production in

---

9 Ibid., 29.
10 My discussion is based on Christine Keitz, *Reisen als Leitbild. Die Entstehung des modernen Massen-
    tourismus in Deutschland* (Munich, 1997), 248–9.

the Harz forest." The result: "It seems as if fate overtook not only human beings but also nature."[11] West Germans seemed to have felt more affected emotionally by the years of postwar reconstruction than by the prewar years of the Third Reich.[12]

At the same time, tourism rhetoric represented the Nazi period in a commingling of distancing and victimhood; the Nazi Party was thus a foreign entity that imposed a dictatorship and a war on an innocent people. The German Central Office of Tourism (Deutsche Zentrale für Fremdenverkehr), founded in 1948 as West Germany's national tourist organization, articulated this creed clearly in the first postwar tourist campaign aimed at foreigners, the "Goethejahr 1949" campaign. The organization complained that the task of bringing tourists to Germany was very difficult "because the years of the Nazi dominion made Germany the least beloved country in the world. . . . The Central Office of Tourism must show foreign tourists a way that will enable them to meet again the true Germany. To be sure, Goethe's Germany was brutally trampled on and degraded in the years of tyranny. But not all Germans took part in this maltreatment. The true Goethe's Germany was, is, and remains immortal and indestructible. In this Germany we believed in the period of rape [*Vergewaltigung*], in this Germany we believe today."[13] Significantly, during the same period when "rape" became an accusatory metaphor to describe the Allied occupation of Germany – as well as a harsh reality for many German women, especially in the Soviet Zone – the Central Office of Tourism chose this same word to describe the Nazi regime. It thus achieved two aims: It distinguished between the Nazis and the Germans, as if Nazis were not "true" Germans; and it drew a semantic likeness between the Allies and the Nazis.[14] West Germans made tourism a medium to consider the nation an innocent victim of war and occupation.[15] According to this view, National Socialism was an aberration in the normal German history of cultural and artistic accomplishments.[16]

---

11 R. Irmer, "50 Jahre Harzer Verkehrsverband," *Der Fremdenverkehr* 6, nos. 7–8 (1954): 3–4.

12 Elizabeth D. Heineman, "The Hour of the Women: Memories of Germany's 'Crisis Years' and West German National Identity," *American Historical Review* 101, no. 2 (Apr. 1996): 387.

13 *Mitteilungen der Z.F.V.: Warum Deutschland-Werbung mit Goethe*, n.d., 1–2 (Ncm, IfT).

14 On rape in postwar Germany, see Heineman, "Hour of the Women" and Atina Grossmann, "A Question of Silence: The Rape of German Women by Occupation Soldiers," *October* 72 (Apr. 1995): 43–63.

15 See Michael Hughes, "'Through No Fault of Our Own': West Germans Remember Their War Losses," *German History* 18, no. 2 (2000): 193–213.

16 The Goethejahr campaign should also be seen against the background of the Cold War and the transformation of the Soviet occupation zone into East Germany. For the Central Office of Tourism, Goethe symbolized the true German spirit not only in contrast to the Nazi regime but also in contrast to East Germany's communist regime, which celebrated the Goethe anniversary in Weimar. The Central Office of Tourism attempted to delegitimize the attempted appropriation of Goethe by the East German communists. In this respect, the celebrations in West Germany, which claimed

I have described the discourse of tourism after the war as a way to embrace as well as deny the Third Reich. The previously common argument in historical literature that the Germans kept the Nazi past hermetically sealed and silenced cannot stand up to historical evidence. We may not like everything that Germans had to say about their experiences during National Socialism, but they were not silent about them. At the same time, they remembered the past selectively because distortions, lies, and evasions are the bases of identity. But what kind of identity? We should not just criticize the distortions as misunderstandings of reality or attempts to repress and conceal, but instead try to illuminate their function and meaning.

II

Was the meaning of post-1945 tourist revival a flight from reality into a nostalgic past? The problem with this view is that the subjective meaning of the tourist experience is largely lost, whereas concepts such as irrationalism, repression, and manipulation take center stage as explanatory devices. Tourism, like festivals, religious ritual, art, and cinema, is not a flight from reality but a symbolic practice and representation to understand and negotiate with it. Tourists are not social scientists: "The claim that they should understand the world in an objective way fails to appreciate their motivations for and the character of modern traveling."[17] Rather, the question is why did Germans choose tourism as a medium to think about the Third Reich? What kind of emotions and recollections did Third Reich tourism evoke in the post-1945 era? To answer this question we have to go back to the tourist experience in the Nazi era.

After 1933, as a result of the cumulative effects of Nazi policies and the improved world economy, German tourism flourished. The Nazis' tourist activities ranged broadly; more Germans traveled, an experience that stood in stark contradiction to the Depression years. The 1934 Oberammergau Passion Play, for example, attracted 400,000 tourists (including 60,000 from abroad). The 1936 winter and summer Olympic Games in Garmisch-Partenkirchen and Berlin put Germany on the map and attracted, in Garmisch-Partenkirchen alone, more than one million tourists.[18] Between the Depression and the early 1960s, 1937 was the best tourist year.

the mantle of the true Germany, took place against a perceived background of two "abnormal" Germanys, the Nazi as well as the Communist regimes. This important topic cannot be discussed here at any length.

17 Christoph Hennig, *Reiselust: Touristen, Tourismus und Urlaubskultur* (Frankfurt am Main, 1997), 11.

18 For Oberammergau and tourism, see Ian Kershaw, *Popular Opinion and Political Dissent in the Third Reich: Bavaria, 1933–1945* (Oxford, 1983), 136, 197.

More important, the improvement of tourism between 1933 and 1939 reflected on the ability of the Nazis to improve social, material conditions. For ordinary Germans, "Strength Through Joy" (Kraft durch Freude or KdF) – the plan to give every worker a paid vacation – became the most popular program instituted by the regime. This sentiment is well illustrated in the detailed reports of opposition groups that reached the exiled leaders of the Social Democratic Party (SOPADE). The SOPADE reports are, as is well known, an excellent source on life in Nazi Germany, although they have one significant problem: They naturally emphasized prevalent opposition to and discontent with the regime. The reports on the KdF, however, are different in tone and content, which makes them a valuable source to understand the attitudes toward the KdF and, more generally, the link between tourism and the Nazi regime. One report stated that "some KdFlers say: 'never before did we receive such a thing from the state. Never before could we go out from our hole.' Especially women keep telling for months on end about the beautiful trips and thus also excite their friends and companions."[19] Certainly, many long-time socialists refused to be impressed by the "KdF ballyhoo,"[20] but many saw no contradiction in holding both views, namely, that unions were important but that KdF tours were a positive novelty. "It was like a Grimm fairy tale, we were like one big happy family," gushed one KdFler about his trip years after the fact, in the 1980s – when it was not "politically correct" to praise National Socialism.[21] The KdF program, and the improvement of tourism in general, endowed the Nazi regime with legitimacy and associated the prewar years with improvement.

Traveling raised the expectations for those who traveled, and even more so for those who did not. One important result of the KdF was that by 1939, although most workers still did not travel, vacation was perceived by workers as an established right, an entitlement. Tourism for workers was thus associated with social progress and mobility. "For young and old alike," Mary Nolan has perceptively argued, "perceptions of the 'good' and the 'bad' times were based more on the availability of employment and the prospects of security than on political events."[22] Significantly, KdF travel was not necessarily associated with Nazi ideology. One worker, who was

---

19 Cited in Hasso Spode, "Arbeiterurlaub im Dritten Reich." In Carola Sachse, Tilla Siegel, Hasso Spode, Wolfgang Spohn, eds., *Angst, Belohnung, Zucht und Ordnung: Herrschaftsmechanismen im Nationalsozialismus* (Opladen, 1982), 314.
20 Cited in Spode, "Arbeiterurlaub im Dritten Reich," 314.
21 " 'Wir waren wie eine einzige glückliche Familie!' " *Der Enztäler: Wildbader Tagblatt*, Aug. 24, 1996.
22 Mary Nolan, "Work, Gender, and Everyday Life: Reflections on Continuity, Normality and Agency in Twentieth-Century Germany," in Ian Kershaw and Moshe Lewin, eds., *Stalinism and Nazism: Dictatorships in Comparison* (Cambridge, 1997), 324. Nolan's essay is excellent.

a Communist sympathizer until 1933, recalled after the war that the KdF "was a real vacation. It had usually nothing to do with [propaganda and politics]. It was similar to the way one goes on vacation today. People were together, laughing, singing, dancing."[23] Valued as an entitlement, traveling belonged in a realm beyond politics and ideology, as part of modern life.

After 1945, to return to where this discussion began, talking, thinking, and practicing tourism was, among other things, a medium to capture the perceived good years of the Nazi past, the prewar years.[24] The revival of tourist activities after 1945 was often viewed as a return to the good old traveling days of the late 1930s. This is why tourism and the KdF always figure prominently in post-1945 oral histories about personal experiences under National Socialism: They were viewed as a measure of normality and improvement. In a 1951 opinion poll, half of the West Germans questioned viewed the Nazi prewar years as Germany's best years.[25] There was no more talk, according to the Public Opinion Institute (Institut für Demoskopie), "of German rebirth or of racial awakening...these bits of Third Reich are antiquated." Many Germans put what they considered the "politics" of the period aside, that is, the terror, mass murder, and war, and remembered the prewar years as positive: "guaranteed pay packet, order, KdF, and the smooth running of the political machinery...thus 'National Socialism' makes them think merely of work, adequate nourishment, KdF, and the absence of 'disarray' in political life."[26] It is therefore not surprising that tourist brochures of the 1950s looked purposefully similar to those of the 1930s to associate a familiar experience, while the first postwar production of the Oberammergau Passion Play in 1950 was directly modeled on the 1934 production, the poster for which was adopted as well.[27]

23 Kaspar Maase, *Grenzenloses Vergnügen: Der Aufstieg der Massenkultur 1850–1970* (Frankfurt am Main, 1997), 209–10.

24 I cannot discuss here the topic of German tourism in uniform between 1939 and 1945, namely of Wehrmacht soldiers being tourists in conquered countries. This subject is fundamental to provide background and meaning to the postwar German tourism. I discuss it in "Traveling as a Culture of Remembrance."

25 This discussion is based on Ulrich Herbert, "Good Times, Bad Times: Memories of the Third Reich," in Richard Bessel, ed., *Life in the Third Reich* (Oxford, 1987), 97.

26 Ibid.

27 On the brochures, see Axel Schildt, " 'Mach mal Pause!' Freie Zeit, Freizeitverhalten und Freizeit-Diskurse in der westdeutschen Wiederaufbau-Gesellschaft der 1950er Jahre," *Archiv für Sozialgeschichte* 33 (1993): 397. On Oberammergau: *Niederschrift über die Sitzung des Verwaltungsrats der Deutschen Zentrale für Fremdenverkehr am 5. Februar 1949 im Hotel Lang, Oberammergau.* Feb. 5, 1949, 2–3 (Ncm IfT); *Deutsche Verkehrsblätter*, no. 1, Apr. 8, 1949, 4; and Kershaw, *Popular Opinion*, 136, 197. The 1934 Oberammergau Passion Play was, as mentioned above, a big success. Significantly, in the second half of the 1930s, when relations between the Nazi party and Bavarian Catholics were tense, attending the Oberammergau Passion Play became at times an act of defiance and support of the

This was, then, the meaning of Luft's statement that the beginning of postwar travel was associated with normal travel during the pre-1939 period, interspersed with years of war and occupation. Viewed in this light, the discourse on tourism appears not so much a dissonance but a link to connect the present aspiration to normality with what was perceived as the past experience of it.

But why was tourism perceived as a measure of normality? One reason is that identification with tourism was based on the intimate link between it and everyday life. Tourism is a refuge from the routine and standardization of modern everyday life, but at the same time it also is a practice that (sometimes) confirms one's way of life in comparison between oneself and the other. The cultural process behind tourism, therefore, is similar to the one behind normality. In traveling, we do not appraise an objective condition of the other but our own subjective image of it. Traveling is based on a process of comparison and analogy between our own values and those of the other. As a result, and as a practice of everyday life, tourism places subjective meanings and experiences of concrete settings within larger contexts and bigger developments. It places our daily life and practices – of small occurrences, norms, behaviors, and ways of thinking – within the history of "big events."

Traveling, as a desire or an actuality, reflected in a sense the ways personal experience shifted with the tide of big historical events and developments between 1933 and the postwar period. In the normal life of peace, between 1933 and 1939, things improved, one could travel, and more people did travel. Then came the first years of war, between 1939 and 1941. These were peculiar years: The war was a source of obvious anxiety, but Germany did win on all fronts; fewer people traveled, but travel did take place.[28] This period was followed by the years of total war, defeat, and occupation: At the end, there was no Reich, no sovereign Germany, and certainly no travel. Finally, there came the economic recovery, political sovereignty, material improvement, and the resumption of travel in the 1950s. Thinking about German history using the metaphor of tourism thus corresponded to certain personal experiences and conditions of everyday life.

Moreover, because tourism was perceived as apolitical, it was a useful image in thinking about the Nazi period: It made it possible to hold on to one's life experience in the prewar years while dissociating oneself from

Church. But in 1934, relations between the Church and the party were good. Thus, the fashioning of the 1950s Passion Play after the 1934 Play was not an act of remembering resistance to the Third Reich, but instead of a great tourist season made possible by the Nazis.

28 "Less people traveled" – again, not considering the soldiers.

the "politics" of the regime. This is perhaps the reason why the connection between travel, as an image of normal life, and National Socialism became a fundamental mainstay in the way Germans, after 1945, have described their lives in the 1930s. This link was used, as we have seen, by tourist associations until the 1950s; it was confirmed in the 1970s and 1980s by the oral history project under the direction of Lutz Niethammer, and was again on display most recently in the television series *Heimat Front*.[29]

More broadly conceived, the link between tourism and normal life appears fundamental in the modern world because tourism functions as a social and cultural activity with enormous symbolic power to legitimize political systems. It is viewed as an entitlement that reflects on the ability of the system to keep the promise of a better life. East and West Germany provide good examples: In 1953, 83 percent of West Germans said in an opinion poll that travel was not a luxury anymore. Still, even in 1960 only one-third of West Germans actually traveled. Thus, although most West Germans did not travel in 1960, most were convinced of the ability of the social market economy to make travel a normal part of modern life. In East Germany, by contrast, the desire to travel subverted the state that prevented its citizens from traveling freely. The end is well known: The East German state collapsed in 1989 as people marched through its cities shouting "Visafrei nach Hawaii" (visa-free to Hawaii). In short, in the modern world people view the ability to travel as a mark of normality.

A word of caution is in order here. Tourism means different things to different people. Traveling has many motivations: People may travel to get away from it all, to forget the past, or just to have fun at the seaside or an Alpine resort. Obviously, I do not argue that all Germans traveled after 1945 to remember the Third Reich, or that my interpretation in any way exhausts the varied meanings of travel in modern society. My aim has been to present one aspect of travel, and how it can illuminate attitudes toward the Third Reich.

The argument posed in this chapter, namely, the links among travel, normality, and perceptions of the past, is certainly speculative. Its essence, in a way, is about the importance of historical investigation into the relative sensibility of happiness between the 1930s and 1950s. It requires further empirical evidence that may, in turn, alter some of its conceptualizations. I am aware of the dilemma I have faced in writing this essay: to provide a solid evidentiary base in order to achieve limited results or to provide a weak

---

29 On Niethammer's project, see Herbert, "Good Times, Bad Times," 97–110. See *Heimat Front,* ARD, pt. 1: *Die Mobilmachung* (1998).

evidentiary base in order to achieve original results.[30] My aim was to open new doors and propose new connections. There are several methodological rewards to the argument as well as the approach of this essay, I would argue, when one uses it to think about the period of the 1930s to the 1950s. It is to this topic, then, that I would like to turn now.

III

Until recently, the common view in the historiography has been that West Germans after 1945 repressed the Nazi past. Wolfgang Benz reflects the thinking of a whole interpretive school when he argues that "National Socialism was treated by a whole generation with collective silence and widespread amnesia."[31] The body of work produced by this approach has significantly illuminated how Germans attempted to master their past and how most of them refused to own up to it. In principle, the argument that (some) Germans repressed (some aspects) of the Nazi years is unassailable. But the repression thesis appears to be an exemplary case of the dangers of imposing a laudable moral cause on the vicissitudes and contingencies of historical and human affairs; it has been less successful in explaining Germans' changing attitudes toward National Socialism than in providing a sweeping condemnation of post-1945 German society. As a consequence, the repression approach was often content with an explanation that ignored the complex negotiations between remembering and forgetting. It paid little attention to what Germans did remember of the Nazi past and was quick to use as explanatory devices the terms *denial* and *repression*, which are infinitely tricky in elucidating human motivations. Most Germans instead commingled silence and expression in multiple ambiguous ways. By looking at relative sentiments of happiness and different perceptions of normality, we may learn more about human values and beliefs, and open new possibilities for studying how Germans came to terms with the past.

Moreover, most studies on coming to terms with the past focus on artifacts made specifically to represent the Nazi past (such as novels, films, museums, monuments, and so forth) after 1945. This is certainly an important approach, but it has clear temporal and subject-matter limitations. A

---

30 See Alain Corbin, "A History and Anthropology of the Senses," in *Time, Desire, and Horror: Towards a History of the Senses* (Cambridge, Mass., 1995), 186.

31 Wolfgang Benz, "Postwar Society and National Socialism: Remembrance, Amnesia, Rejection," *Tel Aviver Jahrbücher für deutsche Geschichte* 19 (1990): 12. The essayist Jane Kramer, who argued that Germans "buried the past...without a reckoning, without committing the past to history," popularized this view on the pages of the *New Yorker*. See, Jane Kramer, *The Politics of Memory: Looking for Germany in the New Germany* (New York, 1996), xv.

true history of coming to terms with the past, it seems to me, implies writing a history of sensibilities: It implies discovering the configuration of what is and what is not considered being normal and happy within a culture at a given moment. This kind of history should, first, encompass the peace and war years, and the postwar era. In other words, studying how Germans came to terms with the Nazi past is a historical topic that should not be bound to the post-1945 era. Patterns of remembrance, perceptions, and sensibilities existed across 1945. In the 1950s, explicit ideological support of National Socialism and anti-Semitism became taboo.[32] But did public silence mean self-conviction in private? Were the 1950s closer in this respect to the Third Reich or to the emerging West German political culture of post-1968? These are important questions that are not always posed by new studies that have recently shifted the argument concerning postwar German memories from the emphasis on repression to the complex argument about different uses of the Nazi pasts.[33] These studies are mostly interested in how things happened in the postwar era, whereas a history of sensibilities of normality and relative happiness could trace values and beliefs across the signposts of political history (1933–1945–1949).[34] A history of coming to terms with the past as a history of sensibilities should go beyond the predictability of certain cultural practices and artifacts. In West Germany, as stated, a candid discussion of National Socialism could not take place in the public sphere. Discretion dictated that certain views about the Nazi regime could not be expressed in public, although they were the norm in private life and everyday behavior. Consequently, we should look for traces of National Socialism not only in artifacts and practices created intentionally to represent it. Instead, we should look for its expression in social practices and representations

---

32 Norbert Frei, *Vergangenheitspolitik: Die Anfänge der Bundesrepublik und die NS-Vergangenheit* (Munich, 1996), 23.

33 See, e.g., Robert G. Moeller, "War Stories: The Search for a Usable Past in the Federal Republic of Germany," *American Historical Review* (Oct. 1996): 1008–48; Heineman, "Hour of the Women"; Heide Fehrenbach, *Cinema in Democratizing Germany: Reconstructing National Identity after Hitler* (Chapel Hill, N.C., 1995); Frank Biess, "'Pioneers of a New Germany': Returning POWs from the Soviet Union and the Making of East German Citizens, 1945–1950," *Central European History* 2, no. 2 (1999): 143–80; Catherine Epstein, "The Production of 'Offical Memory' in East Germany: Old Communists and the Dilemmas of Memoir-Writing," *Central European History* 2, no. 2 (1999): 181–202; and Maria Mitchell, "Materialism and Secularism: CDU Politicians and National Socialism, 1945–1949," *Journal of Modern History* 67 (June 1995): 278–308.

34 I do not mean to imply that these studies subscribe to the argument of zero hour, namley of 1945 as a wholly new beginning in German history. They are sensitive to the social relationships and culture negotiations across 1945. But they do mostly focus on post-1945. For a useful critique of the concept of zero hour, see Robert G. Moeller, "Introduction: Writing the History of West Germany," in Robert G. Moeller, ed., *West Germany Under Construction: Politics, Society, and Culture in the Adenauer Era* (Ann Arbor, Mich., 1997), 12.

where they were not directly discernible, but fairly unpredictable. These kinds of sources, practices, and representations may ultimately reveal more about attitudes and beliefs.[35]

It is in light of this consideration that I chose to undertake a study of tourism. Tourism is a social practice that takes place in public but has an essential component linked to private life and individual decision making, for the motivations, the impressions, and the experiences of traveling are absolutely private (although the tourist may decide to share them with others). Moreover, tourism, while supported by governments in all political regimes, is a pillar of modern popular culture; it thus enables us to explore intimate values as well as, of course, official posturing. As a social and cultural practice that is determined by experienced memories, not only by the raison d'être of raison d'état, tourism may reveal what people intimately thought about National Socialism (West German government officials, by contrast, *had* to make certain critical statements about the Nazis for foreign consumption). Regimes can forbid people from traveling, but no regime has yet found the trick to force people to travel; there is an element of free will and agency in traveling that is advantageous for the historian who looks for clues about motivations and beliefs.

We have found some of these clues in the pages that describe the multiple attitudes toward National Socialism. The German Central Office of Tourism, an official mouthpiece of West Germany's newly instituted democracy, depicted the Nazis as outsiders, invaders of the true Germany symbolized by Goethe. But the members of the Harz Tourist Union, by contrast, remembered fondly the Nazi prewar years, whereas others viewed the years of war and occupation as terrible but were uncritical of the pre-1939 dictatorship. Thus, in a society that silenced public expressions of support for National Socialism, thinking of tourism functioned as a medium to recapture the inalienable personal experience during the Third Reich. In this respect, the fact that tourism was viewed as apolitical was an important factor, for thinking of tourism was a way to connect with one's experience under National Socialism without being politically incorrect.

IV

I would like, finally, to use this discussion of dissonance and normality as an occasion to reflect on the procedures by which we understand the Nazi

---

35 Excellent in this regard is Paul Betts' analysis of industrial design in the 1950s as a way to link Nazi and post-Nazi commodity culture. Paul Betts, "The *Nierentisch* Nemesis: Organic Design as West German Pop Culture," *German History* 19 (2001): 185–217.

past, and, in particular, on the problem of the place of the Third Reich and the Holocaust within history. Few if any historical periods have been documented and studied so comprehensively as the Nazi era. Our knowledge of the period is so vast that it is difficult to see how the unearthing of new documents can revolutionize our interpretations. (Interpretative revolutions in the study of National Socialism may happen, but they depend on asking new questions, not on finding new documents.) Even the finding of the single most coveted document in modern German history – an order signed by Hitler ordering the Final Solution – will change little. Who, among people who seek truth and who look at the evidence with an open mind, will doubt the centrality of Hitler in the extermination of the Jews? But in spite of this vast knowledge, the Third Reich and the Holocaust present enormous problems of historical understanding and explanation. Our interpretation of the Nazi regime, therefore, is not dependent on finding new evidence but on thinking critically on the methods we use to approach this past.

In this respect, the notion of normality has been central to thinking about the Nazi regime. But using the notion of normality in German historiography has been less fruitful in producing new insights and novel approaches than in illustrating the problems of this historiography.[36] Let me discuss briefly the work of three historians whose work I hold in high regard. In his debate with Martin Broszat over the historicization of the Nazi regime, Saul Friedländer argued that the Third Reich could not be regarded or analyzed with the same methods as normal history. "Writing about Nazism is not like writing about sixteenth-century France."[37] With this statement, Friedländer is making two points: First, we lack a sense of detachment from the Nazi era, because the enormity of the crime prevents an honest historian from writing about it with a sense of neutrality. This is true but not unique

---

36 Exceptions are the perceptive discussions of Nolan, "Work, Gender, and Everyday Life," 311–42; and Ian Kershaw, *The Nazi Dictatorship: Problems and Perspectives of Interpretation*, 3d ed. (London, 1993), chap. 9, although Kershaw's discussion, as we shall see below, is not without problems. The notion of normality had different implications on historical writing on the Third Reich. Nolan identified three such implications in the disagreements over whether National Socialism can be historicized. The first question concerns the place of Auschwitz in the historical evaluation of the Nazi regime; the second problem involves whether the Nazi era can be at all understood historically; and the third issue is the place of National Socialism in twentieth-century German history (Nolan, "Work, Gender, and Everyday Life," 317). My discussion below touches on all these issues, though especially on the problem of historical explanation and the place of the Nazi regime within the historical method.

37 Saul Friedländer, "Some Reflections on the Historicization of National Socialism," in Peter Baldwin, ed., *Reworking the Past: Hitler, the Holocaust, and the Historians' Debate* (Boston, 1990), 98. My critique notwithstanding, I found Friedländer's body of work on the Holocaust to be highly insightful. It stands out as a combination of original thinking, historical writing, and moral voice.

to the Holocaust. Other historical cases present a similar problem of lack of detachment. One can think of the Palestinian catastrophe of 1948–9, of Vichy France, and of Stalin's Russia. Religious history may provide the best examples: Jews and Christians still argue over the historical meaning of a Jewish prophet who founded a church, whereas Catholics and Protestants still argue over the meaning of a heretic who split the Church to re-found Christianity. In a sense, Friedländer is correct, for all agree that Nazism is relevant to our lives in a way sixteenth-century France is not while acknowledging that writing on any historical event is, on a fundamental level, unlike writing about another. But it seems more accurate to argue that, on a spectrum of events that test our interpretative abilities that prevent the detachment necessary for the historian's craft, the Holocaust is an extreme case but not a case *sui generis*. Second, for Friedländer the meaning of his statement is moral: The Nazi regime was unique because it determined who should and who should not inhabit the world. "*This, in fact, is something no other regime, whatever its criminality, has attempted to do.*"[38] This is also true, but not without problems. Criminality is not a useful yardstick to determine what is or is not part of history; it is part of history, not extraneous to it. Immoral things are also human, although not humane. However big our moral repulsion, this in itself cannot be a historical yardstick to determine what was normal. Normality is thus used by Friedländer as a powerful moral metaphor and yardstick, but not as a historical tool.[39]

Other historians have seen the Holocaust as abnormal to a degree that puts it beyond the human ability to understand and explain. Dan Diner

---

38 Friedländer, "Some Reflections," 100. Emphasis in the original.
39 Our difficulty in understanding Auschwitz is enormous, but sixteenth-century France presents its own violent cases. The Wars of Religion saw unparalleled Catholic zeal for religious massacres. Disfigurement of the dead and mutilation of bodies, expressing a theatricalization of godly damnation, were common, but also common was cannibalism. Catholic killers ate the livers of the Huguenots they murdered, while the fricassees of human ears and grilled hearts were served up during the Saint Bartholomew massacres; human flesh was auctioned in the city of Romans in 1580. Although these facts are monstrous, we don't doubt our ability to explain them. Perhaps the reason lies in our detachment from these events in historical time and space, in spite of our moral revulsion. And so, perhaps, will be one day the case with an explanation for the Holocaust: The distance in time and space will provide the necessary detachment to explain it, while the moral revulsion will remain. But lack of detachment does not make the Holocaust abnormal while cannibalism normal. Indeed, it should be added that genocide and ethnic cleansing were much more common in the twentieth century than cannibalism in the sixteenth. Which case, in truth, better reflects its age?

I have taken the details on sixteenth-century cannibalism from Alain Corbin, *The Village of Cannibals: Rage and Murder in France, 1870* (Cambridge, Mass., 1992), esp. 88–9, an insightful book helpful for thinking about extreme violence and the Holocaust. For the cannibalism cases see Frank Lestringant, "Catholiques et cannibales: Le thème du cannibalisme dans le discours protestant au temps des guerres de religion," in Université François Rabelais, Centre d'études supérieures de la Renaissance, ed., *Pratiques et discourses alimentaires à la Renaissance: Actes du Colloque de Tours de mar 1979* (Paris, 1982), 233–47.

wrote: "Auschwitz is a no-man's land of understanding, a black box of explanation, a vacuum of extrahistorical significance which sucks in attempts at historiographic interpretation."[40] This statement postulates two kinds of histories: the history of all human events and the outside-of-history story of the Holocaust. Abnormal, outside of time, and in a sphere all its own, the Holocaust thus becomes a matter of belief.

But even historians who pleaded to historicize the Nazi regime found it, in parts, abnormal. Thus, Martin Broszat argued in a seminal essay that alongside the barbarism of the regime were patterns of social "normality" – long-term modernization tendencies, such as patterns of leisure, social policy, and plans for universal insurance – that were influenced by Nazism in various ways but existed before and remained after.[41] This context of a normality of everyday life, stated Broszat, cannot be reduced to being simply an epiphenomenon of Nazi ideology. At the same time, Broszat conceded that "regarding the crimes perpetrated against the Jews . . . everyday life in the Nazi period was probably not as normal after all as it might appear to have been on the surface."[42] But because normality is used but never defined, one wonders what is normal everyday life and where can it be found in the 1930s? In Communist Russia, with the terror, trials, and Gulags? In Fascist Italy? Or in America's Jim Crow South? By arguing that everyday life connected to racism and extermination was not normal, Broszat sharply separates normality from barbarity and assumes a schizophrenic existence of everyday life.[43] Perhaps more important, by arguing for the abnormality of some aspects of everyday life and, by extension, of the Nazi period, Broszat undermined his own argument about the integration of the Nazi period into history: Either the Third Reich is part of European historical development or it stands outside it as abnormal; it cannot be both.

The notion of normality used by these historians works much better as a moral metaphor than as an analytical tool; as an abstraction whose

---

40 Dan Diner, "Between Aporia and Apology: On the Limits of Historicizing National Socialism," in Baldwin, ed., *Reworking the Past*, 144. Paradoxically, Diner's insightful work on the Holocaust serves as a testimony to its historicity. One reading of his work can be in terms of the negotiations of the tension between the Holocaust as history and as a "black box."

41 Martin Broszat, "A Plea for the Historicization of National Socialism," in Baldwin, ed., *Reworking the Past*, 77–87. See the judicious discussion of Kershaw, *The Nazi Dictatorship*, 180–96.

42 Broszat, "A Plea," 125.

43 The work of Detlev Peukert has been fundamental in integrating normality with barbarism, everyday life with racism. See *Inside Nazi Germany: Conformity and Opposition in Everyday Life* (London, 1987); "Alltag und Barbarei: Zur Normalität des Dritten Reiches," in Dan Diner, ed., *Ist der Nationalsozialismus Geschichte? Zu Historisierung und Historikerstreit* (Frankurt am Main, 1987), 51–61. But, then, Peukert helps to normalize the Nazi regime in one theoretical move, while making it abnormal again in another, for he sees the period as a whole as a prototype of the pathologies of modernity. Normalities and pathologies thus dominate the historical discourse on the Third Reich.

consequence is to make the Holocaust autonomous of time, space, and agency, than as an illuminating concept. The problem is that normality is taken as a presupposition, not as an object of study; a definition of normal history is assumed to be self-evident and universally accepted. The assertion of abnormality thus becomes a self-fulfilling prophecy. The three cases above impose a morally clear although analytically vague category on a society that had in fact quite different ideas about normality. I wonder whether these historians do not write a history that is quite different from the history that was actually created by people in the past.[44] The Holocaust poses a profound challenge to our ability to understand and explain the human condition; we do often describe it, struggling in vain to find the right words, as abnormal, impossible to grasp and to fathom. But, and this is the main point, we should not mistake a term that best describes our own problems in understanding the Nazi regime as a term that actually explains the Nazi regime (or, in the case of Diner, that explains why it is impossible to explain it). Our use of the notion of normality reflects our own thinking about the Holocaust and the perceived enormity of the event.[45]

Instead, the notion of normality can be useful for our historical understanding, first, when we approach it not as a being but as an object of exploration.[46] We need to investigate the relation between historical understanding to the problematizing of normality, to write the history of the formation of normality as an analytical category and heuristic device in our thinking about the Nazi regime. For there is nothing obvious or self-explanatory about the claim, by historians who are trained to look at the past critically, that the Nazi regime was abnormal. The problem is not whether the regime was really abnormal but whether normality (as it is used) has any value as an explanatory device and how and why has it come to be so prevalent in the historical discourse about the Nazi era. The idea that the

---

44 Paradoxically, Saul Friedländer's masterful narrative of the years of persecution belied his own moral, theoretical view of the incomprehensibility of the Third Reich and of its uniqueness. He could conceive and write his study, and we can understand it, only on the basis of a shared historical discourse (of history as a discipline, I mean) and of a shared notion of what modern history has been like, excesses, crimes, and mass murders included. Had the Nazi era been abnormal and unique it would have left us no methods, narratives, and approaches to write about and comprehend it. While it is difficult to write about the Nazi regime, and problems of representation and language are significant, it is not wholly impossible, as Friedländer's book successfully demonstrates. See *Nazi Germany and the Jews: The Years of Persecution, 1933–1939* (New York, 1997).

45 Using the notion of abnormality also serves, perhaps, as a mechanism to distance us from the Holocaust by labeling it as the absolute other, utterly different from our own values, ways of life, and conditions of modernity.

46 See the original attempt of Andrew Bergerson, "Hildesheim in an Age of Pestilence: On the Birth, Death, and Resurrection of Normalcy," in Alon Confino and Peter Fritzsche, eds., *The Work of Memory: New Directions in German History* (Urbana, Ill., 2002).

Nazi period was not normal (or not entirely normal) has become a ritualistic statement that is at times contradicted by the very analysis of those who argue it. In his balanced book *The Nazi Dictatorship*, Ian Kershaw gives a masterful analysis of our understandings and interpretations of the Nazi regime since the war. His book demonstrates how our thinking about the dictatorship and its crimes, in spite of the profound problems it poses, has developed and been refined. Still, he adds that "Arguably, indeed, an *adequate* explanation of Nazism is an intellectual impossibility."[47] This is true, but, as I noted above in a different context, has the disarming validity of common sense. Arguably, an adequate explanation of the rise of Christianity or the Reformation is also an intellectual impossibility. And was there an adequate explanation of the Reformation sixty years after 1517? Is there now, for that matter? My point is not that an adequate explanation of the Holocaust is possible but that – assuming that adequate historical explanations are at all possible, which is open for debate – the Holocaust is not governed by different explanatory categories from other epoch-making historical events. It seems more fruitful to recognize that historical explanations are always complex, incomplete, and still under construction, and that in this respect, again, the Holocaust is an extreme case but not one that stands alone. Kershaw further argues that "it seems plain that . . . the Nazi era . . . cannot be regarded as a 'normal' part of history in the way that even the most barbarous episodes of the more distant past can be viewed. The emotions which rightly still color attitudes to Nazism obviously rule out the detachment with which not only sixteenth-century France (Friedländer's example) but also many more recent events and periods in German history and in the history of other nations can be analyzed."[48] But Kershaw's own book demonstrates that, with all the difficulties, a great amount of historically detached work has been done, also about the Holocaust. And why should we accept detachment from subject matter as a yardstick to determine historical normality? This way of relating Nazism and history seems to invert the relations between cause and effect in historical explanation. It is not that historians argue that National Socialism is abnormal because they have succeeded in explaining it as such, but that they argue that it is abnormal because all our other explanations are unsatisfactory.

I chose to discuss Kershaw's work because he is one of the most distinguished historians of Nazi Germany of his generation. That he also clings to ritualistic statements about the abnormality of the Nazi regime, which

---

47 Kershaw, *Nazi Dictatorship*, 3. Original emphasis.
48 Ibid., 193.

add little to historical understanding, is illustrative of a problem of historical argumentation. In the same paragraph where he argues that the Nazi era cannot be regarded as normal, Kershaw writes that the problem of detachment

does not rule out the application of 'normal' historical method [are there abnormal historical methods?] to the social, as well as to the political, history of Germany in the Nazi era.... [A] wide-ranging interpretative analysis of the Nazi era based on such methods ... [can] be written. And, while the historian's relationship to his subject of study is different in the case of Nazism than, say, in that of the French Revolution, it could be argued that, even accepting the uniqueness of the Holocaust, the problems posed by "historicization" are little different in theory to those facing the historian of say, Soviet society under Stalin.[49]

If we can write a wide-ranging interpretative analysis of the Nazi regime, why assume that adequate explanation is an intellectual impossibility? If the problems the Nazi era poses are shared by other historical cases, what is the historical significance of viewing it as abnormal? If a historical topic, however extreme, can be put into a narrative, subjected to interpretative analysis, and compared to and contrasted with other historical cases, what, then, is the meaning of arguing that it "cannot be regarded as a 'normal' part of history"?

In fact, the idea of normal history is inadequate. Let us assume, for the sake of argument, that Stalinism and Nazism represent abnormal European histories. One would like to know, then, which countries represent the "norm": Belgium and Portugal? No offense, but Russia and Germany do seem more consequential to modern European history. As for England and France, the view that their history should be seen as normal was demolished two decades ago by David Blackbourn and Geoff Eley. Moreover, to write the history of twentieth-century Europe as a self-congratulatory, teleological story of freedom and democracy is a mistake. From the vantage point of 1940, the future of Europe was seen as one of totalitarianism, utopian ideologies, and radical attempts at social engineering based on class and race.[50] The notion of normal history is linked to the Third Reich by a moral concern, which is laudable but has little to advance historical clarification. Kershaw's analysis is always historical, but there exists a point in his discussion after which the logical conclusions of his own argument are not drawn, and instead we fall into a language that has become so familiar in describing the Nazi era, a language that, in one way or another, against

---

49 Ibid., 194.
50 David Blackbourn and Geoff Eley, *The Peculiarities of German History: Bourgeois and Politics in Nineteenth-Century Germany* (Oxford, 1984). On a history of Europe without the teleology of freedom and liberty, see Mark Mazower, *Dark Continent: Europe's Twentieth Century* (New York, 1999).

the best of intentions, puts the Nazi era beyond history. By questioning our own historical understanding and use of categories, we may cross the impenetrable threshold that sanctifies the Holocaust and puts it and the Nazi era in a historical plain all their own.

The notion of normality can be useful in another, closely related way, namely, by writing the history of the notion from the subjective point of view of perpetrators, survivors, and subsequent generations, as well as in its manifestations in popular culture. For the Nazi regime, and the Holocaust in particular, were viewed by many people as singular right from the beginning. Heinrich Himmler expressed this sentiment when he addressed a group of SS men at Posen in 1943 about the extermination of the Jews: "In our history, this is an unwritten and never-to-be written page of glory."[51] Survivors experienced the concentration camps as, to use the evocative description of the author K. Tzetnik in the Adolf Eichmann trial, another planet, "Planet Auschwitz. Its inhabitants have no names, they were not born and did not give birth; did not live and did not die. They breathed according to different laws of nature." After the war, but especially from the 1960s and 1970s onward, the uniqueness of the Holocaust became a mainstay of public memory in Israel and among American Jews, among others.[52] This sentiment has been represented in popular culture by annual trips to Poland's concentration camps by young Israelis and American Jews, in films, novels, and in the sanctified place awarded to survivors' testimony. Rather than simply citing these views on the uniqueness of the Holocaust, we need to explore the history of this notion, how it evolved from the perceptions of perpetrators and survivors between 1933 and 1945 and our own days, what have been its ideological and political uses in different contexts and countries, and how it has been linked to popular culture.

I raised doubt about the use of the notion of normality as a historical explanatory device while at the same time, given the centrality of the notion of normality and uniqueness in thinking about the Nazi regime, pleading to write the history of this term. To avoid misunderstanding, let me state my argument again, in different words: The Nazi era and especially the Holocaust are historical cases that test the limits of our interpretations, extreme events that call into question our ability to explain the past in any satisfactory way.[53] This, I believe, is beyond doubt, and to argue differently is either naïve or sinister. The question is, where do we go from here?

---

51 Cited in Klaus Fischer, *Nazi Germany: A New History* (New York, 1995), 513.
52 See the critical view of Peter Novick, *The Holocaust in American Life* (New York, 1999).
53 On this, see the excellent collection by Saul Friedländer, ed., *Probing the Limits of Interpretation: Nazism and the "Final Solution"* (Cambridge, Mass., 1992).

One way would be to negotiate, based on this premise, between the Nazi era and the historical method while arguing, at one point along the way, that our ability to understand is not simply limited but that in fact the era stands beyond our comprehension. This view operates within a territory that interprets National Socialism within history while at the same time assigning it, implicitly or explicitly, to an ahistorical realm. A second way is to remain, however difficult it is both emotionally and historically, within the territory of the historian and to attempt to elucidate the era only by negotiating between it and history. There will be many frustrations along the way, many false starts and dead ends. The consolation of assigning the era to a land beyond history is unavailable. The task of remaining within the territory of the historian is more difficult, at times unforgiving, and always unsatisfactory because historical explanations are always complex, incomplete, and still under construction, and with the case of the Nazi era and the Holocaust an explanation, however convincing, will continue to evoke in us a sense of moral inadequacy, for the victims of the Holocaust died in complete innocence.[54]

The argument that a historical event, enacted by men and women within known boundaries of space and time, should be regarded as an integral part of history, not as abnormal or as "a vacuum of extrahistorical significance," is so obvious that if one were to make it about any historical event one would be viewed as naïve. But the Holocaust is one historical event about which this statement needs to be said. The reason is that, with regard to the Holocaust, we tolerate statements that are in the realm of faith, therapy, and theology but not in the realm, *sensu strictu*, of history. Arguing that the Holocaust is unique and incomprehensible has become part of civic liturgy and, in some quarters, indeed a demonstration of profundity and thoughtfulness. But certainly the Holocaust, as a historical event, stands not as a vacuum of extrahistorical significance. The fact that the regime and especially the Holocaust have been viewed as extraordinary is significant: It tells us about the depravity of the event and its meaning for the human condition. But the fact that people saw it as unique does not make it, from the historian's point of view, unique. The meaning of history, as a discipline based on methods,

---

54 Eva Hoffman put it eloquently: "However one understands the motivations of the Nazis in carrying out the Holocaust, their perverted ideology, technological prowess, or their sheer sadism, the victims of the Final Solution did not have a chance to die for a cause or for a belief. They died in innocence." Eva Hoffman, "The Uses of Hell," *New York Review of Books*, Mar. 9, 2000, 23.

Of course, historical descriptions of sensitive historical events, and perhaps of all historical cases, often commingle elements of faith and elements of the historian's craft. The Holocaust is not singular in presenting this mixture. But descriptions, by historians and other scholars, that put the Holocaust, in various degrees, beyond history are more prevalent in Holocaust historiography than in others.

theories, and evidence that attempts to find meanings over time and across cultures, cannot be reduced to the subjective sentiments of people. I myself pursue in this chapter an approach that explores the subjective beliefs of post-1945 West Germans with regard to notions of dissonance and normality. But this evidence was not taken at face value; rather, it was subjected to historical questions. Writing the history of the relations between the Holocaust and the notions of uniqueness and incomprehensibility may enhance our self-consciousness as to our own relations to the Holocaust.

I should say what my own view about the Holocaust and history is: The Holocaust is a part of German history, an extreme part but an integral part nonetheless, that is bound, similar to all other historical events, by patterns of explanations based on evidence. To arrive at such an explanation is, as we all know, an arduous task, but is ultimately possible. The Holocaust represents a rupture in modes of representation and speech, in the faculty to describe meaningfully that which happened, and yet this rupture cannot be, in fundamental terms, considered total and absolute, for the language of rupture itself is intimately connected to the set of images, representations, experiences, and languages that existed before. Survivors, perpetrators, subsequent generations, and even scholars have often perceived "Planet Auschwitz" as outside of time. But the sense of rupture is predicated on the ability to articulate past experience, from which one is severed. The sense of being outside time, outside of history, is predicated on the ability to articulate the notion of being inside time, of being part of history. In this sense, continuity and the notion of being within time – that is, the notion of living within history – is constitutive of the sense of rupture itself.

Admittedly, this has been a long journey from post-1945 tourism to the place of the Nazi era in history. What began as an exploration of a dissonance turned into a reflection on normality. The thread of this chapter was how to think about normality as a historical object, namely, the ways it was perceived by Germans from the 1930s to the 1950s, and as a historiographical object, namely, the ways it was used by historians. The topic of travel was my vehicle for this discussion. What links the theme of traveling and May 8, 1945, with the historical explanation of the Nazi past? One link, on the historical level, is the Germans' sense of having been victims while having been perpetrators. The search for normality after violence (done to Germans and done by Germans) may be seen as a way of putting those difficult and uncomfortable experiences behind them; the selective view of tourism seems to fit in well here. Another link, more broadly, is an awareness, via a discussion of normality, of the danger of psychological anachronism, the greatest historical error, to my mind. Normality, however defined and understood, has been posed as a problem by Germans in the 1940s and 1950s as well as by historians since; it has a past and a present. Historians have explored in the last generation a dazzling array of new topics, such as miracles, sexuality, asylums, witchcraft, and fear, but a history of normality, as far as I know, has yet to be written. The philosopher Georges Canguilhem, Michel Foucault's mentor, observed in his classic essay *The Normal and the Pathological* (1943) that "The normal is not a static or peaceful, but a dynamic and polemical concept."[55] This chapter, I hope, elucidated precisely that, although I am well aware that there are no final words on normality, however lucid, or shall we say "normal," they may seem.

55 Georges Canguilhem, *The Normal and the Pathological* (New York, 1989), 239.

Index

349